Fashions of the Gilded Age

Volume 2

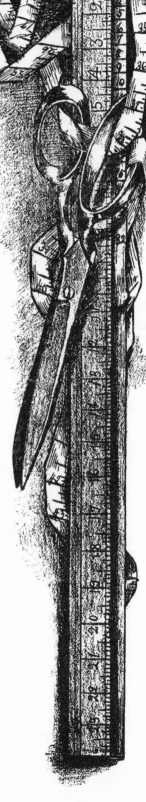

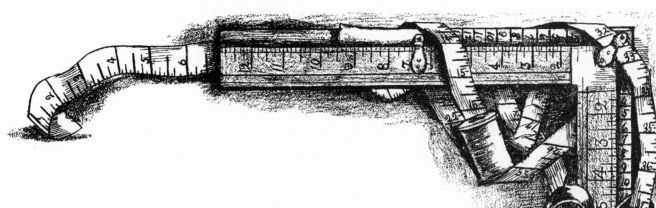

Fashions Of The Gilded Age

Volume 2

Evening, Bridal, Sports, Outerwear,
Accessories, and Dressmaking
1877–1882

Edited and with Additional Material by
Frances Grimble

Lavolta Press
20 Meadowbrook Drive
San Francisco, CA 94132

Fashions of the Gilded Age: Evening, Bridal, Sports, Outerwear, Accessories, and Dressmaking 1877–1882 is a new work first published by Lavolta Press in 2004. All translations; new text and illustrations; the selection and arrangement of period text, illustrations, and patterns; and revised versions of the period materials are protected by copyright. They may not be reproduced or transmitted in any form without prior written permission from Lavolta Press.

First edition

ISBN: 0-9636517-6-5

Published by
Lavolta Press
20 Meadowbrook Drive
San Francisco, CA 94132
http://www.lavoltapress.com

Book design, cover design, scanning, scan editing and coloring, page layout, and production management by Frances Grimble and Allan Terry

Printed and bound in the United States of America

Publisher's Cataloging-in-Publication Data
(Prepared by The Donohue Group, Inc.)

Fashions of the gilded age / edited and with additional material by Frances Grimble. -- 1st ed.
  2 v.
  Includes bibliographical references and indexes.
  Contents: v.1. Undergarments, bodices, skirts, overskirts, polonaises, and day dresses, 1877-1882 -- v.2. Evening, bridal, sports, outerwear, accessories, and dressmaking, 1877-1882.
  ISBN: 0-9636517-5-7 (v.1)
  ISBN: 0-9636517-6-5 (v.2)
1. Dressmaking--Patterns. 2. Dressmaking--Pattern design.
3. Dressmaking--History--19th century. 4. Costume--History--19th century. 5. Fashion--History--19th century. 6. Millinery--History--19th century. 7. Vintage clothing--Collectors and collecting. 8. Vintage clothing--Repairing. I. Grimble, Frances.

TT520 .F37 2004
646.4'07--dc21   2003114921

Acknowledgments

Foremost thanks go to Theresa Reinhardt, who translated the entire text of *Vollständige Schule der Damenschneiderei* from German to English. Although I have used edited selections from her work, it forms the basis for much of this book. Ema Wirz-Fischinger also provided translation assistance.

My husband, Allan Terry, helped to design the cover and interior, and to scan the illustrations and patterns. He edited and colored the cover scans, and drew the apportioning scales. He also did prepress work, built a metric conversion spreadsheet, kept my computer running, and performed countless other tasks.

My brother, Robert Grimble, gave legal assistance with contracts and copyrights. Pete Masterson of Aeonix advised us on printing our images. Sean Alemzadeh of Consultex provided color proofs. Our printer, McNaughton & Gunn, did their usual high-quality job. Special thanks to our account rep Karl Frauhammer.

To Allan, who I love more than anything

 **Contents**

Volume 1

Contents

Contents

 **Contents**

6 Evening Bodices   246

7 Overskirts   277

Contents

Contents

Volume 2

Contents

Contents

Contents

Contents

Contents

Introduction

Fashions of the Gilded Age concentrates on a 19th-century silhouette sometimes called the "cuirass bodice and natural form." From the late 1860s into the mid 1870s, the silhouette had been that of a hoopskirt with a large bustle, with puffy skirt drapery on top. Some fashion historians call this the "first bustle period." In the second half of 1876, clothing became significantly narrower and closer to the body. Although dresses still had back emphasis, any bustle worn was smaller, with the skirt often flowing gracefully into a long train. By late 1882, back and hip drapery had increased and begun to evolve into the prominent bustle of 1883 into 1889, sometimes called the "second bustle period."

Although the "form" of 1877 through 1882 looked natural in comparison to the preceding and following bustle periods, it usually required artificial aids. The torso was fashionably supported by a boned corset, such as the Spoon Busk Corset in volume 1, chapter 2. Adherents of the rational dress movement and the aesthetic movement sometimes substituted a soft underbodice with buttons to support the petticoats (they considered it healthful to depend garment weight from the shoulders). Or they used an alternative corset such as the Japanese Corset given in volume 1, chapter 2. Bustles and even hoopskirts were still worn to some extent, as evidenced by the Dimity Bustle and the Muslin Hoopskirt (see volume 1, chapter 2). The skirt might instead be supported by petticoats with back flounces of either heavily starched fabric (such as the Muslin Petticoat in volume 1, chapter 3) or of crinoline. Sometimes similar flounces, or even hoop wires, were attached to the underside of the dress skirt in back (as with the Embroidered Camel's Hair Dress in volume 1, chapter 9).

Although not mandatory, it was common to wear an undervest next to the skin (wool was considered particularly healthful). Next came the drawers and the chemise (volume 1, chapter 3 shows 19 chemise styles). A corset cover or underbodice (such as the Underbodice with Round Neck in volume 1, chapter 3), was worn over the corset. The petticoats were also worn over the corset.

The narrow fashionable line made it desirable to reduce the bulk of undergarments, and there were several means to this end. One was the fitted, or princess, chemise (see the Princess Chemise in volume 1, chapter 3). Another was the combination garment, which could combine the chemise and the drawers, the chemise and the corset cover, or the chemise and a petticoat. Wide yokes on petticoats (such as the Long Underskirt in volume 1, chapter 3) and drawers shifted gathers to below the waist. Or, instead of having separate yokes, several petticoats (arranged vertically) could be buttoned to one yoke or to an underbodice.

There were three basic types of fashionable dress. One was the separate bodice, skirt, and overskirt, such as the Sateen Dress in volume 1, chapter 9. The bodice was usually a basque. This had a short skirt (what we would call a peplum) that was either cut in one with the rest of the bodice or sewn on. The cuirass bodice was a basque that was so long waisted and close fitting that it was reminiscent of armor. The dress skirt was simply cut, with four to six gores. It was often merely a foundation of cheap fabric with trimmings mounted on the areas exposed by the overskirt. It was furnished with several inside elastics or pairs of tape ties in back to keep the fullness there. (Contemporaries sometimes called this style the "tie-back.") The overskirt was cut in a variety of ways, but the starting point for most seems to have been either the gored skirt pattern, or plain rectangles. The real interest lay in the draping. By "draping" I mean the manner in which the overskirt was pleated, looped up, and turned up, tacked together and held

by tapes, even if the style was taken from a published pattern rather than developed on a three-dimensional form. (See the Overskirt for Directoire Basque and Round Skirt in volume 1, chapter 7.) For some overskirts made of washable materials, the drapery was secured mostly by tape ties, or by buttons and buttonholes, so the overskirt could be laid out flat for ironing. The overskirt was omitted in some simple dresses such as the Grosgrain Reception Dress in volume 1, chapter 9.

The second type was the princess dress, a basic pattern for which is the Princess Dress in volume 1, chapter 9. The princess was a long, close-fitting style with continuous pieces from neck to hem—a darted front, one or two side pieces, and the back. The basic style was especially popular for simple house dresses and for outer coats. The princess was sometimes trimmed to resemble a separate basque and skirt. It was often elaborated to include waist seams partway around and/or skirt drapery, as with the Satin Bridal Toilette in volume 2, chapter 3.

The third type was the polonaise, which was worn over a skirt as an alternative to a separate bodice and overskirt. Some polonaises were shorter princess dresses. These were pleated up in a variety of ways (for example the Overdress for Mousseline des Indes Dress in volume 1, chapter 8). Other polonaises were bodices with the overskirt attached (for example the Velvet and Satin de Lyon Basque in volume 1, chapter 5). The inspiration for these, particularly when combined with a square neckline and elbow-length ruffled sleeves, was 18th century.

As well as being constructed separately, garment sections were at times worn separately to extend the size of the wardrobe or the useful life of specific garments. A new dress often included day and evening bodices, or two evening bodices of differing formality, to match a single skirt. Last year's bodices were rejuvenated by being worn with contrasting skirts, and vice versa. The overskirt could be attached to its own waistband, rather than the skirt's, so that both were usable as parts of other outfits. The ingenious detachable train swiftly converted a practical walking dress into a trained house dress, or an evening dress into a more formal one. Such trains were used for both dress skirts (such as the Evening Dress with Removable Train in volume 2, chapter 2) and petticoats (such as the Underskirt with Buttoned-On Train in volume 1, chapter 3).

Even though some garment parts could be worn as "separates," a number of different outfits were required for different occasions. Day dresses typically had high necklines and long sleeves, although in summer sleeves might be elbow length or even short (see the Bodice for Striped Percale Suit in volume 1, chapter 5). Etiquette recommendations (quoted at the beginnings of chapters in this book) were made for walking dresses, carriage dresses, dresses for social calls, dresses for luncheons, church dresses, and other functions.

Evening dresses tended to have lower necklines (oval, narrow or broad square, or V) and shorter sleeves (from cap sleeves to elbow length). The amount of flesh exposed varied with the formality of the occasion. Only the most elaborate events, such as balls, required the lowest neckline, the smallest sleeves, and often, back lacing (see the Satin Dress in volume 2, chapter 2). Casual evening calls, informal parties, and even formal dinners required the bosom and arms to be more covered (see the Basque Bodice with Square Neck in volume 1, chapter 6).

Outfits made for specific occasions included traveling dresses, sports outfits, and wedding dresses. Traveling dresses were plain, practical suits with a separate jacket, skirt, and simply draped overskirt. (See the Overskirt for Traveling Costume in volume 1, chapter 7.) Riding habits, also plain and practical, required trousers under the skirt rather than a petticoat, in case of accident. The skirt, and sometimes the trousers in addition, was cut asymmetrically for riding sidesaddle (see the Modern Riding Trousers in volume 2, chapter 4). Bathing (swimming or wading) outfits were belted tunics worn over trousers (see the White Serge Bathing Suit in volume 2, chapter 4).

Because a wedding dress was as expensive and fashionable as the bride's family could afford, it was worn after the wedding (minus bridal trimmings

such as wax orange blossoms). Often elaborate decoration and nonwashable white fabric made it best suited to formal evening wear (see the Satin Merveilleux Bridal Toilette in volume 2, chapter 3). However, a low neckline and short sleeves were considered inappropriate for a wedding dress. This problem was solved by using some detachable parts, such as a plastron to fill in a square neckline, or by remodeling the bodice after the wedding, for example to replace long sleeves with short ones.

A woman's wardrobe included a variety of outerwear to suit not only the occasion but the weather. If it was not too cold or wet, the jacket of a walking suit served simultaneously as a bodice and an outer covering. (See the Basque for Brocade and Velvet Visiting Dress in volume 1, chapter 5.) Some styles were so similar that a jacket-bodice pattern could be adapted as an additional layer merely by cutting it larger and perhaps longer. There was an array of coats, close fitting, half fitting, or loose (sacques), the fit controlled by the number of darts and seams. Waterproofs (raincoats) and traveling mantles could have pelerines (shoulder capes over the main part of the coat), like the Mantle with Optional Pelerine and Hood in volume 2, chapter 5. Circular capes, sometimes hooded, were also worn. A unique wrap of the period was the dolman, which had the sleeve cut in one with the side piece and hanging over the arm. Dolmans were made for both day and evening (see the Camel's Hair Opera Cloak in volume 2, chapter 5).

Some wraps were fashionable finishing touches rather than protection from the elements. These included mantelets and mantillas, shaped rather like shawls with material on the sides removed (see the two Mantelets for Evening in volume 2, chapter 5). In fact some were made from shawls. The cashmere shawls that had been a wardrobe staple for decades had mostly gone out of fashion. Because they were very expensive, women were loath to discard or cut into them. Folding and tacking a shawl into a mantle, in a way that allowed reconversion to a shawl, was a sensible course. This was also done with lace shawls. (See the India Shawl Worn as a Cloak and the Lace Shawl Worn as a Mantle in volume 2, chapter 5.)

Because most dresses were custom made (by a dressmaker or at home), women were deeply concerned with materials. (See volume 2, chapter 8, which is essentially a dressmaking manual.) Materials represented the greatest cost for an outfit and were reused till they wore out. They too varied with the season and occasion. Day dress fabrics for fall and winter included wool, cloth, cashmere, plush, velvet, and repped silk. (See the glossary in appendix C of this volume.) For spring and summer they included muslin, gingham, percale, sateen, batiste, lawn, bunting, nun's veiling, cashmere, camel's hair, grenadine, pongee, louisine, foulard, faille, and grosgrain. For evening dresses they included velvet, brocade, satin, faille, gauze, crape, and tulle. Outerwear fabrics for winter included homespun cloth, lamb's wool cloth, cheviot, cashmere, camel's hair, sicilienne, velvet, and satin. Summer wraps used beige, vigogne, cashmere, mohair, pongee, lace, and tulle.

Black was worn a great deal for both day dresses and outerwear. It was considered to look good on most people, be suitable for most occasions, and coordinate with most other colors. Other colors tended to be earth tones. Popular colors included ecru, beige, tan, brown, olive green, light gray, light drab, several shades of light and dark blue, and a few reds—terracotta, peony, claret color. Colors for evening dresses included ivory; pastels such as pale green, pale blue, and pink; a few darker yellows and browns such as canary yellow, old gold, and bronze; and of course black.

Most dresses used two or more fabrics contrasting in texture, and two or more shades of one color or contrasting colors (which was convenient for recycling partly worn dresses). For example, the Scotch Plaid Dress in volume 1, chapter 9 is composed of blue and green plaid (probably wool), with black velvet imitation vest, overskirt trimmings, pocket flaps, and cuff trimmings. The Ottoman Silk and Figured Plush Dress in the same chapter uses these two differently textured materials in the same

 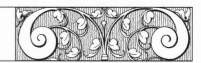

dark shade of terracotta. The Velvet and Brocaded Gauze Evening Dress in volume 2, chapter 2 has a shrimp pink satin skirt covered with brocaded gauze, and a golden brown velvet bodice, pannier drapery, and train.

When smallish garment parts such as pocket flaps were made from contrasting fabric they were referred to as "trimmings." Popular applied trimmings included kilt-pleated flounces, machine lace (white, black, and with colors), machine-embroidered fabric, passementerie, and beading. (See the trimmings in volume 2, chapter 7.) Lingerie was lavishly trimmed with machine lace, hand-crocheted and -knitted lace, and hand and machine embroidery (sometimes colored). Closures and clasps, such as buttons and bonnet pins, were also forms of decoration.

Accessories were important to provide variety and finish an outfit. Married women wore breakfast caps in the morning, though only elderly women wore caps all day. Outdoors, women usually wore a bonnet or hat, such as the Black Chip Bonnet in volume 2, chapter 6. Formal evening headdresses consisted of wreaths and sprays of artificial flowers and ribbon. A hood was often worn over these outdoors; it disarranged the hair less than a bonnet.

There was a great deal of pretty neckwear. Most bodices had a firmly attached, narrow standing collar. Additional white collars and cuffs, made with lace and/or embroidery, were basted to the bodice for easy removal. (See volume 2, chapter 6 for neckwear patterns.) Other neckwear included cravats (neckties), jabots, fichus, and scarves.

It was fashionable to wear a belt with various items dangling from it, a medieval-inspired arrangement called the chatelaine. The items could include a reticule, a fan, and for evening, ivory ball tablets (a sort of erasable dance card). Women carried a parasol or perhaps a muff outdoors, depending on the season.

Metal jewelry tended to be massive and Etruscan inspired in design. Homemade fabric jewelry included lace necklaces, beaded velvet necklaces, and painted silk button jewelry such as the Silk Necklace in volume 2, chapter 6.

Stockings, even for ordinary day wear, were rather ostentatious. They had multicolored narrow stripes, or were embroidered with clocks or other patterns, or were beaded. Indoor shoes were slippers, in a style we would call pumps. They often had a Louis XV heel and 18th-century-inspired embroidery or a large rosette. Buttoned ankle boots, also with the Louis XV heel, were worn outdoors.

Despite minor regional differences, styles and construction techniques were international. Fashion plates, sewing and needlework patterns, sewing instructions, and information from fashion columns circulated among German, French, English, and American magazines and books. Some basic information, such as illustrated instructions for stitches and seams, was repeated in different venues for years. *Fashions of the Gilded Age* draws from German, American, and English sources. (See the attributions for specific material, the bibliography in appendix D of this volume, and chapter 1 of this volume.) Its purpose in doing so is to give a wide view of fashionable women's clothing, a large selection of patterns and fashion plates, and hard-to-find details on garment construction.

Frances Grimble, 2004

1. Enlarging the Patterns

The primary pattern sources used in this book are an 1883 manual titled *Vollständige Schule der Damenschneiderei*, 112 issues of *Harper's Bazar* from 1877 through 1882, and an 1877 annual volume of the *Englishwoman's Domestic Magazine*. (See the bibliography in appendix D.) The chapters in this book are organized by garment type. Because each source is strong in different garments and even garment parts, you may want to use patterns from several sources (as well as chapters) in assembling one outfit. Feel free to combine and substitute bodices, skirts, overskirts, sleeves, collars, etc. to achieve your desired result.

At the beginning of each chapter is a section containing substantial "quotes" drawn from original fashion magazines and etiquette manuals. (I edited the quotes for focus and brevity.) In addition to describing appropriate ensembles for different occasions, the quotes contain useful details on garment construction. Some are recipes for drafting simple accessories and garments. The dressmaking manual in volume 2, chapter 8, which was reworked from such a wide variety of sources that it became too difficult to quote, will also reward study prior to drafting a pattern.

Using Patterns from Ladies' Garment Cutting

Vollständige Schule der Damenschneiderei, by Henrich Klemm, may be loosely translated as *The Complete Guide to Ladies' Garment Cutting*. Despite the 1883 publication date of this edition (the 11th), the styles are from the "cuirass bodice and natural form" period of 1876 through 1882. A few may be earlier. It is likely that some patterns were also published in previous editions and/or a magazine that Klemm edited, *Zeitung für die Elegante Welt* (*Journal for Elegant Society*). As far as I know, Klemm never published his material in English.

The Complete Guide to Ladies' Garment Cutting also contained many patterns for children and a few for men, which have been omitted from this book. The women's patterns comprise a rich selection of bodices, outer coats and wraps, undergarments, and the main skirt shapes. Klemm's drawing style is technical, which tends to make his garment styles look tailored. However, many patterns are suitable for fabrics and trimmings not usually thought of as tailored.

Klemm was the director of the Europäische Moden-Akademie (European Fashion Academy) in Dresden. His book seems to have been used as a text, and to have at some point superseded large unbound pattern sheets (although the book included one life-size practice draft, shown reduced in figures 5 and 6). The book format did more than provide the Academy's students with a more easily handled text. It made Klemm's material available to a much wider audience as a self-study guide. Judging from his introduction (omitted here), he views his readers as female, as including both professional and amateur dressmakers, and as beginners at pattern drafting.

In addition to providing drafts of specific garments, Klemm teaches his readers several different pattern-making methods. These are drafting with his system of apportioning scales, drafting with ordinary measuring tools, and developing more complex styles from an existing pattern.

Apportioning scales were a common 19th-century method of obtaining many garment sizes from one printed draft without doing arithmetic. They are special rulers that make it easy to enlarge patterns designed for that system to an individual's body measurements. Each scale has units of a different size (see appendix A). Scales for smaller sizes have smaller units, and scales for larger sizes have larger units. Thus the units on the pattern can be used to draft any size.

Patterns with ordinary units are drafted following much the same procedure as for patterns with apportioning scale units. However, all size adjustments must be made after drafting. Since many Americans do not use the metric system, I provided conversions to imperial units in parentheses on the patterns and in the instructions.

Klemm's method of developing new styles from an existing pattern is more oriented toward drawing around the pattern outlines than modern slash-and-spread or pivot-and-slide techniques. Any measurements given are metric (with imperial equivalents). Sometimes the starting pattern is a simple close-fitting bodice (what we would call a sloper). Sometimes it is more similar to the final desired pattern. His detailed diagrams make his method simple and, once learned, it can be used to produce additional styles not included in this book.

Klemm's directions for these three methods are given below from "Taking the Measures" through "Preparing a Bodice." I rewrote them for clarity and provided introductory information.

Using Patterns from Harper's Bazar

Harper's Bazar was a stylish, up-to-date weekly fashion magazine. Each issue contained fashion plates, fashion columns, and patterns for fancy needlework (such as crochet and embroidery). Many contained advertisements for sewing patterns readers could order from the magazine. Alternate issues included oversized supplement sheets printed with full-size sewing patterns, distinguished by different line types. (Figure 1 shows a scaled-down supplement.) Because these patterns, unlike Klemm's, convey the nuances of seasonal style changes, I labeled the instructions for each one I chose with the month and year of original publication.

Although *Harper's Bazar* was published in New York, most of its sewing and needlework patterns were licensed from *Der Bazar* in Berlin. The cuts are similar to Klemm's, but contain more ephemeral variations. Patterns are given for more specialized garments such as wedding gowns and bathing suits. The *Harper's Bazar* patterns give more detail on fabrics, trimmings, and construction methods.

Many *Harper's Bazar* dress patterns are for ensembles—a bodice, overskirt, and sometimes a skirt—rather than separate garment parts as with Klemm. The overskirts and polonaises are particularly useful to combine with Klemm's bodices, because he provides very few patterns for the former. The *Harper's Bazar* ensembles do not always include skirts, but Klemm's may be freely substituted.

As figure 1 shows, it was essential for me to separate out, scale down, and redraw the *Harper's Bazar* patterns. The scales used are 1/16, 1/8, 1/4, 1/2, and occasionally 1:1. My choice of scale was based on whether the pattern piece was small enough to fit on the page and large enough to contain its labels. I labeled each pattern piece with the scale used. Where possible I kept all pieces for a garment to the same scale. No allowances are given for seams, hems, or facings unless the pattern instructions explicitly say otherwise.

The *Harper's Bazar* patterns can be enlarged by projection, by gridding, and in some cases by photocopying. (As can the scaled patterns I drew from other sources.) Projection is the most flexible method, because it enables you to enlarge the pattern to any desired size. Gridding allows you to scale up the pattern to its original size (and make fitting alterations later). Photocopying works best for pattern pieces small enough to fit on one sheet of paper after enlargement. It is the easiest method for patterns with designs for surface decoration such as embroidery.

Pattern pieces are not given for some simple sections such as skirt waistbands. These can be drafted to the wearer's measurements in ordinary units. In some cases you may be able to borrow a piece from another pattern.

Using Patterns from the Englishwoman's Domestic Magazine

The patterns from the *Englishwoman's Domestic Magazine* are meant for cutting by the cloth. This is a traditional pattern-making method that by the late 1870s was used only for some undergarments and skirts. The pattern shapes are determined primarily by the fabric width, so most are geometric. The

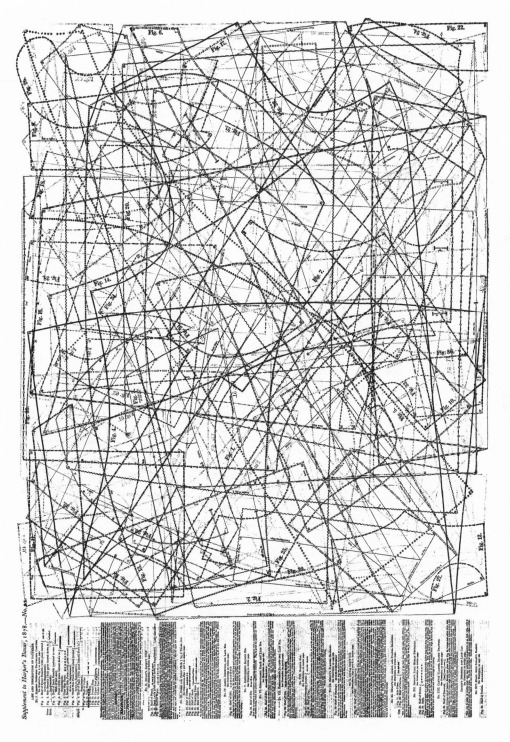

Figure 1. One side of the original pattern supplement for June 1, 1878

finished garments are only roughly sized. The wearer's exact measurements are unimportant except for a few more fitted pieces such as chemise yokes and skirt waistbands.

The *Englishwoman's Domestic Magazine* gives sketches, measurements, and instructions rather than scale patterns. Readers were expected to cut directly into the cloth. However, it was customary to copy measurements from a similar garment in the wearer's wardrobe, which is not an option for most modern readers. I suggest drafting these patterns onto paper (using ordinary units) and doing a rough fitting before cutting into fabric.

Frances Grimble, 2004

Taking the Measures

Measures should only be taken over the corset intended to be worn with the garment for which the measures are taken, including the desired wraps underneath, and over a close and neat-fitting body garment. If the body is covered by heavy goods–even if close fitting–their texture and weight must be considered. These touch the degree of tightness or looseness with which the tape measure is drawn, in comparison with measuring over lighter fabrics.

Encyclopedia of Scientific Tailor Principles, 1885

To draft a well-fitting pattern, it is essential to measure the body accurately. Taking the measures does more than determine the width and length of the most important garment parts. These measures also provide precise information about the lady's figure and posture.

There are 20 measures for all garments, with no more than 12 for the bodice pattern, so that you must not think of this as at all tedious or complicated. All positions of the measures are shown in figure 2, numbered in the order in which they are taken. To make it all easier, you only need a well-organized measure book, in which all measures are already printed, so that only the figure for each must be entered.

An essential tool is an ordinary measuring tape. Also necessary is a belt or strong tape. This is fastened closely around the lady's waist to create

an accurate horizontal line, which helps to mark where the most important length measurements end.

Measure 1: The breast circumference. This measure is taken directly under the arms in a horizontal line around the upper body and in front across the largest part of the bust, and without having the bust held in or pushed out unnaturally. The measuring tape must not be held too loose nor too tight. Care must be taken that it runs correctly over the largest part of the shoulder blades in the back, for if it is left to slide down carelessly, the breast circumference will be too small. The latter would be just as great a disadvantage as if the measure had been taken too large, because the entire drafting system is based primarily on this measure.

The breast circumference is always written down in half. Half centimeters need not be taken into account. If the total circumference were for example 89 cm (35 1/16 in.), do not note 44 1/2 (17 1/2), but round up to 45 (17 11/16), because such a small increase makes no difference in an otherwise correctly drafted pattern.

Measure 2: The waist circumference. This is taken where the waist is narrowest, and it is also written down as half. This measure is taken rather close even when the person desires the garment unusually loose or tight, in which case a special note should be made in the measure book and the appropriate amount later added or subtracted when drafting. The same applies for outer garments. For corsets, the waist circumference should be assumed 3 to 4 cm (1 3/16 to 1 9/16 in.) per half smaller than what it is above the dress.

Measure 3: The high bust width. This measure is indispensable for making the bodice pattern fit each lady. The form of the bust is infinitely variable, which often results in alterations to the regular patterns.

The high bust width does not run in a straight line, but somewhat downward in a curved line from the arm across the largest part of the bust. Occasionally it must be measured even deeper should the largest part of the bust be very low. Figure 3 shows the location of the high bust width.

Figure 2. Taking the measures in front and back

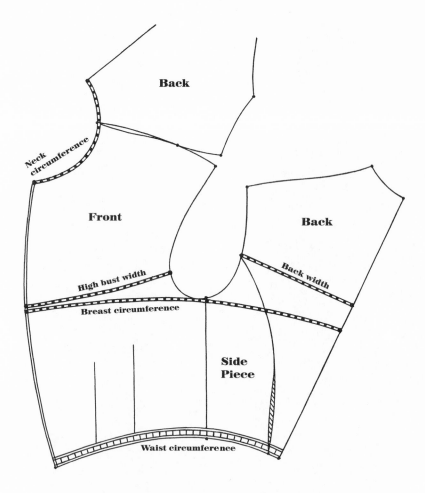

Figure 3. Measuring widths and circumferences on the pattern

Allowance for ease is included in the pattern where necessary. Thus the high bust width may be used exactly as measured, as long as the garment worn by the lady is not too tight in the front. If this measure must be taken over garments that are very full or of such a style that you cannot see the center front exactly, the measure should be taken across the entire bust in the necessary curved line from one arm to the other. Half of that is then written down as the high bust width.

Measure 4: The neck circumference. The neck circumference is only necessary for garments that are tight around the neck and must fit there exactly. It should, if at all possible, be measured on the bare neck–not over the garments or around a stiff collar–although the small amount the collar would add

must always be included. The measuring tape must be applied so that it touches the vertebra in back and the hollow of the throat in front. This measure is taken around the neck, but only half is written down.

The standard patterns assume the standard size of the neck measure. It may, however, be as much as 2 or 3 cm (13/16 or 1 3/16 in.) less in thin, and usually too long, necks. For very thick necks, it may be up to 3 cm (1 3/16 in.) more. Consequently, the neck opening must be modified accordingly.

Measure 5: The back width. It is advisable to measure the back width with the lady's arms hanging down straight. It may then be seen more precisely and easily whether the back of the garment she is wearing is too narrow or wide, or whether

you may use exactly the same back width. The back width is also strongly determined by the prevailing fashion. The back width is always defined in the pattern. You may follow the pattern whenever the correct measure could not be obtained.

The amount by which the high bust width and back width are smaller than half the breast circumference results in the horizontal armhole diameter, if you add the amount by which every well-fitting dress bodice is bigger in the breast circumference than the body measure.

Measure 6: The back length. The measuring tape is placed at the neck vertebra of the lady and continued to the lower edge of the belt, which will then show the exact back length. Measure 6 is shown on the pattern in figure 4.

If the waist is to be lengthened in the garment, the measuring tape will be continued past the belt. Both the measures above and below the waist must be recorded in the measure book. For example, a

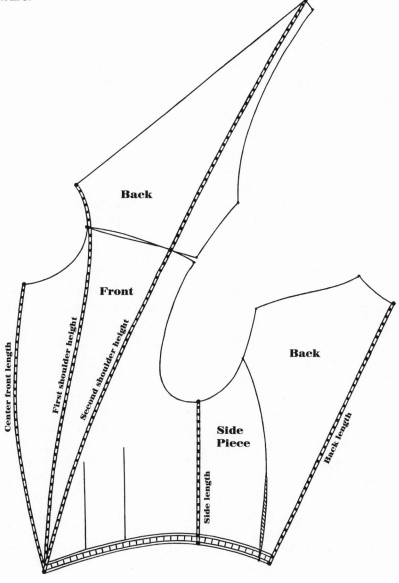

Figure 4. Measuring lengths on the pattern

38 cm (14 15/16 in.) unlengthened and a 43 cm (16 15/16 in.) lengthened waist in the back would be written as 38/43.

Measure 7: The center front length. This measure goes from the hollow of the throat straight down to the lower edge of the belt. With its help, you may find the center front of the waistline more precisely, and also the exact upper edge of the high dress bodice. The center front length also helps to determine necessary darts and their size, especially for very large, rounded busts.

Measure 8: The first shoulder height. This measure starts where the neck joins the shoulder and continues in a slanting line to the center front of the waistline. It must be taken carefully because many ladies need an unusually long front pattern piece. This is sometimes caused by the size of the bust, sometimes by the posture of the upper body.

Measure 9: The second shoulder height. This measure proceeds in a slanting line from the center back of the waistline over the shoulder to the center front of the waistline. The second shoulder height is very important for assessing the shape of the shoulders, in which there may occur great variations. Some shoulders slope considerably, which is commonly called "low" shoulders, and some shoulders are square or "high." If the shoulders are low, the measure of the second shoulder height will be smaller than usual. If they are high, it will be larger.

Measure 10: The side length. This measure is taken from under the arm to the waistline, unless the garment is to have a lengthened waist. It is preferable to add any extra length when drafting, following the prevailing fashion. If the extra length is instead measured on the body, the two side lengths are written down one above the other. For example, 17/23 would mean a 17 cm (6 11/16 in.) side length and a 6 cm (2 3/8 in.) extension.

Measure 11: The arm length or sleeve length. This is measured from under the arm straight down to the wrist, or as long as fashion or taste dictates. If you want to also measure the length to the elbow for reassurance, its number is written above the number for the entire arm length; for example, 21/44.

Measure 12: The armhole circumference. This measure is taken around the armhole following the seam where the sleeve is inserted into the bodice; for in narrow shoulder widths, the armhole is larger than if the shoulders are so wide as to fall on the upper arm. The tape is held taut, but without pinching or being stretched. For a very thin lady it is advisable not to take this measure as closely, as a larger armhole will lend her arms a somewhat fuller appearance.

Persons with very muscular shoulders and upper arms often require a larger armhole than the standard pattern. Where the measure differs by more than 1 cm (3/8 in.) from the standard, you can cut the armhole a little lower. Care must be taken, for damage is often done by enlarging the armhole unnecessarily.

In persons who work much, and mostly with the right hand while the left remains idle, there is often an unevenness in the size of the shoulders. This is because the entire right side of the upper body develops more strongly, while the left side is smaller. You may immediately see this in back by looking at the shoulder blade. If you failed to take this into account, the garment would hinder the right shoulder continously. In these cases measure the armhole circumference separately on each side and adjust the pattern accordingly. However, this will only be necessary when the unevenness is clearly visible.

Measure 13: The elbow circumference. This measure is taken where the elbow is the thickest. It is not noted down as half, but in its entirety.

Measure 14: The wrist or sleeve circumference. This measure is taken at the wrist if the sleeve is to end above the hand. For long sleeves without a slit, which are to go to the wrist and are not supposed to be overly wide, it is better to take this measure around the widest part of the palm, so the hand will fit through the sleeve.

This measure is noted down in its entirety. Since there is a difference of several centimeters between the wrist and the palm, there cannot be any confusion later. You may also measure in both places and write the two figures above each other, for example, 12/18.

For close-fitting sleeves, you will occasionally, in addition to the elbow circumference, measure the upper arm in the middle between shoulder joint and elbow, where the muscle is the strongest. This measure is also entered into the measure book in the following way: 31 1/2/32.

For sleeves that are short, wide at the end, or very full, all sleeve circumference measures are superfluous.

Measure 15: The back skirt length. Measuring and drafting a correct skirt length is more important than it seems. Not only must fashion be taken into account, but also the appearance of the lady, her position in society, the material used, and the purpose of the garment.

It is best not to measure the finished skirt length, but to take the body measures from the waist to the floor. You can then draft any skirt length by subtracting or adding for the style of dress.

For dresses with long trains it is, however, advisable to take measures for the finished skirt length. Some dressmakers believe they are proceeding correctly if they measure the length for the train from the waist straight to where the lower edge of the train will touch the ground. This will not suffice, since this measure forms a straight line. The dress with a train will be compressed toward the bottom, so that part of the length is absorbed. It is therefore necessary to either take the measure as loose as the dress will fall, or, depending on the length of the train, to add 10 or 20 cm (3 15/16 or 7 7/8 in.) to it, as the train is supposed to look when worn.

Measure 16: The side skirt length. This measure is taken at the side, continuing the line of the side length, from the waistline to the floor.

With trained dresses, it is entirely sufficient to measure the back and front skirt lengths, because the side skirt length can never be determined exactly. Instead, it must be worked out when drafting the skirt how long the sides may be while following the even flow of the edge.

Measure 17: The front skirt length. This measure is taken at the center front, from the waistline to the floor.

Measure 18: The shoulder width. The shoulder width results from the standard pattern. This measure is consequently required only if fashion prescribes narrower or wider shoulders, and for highly irregular figures.

Measure 19: The hip circumference. This measure is required for garments that fit closely at the hips—basque bodices, jackets, coats, princess dresses, and close-fitting skirts. At times it is also advisable to take a separate measure for the lower skirt circumference.

Measure 20: The back skirt length for basque bodices, jackets, coats, and the like. This measure is rarely necessary, for usually the length is determined by fashion.

For many undergarments, our system requires at most three measures: Breast circumference, neck circumference, and whole garment length, which depends on the lady's height. The neck circumference is only necessary for garments worn high at the neck. The garment length measure may also be dispensed with as long as a medium size is desired. For drawers, the measures are the waist circumference and the length of drawers.

Complete Guide to Ladies' Garment Cutting, 1883

Gathering Tools and Materials

To enlarge a pattern you will need the following:

Measuring tools. A yardstick or meter stick, and a 6- or 12-in. ruler or its metric equivalent. Clear plastic is best. For patterns that use apportioning scales, the scales in appendix A.

A large L-square. Handy for drawing perpendicular lines, but optional; you can use a yardstick instead.

A set of French curves. Available in art stores.

A hip curve. The top often works for armholes.

A flexible or "spline" curve. For curves that don't match any of your French curves well. Optional but useful.

Pattern paper, plain or marked in 1 in. squares. Or pattern-tracing cloth, a gridded lightweight interfacing that can later be used as the muslin.

Writing tools. A soft writing pencil and an eraser.

Cheap scissors. For cutting paper.

A transparency or opaque overhead projector if you are projecting the pattern.

Transparent graph paper if you are adding a grid to the pattern. A gridded mylar is sold in art stores, or you can make your own by copying graph paper onto transparency film.

A double tracing wheel. For adding seam allowances; optional.

Drafting with Apportioning Scales

In Klemm's system, the only scale used is the apportioning scale that corresponds to the individual's half breast circumference. The half breast, rather than the full breast, was chosen because each pattern piece is cut out either double or on the fold of the material. All sizing other than the breast circumference is built into the pattern, although Klemm recommends using ordinary units to draft or correct some measurements.

The Complete Guide to Ladies' Garment Cutting was originally sold with a large separate sheet printed with 43 apportioning scales. Klemm says these are sufficient to draft patterns for any size "from the smallest child to the stoutest lady." Redrawings of all 43 scales are supplied in appendix A. Each scale is labeled (in both metric and imperial units) with the half breast circumference it is used for. Because scale lengths are limited by the book size, only as many units are given as fit on the page, in groups of 10. You can create a scale long enough to draw any line by making several photocopies. Cut out the copies. Lay the first copy of the scale on a table with the label at the top. On the second copy, cut off the label and paste the top of the scale over the blank tab at the bottom of the first copy. Use a pen to change the "0" on the first copy to a "10" and the "0" on the second copy to a "20." Paste any additional copies the same way. The scales may then be pasted onto cardboard and used for drafting. Or they may be used for measurement only, and lines drawn with a yardstick.

Each pattern has a vertical baseline, marked "a" at the top. The line intersecting it at *a,* and perpendicular to it, is the first crossline. The first drafting step is to use your L-square or yardstick to draw both these lines to the lengths indicated. Measure down from *a* to the place where the second crossline starts and pencil a point. Klemm calls a point in general a "drafting point" or "point," a point indicating a vertical distance a "length point," and a point indicating a horizontal distance a "width point."

Repeat for the third crossline, and so on till you have marked where all crosslines start. Always measure from *a,* not the previous crossline (unless the instructions say otherwise). Then draw the crosslines from the points you marked on the baseline, measure across, and mark the points on them. Start with the second crossline and work down. Klemm also uses "auxiliary lines," straight drafting lines that are neither baselines nor crosslines, and calls the points marked on them "auxiliary points."

Finally, connect the points. When drawing curves, choose a French curve that fits to the ends of the lines you drew and looks like the pattern shape. You may need parts of two curves. Transfer all labels and marks given on the pattern.

For many patterns I have separated pieces that overlapped each other in the original diagrams. But for others this was impossible because multiple pieces were laid out using the same vertical baseline (see figure 6). Where these overlap, even slightly, each piece should be drawn separately, following the printed measurements but with its own baseline.

The Complete Guide to Ladies' Garment Cutting gives detailed step-by-step instructions for drafting a plain bodice pattern. Plain bodice patterns are given for different figure types in volume 1, chapter 5. The one most appropriate to yours may be used to practice drafting.

Detailed directions are then given for altering the standard pattern during drafting, to fit a variety of irregular figures. You may not need any of these alterations. If you do you may wish to draft the pattern as given, then use the alteration techniques

you use with modern commercial patterns. Or you may prefer to do all fitting in the muslin. I recommend making a muslin regardless of whether you altered the pattern.

Frances Grimble, 2004

Drafting the Plain Bodice Pattern

The drafting method is not at all difficult, and the same basic rules apply to each pattern. For practice, draft the plain bodice pattern shown completed in figures 5 and 6 for a lady with a half breast circumference of 48 cm (18 7/8 in.). First choose the scale labeled "48."

Figure 7 shows the baseline and first crossline with which all drafts start, and which is marked *a* at the upper corner. This is the baseline and first crossline for both the front and back because these pieces are drafted together. Across the top, the line in figure 7 must be lengthened past *ck* as necessary, as shown by figure 8 in more detail.

The scale is placed at corner *a*, then the length points 4 1/2, 9, 16, 22, 23, 28, and 29 are marked vertically down. That is, starting from *a*, that many units are measured to *b*, *c*, *d*, *e*, *f*, *ff*, and *g*, a point being marked every time.

Then the side length is marked in centimeters (as measured on the lady) from point *f* down to *h*, which is 17 cm (6 11/16 in.) here, and then 3 units are measured on the scale from *hx* to *ch*. All length points are now marked correctly from *a* to *ch*.

Figure 8 shows how to measure the width points, auxiliary lines, and auxiliary points. The dashed outline shows what the pattern will look like when drafted.

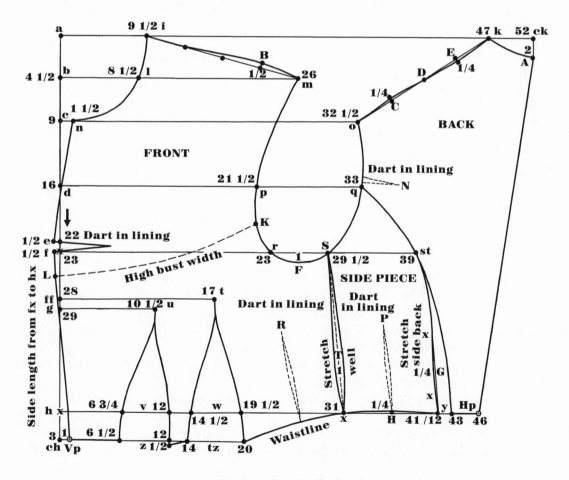

Figure 5. Practice bodice

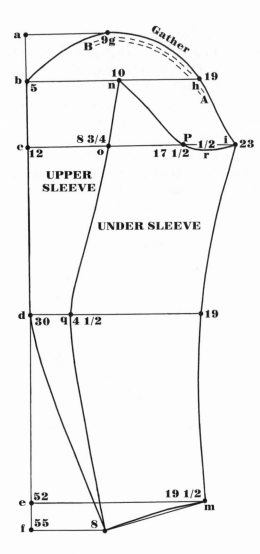

Figure 6. Practice sleeve

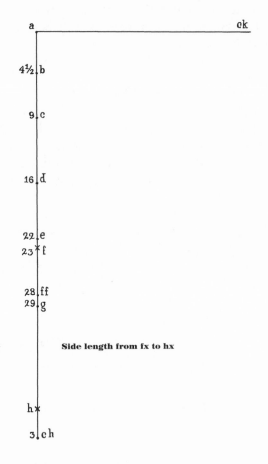

Figure 7. The baseline, first crossline, and length points

With the help of the square, the horizontal crosslines are drawn to the right. Then the width points are measured. This must be done in order, first measuring the distances *i* 9 1/2, *k* 47, *ck* 52 on the first crossline, starting from *a*. On the second crossline starting at length point *b,* lie width points *l* 8 1/2 and *m* 26, and on the third, 1 1/2 units to *n* at the front neck opening, and 32 1/2 to *o*. On the fourth crossline starting at length point *d* are width points *p* 21 1/2 and *q* 33. Then, on the next line, starting from *f* go to *r* 23, *s* 29 1/2, and *st* 39. Thus

all width points are marked from *t* to *tz,* namely: 17, 10 1/2, 6 3/4, 12, 14 1/4, 19 1/2, 31, 41 1/2, 43, 46, 1, 6 1/2, 12, 14, and 20.

The labels "Hp" on the back, and "Vp" on the front, signify "center back point" and "center front point." These points lie exactly on the waist-line.

Also needed are auxiliary lines and auxiliary points. These are intended to make drafting easier for the beginning student. After sufficient practice, most auxiliary points will be superfluous.

The shoulder seam is always slightly curved at the highest point on the shoulder where the clavicle is most visible. For that purpose, draw on the shoulder area of the front a diagonal line from *m* to *i*. At point *B*—which is always one-quarter of the shoulder width from *m* to *i*—measure out 1/2 unit for rounding the seam.

For the back, the auxiliary shoulder line is drawn from *k* to *o;* 1/4 unit is marked at *C* for rounding the seam. Then the auxiliary line is divided into four parts with points *C, D,* and *E.* At point *D,* the shoulder seam intersects the auxiliary line, and at *E* the seam moves inward by 1/4 unit to form a small curve.

From the uppermost width point *ck* 52, 2 units are marked straight down to *A* to mark the neckline at the center back. Auxiliary point *F*1 is marked

for the base of the armhole. Point *H* is marked over the crossline at the bottom of the side piece and moved in 1/4 unit for curving the waistline. In the hollow of the waist at *G,* beginners may mark 1/4 unit for the little curve in the side piece seam.

The high bust width is drawn in a rounded line from point *K* at the armhole down to *L* at the front edge, as shown in figure 5. The rounded line is needed because of the curved shape of the bust.

Special care is needed when drawing the curves of the front neck opening, the lower front darts, the armhole, and the shoulder seams.

Points *e* and *f* are marked partway down the center front and moved out by 1/2 unit each for the small horizontal front dart. Its purpose is to shape the bodice to the bust (in connection with the two lower darts). It is made only in the lining.

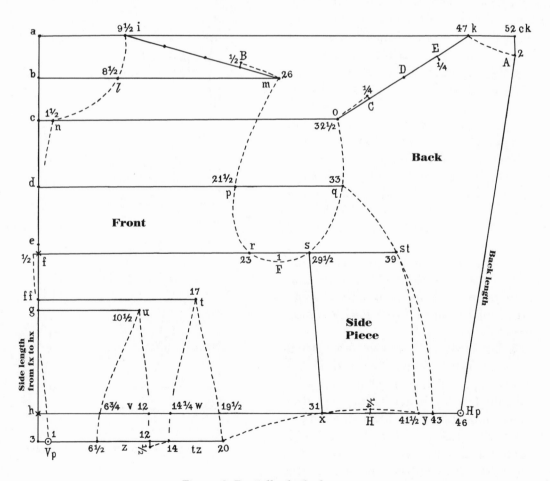

Figure 8. Partially drafted pattern

The upper material is sewn so that the front edge is a little drawn in, but as flat as possible. Sometimes the dart is replaced by pulling up the lining a trifle and pressing it.

The side piece seam is usually stretched somewhat in the bend of the waist at *G*.

The small dart in the back near *q* is essential for a well-fitting dress bodice. Its purpose is to achieve a better fit at the back of the armhole and around the shoulder blade. It is made only in the lining, and the upper material is smoothed carefully over it. This results in having to take in the upper material slightly when inserting the sleeve.

To curve the bodice to the figure, a small horizontal dart, usually called a fish dart, is made from *H* to *P* in the lining of the side piece. It is advisable to place a similar dart in the front piece at *R*, especially if the waist is lengthened toward the front.

This careful work is most essential for a perfect fit; especially if the bodice is not to wrinkle at the sides and in the hollow of the back. This is greatly aided by keeping the lining rather long, especially in those places, but rather narrow in circumference.

The lining may be 1/4 cm (1/8 in.) longer than the upper material for bodices that are unlengthened, but close fitting on the hips. For lengthened and thus more curved waists it may be 1/2 cm (3/16 in.) longer. The most careful smoothing and working of the upper material is essential, especially if the material is hard to shape by stretching and shrinking.

For ladies with a very large bust, occasionally a small dart is placed in the front of the armhole at *K*, but only in the lining. Many believe that a small dart should be placed in the front neck opening between *l* and *n*.

When a dart is added, the shape of the edge it is placed on is always significantly changed. Therefore, when cutting the lining, something must be added so that the line will be correct after the dart has been sewn, and without any loss to the dimensions of the basic pattern. For example, once the dart between *e* and *f* has been sewn, the edge sharply bows toward the inside instead of the

outside, and what was lost at the edge must be added again. That is why the front edge is moved out by 1/2 unit. The completed pattern is shown in figure 5.

The sleeve is also drafted with the scale for the half breast circumference. Figure 6 shows the common two-piece, half-fitting sleeve. Figure 9 shows a close-fitting sleeve. If the standard pattern is not wide enough at the elbow, the elbow circumference measured on the body should be used.

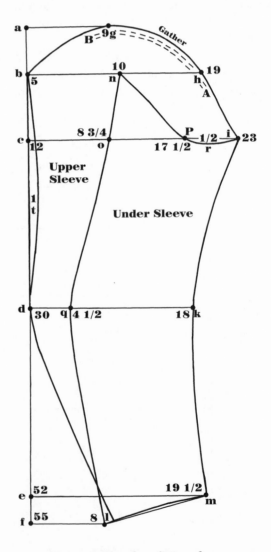

Figure 9. The close-fitting sleeve

The outline of every pattern represents the edge or the finished seam as it will look after the garment is constructed. All seams and hems, whether for the finished garment or larger ones for fitting, must be added to the pattern after drafting.

Refining the Pattern For Irregular Figures

Figures 3 and 4 have already shown how the measures are applied to the pattern once they have been taken on the body, for more precise drafting. Should the standard pattern not agree at least approximately, the necessary alterations must be made.

However, do not fall prey to the assumption that the alterations for irregular figures are all that frequent, and that you must approach each reasonably well-proportioned lady with hesitation. It is not advisable to partly mutilate the standard and perfectly drafted pattern because of a negligible difference, especially if you are not entirely certain that the measures have been taken with the utmost accuracy. To the extent possible, strive to respect the shape of the pattern. It will often be found in fitting that this is quite possible, and that you have done well to retain the standard pattern and adjust it to the figure as long as the pattern corresponds to the body in its most essential measures.

Fitting the Bust and Waist. The small horizontal dart at the front edge, marked by points e and f, may be made larger or smaller, eliminated, replaced with two darts, or moved, depending on the size and shape of the bust.

If the front edge is drafted rounded as shown, on comparing the front length of the pattern, from the hollow of the neck n to point Vp, with the front length of the body, the body measure will be somewhat smaller. The difference in length will yield the requisite size and number of darts. The dart in this standard pattern is 1 cm (3/8 in.).

It may be assumed there is a flat bust if the high bust width body measure is less than 21 to 22 units of the scale for the half breast circumference. A high bust width of more than 23 units indicates a larger bust. The high bust width is 23 cm (9 1/16 in.) here and thus a regular proportion.

Enlargement of this dart may be required by a very curved rib cage carried erect, rather than a highly developed bust. If the dart is enlarged, two darts may be used to better distribute the amount. The second dart should be located near point fx.

If the lady has a flat bust, this dart may be omitted. In that case the front edge will be drafted fairly straight by not moving out 1/2 unit at e and f. In such figures, the back is always wider and the breast narrower. What, if anything, might have to be widened in the back would be subtracted in the front. The lower bust darts will also never be as large as for a completely regular figure.

In many ladies the rounding of the bust is located lower, at the top of the two large, lower bust darts marked u and t. The horizontal dart should then be placed a few centimeters lower.

The purpose of the lower bust darts is to adjust the difference between the waistline and breast circumferences while shaping the bodice to the bust. Our pattern is intended for a 32 cm (12 5/8 in.) half waist circumference. However, many ladies with a 48 cm (18 7/8 in.) half breast have a smaller half waist circumference, as small as 28 cm (11 in.). This often indicates that the bust is unusually large. Darts u and t must be widened at the bottom. To achieve a half waist of 28 cm (11 in.) in this pattern, 2 cm (13/16 in.) more must be taken in at the bottom of each dart.

Only if an unusually large high bust width has been measured on the body with a correspondingly narrower back circumference, may it be assumed with certainty that a highly developed bust is the sole cause of the greater difference between breast and waist circumferences. Sometimes the lady's waist is very curved in back and at the sides. In this case the high bust width will not be as large compared to the standard pattern. The entire amount should not be taken in by the front darts, but part of it also at the side seam at x. The back may also be made 1/2 unit smaller at point Hp 46, while, for a very large bust, 1 more unit may be taken in at point Vp.

19

Figure 10. Lady with a wide back and narrow bust

Some experts prefer to make three lower bust darts. This makes the difference easier to divide up. Three darts are often preferred for very stout ladies.

Altering for a Wide Back and Narrow Bust. For a narrow-busted lady, the measures to be considered are the high bust width, back width, first shoulder height, second shoulder height, back length, and center front length. (See figure 10.) When comparing these to the standard pattern, in most cases the lady will require the alterations shown in figure 11, though perhaps to a greater or lesser degree.

Figure 11 assumes a moderate alteration. The back from *g* to *B* is 1 cm (3/8 in.) wider than the standard pattern. This amount is added to the center back as shown by the dashed line from *a* down to *Hp*. To prevent the back neck opening from becoming too large from *a* to *b*, 1/2 cm (3/16 in.) is subtracted from *b* to *c* following the dashed line.

Half a centimeter (3/16 in.) is removed from the lower back width at the side piece seam at *tz*. Then the same amount is added to the other side of the seam at *y*. In all other respects, the shape of the back will remain unchanged unless the second shoulder height necessitates another alteration, which would then be done according to figure 19 or 21.

The front shoulder is shortened by 1 cm (3/8 in.) from *p* to *h*. Since the shoulder point has

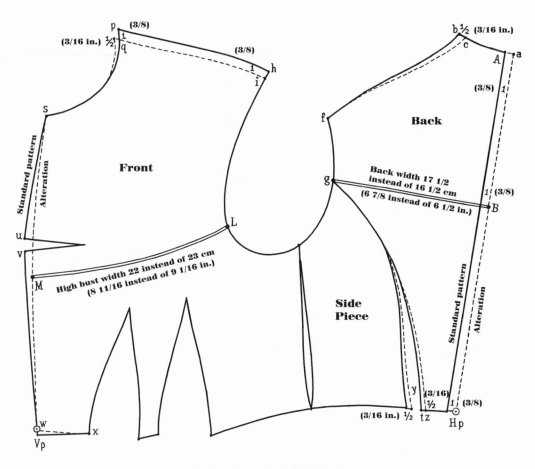

Figure 11. Altering for a wide back and narrow bust

been moved forward at *h,* the point of the neck opening should also be moved forward by 1/2 cm (3/16 in.).

The high bust width from *L* diagonally to *M* is 1 cm (3/8 in.) narrower than the standard pattern. The front is reduced starting at the bottom from *Vp,* according to the center front length, while observing the second shoulder height. The latter is drafted as in figure 19 or 21, which may make the shoulder height too small at point *i* in figure 11 depending on whether the lady's shoulders are more high or low. Removing 1 cm (3/8 in.) from the center front also softens the strong curve of the edge. The dart between *u* and *v* is omitted because

of the narrow bust. To make up for that, 1/2 to 1 cm (3/16 to 3/8 in.) is removed across the bottom at *Vp.*

Ladies with a wide back and narrow bust are often too thin overall. The shape of the shoulders and upper arms will sometimes require a smaller armhole, which has already lost 1 cm (3/8 in.) by the shortening at *h.* Comparison of the armhole circumference measure will leave no doubt as to the required size of the armhole. Such ladies also frequently have stooping figures. The alterations for a stooping figure must then be combined with those shown in figure 11.

Figure 12. Lady with a narrow back and full bust

Altering for a Narrow Back and Full Bust.
The lady in figure 12 has a flat, narrow back, very rounded bust, somewhat long center front length, but does not have extra-erect posture. The pattern in figure 13 shows that the back is narrower by 1 cm (3/8 in.), and the center back has been brought in by that much all the way down. The back length is the standard of 38 1/2 cm (15 1/8 in.), so does not require alteration. The side piece seam has been adjusted by adding 1/2 cm (3/16 in.) to the back and removing it from the side piece at *tz*. The back neck opening has been moved by 1/2 cm

(3/16 in.) at *c;* the addition is tapered into the shoulder seam.

The high bust is wider by 1 cm (3/8 in.), so the front requires more rounding than the standard pattern. Because of the erect and often even extra-erect posture of ladies with full busts, the neck opening should be moved forward somewhat starting at *p*, in conjunction with moving forward at the dashed line at *t, u, v,* and *Vp*.

Because the lady's first shoulder height is 50 cm (19 11/16 in.) instead of 49 1/2 (19 1/2 in.), the front is lengthened 1/2 cm (3/16 in.) at the

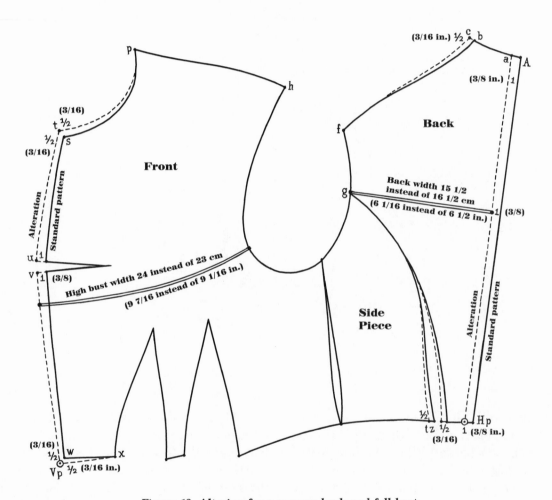

Figure 13. Altering for a narrow back and full bust

bottom from *w* to *Vp*. If the first shoulder height and center front length are more than 1 1/2 cm (9/16 in.) longer than the standard pattern, two-thirds is added at the top at *p*, and one-third at the bottom at *Vp*, to make the front conform to the actual measures.

Whether the shoulder must be enlarged at *p* or *h* will become obvious when the measure is

applied to the second and first shoulder heights. This alteration is not uncommon for this figure. When it is necessary to change the shoulder height and the position of the shoulder seam, the neck opening should be adjusted to the neck circumference to ensure that its changed position does not render it too large or too small.

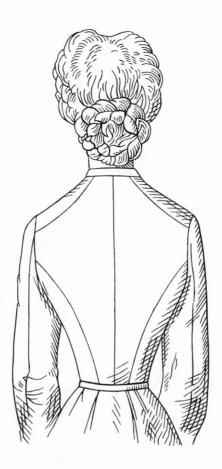

Figure 14. The overly tall, slim figure

Fitting a Tall, Slim Lady. The basic pattern ends at the natural waistline, which style is most suited to tall, slim figures. When the lengthened waist is more fashionable, it is best to give the plain bodice a curved shape that merely appears to be lengthened.

The waist length of a tall lady may differ significantly from the standard proportions. (See figure 14.) Because the distance from f down to h is drafted in ordinary units, using the actual side length of the lady, the pattern will usually be as long as necessary. However, for very tall ladies, or if you have not used the actual side length, the pattern may need to be lengthened. To see if everything is correct, the back is compared to the back length of the lady, from A down to B in figure 15. Then the first shoulder height is compared, from A via r to Vp, and the side length.

Figure 15 shows how to alter a bodice pattern of standard length for a tall, slim lady. The back length and the first shoulder height are each 2 cm (13/16 in.) longer than the standard figure, while the side length is 1 1/2 cm (9/16 in.) longer. The entire waist length is therefore 2 cm (13/16 in.) longer. The alteration is very simple; the pattern is lengthened by 2 cm (13/16 in.) all around the bottom.

However, the lower part consists of three-quarters of the whole, while one-quarter is for the part above the armhole. Therefore the amount added must be divided by 4. The armhole is cut lower at point n by that amount (in this case 1/2 cm or 3/16 in.), as indicated by the dashed line. It is well, when finished, to compare the side and center front lengths of the altered pattern to those of the lady.

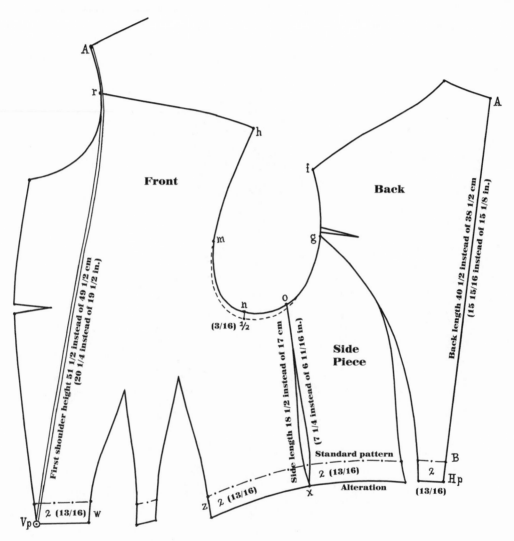

Figure 15. Altering the waist length

No changes are necessary at the shoulders unless there are other irregularities such as high or low shoulders, or a stooping or extra-erect figure. In those cases the appropriate alterations must be combined with the ones described here.

In tall ladies, the neck may be exceptionally thin, or more pronounced because of a larger bone structure. For dresses closed high at the neck, the neck circumference must be compared. If the neck is thin, the neck opening is best reduced by adding 1/2 to 1 cm (3/16 to 3/8 in.) all around, which also increases the shoulder width somewhat. For a larger neck, an equal amount is cut away, which makes the neck opening larger and the shoulder width narrower. This does not only apply for overly slim ladies, but whenever the body measure requires a larger or smaller neck opening than that of the standard pattern.

In general, it is advisable to make a bodice for an overly slim lady rather loose and comfortable, and to keep the shoulder width wider. Keeping the sleeve rather full toward the top will contribute greatly to a fuller appearance. The entire bodice has been made somewhat fuller here, including the waist circumference.

Do not exclude adding some padding for very flat busts, or at least using a stronger interlining to round the front more.

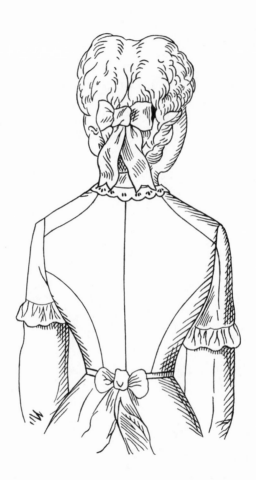

Figure 16. The short-waisted figure

Fitting a Short Lady. The standard pattern must be altered for a short-waisted lady if the correct side length was not used at the outset. Even so the upper part of the pattern may need to be shortened.

A lady with a short-waisted figure is shown in figure 16, and the alterations for it are shown by dashed lines in figure 17. A moderate alteration is assumed; that is, a waist length 2 cm (13/16 in.) shorter than the standard pattern.

First the back length of the short lady is compared with the standard pattern from *a* down to *Hp*. The standard pattern has a back length of 38 1/2 cm (15 1/8 in.). The measure of the lady is only 36 1/2 cm (14 3/8 in.). Three-quarters of the difference–1 1/2 cm (9/16 in.) in this case–is always removed around the bottom from *B* to *F;* that is, the bodice is shortened evenly all around. The remaining 1/2 cm (3/16 in.) must be removed from the shoulders without changing the actual shape.

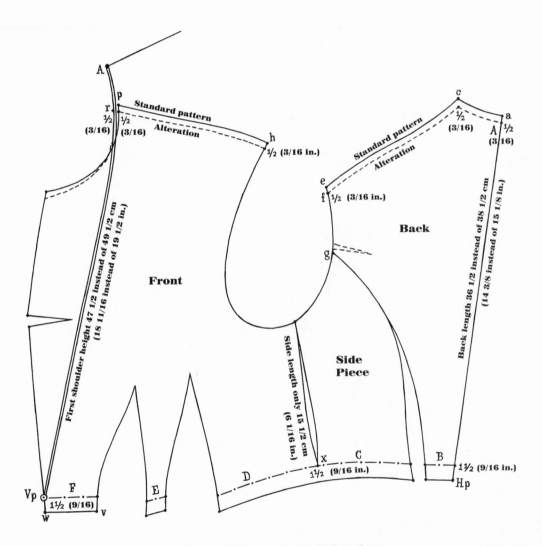

Figure 17. Altering the waist length

Starting at *A*, and under *c* to *e*, the back shoulder and neck are drafted 1/2 cm (3/16 in.) shorter. Likewise at the front shoulder under *h* to *p*, moving the shoulder point at *p* by 1/2 cm (3/16 in.) toward the front at *r* to restore the full length of the shoulder seam.

The measures for the neck and armhole circumferences should be compared to the body measures. In short-waisted figures, the neck and shoulders are often larger, which necessitates a larger armhole and neck opening.

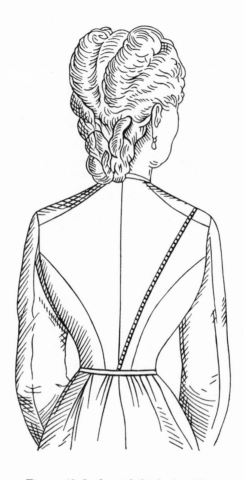

Figure 18. Lady with high shoulders

Altering for High Shoulders. The measures that are especially important for high, square shoulders are the first shoulder height, the second shoulder height, the back length, and the side length. (See figure 18.) The first shoulder height is measured on the pattern starting from Vp at the center front, as shown in figure 19. The second shoulder height is measured from Vp, across the highest point of the shoulder at B and C, to Hp at the center back. The entire measure, including the front and back, determines how large the alteration must be.

Figure 19 assumes a moderate alteration of 2 cm (13/16 in.) at B and C. This is divided between the front and back as shown by the dashed line. Raising the shoulder enlarges the armhole at i and e. The side length becomes 17 1/2 cm (6 7/8 in.) instead of 17 (6 11/16 in.). This requires the base of the armhole to be raised at n by one-quarter of the total, or 1/2 cm (3/16 in.). For very long side lengths, this elevation may be up to 1 1/2 cm (9/16 in.) without the shoulders being any higher than here.

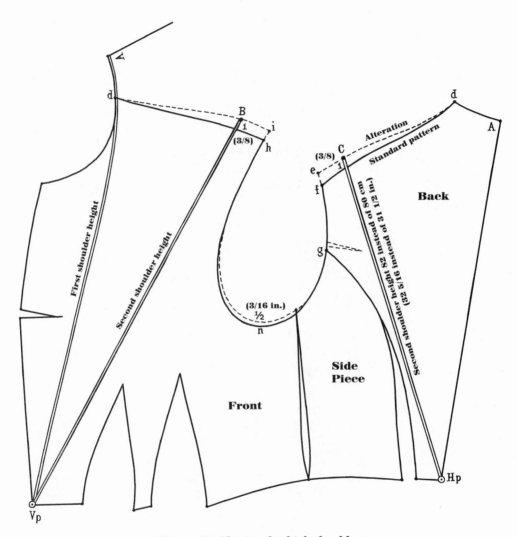

Figure 19. Altering for high shoulders

The small area of the back behind the armhole from *f* to *g* may become larger. To retain the original shape, *g* may be raised in proportion. This little alteration is not shown in figure 19.

Since the shoulders may be thinner or plumper, the armhole circumference must be measured, and the armhole enlarged toward the front, or else made smaller.

High shoulders are often found in ladies with a stooping figure. In this case the alterations for high shoulders and the stooping figure must be combined.

29

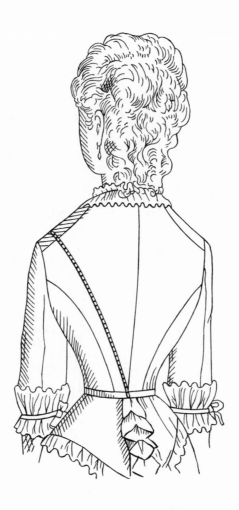

Figure 20. Lady with low shoulders

Altering for Low Shoulders. The alteration for low, sloping shoulders is shown in figures 20 and 21. Figure 21 assumes a moderate alteration of 2 cm (13/16 in.), as is most common. The front and back shoulders will each be lowered 1 cm (3/8 in.) at *B* and *C*, as shown by dashed lines.

Lowering the shoulders will also lower the armhole, especially more toward the front. One-quarter of the total amount, or 1/2 cm (3/16 in.), must be taken out at *n*, which is positioned further forward than when raising the shoulders. The side length is usually also about 1/2 cm (3/16 in.) shorter.

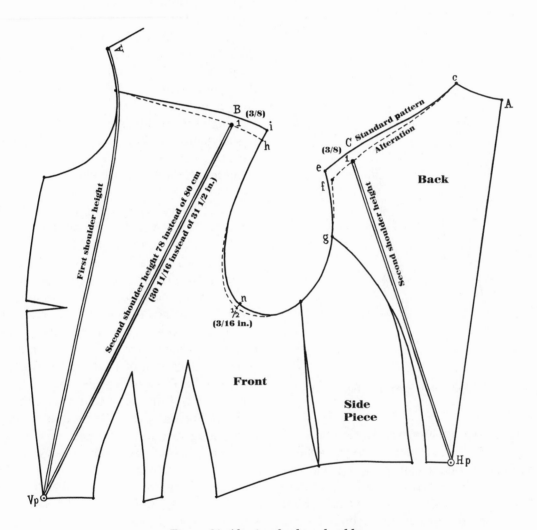

Figure 21. Altering for low shoulders

The small area of the back behind the armhole from *f* to *g* may become smaller; point *g* may lowered in proportion to retain the shape. This alteration is not shown in figure 21.

Often low shoulders are found in ladies with extra-erect posture. In this case, the alterations for low shoulders and extra-erect posture must be combined.

31

Figure 22. Moderately stooping figure

Fitting Stooping Figures. The category of stooping figure includes all ladies whose ratio of first shoulder height to back length is smaller than that of the standard bodice pattern. There the first shoulder height is always 10 to 12 units (of the half breast circumference scale) larger than the back length. For the medium figure of 48 cm (18 7/8 in.) half breast, the difference is 11 units. However, a clearly defined limit may not be assumed because the first shoulder height is determined not only by the posture, but by the fullness of the bust.

A stooping figure is not always a visibly bent-over posture. The first shoulder height may appear too short compared to the back length because the lady has a rather large, wide back and a flat bust. However, the cause of the difference between the two measures is immaterial.

The lady in figure 22 shows a moderate degree of stooping. Her back is somewhat rounded and long, her bust compressed and hardly developed, her neck tilted forward a trifle. Her first shoulder height is 48 cm (18 7/8 in.) instead of 49 1/2 (19 1/2 in.); 1 1/2 cm (9/16 in.) is a moderate degree of stooping. Her back length is 40 cm (15 3/4 in.) instead of 38 1/2 (15 1/8 in.). Her center front length is 31 1/2 cm (12 3/8 in.), rather than the standard of 33 (13 in.). Her side length is 16 1/2 cm (6 1/2 in.) rather than 17 1/2 (6 7/8 in.). Her high bust width is too small by 1 cm (3/8 in.). In such figures the back is often wider than the standard by 1/2 to 1 cm (3/16 to 3/8 in.). The second shoulder height is often smaller by 1/2 to 1 cm (3/16 to 3/8 in.).

The alteration procedure for a stooping figure is the same whether the alteration is large or small. It is shown in figure 23. The standard pattern is drawn in a solid line, while the altered one is shown by a dashed line.

First, the back length is measured from *Hp* up to *A*. If the lady's back length is longer, the back is changed at the neck to *a* and *c*, as well as moved higher at the shoulder seam from *d* to *e*. Figure 23 shows an alteration of 1 1/2 cm (9/16 in.).

The back neck, shoulder seam, and armhole are then given the same shape as in the standard pattern. The latter may be used as a template by laying it against *a*, *c*, and *e* and tracing the outline with a pencil, and also from *e* via *d* to *g*.

The small horizontal dart from *g* to *N* may be enlarged a little for stooping ladies for their fuller backs, to make the armhole fit better. It is not uncommon for stooping ladies to have a larger back width. In that case, add the required amount in the center of the back as described for ladies with overly wide backs.

In the front the first shoulder height should be measured from *p* down to *Vp* (after subtracting the addition to the upper back). The standard front shoulder must be shortened by 1 1/2 cm (9/16 in.) from *p* to *q*; that is, by as much as the first shoulder height is shorter. Toward *i* and *k*, the shoulder is usually lower by two-thirds of that amount, or 1 cm

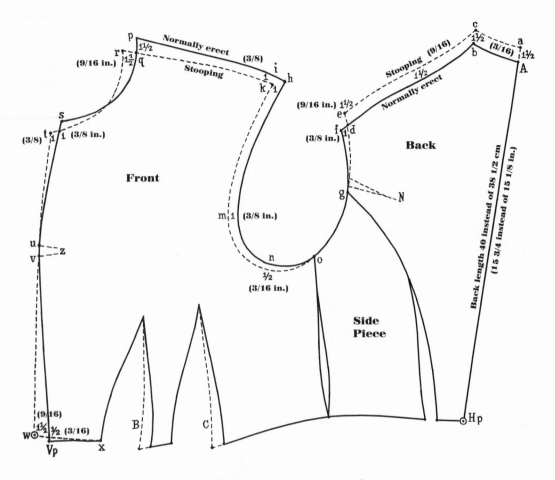

Figure 23. Altering for a stooping figure

(3/8 in.); but the amount depends on the lady's second shoulder height measure. If the front must be shortened more than 2 cm (13/16 in.), two-thirds of the amount should be removed at the shoulder and one-third at the bottom at *Vp*.

The shoulder point is then moved forward from *q* to *r* by as much as the shoulder was shortened, that is, by 1 1/2 cm (9/16 in.). This makes it necessary to move the other shoulder point at *h* 1 cm (3/8 in.) forward to *k*. This amounts to two-thirds of those 1 1/2 cm (9/16 in.), while the increase in shoulder width by one-third from *r* to *k* results from the fact that the back shoulder seam has also increased.

Moving the shoulder point forward from *q* to *r* also determines the other alterations. The front neck opening is lowered by two-thirds of that

amount, here 1 cm (3/8 in.), at *s*. It is also moved forward toward *t* by the same amount, or 1 cm (3/8 in.), so that the line from *t* to *u* becomes straighter. At *m*, according to the high bust width, two-thirds, or 1 cm (3/8 in.), is taken from the armhole, which these ladies require to be larger. The base of the armhole is lowered by one-third, or 1/2 cm (3/16 in.), at *n*.

The horizontal dart is omitted due to the flatter bust. How much the bottom of the front is moved forward from *Vp* to *w* to obtain a straighter bust line from *v* to *w* depends on the lady's waist circumference. In most cases, 1 to 1 1/2 cm (3/8 to 9/16 in.) is sufficient even though the waists of stooping ladies tend to be larger. The lower bust darts are usually made smaller because of the flatter busts of these ladies, as is shown in figure 23 at *B* and *C*.

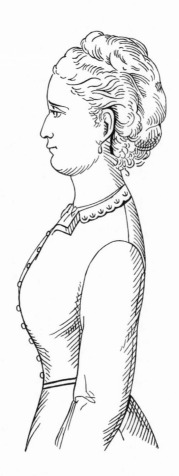

Figure 24. Lady with extra-erect figure

Fitting Extra-Erect Figures. Extra-erect ladies are those whose first shoulder height is more than 10 to 12 units (of the half breast circumference scale) longer than their back length. They are easily recognized by a strained posture of the upper body, a flat and somewhat shorter back, and a somewhat more prominent bust. The entire front of the upper body appears larger than usual compared to the back.

The lady in figure 24 has a back length of 37 cm (14 9/16 in.) instead of 38 1/2 (15 1/8 in.), a first shoulder height of 51 cm (20 1/16 in.) instead of 49 1/2 (19 1/2 in.), a center front length of 34 1/2 (13 9/16 in.), and a side length of 17 1/2 (6 7/8 in.). The necessary amount, in this case 1 1/2 cm (9/16 in.), must be added to the shoulder height from q to p as shown by the dashed line in figure 25. Point r, however, will only move back to q by half as much, that is 3/4 cm (5/16 in.), because i must remain in the same line with h.

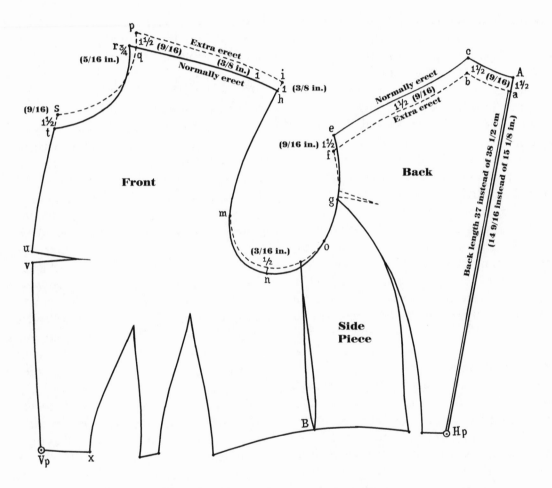

Figure 25. Altering for an extra-erect figure

The back must as a rule be shortened as much as the front shoulder point at *a, c,* and *e.* The amount will be indicated more precisely by the lady's back length. Even if the side length has been drafted according to the lady's measure (which is usually rather long), the armhole must be raised at *n* by 1/2 cm (3/16 in.), which amount should be removed across the lower part of the waist at *B.*

The front neck opening must also be drafted higher from *t* to *s* by the amount the shoulder height was increased. For this, it will suffice to use the lady's center front length starting at *Vp.*

If an extra-erect lady has a narrow back, as is often the case, this alteration should be combined with the one for narrow backs.

35

Altering for Highly Irregular Figures. Often several irregularities are found in combination, for example a stooping figure with a wide back. All that is required is a careful combining of different alterations.

Howver, at times irregularities are not distributed evenly on both sides, but the lady has a crooked figure; or at least, half the body differs in some respect from the other. For example, one shoulder may be lower or higher, half the back may be rounded or hunchbacked, and one side under the arm may appear pushed in, while the other side is more prominent. The entire upper body may also be shifted to one side and entirely crooked. In those cases, it is not rare for half the ribcage to protrude, while the ribs in back below the shoulder blade appear sunk in, forming a completely hollow side.

To fit such figures well, double measuring is indispensable. This is measuring each side separately, then drafting and cutting the two halves likewise. First the exact center line of the back is determined, from the neck vertebra down to the waist; and in the same manner, the center line of the front. Unless the seams of the lady's dress already follow these lines accurately, they should be marked with chalk or a few pins.

Now that the body is divided in half, the usual measures are taken, but separately on each side. Even the circumference measures are taken separately, for these may differ considerably in crooked ladies. Only for the back length and the center front length will it suffice to measure once. It is usually necessary to measure the skirt lengths separately on the sides. The shoulder width measure is also essential. If the two front halves of the body are not equally wide, as shown by the high bust widths, the shoulder width may be measured both in the standard position and further toward the front, running diagonally from the hollow of the neck to the armhole.

The right and left sides of the bodice pattern are drafted entirely separate. Before the pattern is cut from the paper, the shoulder and side seams must be adjusted so that both halves will fit together. Apart from that, the pattern is drafted as for a common, somewhat irregular figure. The same alterations are used as explained above. The basic shape of the bodice pattern may then be easily transferred to any other garment.

Of course, it is necessary to baste the bodice lining first and to fit it carefully. This will also show whether it is advisable and practical to pad the figure for a more even appearance.

Using a Basic Pattern To Draft Other Styles

It is of great advantage to know a method that allows the rapid and simple cutting according to the plain bodice pattern of any close-fitting, half-fitting, or loose outer garment, be it a jacket, coat, mantle, mantelet, pelerine, polonaise, casaque, or the like. Each of these garments, even the fullest, must be based on a pattern corresponding to the body. You merely need to know which modifications are required, and where to reduce or add, lengthen or shorten, to attain a certain fashionable style.

This method may be made easier by cutting out a well-fitting bodice pattern in cardboard, including the sleeve. This may be used as a template when drafting any other pattern. Once the drafting points have been measured and marked, the template is placed first on the neck opening and the shoulder seams. Then the pencil is used to draw around the edges. The template is placed in the same way at the armholes, as well as in the front at the bust point and the other parts of the pattern. It will make no difference whether the template is somewhat larger or smaller than the pattern to be drafted; it may be moved about as needed.

You should also possess the lady's measurements, though the length of many garments is largely determined by fashion. All the numbers on the patterns drafted in this manner are ordinary units. A 48 cm (18 7/8 in.) half breast circumference is assumed, but the patterns can be used for all ladies from 42 to 50 cm (16 9/16 to 19 11/16 in.) half breast. For ladies with a 51 cm (20 1/16 in.) or larger half breast, it may be necessary to change some measurements. Body measures should be used for the hip and lower skirt widths. For girls 10 to 16 years old or from 34 to 40 (13 3/8 to 15 3/4 in.)

half breast, the apportioning scale may be used, again using body measures for the hip and lower skirt.

Drafting a Coat. Detailed drafting directions are given for the close-fitting coat shown in figures 26 through 30. The dashed line shows the bodice pattern, while the solid line shows the finished coat. Where both outlines are the same only the solid line is given. The dashed line of the sleeve in the front piece shows the pocket position. The suggestion of the top of the side piece next to the front shows how the front and side piece fit together.

The first piece to be drafted is the back (see figure 26). A baseline must be established from *a* down to *B* via *C*. The first crossline, which runs across the center of the back to *D*, is not essential; it is only a reference for the eye.

The back of the bodice pattern is placed against the baseline at *a* as shown. At the bottom of the waist at *C*, it is laid against *b* 5 cm (1 15/16 in.) from the baseline. A point is made to the right of *b* 1 cm (3/8 in.) from point 5. From this point down to *B*, the coat length is determined according to the height of the lady or the dictates of fashion; here 91 cm (35 13/16 in.) is assumed.

The back for the coat is made higher by 1 cm (3/8 in.) from *a* to *A;* the distance from *A* to *c* must be 1 cm (3/8 in.) wider than that from *a* to *b*. The back of the coat is also made larger by 1 cm (3/8 in.) from *b* to *E* and from *E* to *D*. Compared with the bodice pattern, the back is made 3 cm (1 3/16 in.) wider at the waist at *G*.

About 2 cm (13/16 in.) above *B*, a crossline is drawn to *F*, to mark the lower skirt width. This should be 18 to 24 cm (7 1/16 to 9 7/16 in.) for the length assumed here. For the current close-fitting style, 18 cm (7 1/16 in.) will suffice.

An auxiliary line, shown by dots and dashes, is drawn from *G* almost up to *D*. This line is then divided in half, and the curve of the back is 2 1/2 cm (1 in.) from the middle. The back skirt length, which must be somewhat curved at the top following the shape of the body, is drawn from *G* to *F*. The coat back may easily be finished by drawing the curves.

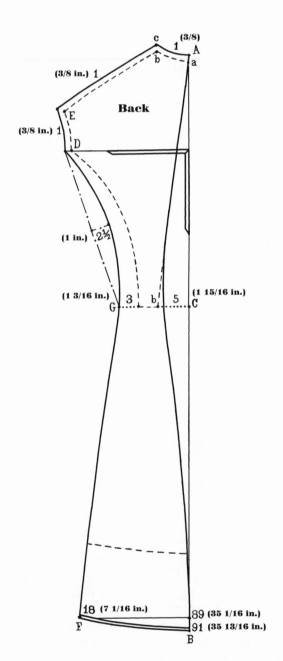

Figure 26. Coat back

The second piece to be drafted is the side piece (see figure 27). The baseline and first crossline are drawn from *A* to *Ff* and from *A* to *D*. The top of the bodice side piece is placed against *C* and the first crossline, with the top of the coat being 1/2 cm (3/16 in.) over at *D*. At *E* the waistline of the side piece is placed 2 cm (13/16 in.) from the baseline. The coat is made 1 cm (3/8 in.) narrower from *H* to *G*.

To measure the curve of the side piece seam, an auxiliary line is drawn from *D* to *G*. It is then divided in half, and the curve is 2 1/2 cm (1 in.) out from the auxiliary line.

The skirt length where the side piece is sewn to the back, from *G* to *F*, is always the same as from *G* to *F* on the back. The skirt length where the side piece is sewn to the front, from *e* to *Ff*, is 1 cm (3/8 in.) longer than *G* to *F*. The skirt width from *F* to *Ff* is 20 cm (7 7/8 in.) here. Now the side may be finished by drawing the curves.

Finally, the front is drafted, starting with the baseline from *a* to *B* and the first crossline from *a* to *A*. (See figure 28.) Then the front of the bodice is placed at *D* 1 cm (3/8 in.) from the baseline; for very thick materials up to 2 cm (13/16 in.). At *J*, the center front bodice point, the distance must be 2 cm (13/16 in.), for thick materials 3 to 4 cm (1 3/16 to 1 9/16 in.). There the front must be curved in 1 cm (3/8 in.) from *K*, returning to the line about halfway between *K* and *B*. In the front, for a single-breasted coat, an allowance of 3 cm (1 3/16 in.) is necessary for the front underlap; for a double-breasted one, 8 to 10 cm (3 1/8 to 3 15/16 in.).

Two darts should be placed as indicated where the waist is most pronounced. These may be 2 to 4 cm (13/16 to 1 9/16 in.) wide, depending on the figure or the desired fit. It is also possible to make only one dart, but more toward the center. The darts may even be omitted if a close fit is neither desired, nor prescribed by fashion.

At the shoulder the coat is moved 1 cm (3/8 in.) forward from *A* toward *a*. The shoulder is lengthened from *A* to *E* by a total of 1 cm (3/8 in.). Next, the shoulder seam is corrected to correspond to that of the back. The front shoulder, however,

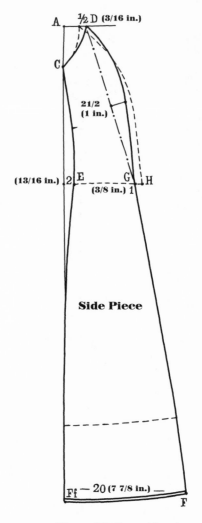

Figure 27. Coat side piece

may be 1/2 cm (3/16 in.) narrower, accounting for the easing of the back.

At *C* the coat and bodice are identical. Point *E* is 2 cm (13/16 in.) out from the bodice pattern. The side seam from *E* down to *Ff* is the same length as *E* to *Ff* of the side piece.

The lower skirt width from *b* to *Ff* is 49 cm (19 5/16 in.) here. It may, however, be 60 cm (23 5/8 in.) or more depending on fashion and the coat length. The front must be lengthened by about 9 cm (3 9/16 in.) from *b* to *B*. Better yet, the finished side piece should be laid where the double line of the lower edge continues to the right. Then

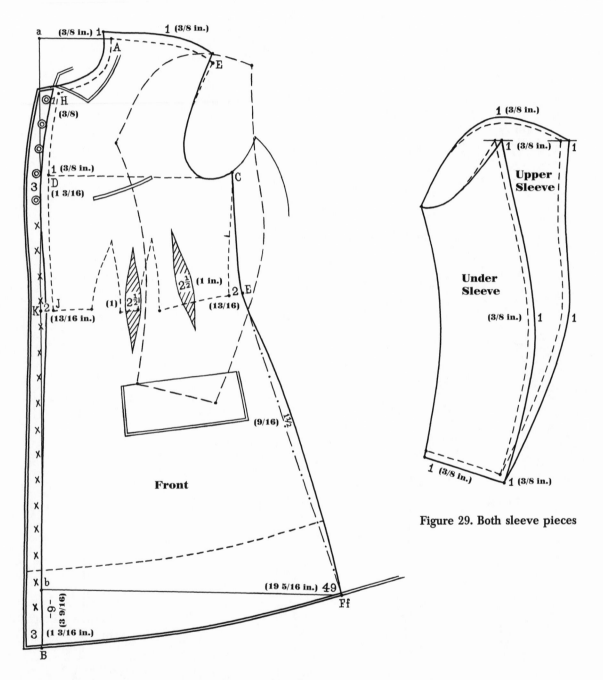

Figure 28. Front, and positions of sleeve and pocket

Figure 29. Both sleeve pieces

the back is added so that all three pieces lie together as if they had already been joined. The lower edge of the coat is then smoothly rounded off.

The coat sleeve head is made 1 cm (3/8 in.) higher than the bodice sleeve. (See figure 29.) The coat sleeve must be made wider overall by 2 cm (13/16 in.), and 1 cm (3/8 in.) longer, as shown on the pattern. The sleeve is then placed on the front piece at *E* as shown, so the skirt pocket can be marked at the correct height.

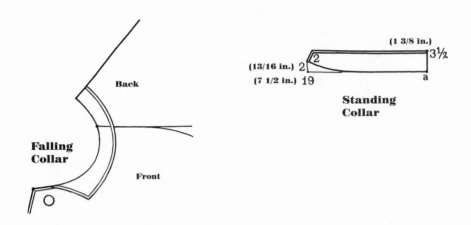

Figure 30. Falling and standing collars

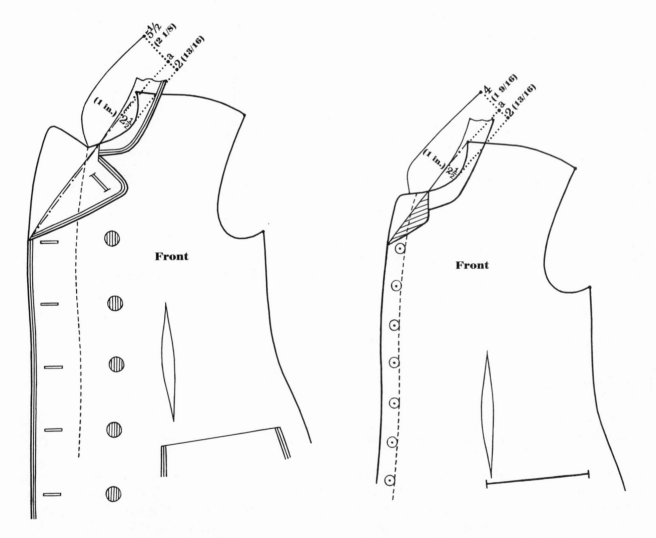

Figure 31. Falling collar   Figure 32. Falling collar

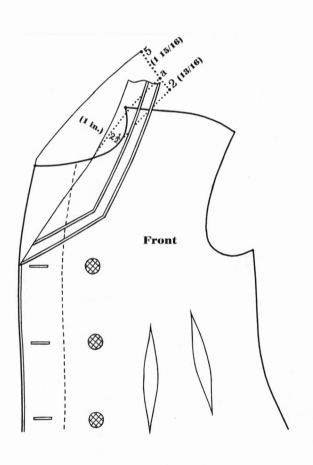

Figure 33. Falling collar

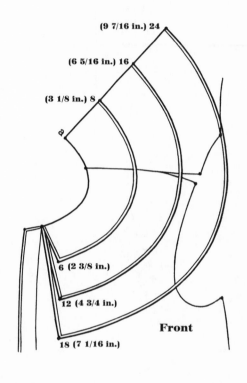

Figure 34. Pelerine-shaped shoulder collars

On the left of figure 30 is a falling coat collar drafted using the plain bodice pattern. On the right is a standing collar drafted 3 1/2 cm (1 3/8 in.) wide, and 19 cm (7 1/2 in.) long; but for the length, the lady's neck circumference measure must be used.

Drafting Collars. Figures 31 to 34 show the drafting of collars in more detail. The depth or height of the revers on the front must be marked first. A line is drawn from that point over the shoulder point at the neck. The width of a standing collar is indicated with a height of 2 cm (13/16 in.) from *a*. Then the back collar seam is drafted following the line of the back, or else running at a right angle to the dotted collar fold *a*. The width of the falling collar depends on fashion. Pelerine collars are drafted to fit the neck opening as shown in figure 34.

Drafting Sleeves. These seven styles of sleeve for coats and mantles are based on the plain bodice sleeve. This is shown by dashed lines. The numbers represent ordinary units. Figures 35 and 36 are half-fitting sleeves. Figure 37 is a sleeve narrow in the elbow, in which the front seam has been moved.

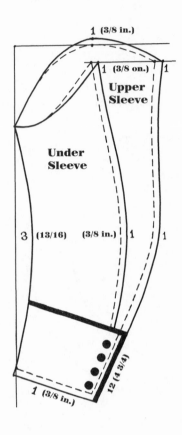

Figure 35. Half-fitting sleeve

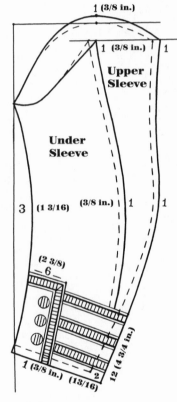

Figure 36. Half-fitting sleeve

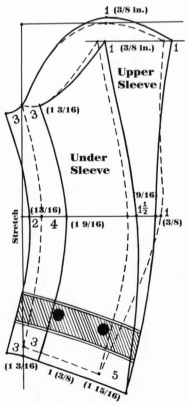

Figure 37. Narrow sleeve

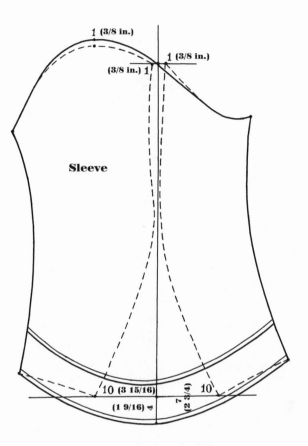

1 (3/8 in.)

1 (3/8 in.)

(3/8 in.) 1

Sleeve

10 (3 15/16)   10

(1 9/16)

7
(2 3/4)

Figure 39. One-piece sleeve

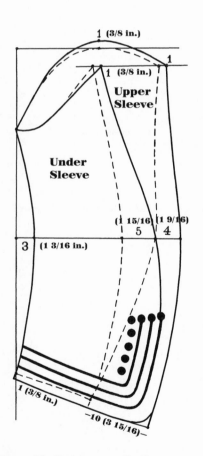

1 (3/8 in.)

1

1 (3/8 in.)

Upper Sleeve

Under Sleeve

(1 15/16)   (1 9/16)
5   4

3   (1 3/16 in.)

1 (3/8 in.)

10 (3 15/16)

Figure 38. Coat or mantle sleeve

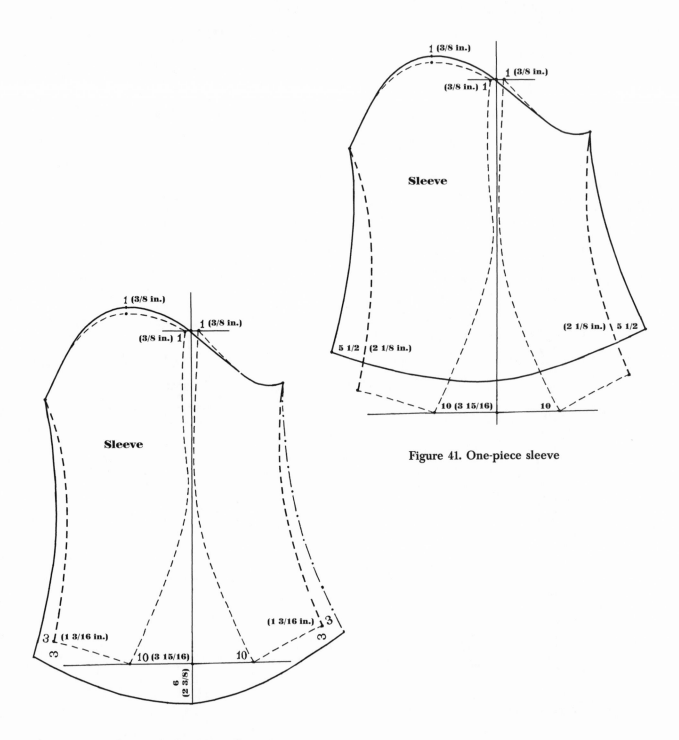

Figure 41. One-piece sleeve

Figure 40. One-piece sleeve

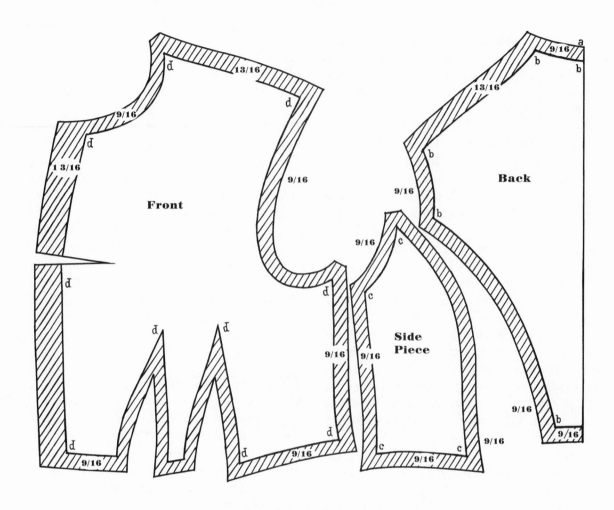

Figure 42. Pattern laid onto lining

Preparing a Bodice

The lining is usually made from linen, fine drilling, or durable cotton. Figure 42 shows the paper pattern laid onto the lining, which is shaded.

Adding Seam and Hem Allowances. The pattern is drafted in the exact shape it is intended to have after completion, so all seams and hems must be allowed in both the lining and the outer material. The allowances facilitate alterations when trying on the basted lining or the bodice. The outer material is of course cut almost as large as the lining, except at the armhole and neck opening, where too much extra would be in the way during fitting and serves no purpose.

The back is generally cut on the fold. Most seam allowances for the lining are 1 1/2 cm (9/16 in.). In the shoulder seam, 2 cm (13/16 in.) is advisable. In the center front, at least 3 cm (1 3/16 in.) must be added, because the left front must be about 2 cm (13/16 in.) wider than the right for the fastener underlap. The more generous allowance also includes the front overlap. For the neck opening and armhole, 1 to 1 1/2 cm (3/8 to 9/16 in.) will suffice.

After basting the bodice or after completion of same, the superfluous seam and hem width may be cut off. This is not advisable until you are certain the finished bodice will not require any further alterations.

45

Stretching and Easing Seams. With regard to the stretching of the side seams in places, and even the lower edge of the bodice in the waist seam, the notes in figure 5 must be borne in mind. (The measurements in figures 5 and 6 are units on the apportioning scale.) The lining and the outer material must be stretched considerably where indicated, for the bodice would otherwise wrinkle on the sides. Especially, the seam where the side piece joins the back must be stretched well in the hollow of the waist. In materials with little elasticity, the lining material must be stretched well in the respective places, and the outer material must then be stretched over the lining tight.

The lining must always be rather long, especially at the bottom, while it is kept tight in width. The outer material remains wider and thus will not be stretched too tight even in a close-fitting dress. The seams in the outer material will not split, for there is no strain as long as the lining does not give.

For ladies with larger shoulder blades, the back part is gathered somewhat around them in joining the back seam. This creates the required slightly rounded shape for the shoulder blade, which is also facilitated by the small horizontal dart in the lining, close above the side seam.

Inserting the Sleeves. In figure 6 the sleeve, when assembled, is 3 cm (1 3/16 in.) wider at the top than the armhole. This surplus is taken up by stretching the armhole in front and back as much as possible before inserting the sleeve. The sleeve head is always gathered somewhat at the top by the shoulder where it appears the most rounded, without causing obvious folds. Thus the sleeve will fit comfortably and not pinch.

The front seam sleeve must be positioned in the underarm area, approximately between points *K* and *r* in figure 5. When basting the sleeve into the armhole for trying on, it will become clear whether the sleeve hangs well, or whether the front seam should be moved about 1 cm (3/8 in.) higher or lower in the armhole. This will result in the back sleeve seam lying between 1 and 2 1/2 cm (3/8 and 1 in.) below the side piece seam. It is impossible

to give a firm rule for positioning, which is often affected by minor variations in drafting or the shape of the lady's shoulders.

The dress material affects the fit of the sleeve. If the material is loosely woven and frays easily, and this is not noticed until after it is cut, it will become necessary to sew wider seams than usual. The sleeve will lose, while the armhole will gain in circumference. The firmness or elasticity of the material is also important. It is highly advisable to stretch the lower part of the armhole before basting the piping around it, or before inserting the sleeve, respectively. The armhole may be enlarged significantly if the material is elastic or soft, but hardly at all if the material is firm. In the latter case, the sleeve may appear too wide when inserted, so that it must be gathered under the arm or taken in at the back seam.

Complete Guide to Ladies' Garment Cutting, 1883

Projecting a Pattern

First decide whether to enlarge the pattern to the key measurements for the finished garment or to the original size. Although enlarging to key measurements is convenient, it is less accurate. Body shapes do not enlarge proportionally. If you enlarge the pattern to its original size, proportions will be preserved. However, you will have to adjust the key measurements after enlargement. The key measurements are the bust for most pieces of bodices, princess dresses, and coats, and the sleeve length for sleeves. The usual key measurement for a skirt without fitted hips is the waistline. However, if there is enough fullness at the skirt waist, you may be able to enlarge to the skirt length and adjust the waistline in the muslin.

Put the pattern on the projector. Tape a large sheet of dotted or gridded pattern paper or pattern-tracing cloth to a wall. Because the key measurement is the entire distance around the bust (for example) the measurements of all relevant pattern pieces must be added up. Note that most pieces are cut twice and others are cut on the fold. Be sure to allow wearing and style ease. Adjust the distance

of the projector from the wall until the key measurement is correct. Make sure the projector is square to the wall to avoid distortion.

If you are enlarging to the original size, and the pattern has no measurements, first add a grid corresponding to the scale. For example, if you are enlarging eight times use a 1/8 in. grid. Place the pattern on transparent graph paper and photocopy it onto transparency film. Put the gridded pattern on the projector. Adjust the distance of the projector from the wall until the grids align.

Draw the projected pattern using clear plastic rulers and French curves (clear tools do not block projection). Or draw freehand and clean up the lines later. Projected lines look thick. You need to decide whether to trace the outsides or the insides.

Transfer all identification and construction labels. On the *Harper's Bazar* patterns, numbers tell you how seams were sewn together. Bullets, asterisks, and *x*s mark joins other than seams, such as pleats and some darts. Pleats are folded with the *x*s on the bullets. When marks are at a distance from the pattern outline, they are connected to it by a straight line, which has no further significance. A dashed line labeled "middle" usually means "cut on the fold of the lengthwise thread." On a corset pattern, a row of parallel dashed lines marks the grain line. Most narrow lines indicate where something is placed. What is placed is explained by a text label or the instructions. It can be a pleat, a corset whalebone, trimming, a pocket, or an overlapping pattern piece. Marks that look like buttonholes, buttons, and eyelets are sometimes used to mark their placement.

Enlarging with a Grid

First add a grid as described above in "Projecting a Pattern." Put an ample piece of dotted pattern paper or pattern-tracing cloth on your worktable. Put the gridded pattern beside it (see figure 43). Plot points from the grid onto the pattern paper. Start at the center front, center back, or a straight line of the pattern piece. On the pattern paper, pencil a mark that represents one end of this line. If the line is perfectly straight, count the squares to the other end on the grid. Count the same number of squares

on your pattern paper and pencil another mark. If the line is curved count the squares, or portions thereof, up (or down) and across to the next point. Mark that point on your pattern paper. Continue counting and marking till you finish the section.

You'll note that you have some choice as to how many points to plot and where. Plot as many as are needed to accurately represent the line. It's best to plot points at grid lines or intersections, but sometimes you'll have to estimate where a point falls in the middle of a square.

Then connect the points to draw the pattern. Use a yardstick or L-square for straight lines. Fit French curves against a curved area till you find the best match. Sometimes you'll need to use more than one curve for an area, or draw it freehand or with a flexible spline.

Transfer all identification and construction labels as described in "Projecting a Pattern."

Enlarging with a Copier

Before enlarging a pattern piece by photocopying, calculate its final size by measuring its length and width and multiplying them by the amount to be enlarged. You may have to enlarge the piece in sections. The sections should overlap slightly, and the overlap area should include one or two distinctive marks. After copying align the sections at the marks and tape.

An alternative is to find a copy shop with a large-format copier. Most photocopiers can enlarge up to 150 or 175 percent. You can enlarge a pattern further by passing it through multiple times.

Finishing a Pattern

No matter what enlargement method you used, you need to proof and finish the pattern. Measure edges that will be seamed together. If they're different lengths, check the original measurements and redraw as necessary. True seam lines where fabric will be folded into darts, pleats, or facings. Fold the pattern like the fabric and redraw nonmatching lines.

Add seam and hem allowances by measuring out from the pattern edge with the plastic ruler. For straight edges measure each end and connect

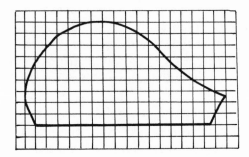

Gridded pattern

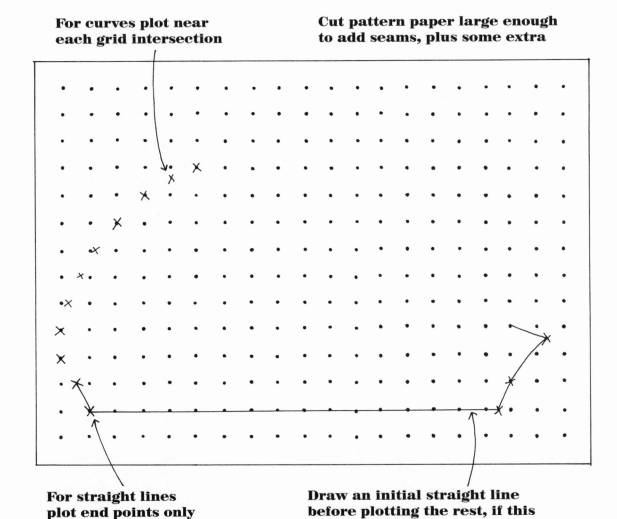

**For curves plot near
each grid intersection**

**Cut pattern paper large enough
to add seams, plus some extra**

**For straight lines
plot end points only**

**Draw an initial straight line
before plotting the rest, if this
makes measurement easier**

Figure 43. Scaling up a gridded pattern

48

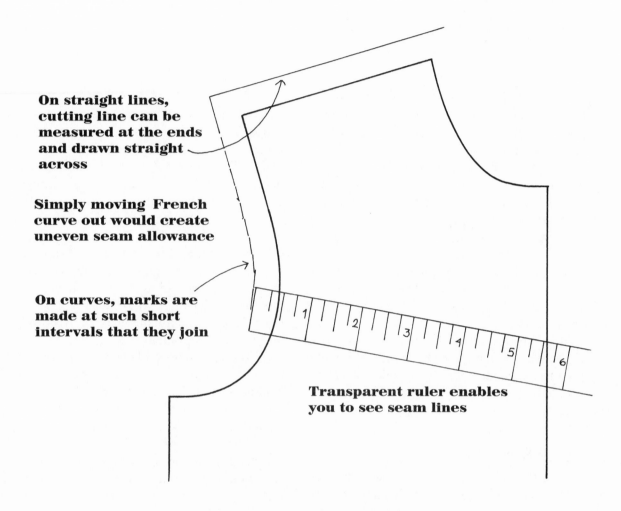

On straight lines, cutting line can be measured at the ends and drawn straight across

Simply moving French curve out would create uneven seam allowance

On curves, marks are made at such short intervals that they join

Transparent ruler enables you to see seam lines

Figure 44. One way to draw cutting lines

the lines. For curved edges draw short lines at such frequent intervals that they connect. (See figure 44.) Or use a double tracing wheel to indent the paper, then pencil over the indents.

For the fitting muslin, I suggest adding allowances of 1 to 2 in. on side seams, 1 in. on tight-fitting sections, and 1/2 in. on loose-fitting ones. For Klemm's patterns, also see "Preparing a Bodice," above. Extra-wide allowances can be trimmed when you are sure the pattern needs no further alteration.

Draw a grain line following a long row of pattern-paper dots. Label the pieces with the pattern source, garment type, and style date. Indicate how many times each piece will be cut from the outer material, lining, underlining, and/or interfacing. Where necessary mark the right, left, top, and/or bottom.

Make a muslin and adjust it till the fit is correct. (Period fitting methods are described in volume 2, chapter 8.) Transfer all corrections to a final version of the pattern for later use.

Frances Grimble, 2004

2. Evening Dresses

A lady should always be prepared for casual visitors in the evening. The house dress should be tasteful and becoming, made with a certain amount of ornament and worn with lace and jewelry. Silks are the most appropriate for this dress. But all the heavy woolen dress fabrics for winter and the lighter lawns and organdies for summer, elegantly made, are suitable. For winter the colors should be rich and warm, and knots of bright ribbon should be worn at the throat and in the hair. The latter should be dressed plainly, with no ornament save a ribbon. Artificial flowers are out of place, and glittering gems are only worn on more important occasions.

Those who pay a casual evening call will dress in similar style, though somewhat more elaborately. More pains may be taken with the coiffure. A hood should not be worn unless it is intended to remove it during the call. Otherwise a full-dress bonnet must be upon the head.

Dress for Social Party

The rules just given will apply, save that somewhat more latitude is allowed in the choice of colors, materials, trimmings, etc. Dresses should be worn covering the arms and shoulders. Or if they are cut low in the neck and with short sleeves, puffed illusion bodices or some similar device should be employed to cover the neck and arms. Dark silks are very dressy, relieved by white lace. Glittering gems are admirable. Gloves may or may not be worn. If worn, they should be white or of some light tint harmonizing with the dress.

Dinner Dress

We do not in this country, as in England, expose the neck and arms at a dinner party. These should be covered, if not by the dress itself, then by a lace or muslin overbodice or cape and sleeves.

The hostess's dress should be rich in material, but subdued in tone, in order that she may not eclipse any of her guests. A young hostess should wear a dress of rich silk, black or dark in color, with collar and cuffs of fine lace. She may wear plain jewelry by daylight, or, if the dinner is by gaslight, glittering stones.

An elderly lady may wear satin, moiré antique, or velvet, with rich lace. If gloves are worn before dinner, they are withdrawn at the dinner table.

The dress of a guest at a dinner party is less showy than for evening. Still, it may be very rich. Silks and velvets for winter and light, rich goods for summer, which latter may be worn over silk, are most appropriate.

Young unmarried ladies should wear dresses of lighter materials and tints than married ones. Middle-aged and married ladies should wear silks heavier in quality and richer in tone. Elderly ladies should wear satins, velvets, and moiré antiques.

All the light neutral tints and black, dark blue, purple, dark green, garnet, brown, and fawn are suited for dinner wear. But whatever color the dress may be, it is best to try its effect by daylight and gaslight both. Many a color that looks well by daylight looks extremely ugly in artificial light.

The Soiree and Ball

These two occasions call for the richest dress. The soiree usually requires dark, rich colors and heavy materials, the ball far lighter tints and goods. The richest velvets, the brightest and most delicate tints in silk, the most expensive laces, low neck and short sleeves, elaborate coiffures, the greatest display of gems, artificial flowers for the headdress, *bouquet de corsage* and ornaments upon the skirt, natural ones in the hand bouquet—all belong more or less to these occasions.

White kid gloves and white satin boots always belong to these costumes unless the overdress is of black lace, when black satin boots or slippers are required.

Dress for the Theater

The ordinary promenade dress is the suitable one for the theater, with the addition of a handsome shawl or cloak, which may be thrown aside if it becomes uncomfortable. Either the bonnet or the hat may be worn. In some cities it is customary to remove the bonnet in the theater. The dress should be, in all respects, quiet and plain, without any attempt at display. Gloves should be dark, harmonizing with the costume.

Dress for Lecture and Concert

Lecture and concert halls call for a little more elaboration in the toilette. Silk is the most appropriate material for the dress, and should be worn with lace collar and cuffs and jewelry. If the bonnet is worn, it should be handsome. If it is removed, the coiffure should be somewhat elaborate, with either ribbons or flowers. White or light kid gloves should be upon the hands. A rich shawl, velvet promenade cloak, or opera cloak is an appropriate finish. The latter may be kept on the shoulders during the evening. The handkerchief should be fine and delicate; the fan of a color to harmonize with the dress.

Dress for the Opera

The opera calls out the richest of all costumes. The lady goes to the opera not only to see but to be seen. Her dress must be adopted with a full realization of the thousand gaslights that will bring out its merits and defects, and of the hundred lorgnettes that will be no less spying.

The material of the dress should be heavy enough to bear the crush of the place, rich in color, and splendid in its arrangement and trimming. Blue and yellow should both be avoided in an opera dress, as neither bears the light well. Green requires gold as a contrasting color; crimson, black. Lace, either black or white, may be adopted with great advantage in an opera dress. Pink, purple, orange, and most light tints require black lace. The neutral shades may be worn with either white or black.

The headdress should be of flowers, ribbons, lace, or feathers—whatever may be the prevailing style—and the head must be uncovered. If, however, it is necessary to protect the head, a bonnet of the lightest, daintiest character must be adopted. If a bonnet is worn, the arms and neck must be covered.

Jewelry of the heaviest and richest description is admissible. There is no occasion when the glitter of gems will be seen to better advantage. White kid gloves or those of light, delicate tints are indispensable. The lorgnette, the fan, the bouquet, and dainty handkerchief must all have due consideration and be in keeping with the other portions of the dress.

A most important adjunct to an opera costume is the cloak or wrap. This may be white or of some brilliant color. White and gold, scarlet and gold, green and gold, or Roman stripe are all very effective when worn with appropriate dresses. White ermine capes are beautiful when lined with white satin or colored silk and finished with heavy white cord and tassels.

Ladies' and Gentlemen's Etiquette, 1877

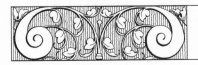 

Satin Ball Dress

This dress is shown by the figure on the left. For the skirt of old-gold-colored satin first cut the breadths of net. Cover the front with wide and narrow pleatings of satin. On the wide pleats set wax beads of the same color. The trimming for the overdress consists of similar beads, box-pleated satin ruffles, and garlands of yellow roses and brown foliage. Similar flowers are in the hair.

To make the overdress, first join part A and part B of the back pattern along the dashed line. Cut of satin two pieces each from the front, side piece, back, and bertha front, and one piece each from the bertha back and the trimming piece. Furnish the fronts, side pieces, and backs with silk lining. In the dress back the lining should only reach from the neck to 1 3/4 in. below the bottom of the waist. Sew up the darts in the fronts. Face the front edge of the right front with a strip of the material 2 1/2 in. wide, and work buttonholes. Set the left front into a double fly 1 3/4 in. wide, on which set buttons. Join the backs, side pieces, and fronts according to the corresponding figures. Pleat the back, bringing *x* on ●. Edge the front and side pieces with piping on the bottom. Trim the back on the sides and bottom with a satin ruffle.

Underlay the bertha with net, trim it with wax beads, and line it with silk. Sew it up according to the corresponding figures. Edge the bertha with a ruffle and folds. Sew it on the neck of the dress. Pipe it, together with the dress, with satin. The neck and sleeves are trimmed with lace. The trimming piece is trimmed to match the bertha. It is sewed to the right half of the overdress according to the corresponding figures, and hooked on the left half.

To drape the overdress, on the wrong side, to each point marked 9 fasten a tape 12 7/8 in. long, the free end of which is fastened to ✳ on the back. On both sides of these tapes, to the points marked 4, set tapes each 12 in. long, and fasten the under end to ●● on the back.

Harper's Bazar, February 1879

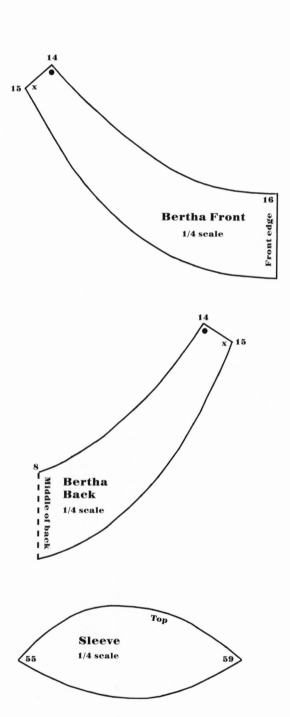

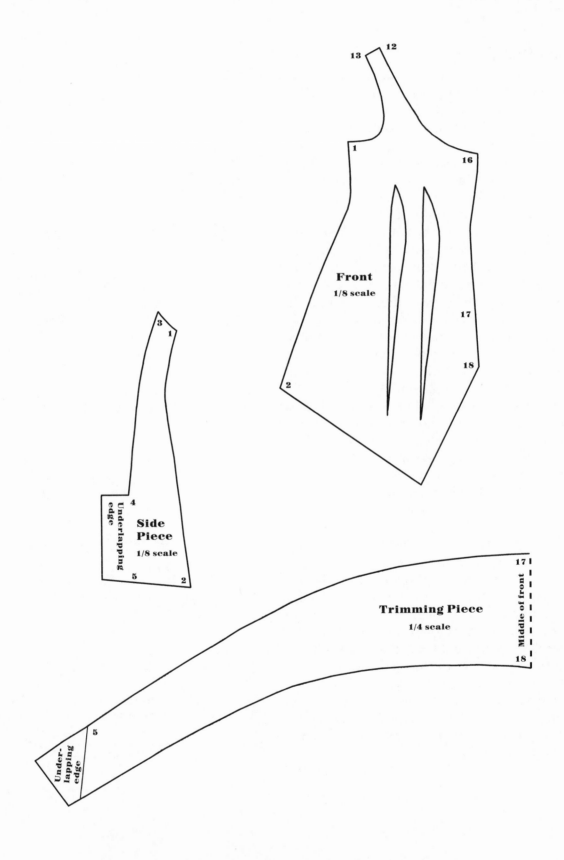

Front
1/8 scale

13 12

1

16

17

18

3 1

2

Side Piece
1/8 scale

Underlapping edge

4

5 2

Trimming Piece
1/4 scale

Middle of front

17

18

Underlapping edge

5

54

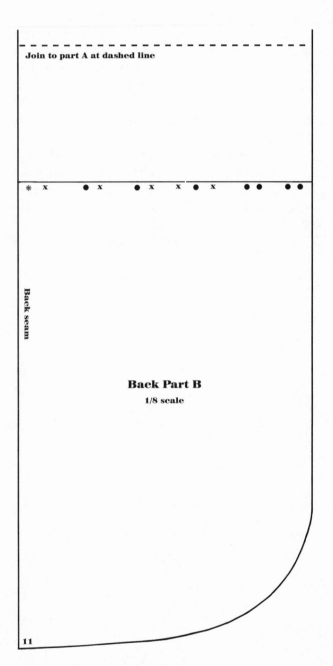

Join to part A at dashed line

Back seam

Back Part B

1/8 scale

11

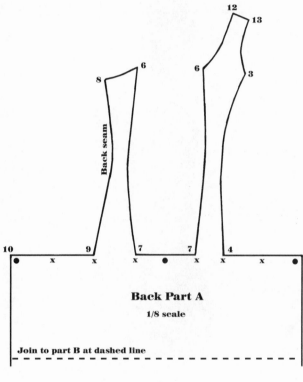

12

13

8

6

6

3

Back seam

10

9

7

7

4

Back Part A

1/8 scale

Join to part B at dashed line

For the overskirt cut a breadth of silk tulle in one piece. Cut the slit indicated, pleat it on the sides, and gather it closely along the narrow lines, to form puffs as illustrated. Sew on the overskirt breadth in the back according to the corresponding figures. Pleat the skirt and the overskirt breadth at the top and set them on a waistband. Trim the skirt with garlands of roses, and loops and ends of satin ribbon, as illustrated.

Cut the bodice of silk tulle, satin, and lining. Furnish the backs with eyelet holes and pink silk cords for closing. Trim the bodice, as illustrated, with ruffles of silk tulle and with flowers. A ruche of white crepe lisse is in the neck.

Harper's Bazar, February 1879

Satin and Tulle Ball Dress

The front of this dress is shown by the figure on the right of the illustration for the Satin Ball Dress. For the skirt cut of pink satin one piece from the front and two pieces each from the side gore and back. Join the front and side gores according to the corresponding figures. Cover them as shown by the illustration and the pattern, on the left side with a shirring of pale pink silk tulle, and on the right side with narrow box-pleated ruffles of the material. Join the back breadths from 46 to 47 and from 48 to 49. Pleat them as indicated on the pattern. Join them with the side gores from 44 to 45. Trim the skirt on the bottom with ruffles of silk tulle.

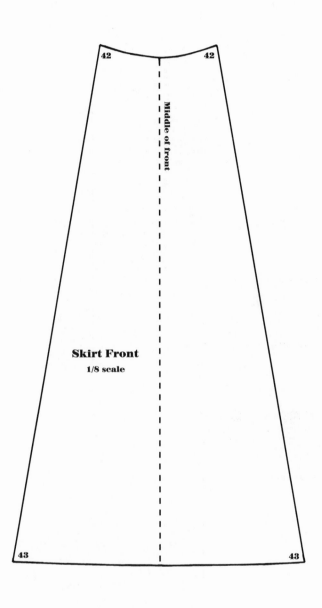

Skirt Front
1/8 scale

Middle of front

42 42

43 43

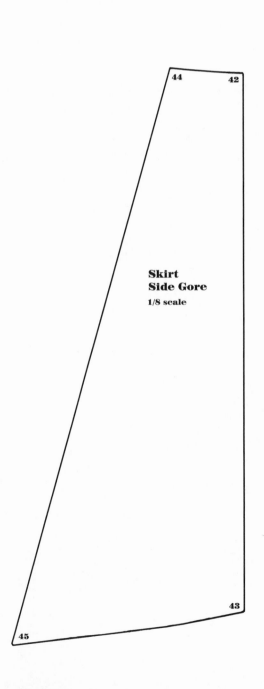

**Skirt
Side Gore**
1/8 scale

44 42

43

45

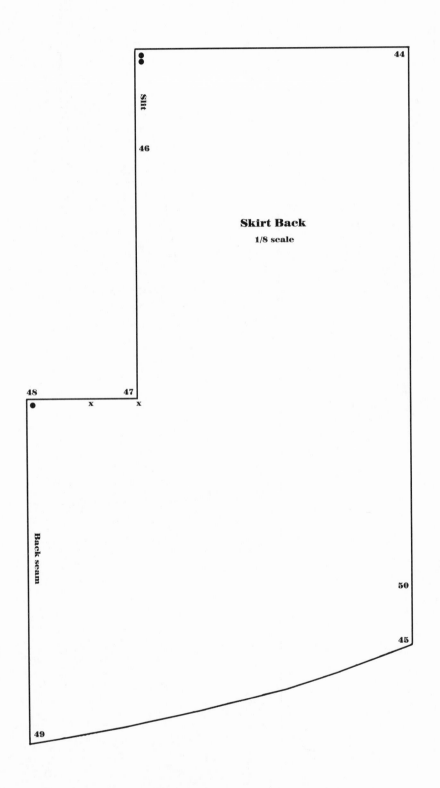

Skirt Back

1/8 scale

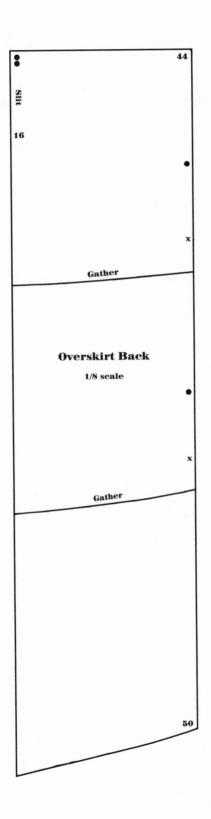

44

Slit

16

x

Gather

Overskirt Back

1/8 scale

x

Gather

50

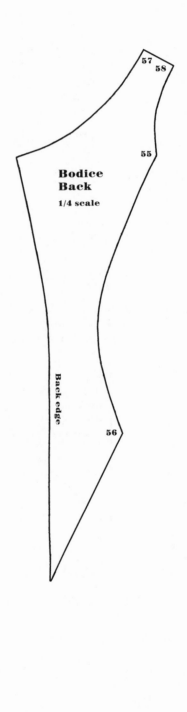

57 58

55

Bodice Back

1/4 scale

Back edge

56

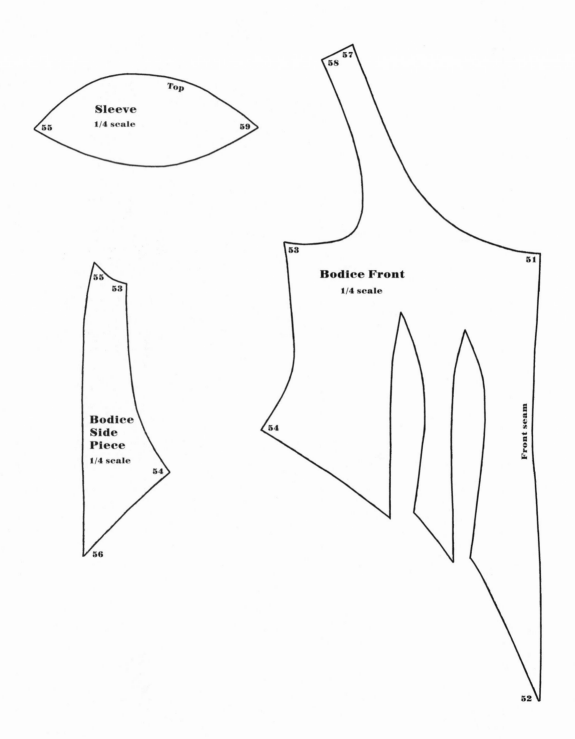

Sleeve
1/4 scale

Top

55

59

Bodice Front
1/4 scale

57

58

53

51

54

Front seam

52

Bodice Side Piece
1/4 scale

55

53

54

56

Tulle Evening Dress

The skirt of this white tulle dress is trimmed with a flounce and puffs of the material and with lace. For the overskirt, cut of tulle one piece each from the front and the back breadths, cutting the back whole. Sew up the hip darts in the front breadth. Gather it on the right side edge from ✳ to 41, and on the left side edge from ●● to 42. Pleat the back breadth, bringing *x* on ●. Join the front and back breadths according to the corresponding figures. Cut a slit in the back breadth 10 in. long, and hem the edges narrow. Set the overskirt on a waistband. Trim it as illustrated.

For the corsage cut of lining one piece from the guimpe and cover it with gathered tulle. Cut of figured goods and lining two pieces each from the front, first side piece, second side piece, back, and sleeve. Sew up the darts in the fronts. Join the back, side pieces, and fronts according to the corresponding figures. Pleat the second side piece as indicated on the pattern. Pipe the edge of the corsage all around. Fasten the right front on the guimpe from 43 to 44 and from 44 to ✳. Set on hooks and eyes for closing. Sew in the sleeves. Trim the corsage with lace, bows of satin ribbon, and apple blossoms, as illustrated. Similar flowers are in the hair.

Harper's Bazar, December 1879

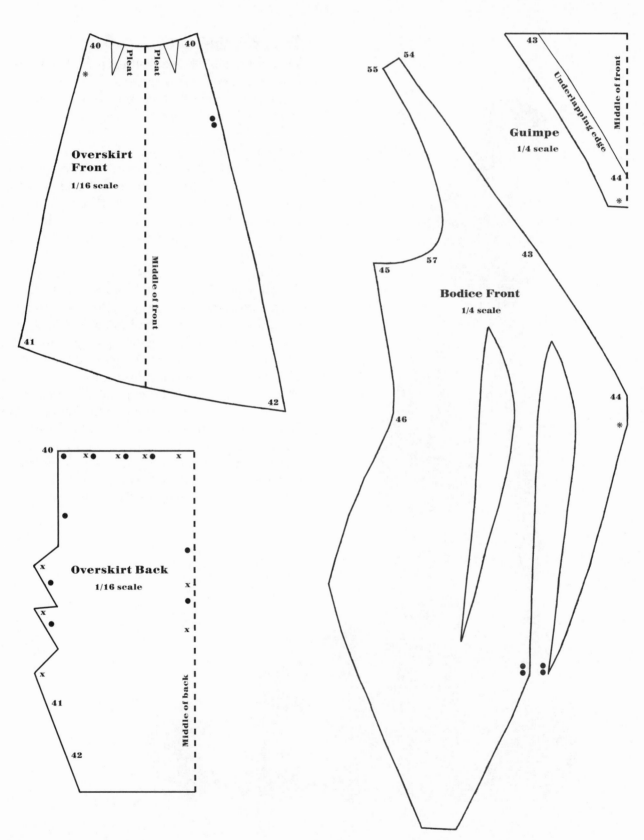

Overskirt Front

1/16 scale

40   Pleat   Pleat   40

*

Middle of front

41

42

Overskirt Back

1/16 scale

40   x   x   x   x

x

x

x

x

41

42

Middle of back

Guimpe

1/4 scale

43

Underlapping edge

Middle of front

44

*

Bodice Front

1/4 scale

55   54

45   57   43

46

44

*

62

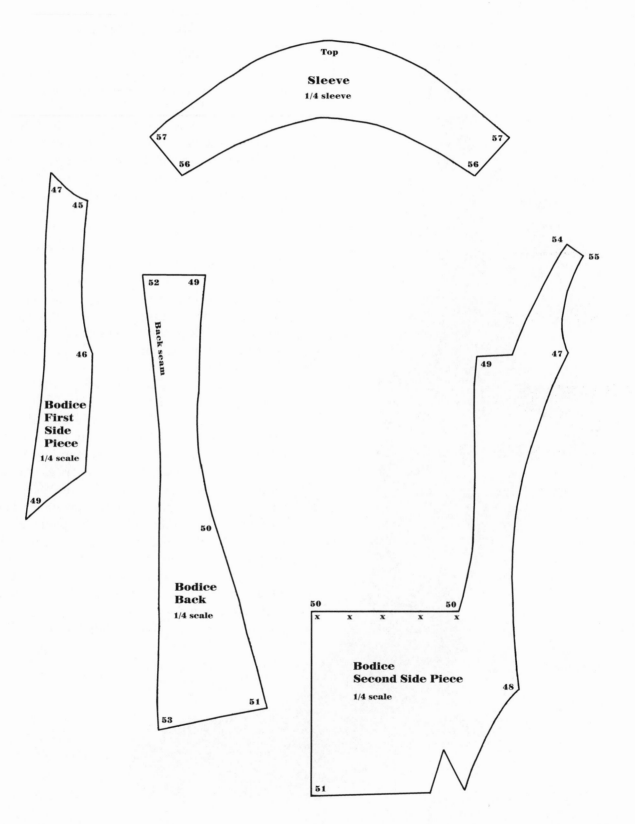

Top

Sleeve
1/4 sleeve

57

57

56

56

47

45

52   49

46

Back seam

54

55

49

47

**Bodice
First
Side
Piece**
1/4 scale

49

50

50   50

x   x   x   x   x

**Bodice
Back**
1/4 scale

50

**Bodice
Second Side Piece**
1/4 scale

48

53

51

51

Velvet and Brocaded Gauze Evening Dress

This dress is of shrimp pink satin and brocaded gauze combined with golden brown velvet. It requires 7 3/4 yd. of satin, 3 1/4 yd. of brocaded gauze, and 6 yd. of velvet. The petticoat front of the skirt consists of a wrinkled drapery of the gauze arranged on a satin foundation. The bottom is edged with a satin pleating. A similar pleating extends around the bottom of the velvet train. The bodice and the pannier sides are of velvet.

For the bodice cut of velvet and lining two pieces each from the front, first side piece, second side piece, and back. Take up the darts in the fronts. Join the fronts, side pieces, and back according to the corresponding figures. Cord the bodice at the top and bottom. Furnish the back edges with silk eyelet holes. Edge the armholes with white lace. Trim the top of the bodice with a gauze drapery and white lace.

For the drapery cut two pieces each from the pannier and back drapery of velvet. Sew up the back drapery from 52 to 54. Line both the back drapery and the pannier sides with thin silk. Face the latter 4 in. deep on the front and lower edges with pink satin. Pleat the back drapery as indicated on the pattern. Tack to each other the ✱s marked with corresponding letters so that the folds will fall on the outside. Gather the top of the panniers from 43 to 52. Set the back on the panniers from 52 to 53. Join the panniers and back drapery to the bottom of the bodice and to the foundation skirt. A garland of large plush flowers and leaves is on the right side of the skirt.

Harper's Bazar, February 1882

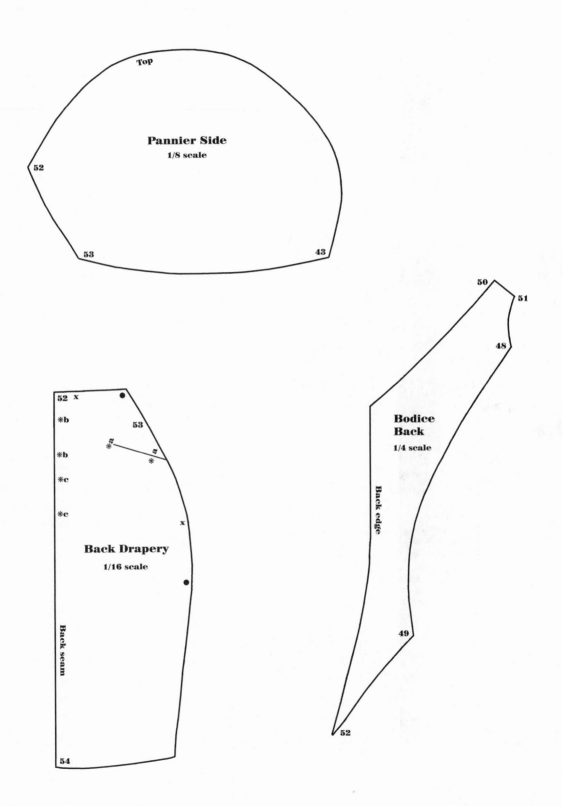

Pannier Side
1/8 scale

Top

52

53   43

50
51
48

Bodice Back
1/4 scale

Back edge

49

52

52 x

*b

53

*a

*b   *a

*

*c

x

*c

Back Drapery
1/16 scale

Back seam

54

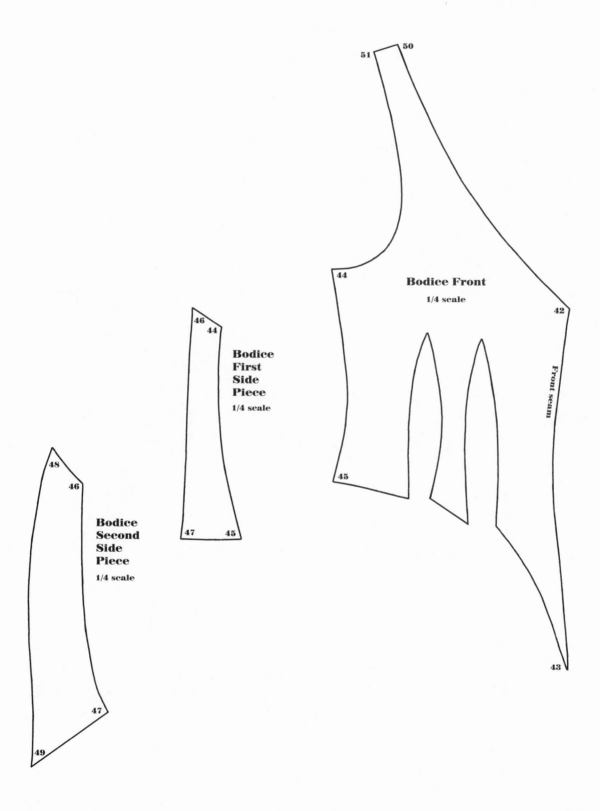

51 50

44 **Bodice Front**

1/4 scale

42

Front seam

45

43

46
44

**Bodice
First
Side
Piece**

1/4 scale

47 45

48

46

**Bodice
Second
Side
Piece**

1/4 scale

47

49

Satin Dress

This dress is of canary yellow embroidered satin. It requires 20 yd. 20 in. wide. It is trimmed with clusters of roses and moiré ribbon bows.

Cut of foundation silk one whole piece from the skirt front and two pieces each from the skirt side gore and back. Join the front, side gore, and back according to the corresponding figures. Border the skirt front with two embroidered flounces. Above these, wherever it is exposed by the front drapery, cover it with similar flounces. Cover the back with broad kilt pleating from the narrow line to the lower edge. Pleat it as indicated on the pattern, bringing *x* on ●.

For the drapery cut of satin one whole piece each from the front and back drapery, and two pieces from the pannier side. Cut the slit in the back drapery and hem the edges. Gather the back drapery at the top and bottom and along the narrow line. Fasten *x* on ● along the side edges. Set the whole on the skirt back according to the signs and figures on the pattern. Face the front drapery at the bottom. Pleat it as indicated on the pattern. Pleat the pannier sides. Fasten both the drapery and the panniers on the skirt according to the signs and figures on the pattern. Then set the skirt into the band.

Cut the bodice of satin and lining from the front, side piece, and back. Join the parts according to the corresponding figures. Cord the upper and lower edges. Furnish the back edges with silk eyelets for lacing.

Cut the sleeve linings. Cover them with satin drapery as illustrated. Set them into the armholes.

Trim the dress with flowers and ribbon bows as illustrated.

Harper's Bazar, February 1882

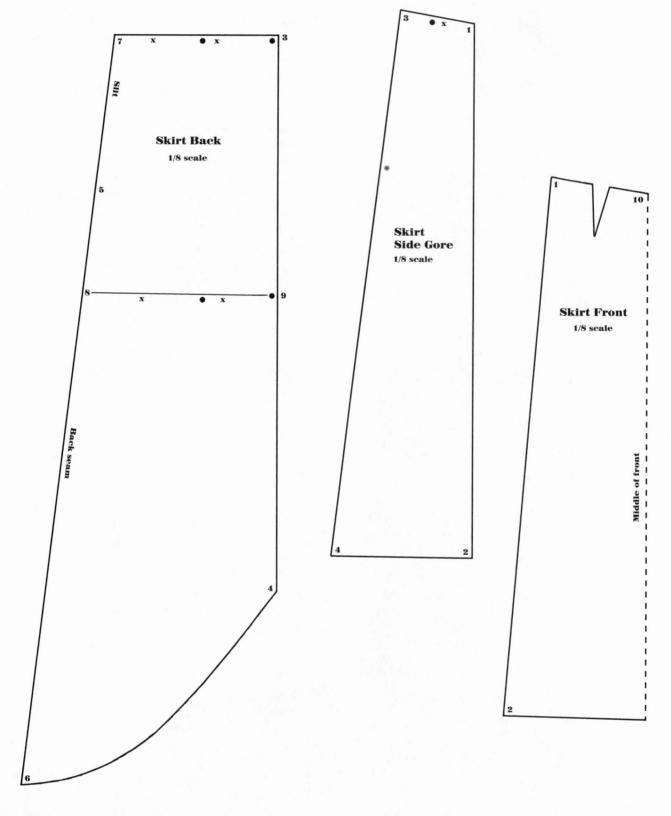

Skirt Back

1/8 scale

Slit

Back seam

**Skirt
Side Gore**

1/8 scale

*

Skirt Front

1/8 scale

Middle of front

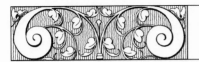 

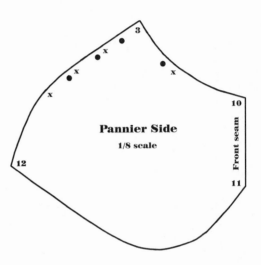

Pannier Side

1/8 scale

3

x

x

x

x

x

10

Front seam

12

11

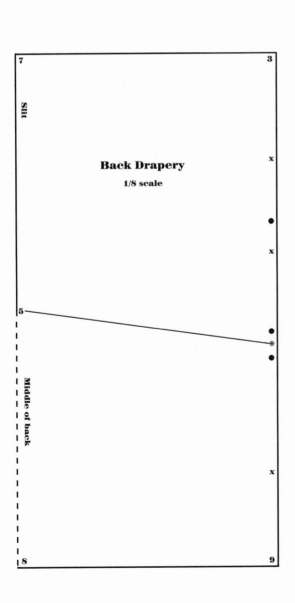

7

3

Slit

x

●

x

Back Drapery

1/8 scale

5

●

✳

●

Middle of back

x

8

9

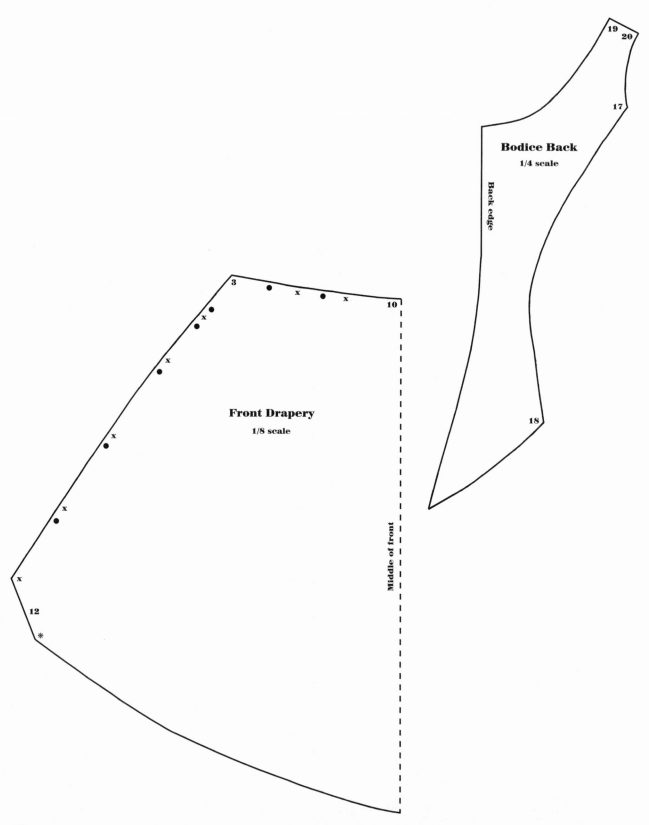

Bodice Back

1/4 scale

Back edge

Front Drapery

1/8 scale

Middle of front

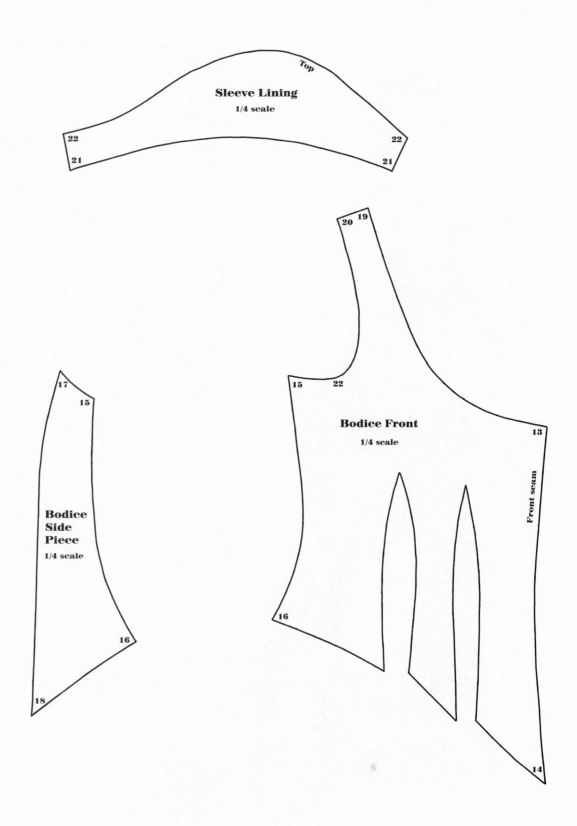

Sleeve Lining
1/4 scale

Top

22
21

22
21

20 19

15 22

Bodice Front
1/4 scale

13

17
15

Bodice
Side
Piece
1/4 scale

Front seam

16

16

18

14

Faille Evening Dress

The foundation skirt of this ivory faille dress is faced with silk for the petticoat front, which is veiled by lapping flounces of white Spanish lace. The fronts of the train, as well as those of the basque, are embroidered with cream-colored silk and chenille and pearl beads. Eighteen yards of faille are required. Patterns for the train, panniers, and basque are given.

Cut two pieces each from the train front and pannier drapery, and one whole piece from the train back. Join the train fronts from 19 to 20. Join them from 24 to 25 with the train back. Pleat the top of the train back as indicated on the pattern. Set the whole on the foundation skirt.

Turn down the lower edge of the panniers along the narrow line. Edge them with gathered lace. Pleat them as indicated, bringing *x* on ●. Set them on the train front as indicated on the pattern. Trim the skirt above the panniers with two lapping rows of gathered lace.

Cut of faille and lining the bodice front, side piece, back, and sleeve. Join the parts according to the corresponding figures. Pleat the back, bringing *x* on ●. Trim the basque and sleeves with lace and satin ribbon bows.

A cluster of ostrich tips and a pompon are worn in the hair.

Harper's Bazar, March 1882

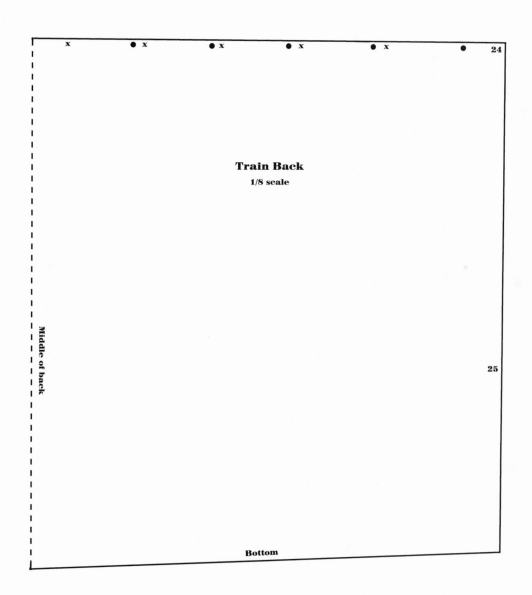

x   • x   • x   • x   • x   •   24

Train Back
1/8 scale

Middle of back

25

Bottom

73

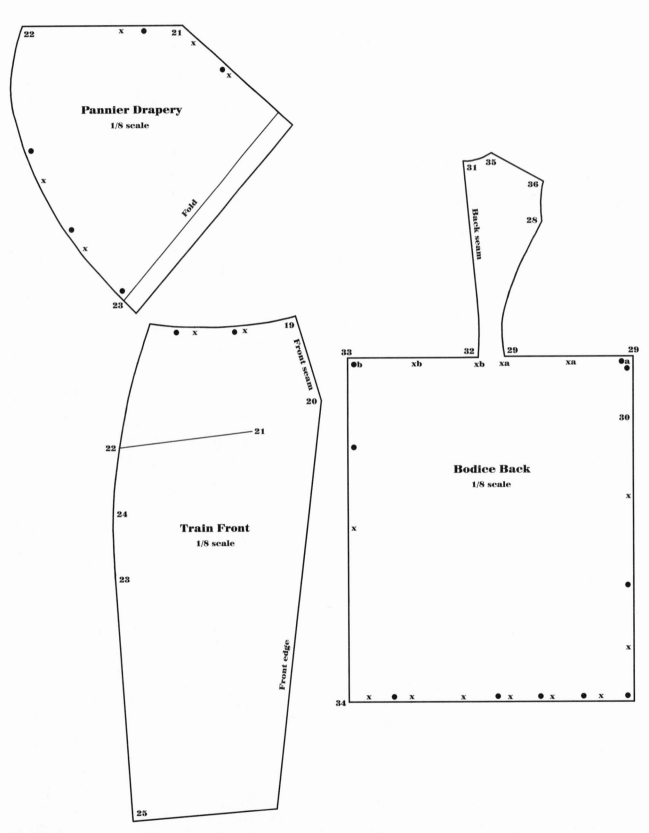

Pannier Drapery
1/8 scale

Fold

22

21

x

x

x

x

x

23

Train Front
1/8 scale

19

Front seam

20

21

22

24

23

Front edge

25

Bodice Back
1/8 scale

31 35

36

28

Back seam

33 32 29 29

●b xb xb xa xa ●a

30

x

x

x

34 x x x x x x x x

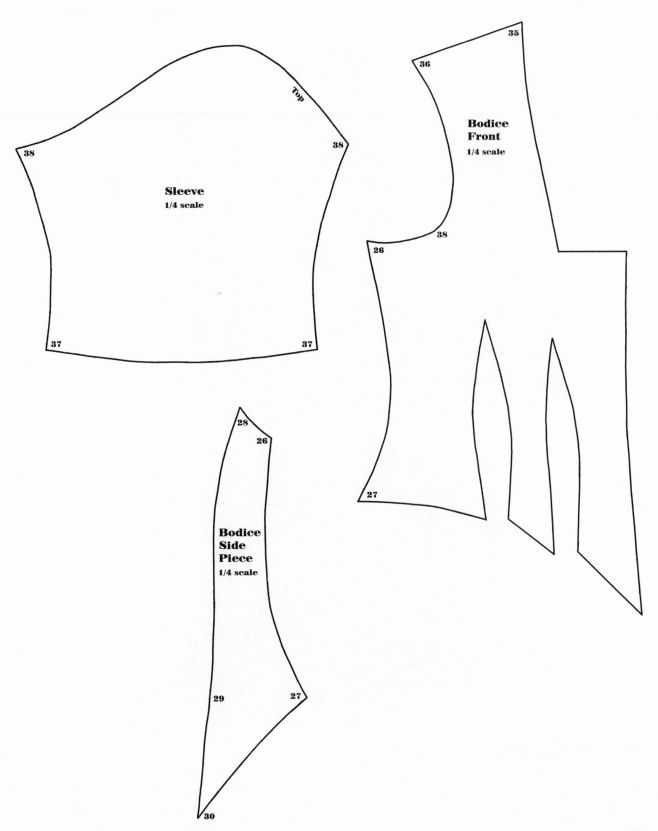

Sleeve
1/4 scale

Bodice
Front
1/4 scale

Bodice
Side
Piece
1/4 scale

Evening Dress with Removable Train

This dress is shown without the train buttoned on in the first figure, and with it in the second figure. It is made of light blue grosgrain combined with gauze of the same color, which has a deep lace-patterned border. The short grosgrain skirt is trimmed with three gathered ruffles of the material.

These are surmounted by a deep gauze pleating with the lace border at the bottom.

Cut the gauze back drapery. Trim it with the lace border. Pleat it as indicated, bringing *x* on ●.

Fasten ✱*a* on ✱*b*. Set the drapery on the skirt.

To make the polonaise, cut two pieces each of grosgrain from the vest, front, back, upper sleeve, under sleeve, and sleeve puff. Line all the parts

except the sleeve puffs, letting the lining in the front and back extend from the top to 3 in. below the waistline.

Take up the darts and seams in the fronts. Pleat them as indicated, bringing *x* on ●. Pleat the backs, and gather them into a space of 14 in. at the bottom. Join them to the fronts according to the corresponding figures. Set the vest underneath the right front from 3 to 4. Set a buttonhole fly underneath the left front. Sew a row of buttons to correspond on the vest. Trim the polonaise with a frill of cream lace headed by a gauze puff.

Sew up the sleeves from 15 to 16 and from 17 to 18. Set on the puff at the top as the figures indicate. Below the sleeve puff there is a shirred gauze puff crossed by two silk folds, and a similar gauze puff borders the bottom.

For the train, cut one double piece of silk and lining from the pattern. Edge the bottom with a pleating headed by a ruche. Continue the latter up the sides. Pleat the top as indicated and set it into a band. Work buttonholes at intervals on the band, by which to button it to the skirt. Set the buttons across the back of the skirt under the drapery.

Harper's Bazar, November 1882

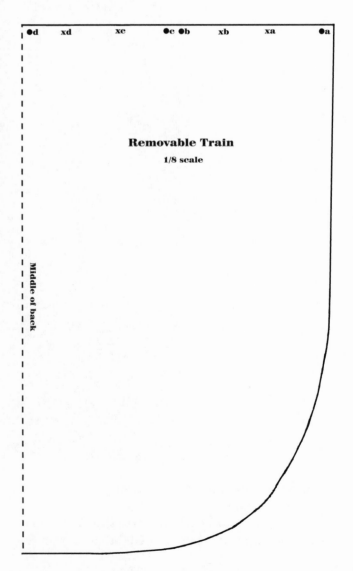

●d   xd   xc   ●c ●b   xb   xa   ●a

Removable Train
1/8 scale

Middle of back

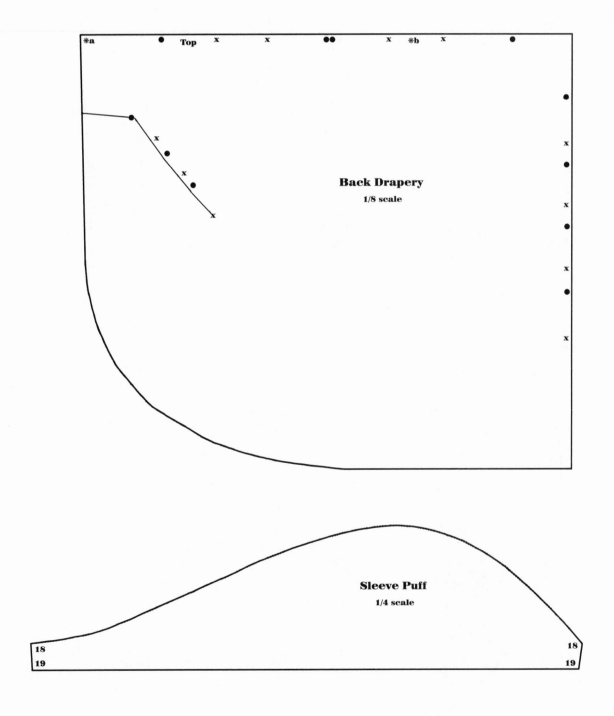

*a   ●   **Top**   x   x   ●●   x   *b   x   ●

Back Drapery

1/8 scale

Sleeve Puff

1/4 scale

18
19
18
19

79

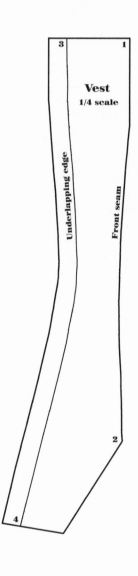

Vest
1/4 scale

Underlapping edge

Front seam

3

1

2

4

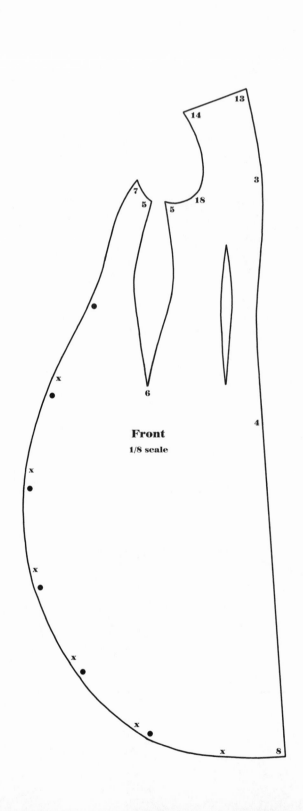

13

14

3

7
5

18

5

6

4

Front
1/8 scale

x

x

x

x

x

8

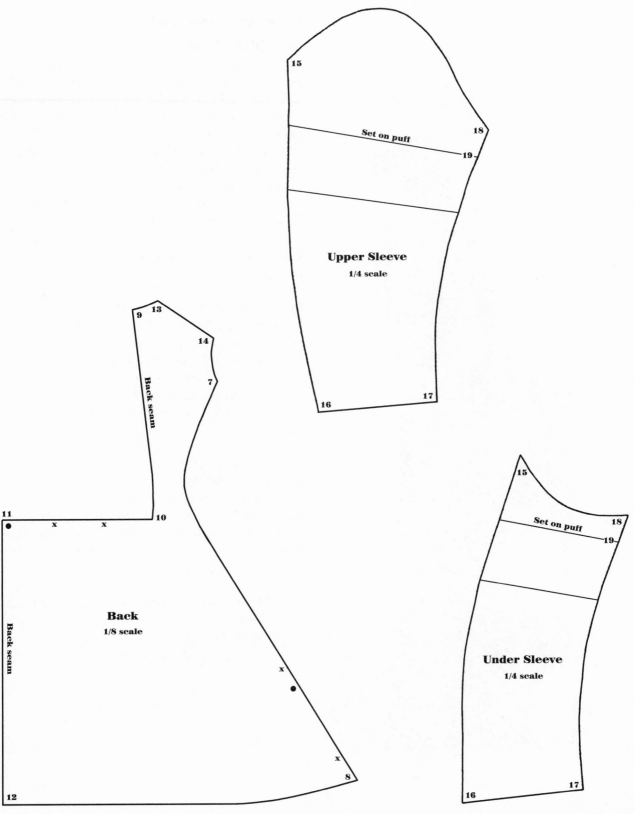

15

Set on puff

18

19

Upper Sleeve
1/4 scale

16   17

9 13

14

7

Back seam

11   10
x   x

Back
1/8 scale

Back seam

x

x

8

12

15

Set on puff

18

19

Under Sleeve
1/4 scale

16   17

81

Satin Duchesse and Brocade Reception Dress

This dress is made of 12 yd. of black satin duchesse and 5 1/2 yd. of black brocade, 24 in. wide. The short round skirt is 2 in. longer behind than in front, and 2 1/4 yd. wide at the bottom. It is bordered at the bottom by two satin pleatings 3 in. wide. Above these is a bias satin flounce. This is gathered and sewn down to form a puff at the bottom. It is shirred in clusters of six rows at intervals of 2 1/2 in., 3 in. from the top, the fullness being tacked to form a heading. The skirt front is faced with brocade.

To make the drapery, cut one piece from the back drapery and two pieces from the lower side drapery of brocade. Cut two pieces from the pannier drapery of satin. Pleat the pannier drapery, lower side drapery, and back drapery as indicated, bringing *x* on ●. Shirr both sides of the back in regular rows in the space enclosed by narrow lines, gathering the fullness into a space 4 in. long. Then join the parts from 3 to 4, face the edges, and drape and sew them on the foundation skirt. The front and bottom are edged with a frill of Spanish lace 4 in. wide.

For the bodice, cut two pieces each from the front, first side piece, second side piece, back, upper sleeve, and under sleeve of satin and lining. Take up the darts in the fronts. Join the fronts, side pieces, and back according to the corresponding figures. Sew up the sleeves and trim them as illustrated. Set them into the armholes, bringing 18 on 18 of the fronts, and fulling in the sleeve top on the shoulder.

The square neck opening is piped with satin and edged with lace. Small round crochet buttons are used for fastening.

Harper's Bazar, November 1882

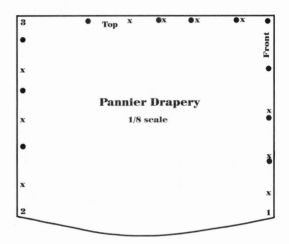

Pannier Drapery
1/8 scale

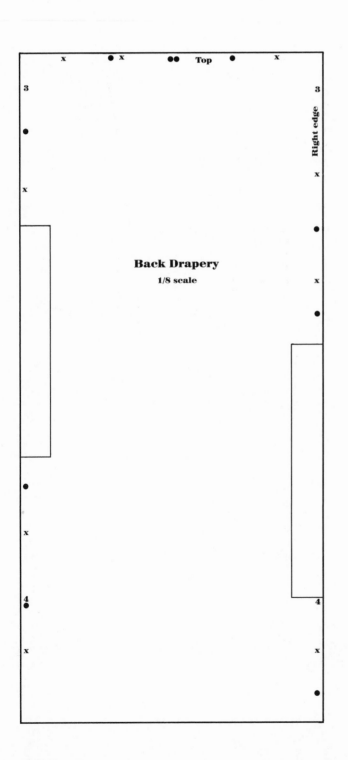

Back Drapery
1/8 scale

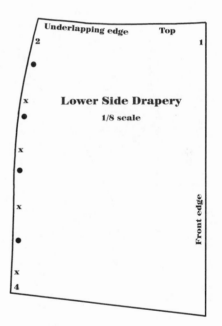

Lower Side Drapery
1/8 scale

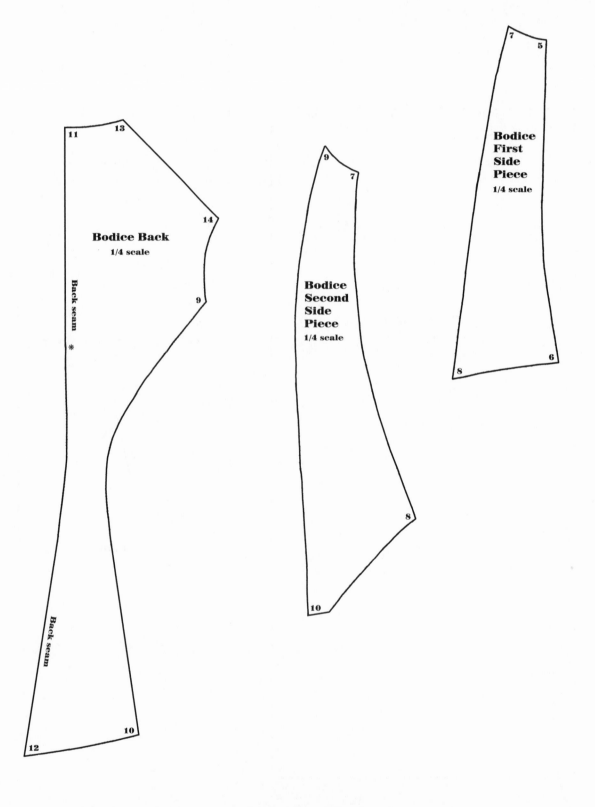

11   13

Bodice Back
1/4 scale

14

Back seam

*

9

Back seam

12   10

9

7

**Bodice
Second
Side
Piece**
1/4 scale

8

10

7   5

**Bodice
First
Side
Piece**
1/4 scale

8   6

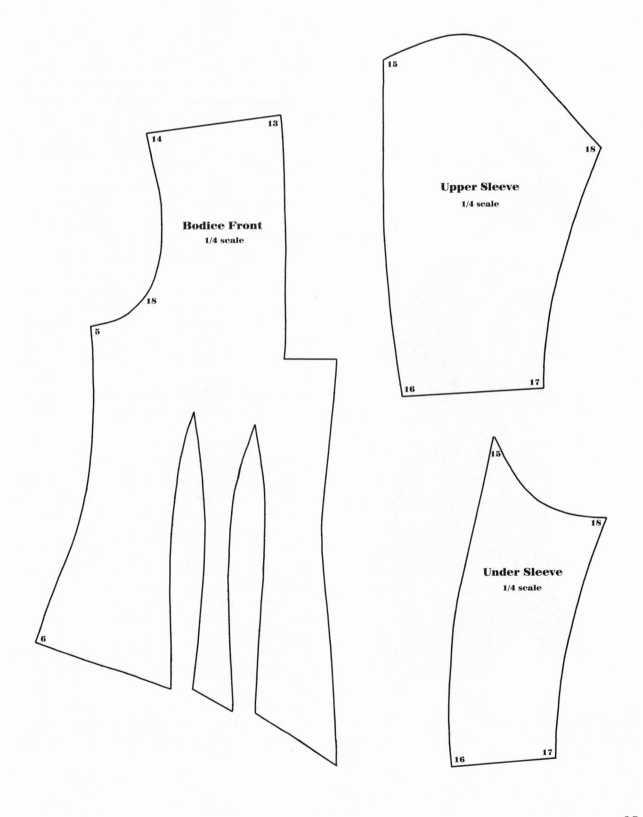

Bodice Front
1/4 scale

Upper Sleeve
1/4 scale

Under Sleeve
1/4 scale

Satin and Brocade Evening Dress

The full-trained skirt of this dress is of light bronze satin, and requires 18 yd. The short pannier polonaise is of brocade with a light blue satin ground and colored flowers; 6 1/2 yd. are required.

The skirt measures 44 in. at the front, 70 in. at the back, and 3 3/4 yd. around the bottom. The bottom is bordered by two narrow pleatings. These are headed by a puff 10 in. deep, which is pleated at the upper edge and gathered at the lower. The front and sides are covered as far as 8 in. from the top with a piece of the material 1 yd. long and 2 1/2 yd. wide. This is side pleated, and is set on with the top and bottom in pleats, and the middle drawn out in a puff. Falling over the pleatings on the front is a deep fringe with mingled strands of bronze silk, light blue chenille, and beads.

For the drapery, pleat the right back and left back as indicated, bringing x on ●. Join them from 1 to 2. Turn down and hem them along the narrow line. Drape them on the foundation skirt, tacking them in place. Sew the top to the skirt waistband. Set a bow at the bottom of the right drapery.

To make the polonaise, cut two pieces from the front of lining. Cut a piece each from the right back and left back, and two pieces each from the collar, upper sleeve, and under sleeve, of brocade and lining. Face the front linings as far as the narrow line on the pattern with bronze satin for the vest, and the rest with brocade.

Take up the darts and seams in the fronts. Join the fronts and back according to the corresponding figures. Pleat the fronts as indicated, bringing x on ●. Set tapes for tying back on the clusters of pleats. Fasten the lettered xs to the ●s marked with corresponding letters on the left back. Tack the ✳s to each other. Pleat the right back as indicated. Sew the pleats on the outside of the left back at the point marked ✳a, covering the raw edges with a rosette of the material. Tack ●●b of the right back to ●●b of the right front. Tack ●●a of the left back to ●●a of the left front.

Join the collar to the neck from 9 to 14. Set a ruche of double bronze satin inside. Sew up the sleeves according to the corresponding figures. Set them into the armholes. The neck and front are bordered with a ruche of silk, chenille, and beads. Satin bows are on the front and sleeves as illustrated.

Harper's Bazar, December 1882

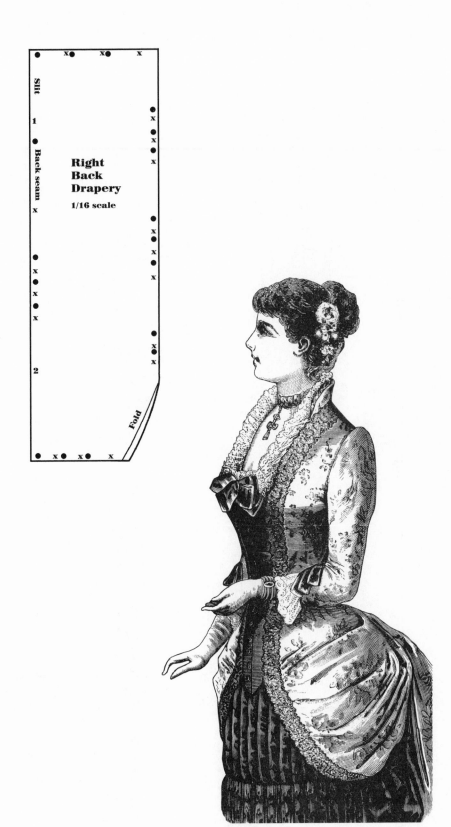

Right
Back
Drapery

1/16 scale

Slit

1

Back seam

2

Fold

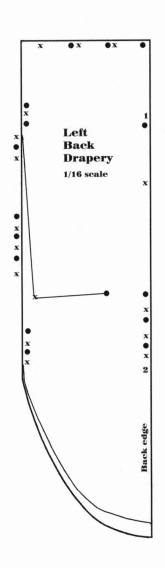

Left
Back
Drapery

1/16 scale

1

2

Back edge

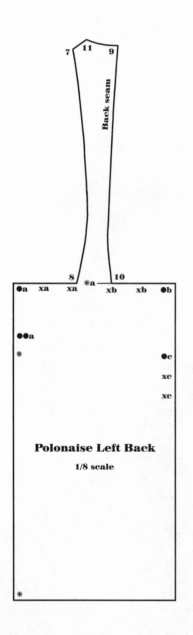

Polonaise Left Back

1/8 scale

Collar

1/4 scale

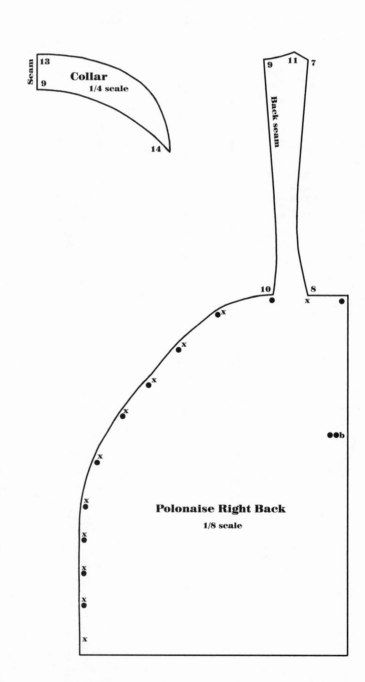

Polonaise Right Back

1/8 scale

 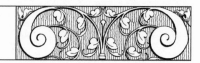

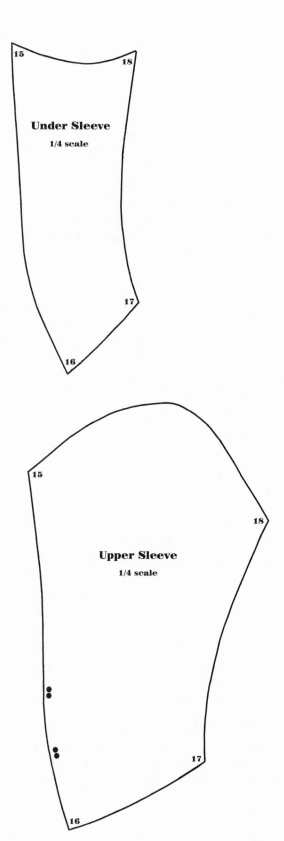

Under Sleeve

1/4 scale

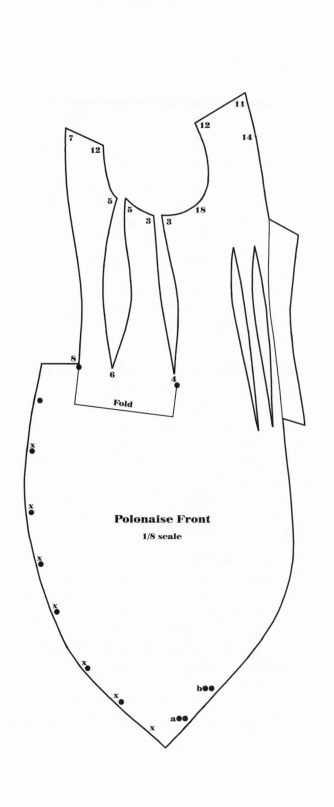

Polonaise Front

1/8 scale

Fold

Upper Sleeve

1/4 scale

3. Bridal Toilettes

A bride in full bridal costume should be entirely in white from head to foot. Her dress may be of silk heavily corded, moiré antique, brocade, satin, or plain silk; of lace, merino, alpaca, crepe, lawn, or muslin. The dress is high and the arms are covered. Her veil may be of lace, tulle, or illusion, but it must be long and full. It may or may not descend over the face. The flowers of the bridal wreath and bouquet must be orange blossoms, either natural or artificial, or other white flowers. No jewelry is worn save diamonds or pearls. Slippers of white satin and gloves of kid complete the dress.

The style of great simplicity in bridal toilettes, adopted in continental Europe, is more commendable than that of England and America, where the bridal dress is made as expensive and as heavy with rich and costly lace as it is possible to make it.

Dress of Bridegroom

The bridegroom wears a black or dark blue dress coat; light pantaloons, vest, and necktie; and white kid gloves.

Dress of Bridesmaids

The dresses of the bridesmaids are less elaborate than that of the bride. They should also be white, but they may be trimmed with delicately colored flowers and ribbons. White tulle worn over pale pink or blue silk, and caught up with blush roses or forget-me-nots, with *bouquet de corsage* and hand bouquet of the same, makes a charming bridesmaid's costume. The bridesmaids may or may not wear veils, but when worn they should be shorter than that of the bride.

Second Marriage of a Widow

A widow is never married in white. Widows and brides of middle age choose delicate neutral tints, with white gloves and white lace collar and cuffs.

The costumes of the bridesmaids must take their tone from that of the bride, and be neither lighter, richer, nor gayer than hers.

Traveling Dress of Bride

This should be of silk, or any of the fine fabrics for walking dresses. It should be of some neutral tint, and bonnet and gloves should match in color. A bridal traveling costume may be somewhat more elaborately trimmed than an ordinary traveling dress.

A bride is frequently married in traveling costume. But when this is the case, the wedding is a private one, and the bridal pair set out at once upon their journey.

Dress of Guests at Wedding Reception

For a morning reception the dress should be the richest street costume, with white gloves. If at the morning reception the blinds are closed and the gas lighted, then evening dress is worn by the guests. The guests at an evening reception should wear full evening dress.

No one should attend in black or wear any sign of mourning. Those in mourning lay aside black for lavender or gray.

The Trousseau

The trousseau may be as large and expensive as the circumstances of the bride will justify, but this expense is mainly put upon outside garments. Of dresses there are required morning dresses, walking suits, carriage dresses, evening dresses, one traveling dress, one waterproof suit, one very handsome suit to return calls, and last but not least the bridal dress. These dresses may be multiplied in number according to the needs and means of the bride.

There are certain requisite articles that must be supplied in a certain number, and of a certain similarity in general character and make. They may be set down as follows:

Four pairs of corsets, one pair white embroidered, two plain white, and one pair colored, the latter to be used in traveling

Twelve chemises, six elaborately trimmed and six more plainly made

Twelve pairs of drawers, made in sets with the chemises, and matching them in trimming

Six corset covers, three finely finished

Six trimmed skirts and six plain ones

Six flannel skirts, three of them handsomely embroidered

Two Balmoral skirts, one handsome and the other plain

Six fine and six plain nightdresses

Four white dressing sacques, two of them of flannel

Two loose wrappers of chintz or cashmere

Six sets of linen collars and cuffs for morning wear

Six sets of lace or embroidered collars and cuffs

One dozen plain handkerchiefs, one dozen fine handkerchiefs, and six embroidered or lace trimmed

One dozen pair of fine thread hose, one dozen of heavy cotton, and one dozen of fine merino

Walking boots, gaiters, and slippers of various styles

Two pairs of white kid gloves, two of light and two of dark tints, with others of thread and cloth

Ladies' and Gentlemen's Etiquette, 1877

Swiss Muslin Bridal Dress

This white Swiss muslin dress consists of a skirt and
bodice. It is trimmed with side-pleated ruffles of
the material, lace insertion, gathered lace, and bows
of white faille. Wreath of orange blossoms and veil
of illusion.

To make the skirt cut one piece from the front
breadth. Cut two pieces each from the side gore,
back breadth, and piece set on. Lay the piece set
on in side pleats at the top. Sew through them along
the narrow line. Gather the back breadth on the
under edge. Sew the pleating to the back breadth
from 23 to 25. Join the front, side gore, back
breadth, and piece set on according to the corresponding figures. Note that the skirt closes at the
left side. Face the bottom with a strip of the material 4 7/8 in. wide. Trim the skirt as illustrated. Set
it on a waistband furnished with hooks and eyes.

For the bodice cut of Swiss muslin and silk
lining two pieces each from the front, side piece,
back, and both sleeve pieces. Cut the collar. Sew
up the darts in the fronts. Furnish the fronts with
buttons and buttonholes. Join the front, side piece,
and back according to the corresponding figures.
Join the neck with the trimmed collar according to
the figures. Trim the sleeves to match the dress. Set
them into the armholes, bringing 40 on 40 of the
fronts. Belt of faille.

Harper's Bazar, May 1878

**Skirt
Front**

1/8 scale

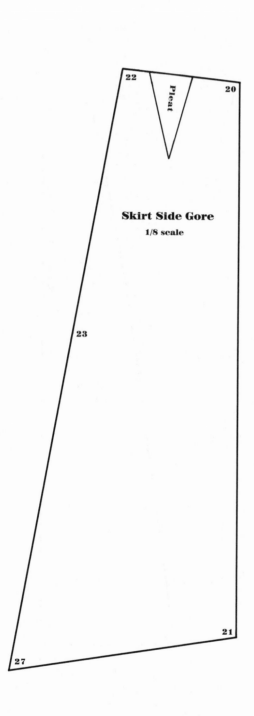

Skirt Side Gore
1/8 scale

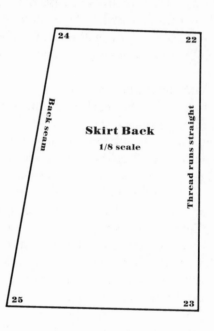

Skirt Back
1/8 scale

94

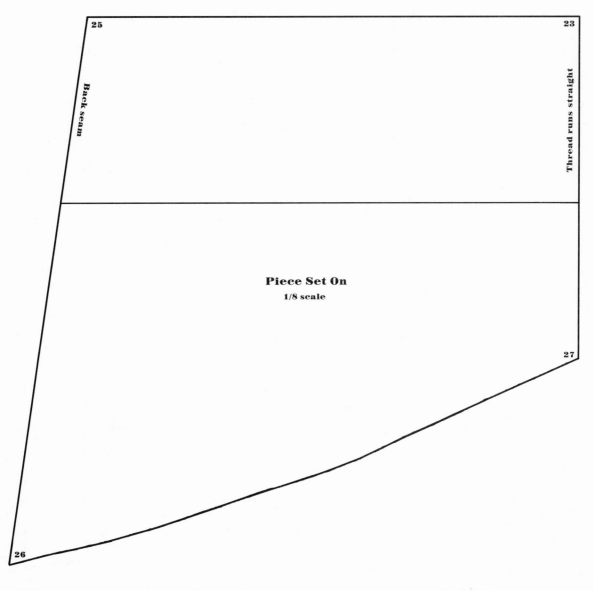

25

23

Back seam

Thread runs straight

Piece Set On

1/8 scale

27

26

95

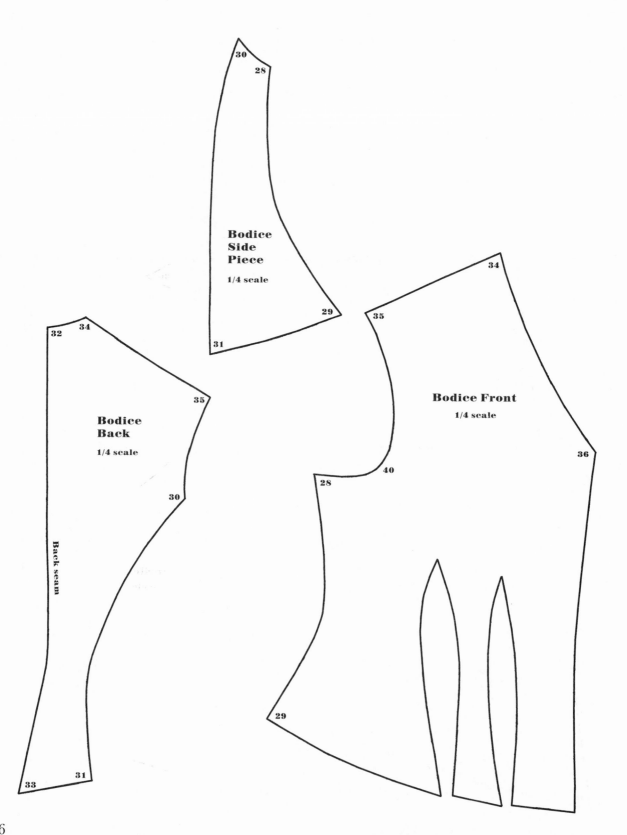

**Bodice
Side
Piece**

1/4 scale

30

28

29

31

34

35

Bodice Front

1/4 scale

28

40

36

29

32   34

35

**Bodice
Back**

1/4 scale

30

Back seam

33   31

Swiss Muslin Bridal Dress

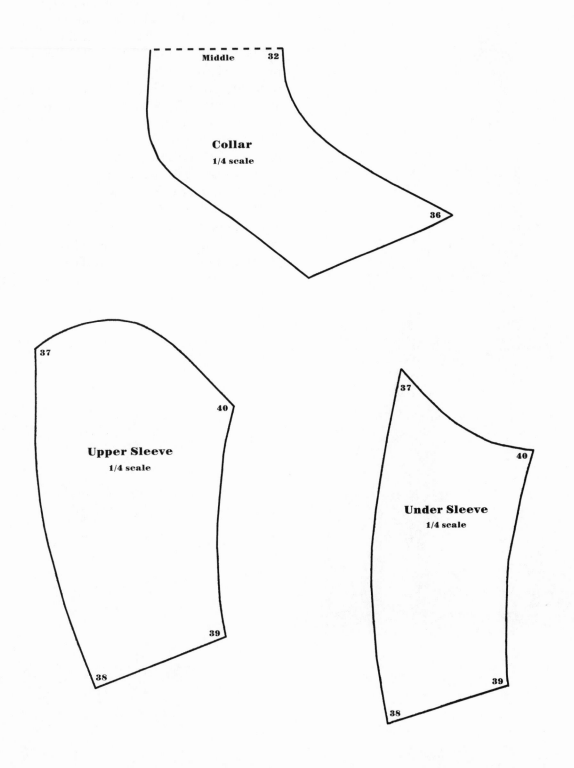

Middle   32

Collar
1/4 scale

36

37

40

Upper Sleeve
1/4 scale

39

38

37

40

Under Sleeve
1/4 scale

39

38

Satin Bridal Toilette

Cut of white satin two pieces each from the front, side piece, and back. Cut one piece from the back breadth. Cut both parts of the sleeves.

Line all the parts. Sew up the darts in the fronts. Join them from 1 to 2. Join the front, side piece, back, and back breadth according to the corresponding figures. Pleat the back and back breadth as indicated on the pattern. Face the bottom of the dress with a strip of the material 4 7/8 in. wide. The fronts are covered with shirred satin in the manner of a jabot as indicated on the pattern. They are closed with buttons and buttonholes. Set on the double standing collar. Sew up the sleeves, trim them as illustrated, and set them into the armholes. Trim the dress with pleated scarves and bows of satin, and with sprays of orange blossoms. Wreath of orange blossoms and veil of silk tulle.

Harper's Bazar, March 1880

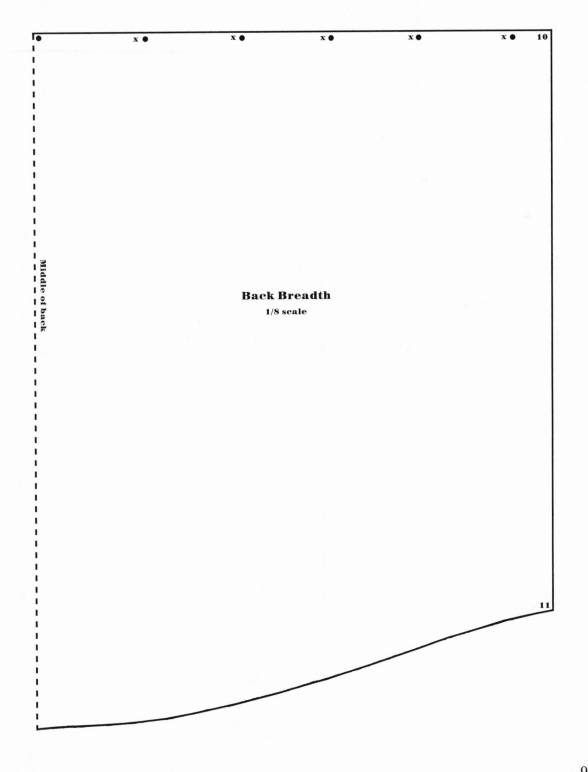

Back Breadth

1/8 scale

Middle of back

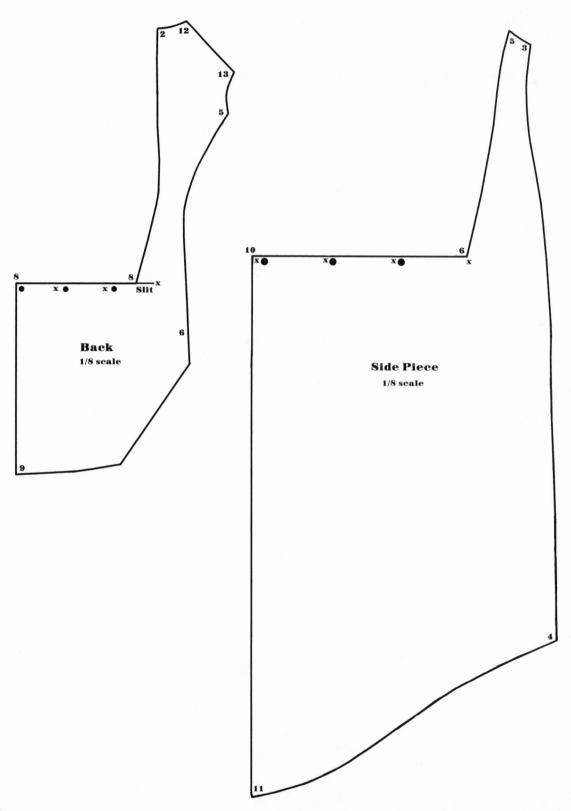

Back
1/8 scale

Side Piece
1/8 scale

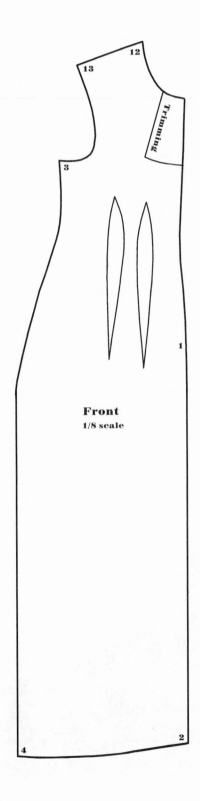

Trimming

Front
1/8 scale

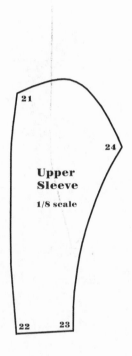

**Upper
Sleeve**
1/8 scale

**Under
Sleeve**
1/8 scale

Satin Merveilleux Bridal Toilette

This dress is of ivory satin merveilleux, the tablier draped with lace-bordered figured silk tulle. The bodice is sharply pointed both front and back. The dress requires 19 yd. of satin, 24 in. wide.

For the trained skirt, cut one whole piece from the front breadth and two from the side gore of satin and foundation lining. Cut two pieces each from the back breadth and the train of white cotton sateen. Face the latter 12 in. deep on the right side with satin. Join the parts of the skirt according to the corresponding figures. Pleat the top of the train and the top of the skirt as indicated on the pattern. Join the skirt to the waistband. Border it at the bottom with a side pleating as illustrated.

Drape the figured silk tulle tablier on the front. Arrange the pannier and back drapery on the skirt. Cut the drapery and join the halves from 22 to 23 in the front and from 17 to 25 in the back. Pleat it as indicated on the pattern, bringing *x* on ●. Tack together the points marked ✳*a* in the middle of the back. Arrange the drapery on the skirt according to the corresponding figures and signs on the pattern. Gather it in somewhat from 22 to ✳, and tack the points marked ● fast to the skirt.

Cut the bodice front, first side piece, second side piece, and back. Cut the sleeves about 4 in. shorter than the pattern. Join the parts according to the corresponding figures. Set the sleeves into the armholes. Trim the bodice with lace as illustrated.

The veil is of figured silk tulle like that on the tablier. Hair and corsage bouquets, and skirt garland, of orange blossoms.

Harper's Bazar, March 1882

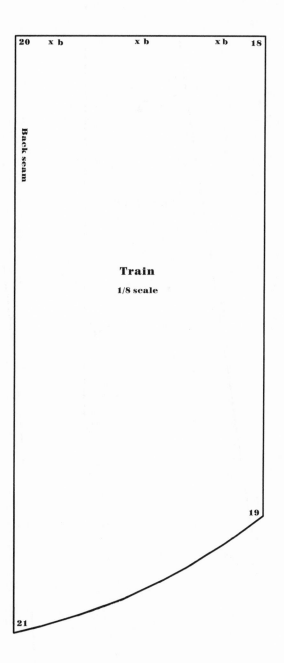

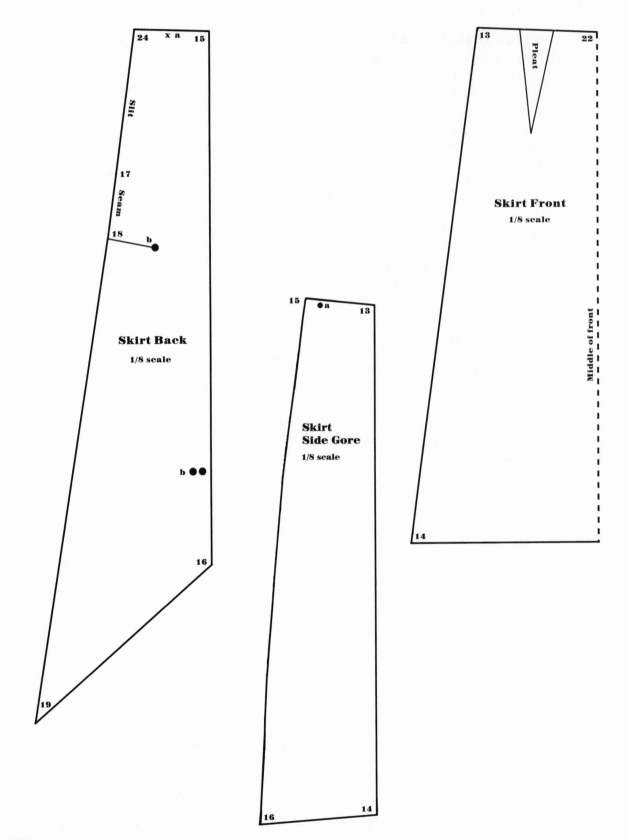

24   x a   15

Slit

17

Seam

18   b

Skirt Back

1/8 scale

b ● ●

16

19

15   ● a   13

Skirt Side Gore

1/8 scale

16   14

13   22

Pleat

Skirt Front

1/8 scale

Middle of front

14

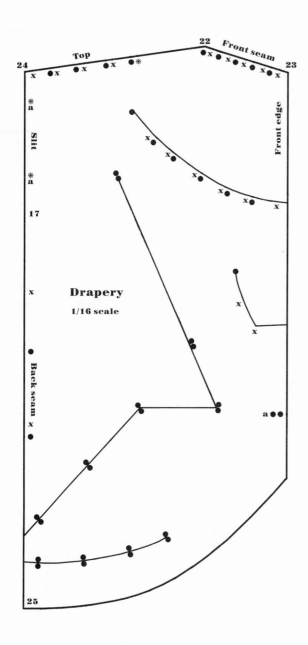

24 Top 22 Front seam 23

Front edge

*a

Slit

*a

17

x

Drapery
1/16 scale

x

Back seam x

a • •

25

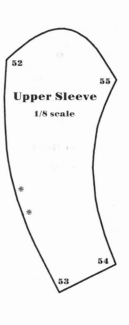

52
55

Upper Sleeve
1/8 scale

54
53

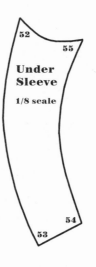

52
55

Under Sleeve
1/8 scale

54
53

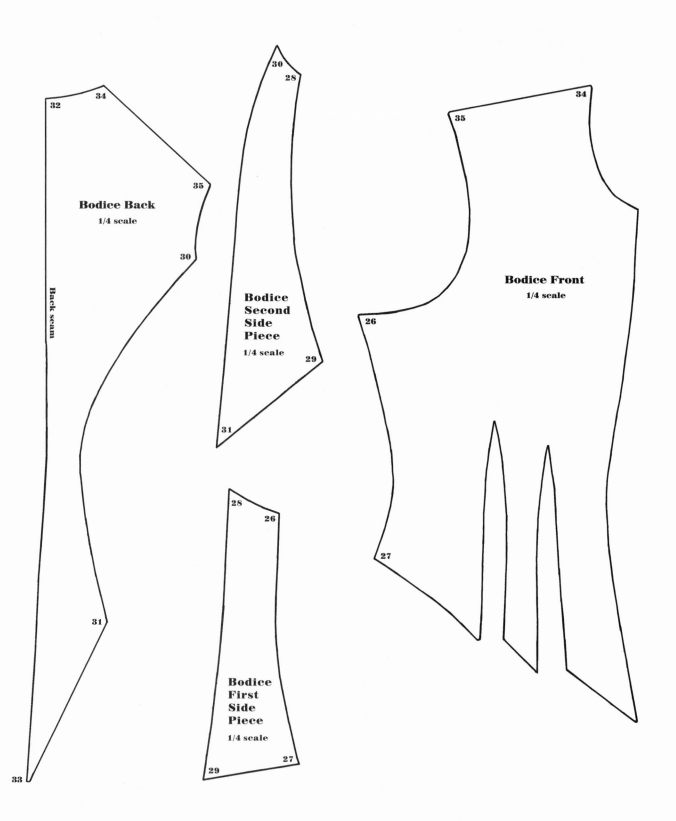

Bodice Back

1/4 scale

Back seam

Bodice Second Side Piece

1/4 scale

Bodice Front

1/4 scale

Bodice First Side Piece

1/4 scale

Brocade and Satin Bridal Toilette

This dress requires 17 1/4 yd. of satin, and 6 1/2 yd. of brocade. It is princess, composed of a trained skirt and a polonaise fastened behind, the drapery of which is tacked on the skirt. The foundation skirt, which has a round train, is cut of white cotton sateen. It measures 43 in. in front, 84 in. to the edge of the train in back, and 5 yd. around the bottom. The front and sides are faced with a strip of satin, bordered with a narrow satin side pleating, and covered with white brocade which is lined with foundation. The back is also faced with satin, and is bordered with a pleating 6 in. wide. Falling over the pleating and partly covering it there is a plain brocade flounce or valance 18 in. deep lined with foundation. This is slashed 5 in. deep at intervals of 4 in. The tabs thus formed are faced with satin, and tacked back on the right side as shown in the small illustration, which gives a section of the skirt trimming.

To make the polonaise, first join the two parts of the pattern for the left back. Cut two pieces each from the front, upper sleeve, and under sleeve. Cut one piece each from the right back, left back, and train drapery.

Line the front, right back, and left back from the top to 4 in. below the waistline. Line the sleeves. Take up the darts and the underarm seams in the fronts, bringing the corresponding figures together. Join them from 1 to 2. Pleat the sides, bringing *x* on ●, and join them to the backs from 7 to 8. Join the backs from 10 to 11, and join the left back and the drapery from 12 to 13. Pleat the right back, left back, and train drapery, bringing *x* on ●. Bring the bottom of the right back over the left back, through the slit left from 12 to the upper edge, and on the wrong side to the side edge of the left back. Fasten ✱*a* of the left back on ✱*a* of the right back, and ✱*b* of the left back on ✱*b* of the drapery. Fasten the top of the drapery on the wrong side of the right back at the waistline.

Furnish both sides of the back with eyelet holes. Set a fly 2 in. wide underneath the left back. Border the front of the polonaise and the train with Venetian lace set on plain with the scalloped edge

turned up. Tack the drapery on the back of the foundation skirt. Trim the elbow sleeves with two pleated satin frills and one of lace. Sew them into the armholes, fulling them in somewhat on the shoulders. The lace scarf veil is 24 in. wide and 3 yd. long. Wreath and corsage bouquet of orange blossoms.

Harper's Bazar, May 1882

Front
1/8 scale

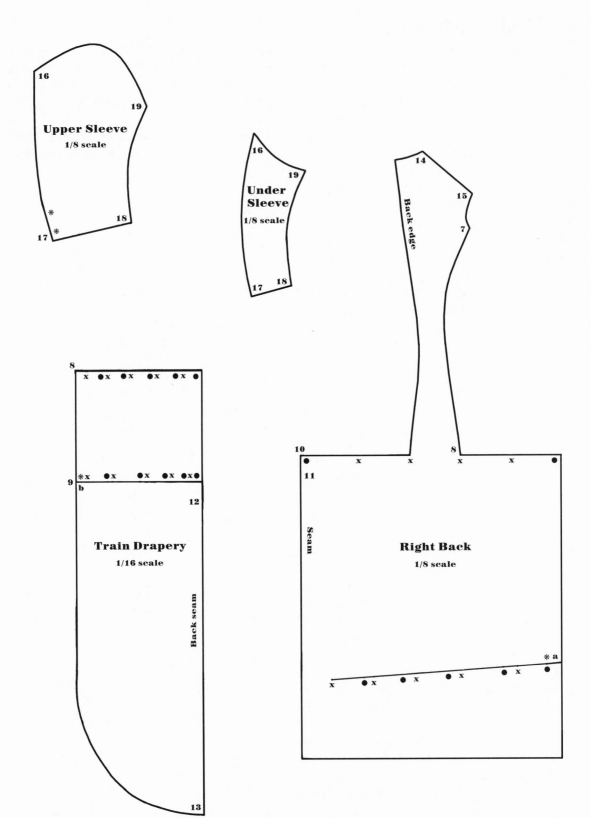

110

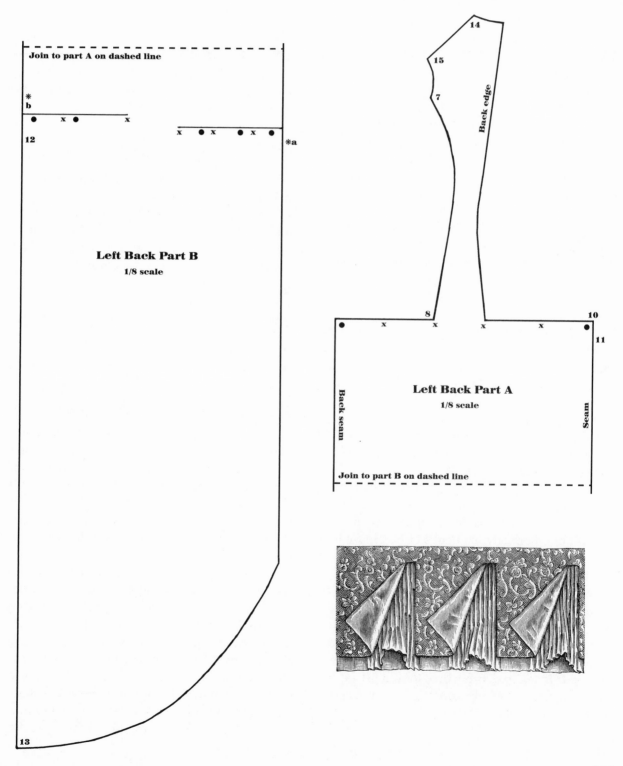

Join to part A on dashed line

*
b
● x ● x
12
x ● x ● x
*a

Left Back Part B
1/8 scale

14

15

7

Back edge

8
x x
x x
10
11

Back seam

Left Back Part A
1/8 scale

Seam

Join to part B on dashed line

13

4. Sports Wear

Waterproof is the most serviceable cloth for a riding costume, though broadcloth is more dressy. Something lighter may be worn in summer. In the lighter costume a row or two of shot must be stitched in the bottom of the breadths of the left side to keep the skirt from blowing up in the wind.

A lady in donning the riding costume must take off all underskirts and put on trousers of the same material as her habit.

The habit must fit perfectly without being tight. It is usually made to fit the waist closely and button nearly to the throat. Above a small collar or revers on the bodice is shown a plain linen collar, fastened at the throat with a bright or black necktie. Coat sleeves should come to the wrist, with linen cuffs beneath them.

The skirt must be full and long enough to cover the feet. It is best to omit the extreme length, which subjects the dress to mud spatterings and may prove a serious entanglement to the feet in case of accident. It is well to have the bodice attached to a skirt of the usual length and the long skirt fastened over it, so that if any mishap obliges the lady to dismount she may easily remove the long overskirt and still be properly dressed.

No lace or embroidery is allowable in a riding costume. All ruffling, puffing, or bows in the trimming is out of place. Trimming, if used at all, must be put on in perfectly flat bands or be of braiding.

No jewelry save that absolutely required to fasten the dress, and that of the plainest kind, is allowable. The boots must be stout and the gloves gauntleted. The hair must be put up compactly, and neither curls nor veil should be allowed to stream in the wind. The shape of the hat will vary with the fashion, but it should always be plainly trimmed. If feathers are worn, they must be fastened so that the wind cannot by any possibility blow them over the wearer's eyes.

Bathing Costumes

A bathing dress is best made of flannel. Any other material becomes limp and unsightly after being worn for a short time. A soft gray tint is the prettiest, as it does not so soon fade and grow ugly from contact with salt water. It may be trimmed with bright worsted braid. The best form is the loose sacque or the yoke bodice, both of them to be belted in and falling about midway between the knee and the ankle. Full trousers gathered into a band at the ankle, an oilskin cap to protect the hair, which becomes harsh in the salt water, and merino socks of the dress color complete the costume.

Boating and Angling

Ladies generally wear some jaunty costume, the skirts of which are rather short. Sometimes blue, or other colored guernsey, and small sailor's hats are preferred. Stout boots with substantial leather uppers are a sine qua non.

Skating and Croquet Costumes

Skating is to winter what croquet is to summer. The requirements of their costumes, in all but material, are similar. Both call for greater brilliancy in coloring than any other out-of-door costume. They should both be short, displaying a handsomely fitting but stout boot. Both should be arranged, by the use of close-fitting sacques, to leave the arms perfectly free.

Velvet trimmed with fur, with turban hat of the same, and gloves and boots also fur bordered, combine to make the most elegant skating costume imaginable. White furs should only be worn by experienced skaters, for they easily become soiled by the novitiate in tumbles upon the ice. Any of the soft, warm, bright-colored woolen fabrics is quite as suitable as fur, if not so rich. A costume of Scotch plaid is in excellent taste. If cold tints, such as blue or green, are worn, they should be relieved

by trimmings of warm, dark furs. Silk is not suitable for a skating costume. The boot should be amply loose, or the wearer will suffer with cold or frozen feet.

Croquet gloves should be soft and washable; skating gloves thick and warm. Kid is not suitable on either occasion. The hat for croquet should have a broad brim, to shield the face from the sun and render a parasol unnecessary.

Lawn Tennis Dresses

These must be cotton, wool, or muslin. If the latter, it must be opaque, not transparent. A strong, not easily tearable material should be selected, such as cashmere, French merino, serge, Mersey shirting, oatmeal cloth, or workhouse sheeting.

Ladies' and Gentlemen's Etiquette, 1877
Ward and Lock's Home Book, 1880

At one time it was thought impossible that anyone but a tailor could make a stylish riding habit, but now many ladies have them made by dressmakers.

The jacket, or habit proper, has a few peculiarities. There should be no seam down the middle of the back. The side piece, back, and front are all cut 1 in. below the natural waistline. The skirt and the back are made some 6 in. long and form a pleat like that upon the skirt of a coat. On no account increase the length beyond the waist without making the necessary allowances for ease over the hips, or the jacket will wrinkle around the waist.

The buttons should be small and round, and the sleeves tightly buttoned at the wrist. The inside of the jacket should be lined with silk, carefully wadded and stitched in close rows. It should have a belt inside stitched to each seam at the waist, to close the jacket tight to the figure. A small square tab with two buttonholes is sewn on the inside at the waistline in back, to hold the train. Small hooks are also sewn on the inside at the bottom of the bodice, which match silk loops on the train.

The lengthening of the waist, which in some seasons finds so much favor, has not been so fashionable recently. The jacket as made now is fastened up to the throat, and has a small standing collar a trifle rounded in front. The jacket skirt is cut in one piece instead of two, as heretofore. It is interlined with something firm to give it substance.

The finish of the jacket may be plain. The edges may be turned in and stitched, and a round, plain lasting or smoked pearl button used. Some, however, trim the edges with a narrow silk braid, sewn on flat, and line the body and sleeves with some light-colored silk. Five or six buttons are sewn on the sleeves, but the lower three only have worked holes.

The train, as now worn, is only a few inches longer than walking skirt length. It is turned up at the bottom, with a narrow hem only, and the cuts taken out at the seams, which are covered with ribbon. The trousers are usually made of the same cloth as the habit. They have a fly front open to the leg seam, or a long opening at each side seam, and a button and hole in the center. A narrow strap is put on the bottom to hold them to the foot.

Dress and Cloak Cutter, 1883

Riding habits have short postilion bodices entirely without trimming, and the scant short skirts that were introduced by Englishwomen. The rule now is to have them just touch the floor when the wearer is standing. There are two breadths of double-width cloth in these skirts, sloped toward the top to fit plainly without fullness at the waistband. The seam on the right side curves outward differently from that on the left, to make room for the knee when it is over the pommel. The tailor takes special measurements for this seam, first making the wearer assume the position in the saddle, then measuring from the waistline to the knee, and from the knee to the foot.

The postilion habit is sloped away in the front about 2 in. below the waistline, is slightly shorter on the sides, and forms a small flat-pleated square basque at the back. The front is buttoned very high, has a straight standing collar, is neatly stitched on all the edges, and is fastened by small crocheted ball buttons. The sleeves are very close, and have three or four buttons at the wrists. Most habits are

slightly padded and interlined with stiff canvas on the shoulders, bust, and, if the arm is slight, in the upper part of the sleeves.

Seven out of ten habits are of very dark blue cloth. Black and invisible green are the colors next in favor. Five and one-half yards of cloth are required. The close trousers that complete the habit are made of more elastic material than habit cloth. Twilled or diagonal cloths are preferred.

A high straight linen collar, fastened by a collar button or a very simple pin, is the only lingerie worn with habits. Cuffs are not needed, as the close sleeves are hidden at the wrists by the long mousquetaire gloves that are drawn up over them. The silk beaver hat has a medium high bell-shaped crown, a very narrow rolling brim, and is worn without a veil. English jockey caps are also worn, of velvet, shirred surah, or the cloth of the habit. The hair is worn plain and low, in a small knot, coil, or close braid.

Harper's Bazar, April 1882

There are three or four ways of making the blouse of a bathing dress. For instance, it may have a yoke, or it may be plain, or it may be double breasted. The plan most liked is that of having the blouse sewed to a belt at the waist, and to this belt the trousers are sewed. For draping the figure a long square overskirt reaching below the knees is buttoned to the same belt. Thus the whole suit is in one piece, and is not liable to drag down when heavy with salt water, as all the weight is suspended from the shoulders. Ladies who swim well can leave off the overskirt if they choose, since it is only buttoned on. There are suits that have sleeves buttoned to the shoulders, so that they too can be easily removed if they interfere with the motions of the arms.

Harper's Bazar, July 1880

If the skirts of a skating costume are made to clear the ground, in fact reach only to the instep, they will greatly facilitate graceful motion. Any street costume can be worn for skating. But if the skirts are the usual walking length, or demitrain, they should be raised with a skirt elevator. Or else by rings sewn at intervals along the inside of the skirt, about 12 or 14 in. from the bottom, and a distance of 4 or 5 in. apart. Through these a silk cord or tape can be run, and a button sewn to each end, to keep the cord from slipping through the rings again. These cords will enable anyone to raise or lower her dress, by passing the ends through buttonholes in the waistband.

Demorest's Mirror of Fashions, December 1877

Vest with Narrow Standing Collar

This pattern is drafted with the scale. It is especially for riding and shooting toilettes. The basque may be lengthened or shortened.

Complete Guide to Ladies' Garment Cutting, 1883

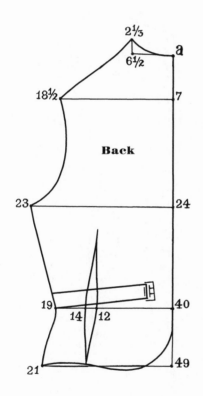

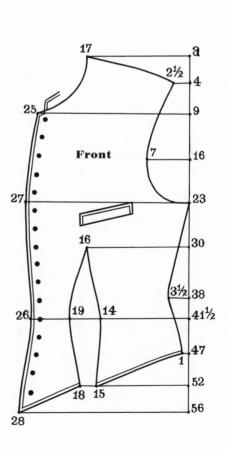

115

Long Vest

Vests are either quite close to the neck, with a narrow standing collar, or they have a shawl collar, or a falling collar. This pattern is drafted using the plain bodice pattern, which is shown by a dashed line. It varies little from the bodice. The numbers signify the differences in centimeters. The underlap for the buttons on the left front is 2 cm (13/16 in.). It may be turned into a double-breasted style by widening. The basque may be made longer, shorter, pointed, or square.

Complete Guide to Ladies' Garment Cutting, 1883

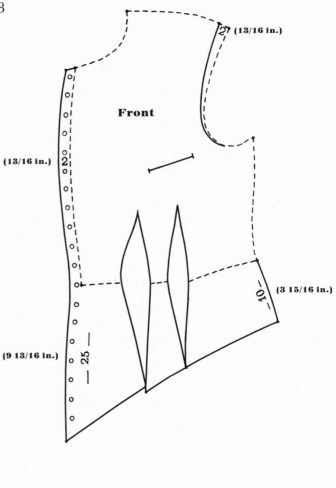

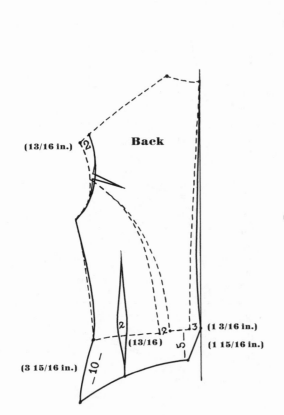

Vest with Falling Collar

This pattern is drafted with the scale. It is especially for riding and shooting toilettes. It has a falling collar cut by the shape of the neck opening. The latter may be higher or lower, depending on the season or the purpose of the vest. The basque may be lengthened or shortened.

Complete Guide to Ladies' Garment Cutting, 1883

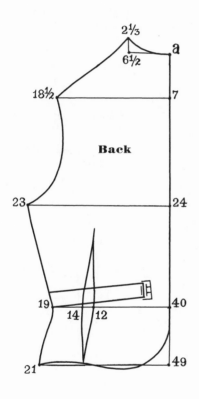

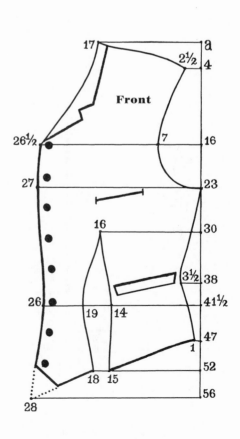

Vest

Vests are used especially in stylish toilettes such as riding habits. They are either quite close to the neck, with a narrow standing collar, or they have a shawl collar, or a falling collar. This pattern is drafted using the plain bodice pattern, which is shown by a dashed line. It varies little from the bodice. The numbers and the letters from *a* through *k* signify the differences in centimeters. The underlap for the buttons on the left front is 2 cm (13/16 in.). It may be turned into a double-breasted style by widening. The basque may be made longer, shorter, pointed, or square.

Complete Guide to Ladies' Garment Cutting, 1883

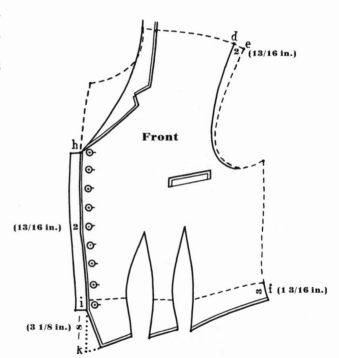

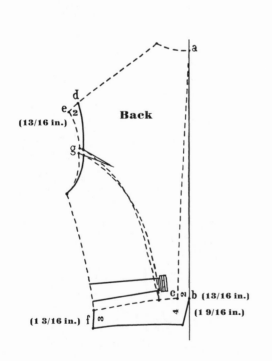

Double-Breasted Vest

This pattern is drafted with the scale. It is especially for riding and shooting toilettes. It is double breasted and has buttonholes in the front edge, which are not shown here, across from the five buttons. It has a falling collar cut by the shape of the neck opening. The latter may be higher or lower, depending on the season or the purpose of the vest. The basque may be lengthened or shortened.

Complete Guide to Ladies' Garment Cutting, 1883

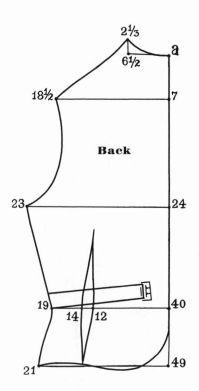

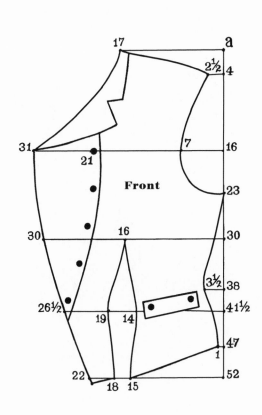

Riding Bodice with Basque

This pattern is drafted with the scale. It is single breasted. It closes high at the neck and has a small standing collar. The dashed line around the bodice in the front piece marks the waistline. A firm band must be inserted in the waistline, to accommodate the vigorous movements of riding. In the side piece, the dashed line is double, indicating a horizontal dart in the lining.

Complete Guide to Ladies' Garment Cutting, 1883

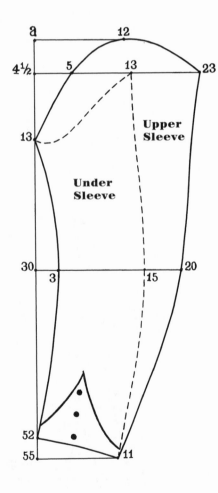

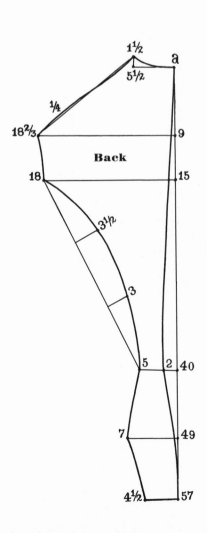

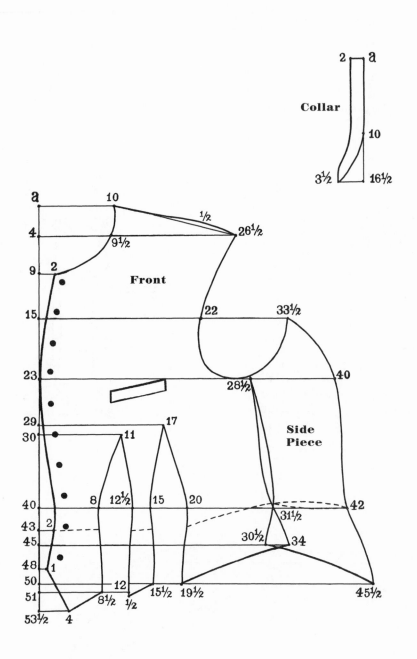

Collar

Front

Side
Piece

Riding Bodice with Short Basque

This bodice with basque is double breasted with a
shawl-like falling collar made with two parts. These
are sewn on flat. This pattern must be drafted with
the scale.

Complete Guide to Ladies' Garment Cutting, 1883

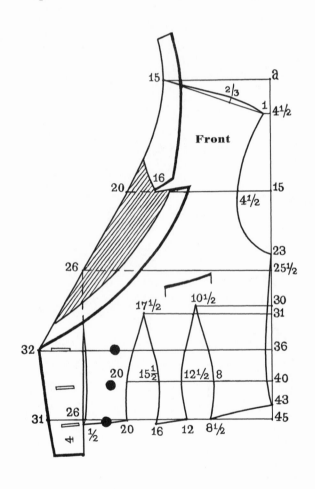

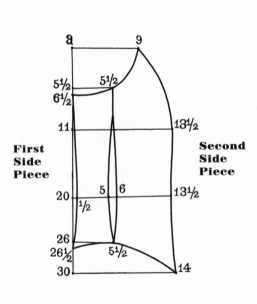

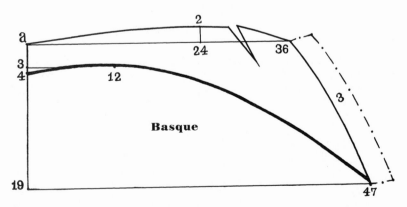

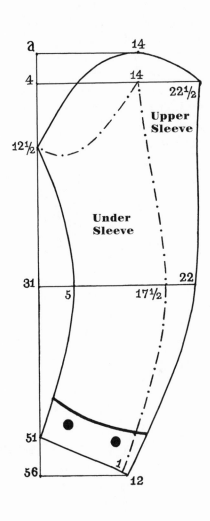

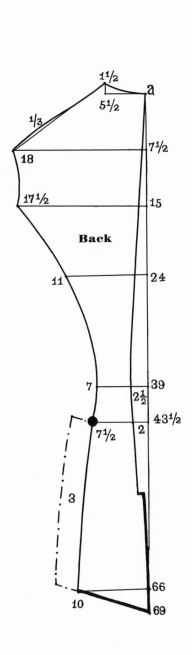

Riding Bodice or Riding Jacket

This pattern is drafted with the scale. It is single breasted with an added basque in front and on the side. The basque forms a stylish tail shape. It is split at the hip; the letters *J* and *K* must meet when the pieces are joined. The seam from *J* to *K* must be pressed well. The basque on the back piece has pleats and waist buttons. The front is closed off by the narrow standing collar.

Complete Guide to Ladies' Garment Cutting, 1883

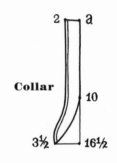

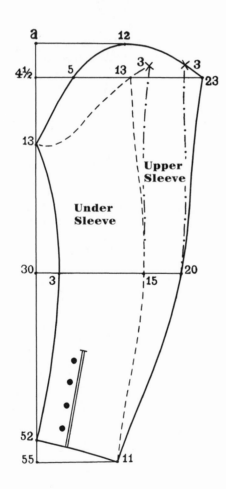

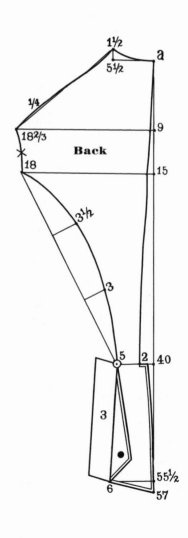

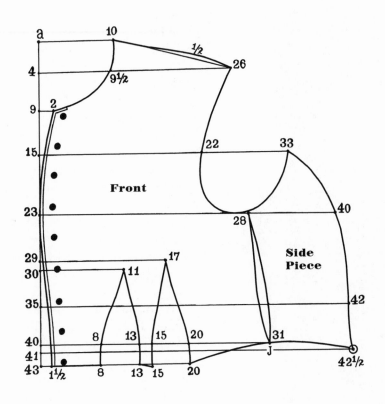

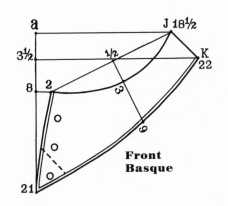

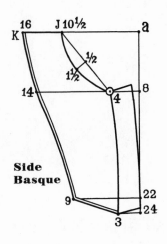

125

To make the basque cut of striped velvet and lining two pieces each from the vest front and pocket. Sew up the darts in the fronts. Set on the pockets according to the illustration and the corresponding signs on the pattern. Face the front edge of the right front with a strip of the material. Work the buttonholes. Set the front edge of the left front into a double fly 1 3/4 in. wide, on which are set the buttons.

Next cut of cloth and lining two pieces each from the front, side piece, and back. Cut the collar of double cloth. Cut both parts of the sleeves. Sew up the darts in the fronts. Baste the vest fronts to the wrong side according to the corresponding figures and signs. Join the vest front, front, side piece, and back according to the corresponding figures.

Pleat the basque below the waistline as indicated on the pattern (the narrow lines indicate the outer folds). Face the bottom and the front edge of the fronts with a strip of the material. Furnish the front with buttons and buttonholes as illustrated. Set the neck into the double collar, and roll the latter along the narrow line.

Sew up the sleeves. Face the slit with a strip of the material 1 3/4 in. wide. Join the sleeves with cuffs as illustrated. Furnish them with buttons and buttonholes along the slit, and set them into the armholes.

On the front of the basque at the left side is set a rose with brownish leaves.

Harper's Bazar, March 1880

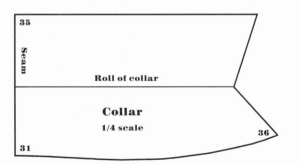

35

Seam

Roll of collar

Collar

1/4 scale

31

36

Blue Cloth Riding Habit Bodice

The basque of this dark blue cloth riding habit is joined with vest fronts of striped velvet. The hat is of felt, trimmed with satin and a bird.

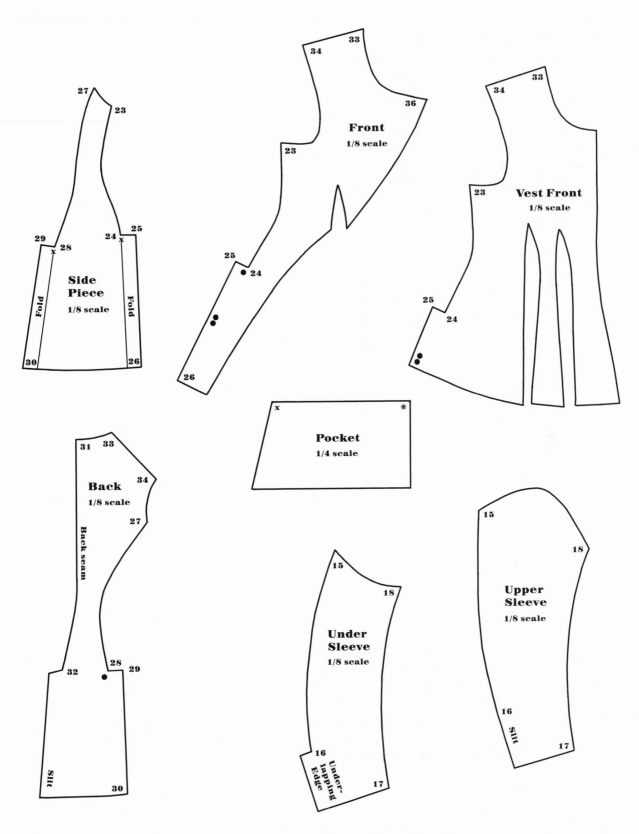

Side Piece
1/8 scale

Fold

Fold

Front
1/8 scale

Vest Front
1/8 scale

Pocket
1/4 scale

Back
1/8 scale

Back seam

Slit

Under Sleeve
1/8 scale

Under-lapping Edge

Upper Sleeve
1/8 scale

Slit

Sports Wear

Modern Riding Skirt

This is a highly recommended pattern, and not too long. It goes with any of the riding bodices given. It is drafted in centimeters. The length is drafted according to the lady's measures. The waist and hip circumference measures are used for making the skirt gores wider or narrower at the top. A narrow waistband holds up the skirt.

Complete Guide to Ladies' Garment Cutting, 1883

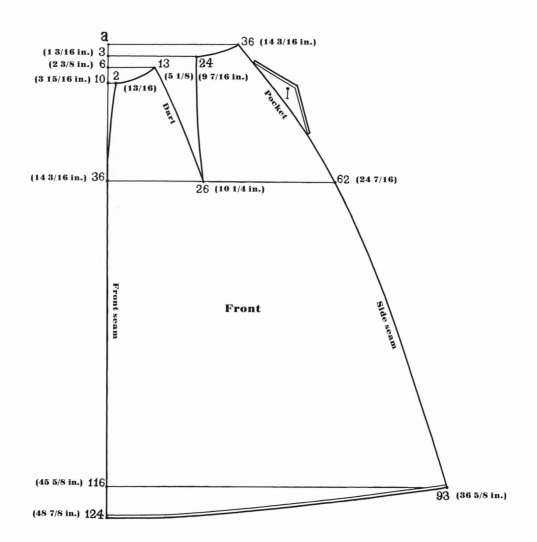

128

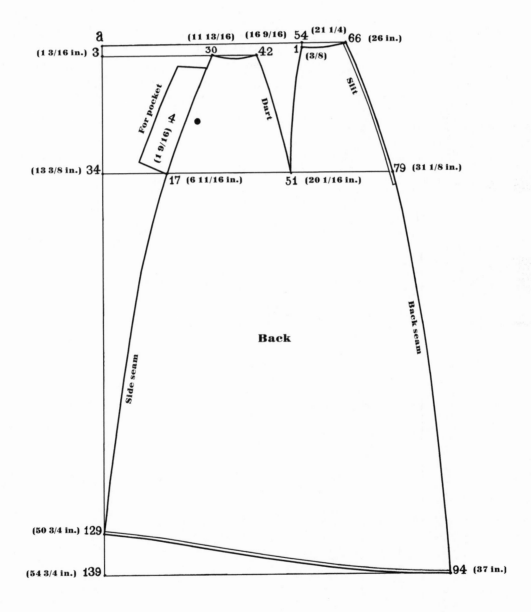

Ordinary Long Riding Trousers

This pattern has been drafted in centimeters for a side length of 100 cm (39 3/8 in.) and a half waist circumference of 32 cm (12 5/8 in.). The illustration shows the front opening and the buckled belt in back. When drafting the belt, the side length must be adjusted according to the lady's measure, as well as the belt circumference. The inseam is lengthened or shortened in proportion to the side length. The legs of this pattern are both identical. The trousers will have sewn-on or buttoned-on, elastic rubber foot straps.

Complete Guide to Ladies' Garment Cutting, 1883

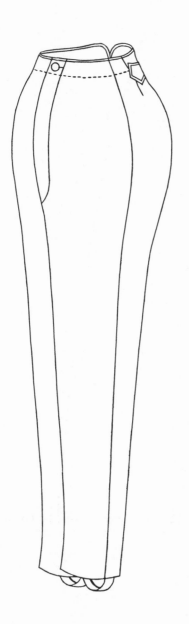

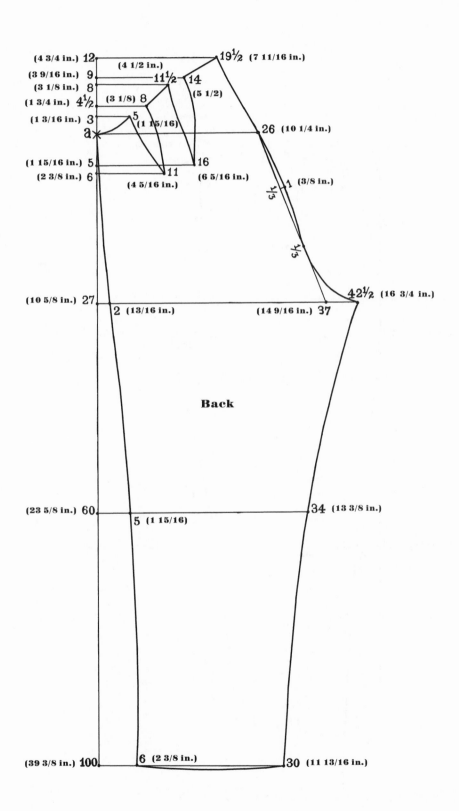

(4 3/4 in.) 12

(3 9/16 in.) 9

(3 1/8 in.) 8

(1 3/4 in.) 4½

(1 3/16 in.) 3

a ✳

(1 15/16 in.) 5

(2 3/8 in.) 6

(4 1/2 in.)

11½ 14

(3 1/8) 8

5

(1 15/16)

11

16

19½ (7 11/16 in.)

(5 1/2)

26 (10 1/4 in.)

(6 5/16 in.)

(4 5/16 in.)

⅓ 1 (3/8 in.)

⅓

(10 5/8 in.) 27

2 (13/16 in.)

Back

(14 9/16 in.) 37

42½ (16 3/4 in.)

(23 5/8 in.) 60

5 (1 15/16)

34 (13 3/8 in.)

(39 3/8 in.) 100

6 (2 3/8 in.)

30 (11 13/16 in.)

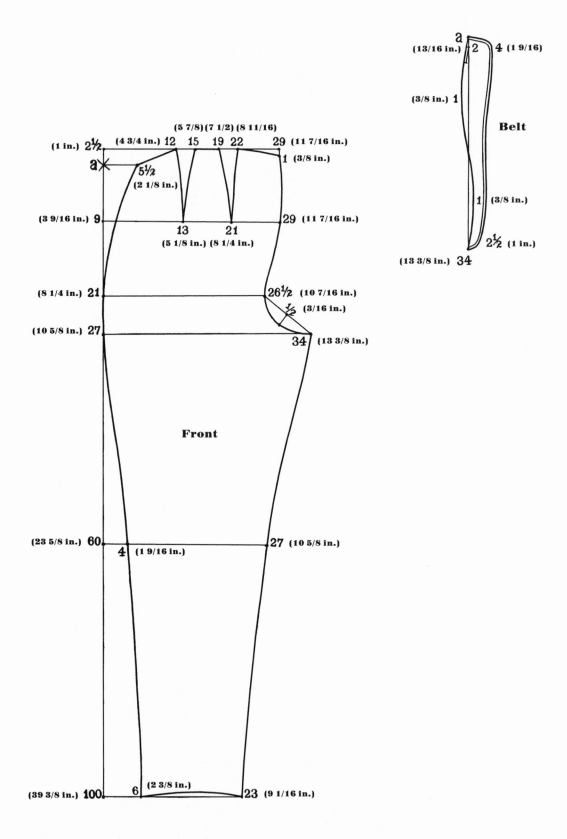

(13/16 in.) 2 4 (1 9/16)

a

(3/8 in.) 1

Belt

1 (3/8 in.)

2½ (1 in.)

(13 3/8 in.) 34

(5 7/8)(7 1/2)(8 11/16)

(1 in.) 2½ (4 3/4 in.) 12 15 19 22 29 (11 7/16 in.)

a 1 (3/8 in.)

5½
(2 1/8 in.)

(3 9/16 in.) 9 29 (11 7/16 in.)

13 21

(5 1/8 in.)(8 1/4 in.)

(8 1/4 in.) 21 26½ (10 7/16 in.)

½ (3/16 in.)

(10 5/8 in.) 27 34 (13 3/8 in.)

Front

(23 5/8 in.) 60 27 (10 5/8 in.)

4 (1 9/16 in.)

(39 3/8 in.) 100 6 (2 3/8 in.) 23 (9 1/16 in.)

132

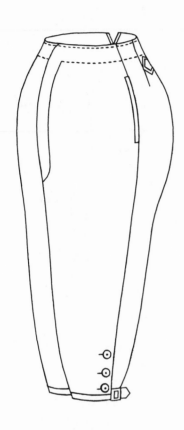

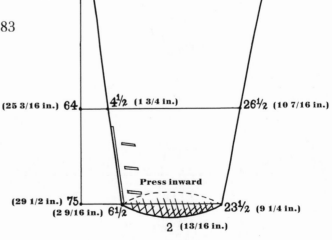

Short Riding Trousers

This pattern is drafted in centimeters for a lady of medium size. It has a small knee band and buckle. These trousers are worn with the Long Gaiters given in chapter 6 of this volume.

Complete Guide to Ladies' Garment Cutting, 1883

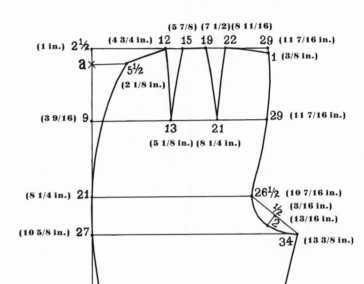

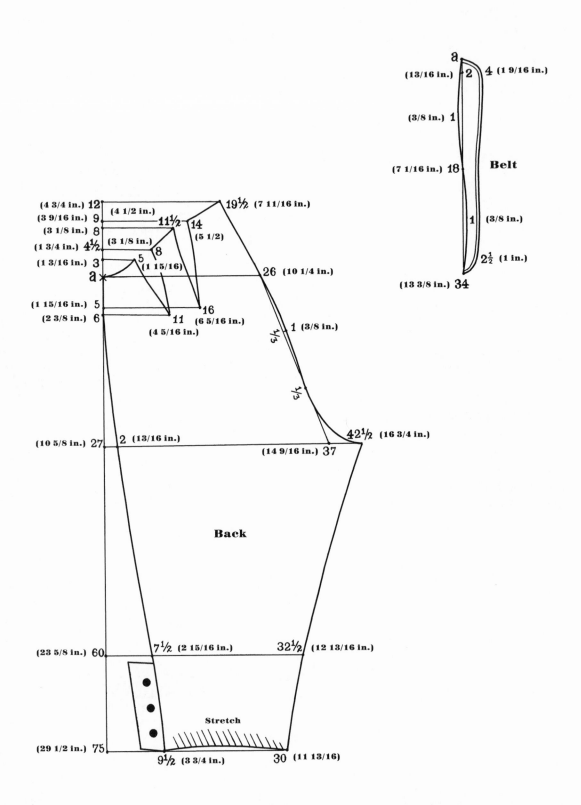

a

(13/16 in.) 2 4 (1 9/16 in.)

(3/8 in.) 1

(7 1/16 in.) 18   **Belt**

1 (3/8 in.)

2½ (1 in.)

(13 3/8 in.) 34

(4 3/4 in.) 12   (4 1/2 in.)   19½ (7 11/16 in.)
(3 9/16 in.) 9   11½ 14
(3 1/8 in.) 8   (3 1/8 in.) 8   (5 1/2)
(1 3/4 in.) 4½
(1 3/16 in.) 3   5
a *   (1 15/16)   26 (10 1/4 in.)
(1 15/16 in.) 5   16   1 (3/8 in.)
(2 3/8 in.) 6   11   ⅓
(4 5/16 in.)   (6 5/16 in.)
⅓
42½ (16 3/4 in.)
(10 5/8 in.) 27   2 (13/16 in.)
(14 9/16 in.) 37

Back

(23 5/8 in.) 60   7½ (2 15/16 in.)   32½ (12 13/16 in.)

Stretch

(29 1/2 in.) 75
9½ (3 3/4 in.)   30 (11 13/16)

Modern Riding Trousers

The fact that the right leg of the rider must be firmly placed around the pommel of the saddle for secure seating, has so far caused ordinary trousers to wrinkle, oftentimes also causing chafing of the leg. This disadvantage is avoided with the following American pattern, whose right leg is cut in the exact shape the right leg of the rider will assume. No wrinkles will form, for the trousers also have elastic rubber foot straps holding them smooth without pulling too much. When walking, the right leg will wrinkle on the outside, but the leg is wide enough overall so that this is not unpleasant. The trousers will also be concealed down to the foot by the long riding skirt.

This pattern has been drafted for a proportionate lady of medium height in centimeters. If the lady is shorter or taller, the measure must be taken loosely to the heel of the shoe. Small differences in the waist may be adjusted by making the belt according to the lady's waist circumference.

The belt is made from a firm, straight band, with a buckle in front. Or it is made from a strip of material 2 to 3 cm (13/16 to 1 3/16 in.) wide in a curved shape (according to the pattern) lest it cause pressure on the hips. If made from material, it is lined with firm linen and has a buttonhole and button in front instead of a buckle.

The back of the trousers will be gathered, or even pleated, by the amount the trousers are wider at the top than the belt. The trousers will sit firmly enough on the hips.

Complete Guide to Ladies' Garment Cutting, 1883

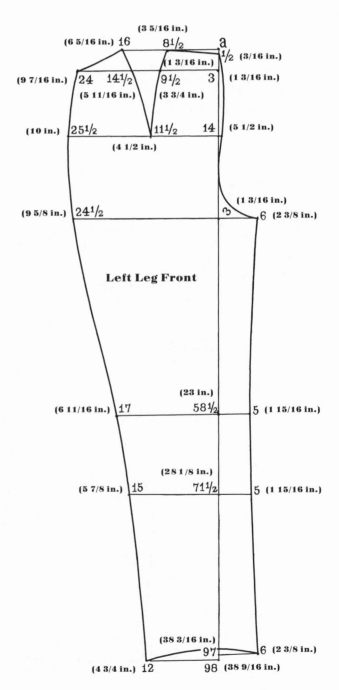

135

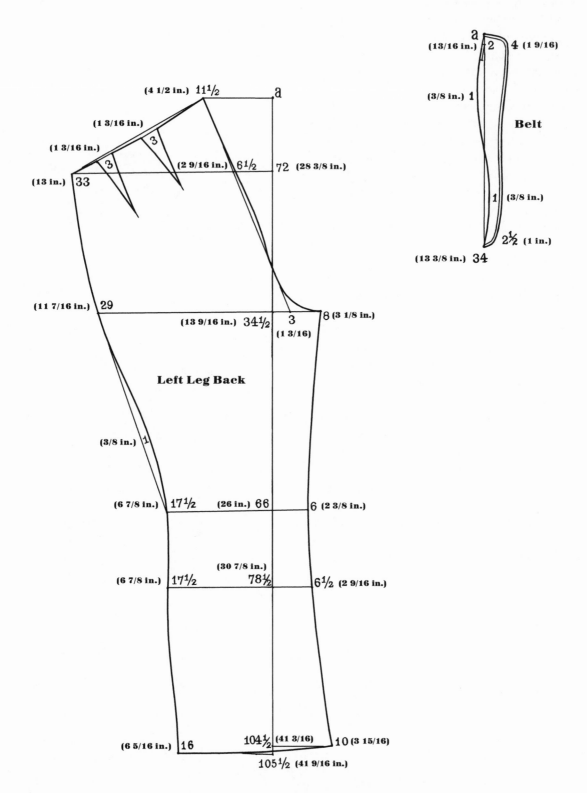

(4 1/2 in.) 11½ a

(1 3/16 in.)

(1 3/16 in.)   3

(13 in.) 33 3 (2 9/16 in.) 6½ 72 (28 3/8 in.)

(11 7/16 in.) 29 (13 9/16 in.) 34½ 3 8 (3 1/8 in.)
(1 3/16)

Left Leg Back

(3/8 in.) 1

(6 7/8 in.) 17½ (26 in.) 66 6 (2 3/8 in.)

(6 7/8 in.) 17½ (30 7/8 in.) 78½ 6½ (2 9/16 in.)

(6 5/16 in.) 16 104½ (41 3/16) 10 (3 15/16)
105½ (41 9/16 in.)

a
(13/16 in.) 2 4 (1 9/16)
(3/8 in.) 1

Belt

1 (3/8 in.)

2½ (1 in.)
(13 3/8 in.) 34

136

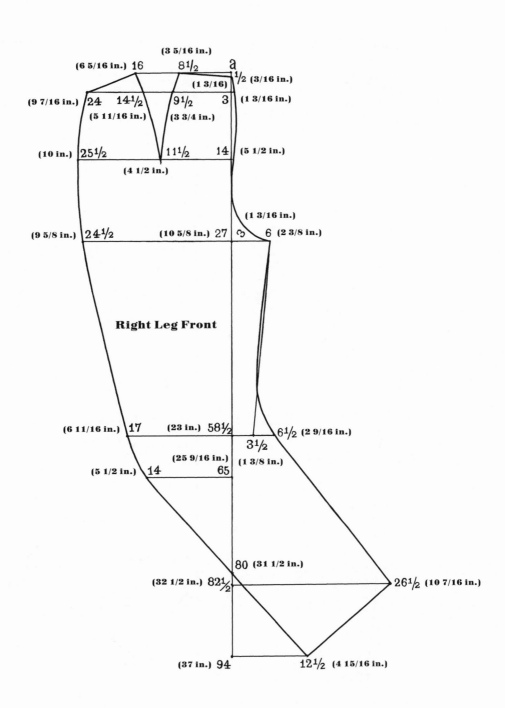

Right Leg Front

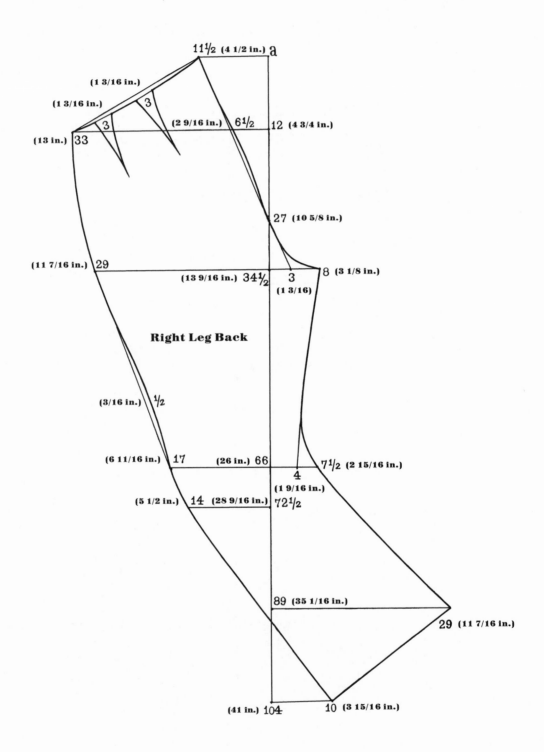

Right Leg Back

White Serge Bathing Suit

This white serge bathing suit, shown by the figure on the left, consists of trousers and a belted frock. Cut two whole pieces from the trouser pattern. Cut a slit in the front along the narrow line. Set the front edge into a double fly 1 3/4 in. wide. Face the back edge with a strip of the material 1 3/4 in. wide.

Sew up each half of the trousers from 1 to 2. Join both parts in the front from 2 to 3 and in the back from 2 to 4. Gather the trousers at the top. Set them into double bands 1 3/4 in. wide, which are furnished with buttons and buttonholes. Gather the trousers on the bottom, and set them on bindings.

For the frock, cut two pieces each from the front, front yoke, and sleeve. Cut one piece each from the back and back yoke. Gather the fronts from ✳ to 8 and the backs from the middle to 9 on each side. Join the front, back, front yoke, and back yoke according to the corresponding figures. Face the lower corners of the fronts with striped serge. Fold the fronts on the outside in revers. Bind the frock 1/2 in. deep on the bottom. Set a fold on the front edges. Furnish the frock with buttons and loops for closing. Cord the neck and trim it with a ruche.

Face the sleeves with the striped material, from the bottom to 1 3/4 in. beyond the narrow lines. Fold them on the outside in revers along these lines. Set them into the armholes according to the corresponding figures.

Harper's Bazar, August 1878

Scarlet Flannel Bathing Suit

This scarlet flannel suit, shown by the figure on the right of the plate for the White Serge Bathing Suit, is made from the same pattern. The trimming consists of a sailor collar and narrow and wide folds of white flannel. On the collar are sewed metal anchors.

Harper's Bazar, August 1878

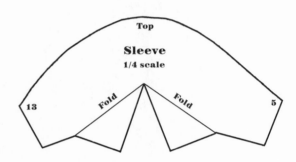

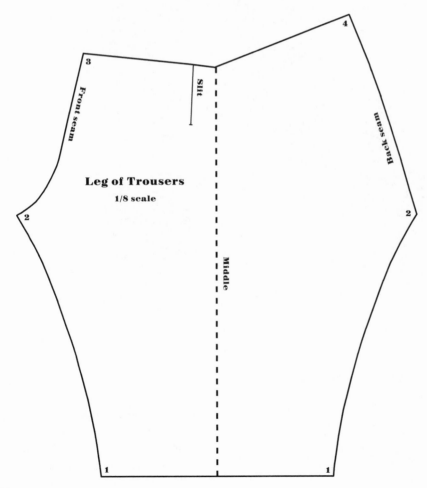

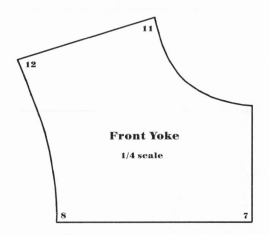

Front Yoke
1/4 scale

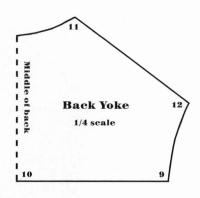

Back Yoke
1/4 scale

Middle of back

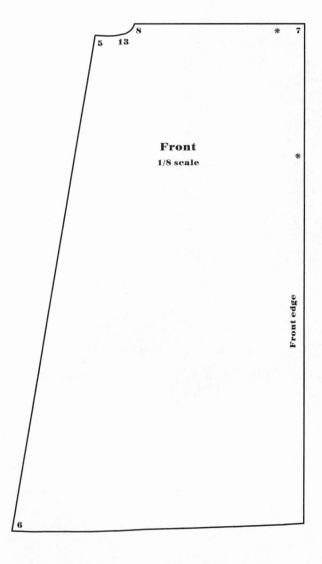

Front
1/8 scale

Front edge

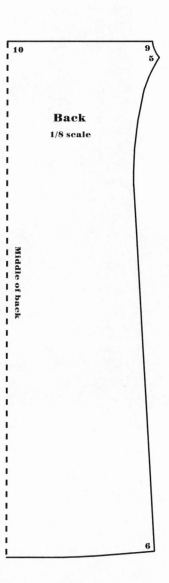

Back
1/8 scale

Middle of back

White Flannel Bathing Suit

The suit, shown on the left of the plate, is composed of trousers, skirt, and bodice. It is trimmed with dark blue worsted braid, and closed with buttons and buttonholes. White straw hat, trimmed with similar braid.

Harper's Bazar, July 1879

Ecru Flannel Bathing Suit

This suit is shown on the right of the plate for the White Flannel Bathing Suit. The trousers are trimmed on the sides with folds of brown flannel and with small shells. For the frock cut of ecru flannel two pieces each from the front and sleeve. Cut one piece from the back. Cut the plastron of brown flannel.

Join the back and fronts according to the corresponding figures. Pleat the frock as indicated on the pattern. Face the front edge of the right front with a strip of the material 1 3/4 in. wide, and set on a buttonhole tab. Set the left front into a double fly 1 1/4 in. wide, which is furnished with buttons. Bind the neck of the frock narrow, and trim it with a side pleating of ecru flannel. Trim the plastron, as illustrated, with large and small shells. Sew it on the right front, and hook it on the left front. Trim the frock on the bottom with a deep kilt-pleated ruffle of ecru flannel.

Trim the sleeves as illustrated. Sew them up from 19 to 20. Set them into the armholes, bringing 20 on 20 of the fronts. A sash of brown flannel completes the suit. Oiled-silk bathing cap, trimmed with brown worsted and shells.

Harper's Bazar, July 1879

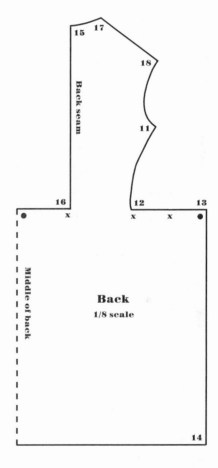

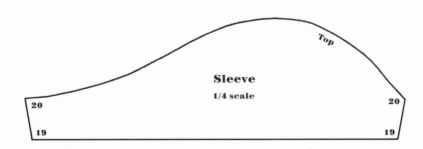

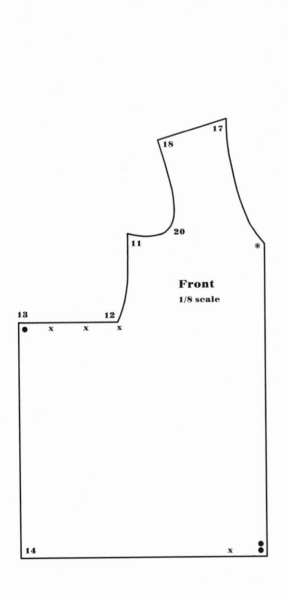

Plastron
1/4 scale

Front
1/8 scale

Middle of front

Embroidered Bathing Suit

deep. Embroider the border. Pleat the top as indicated. Join it to a band 2 in. wide, which is 15 in. long for the front and 16 for the back, where it is furnished with drawstrings. The ends are furnished with buttons and buttonholes.

Cut for the blouse two pieces each from the front and sleeves. Cut one whole piece each for the back and collar. Join the back and fronts according to the corresponding figures. Face the edges. Face the upper corners of the front to 1 in. beyond the narrow line, then roll them to the outside along the line. Furnish the fronts with buttons and buttonholes. Embroider the collar and sleeves, and join them to the blouse. Embroider the blouse as illustrated. Provide it with a flannel belt, which is tacked to the back and buttoned on the front.

Harper's Bazar, July 1882

Embroidered Bathing Suit

This suit consists of trousers and a blouse. It is made of dark blue flannel. It is trimmed with borders worked on the garment with old-gold crewel wool in chain stitch.

Cut for the trousers two pieces from the trousers pattern. Cut the slit indicated on the pattern. Bind the front edge of it with a double fly 1 in. wide. Face the back edge 1 1/2 in. deep. Sew up each half from 1 to 2. Join the front from 2 to 3, and the back from 2 to 4. Face the bottom 1 1/2 in.

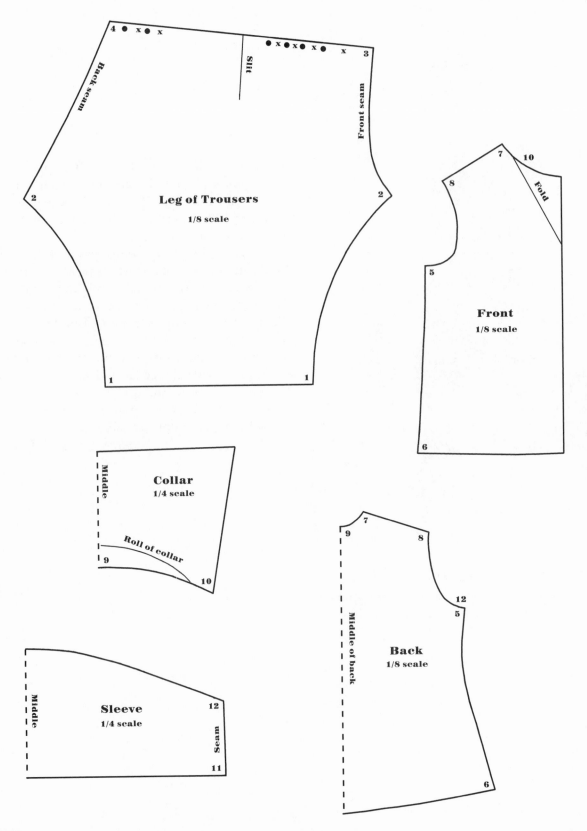

Leg of Trousers
1/8 scale

Back seam

Slit

Front seam

4 ● x ● x

● x ● x ● x x 3

2

2

1 1

Front
1/8 scale

7 10

8

Fold

5

6

Collar
1/4 scale

Middle

Roll of collar

9

10

Sleeve
1/4 scale

Middle

12

Seam

11

Back
1/8 scale

9 7 8

Middle of back

12

5

6

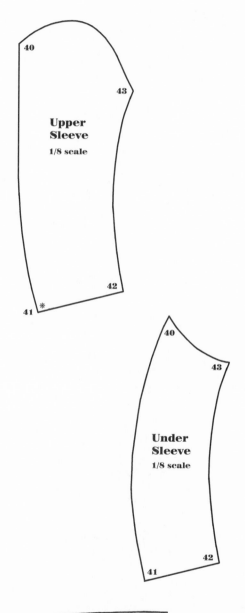

Upper Sleeve
1/8 scale

40
43
42
41 *

Under Sleeve
1/8 scale

40
43
42
41

Sacque for Skating Suit

This brown cloth suit consists of a skirt, overskirt, bodice, and sacque. The skirt is trimmed with a side-pleated ruffle of faille of the same color, headed with a strip of cloth cut into points. The overskirt is trimmed with revers of cloth, and with strips of velvet and oxidized buttons. Similar strips and buttons trim the bodice and sacque. Felt hat, trimmed with a long gauze veil.

Harper's Bazar, January 1878

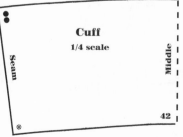

Cuff
1/4 scale

Seam

Middle

42

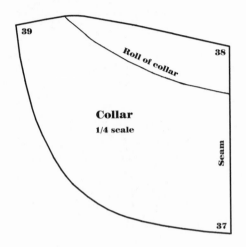

Collar
1/4 scale

Roll of collar

Seam

39
38
37

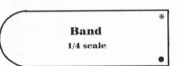

Band
1/4 scale

*

●

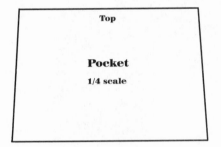

Top

Pocket
1/4 scale

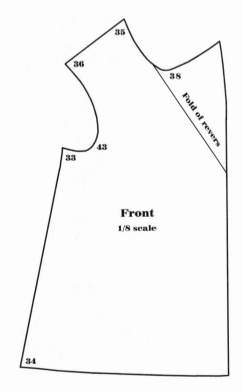

Front
1/8 scale

35
36
38
43
33
34

Fold of revers

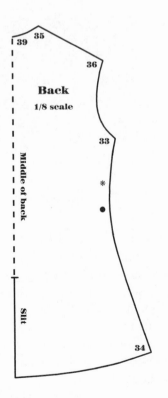

Back
1/8 scale

39
35
36
33
*
●

Middle of back

Slit

34

5. Outer Garments

Wraps are divided into coats, mantles, and long cloaks. The coats are for general use. The mantles are for more dressy occasions. They are made with long square fronts, wide but short square sleevelike openings on the sides, and graceful backs shaped by one, two, or three seams. They differ from dolmans in being as short on the sides as in back. They are made of black camel's hair, sicilienne, figured velvet, or cloth. They are trimmed with whalebone fringe, chenille fringe, passementerie, and pleated lace. The long cloaks are to be worn in the carriage with the demitrained skirts of visiting costumes. They are made of sicilienne, repped silk, or camel's hair. They are lined with squirrel-lock fur, and trimmed with black lynx or silver beaver.

Harper's Bazar, October 1878

The English coat of homespun cloth, with velvet collar, cuffs, and pockets, is the jaunty and comfortable-looking wrap for early fall. It is of medium length, not too long to wear with short skirts, nor too short for carriage costumes. The front is double breasted. The back is in coat shape, with short side pieces that are very broad at the waistline. Buttons define the waist, and there are pleats or revers in the seams below. Their shape and whole appearance are very much like a gentleman's English morning coat. Gray and brown are stylish colors.

Mantles are very large. They have three seams behind, straight across the sides, and long fronts that are caught in tassel ornaments at the end, and almost reach to the feet. Very elegant ones are made of black sicilienne trimmed with pleatings of striped moiré and jet fringe.

Traveling cloaks for autumn journeys are Ulsters of English homespun cloth with three carrick capes, double-breasted fronts, and a belt that crosses the back but not the front.

Harper's Bazar, December 1878

The visite, as its name implies, is a dressy style for visiting and carriage wraps. It is a modification of the dolman combined with the mantelet. There is but one seam at the back, curved in at the waist. The sleeves are cut in one with the bodice, either falling loose over the arm, or arranged in loose square openings.

Young Ladies' Journal, c. June 1879

The newest coats are in the masculine styles worn last year, though the skirt is longer, and often sewed on the hips to give a graceful spring over full tournures. They are shown in black basket-woven cloth that appears to have silk thrown upon the surface, and is tufted inside. The gay trimmings are of the Oriental broché cashmere made into a large collar, cuffs, pocket flaps, and forming lappets in the back. The Japanese buttons are of two sizes, and represent all the rich shades that appear in the cashmere.

There are also many of the jaunty Derby coats. They come in cream- and drab-colored cloths, with collars and cuffs of olive, green, gendarme blue, or black velvet. All of these coat-shaped garments are liked for morning wear and traveling where short costumes are used. The same shapes are also seen in white lamb's wool cloth with Oriental trimmings for the opera and day receptions.

More dressy wraps for midwinter are in the clinging shapes, with square half-long sleeves, and elbow sleeves. The Rumanian cloak is now one of the accepted shapes. There are various mandarin-shaped garments that are straight, yet outline the figure. Some of these cloaks are very long, and are meant to be worn with trained dresses used for the carriage. With short walking costumes cloaks of medium length are preferred, though the shapes remain the same. Many of these cloaks are made of the light drab and pale brown sicilienne, or the finest camel's hair cloths. But the majority are still of black sicilienne, black satin, or embossed velvet.

In circular cloaks the favorite shape has close sacque fronts that keep the breast covered even when the circular front is lifted by the arms. The back is fitted by a seam down the middle, and by underarm seams, and in the latter is sewn the circular front. It is shown in drab, white, or black thick yet soft lamb's wool cloth, all soft fleece on the wrong side. A velvet border of a darker shade, fringe, and great Japanese buttons are the usual trimmings. Plain lustrous satin and satin de Lyon, which is less lustrous, are used for more dressy circular cloaks. These are lined with Oriental silks, or else gay red or old-gold satin that has been warmly wadded and quilted. Jet passementeries and fringes are very effective on these handsome wraps.

Harper's Bazar, November 1879

The mantles imported for spring and summer are regular mantillas, with short round back and long, scarflike fronts. They are little more than scarves. They have but one seam, in the middle of the back. They are fitted to the shoulders with short darts, of which there may be one, two, or three on each shoulder. The back seam is often sloped outward over the tournure, giving a bias effect. In some mantles the whole fabric is cut bias, as it then clings more closely to the arms. This capelike back extends just below the waistline, resting smoothly over the tournure. There it is usually ornamented by a great bow of moiré ribbon. Or there are pleats covering the back seam its entire length, and finished at the end like a fan, to spread out over the tournure. The fronts may each be 1/4 or 3/8 yd. wide, and extend as low as the knees. There the corners may be left square. Or else the end is drawn together, and completed by a passementerie tassel, or lace pleated in the shape of a tassel, and a bow of many loops of narrow moiré ribbon. The neck is cut very high. It is further heightened by a full ruche of lace made in shells like a jabot, or of narrow standing lace frills, with some much wider lace gathered below it to fall deep on the shoulders like a Mother Hubbard collar.

Another style is the half-long shape with square or rounded sleeves cut in one with the back or front. For a compromise between the two, the latest Worth mantle (the pattern for which is given in this chapter) is considered one of the most tasteful and stylish shapes.

Harper's Bazar, April 1882

Ladies who have large shawls of thread or llama lace left over from previous seasons drape them as small pannier mantles, and thus make very dressy wraps. To do this the lower part of the point in the middle of the back is caught up in four or five horizontal pleats deep enough to shorten the back so that it will fall just below the waistline on the tournure. A lengthwise cluster of long loops and ends of black satin ribbon is set down in the middle of these pleats. The pointed ends of the front are then turned back toward the middle. When the garment is put on, the arms are passed between the doubled front that this arrangement forms. If necessary the top edge may be turned over, and the shoulders ornamented with satin bows. This gives a graceful mantle that clings to the front and sides of the figure, and has pannier fullness behind.

Harper's Bazar, July 1879

Ladies who have an old-fashioned Empire or Stella shawl with a large plain center and border, can convert it with little trouble into a stylish wrap. If the ground is black, it can be arranged in visite fashion, with the border around the edge and on the bottom of the Russian sleeves, and also down the middle of the back. If the ground is ivory or blue, it can be transformed, by the same process, into an elegant carriage wrap.

Harper's Bazar, October 1882

Close-Fitting Coat-Jacket

This jacket with a lengthened waist is drafted with the scale. The front has a round skirt.

Complete Guide to Ladies' Garment Cutting, 1883

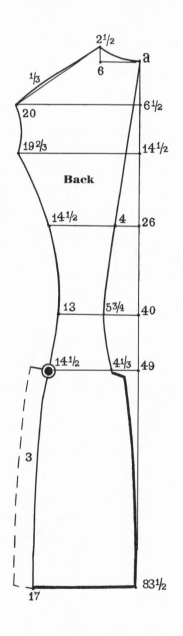

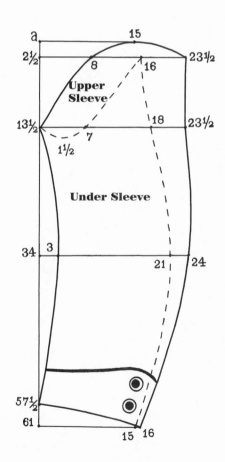

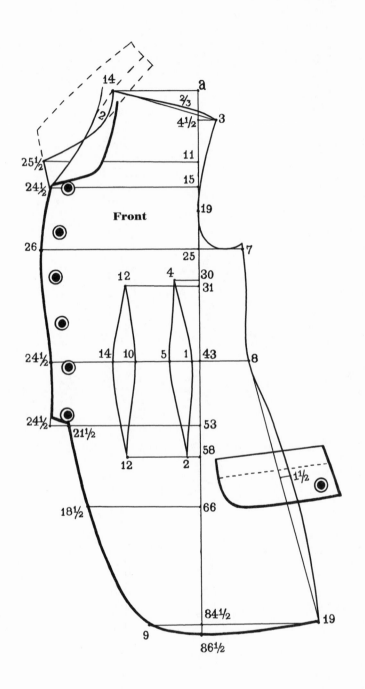

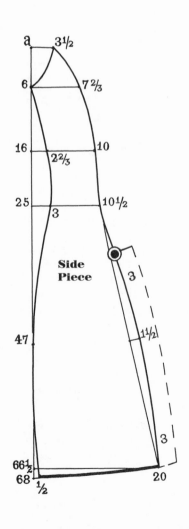

Double-Breasted Winter Coat

This coat is drafted with the scale. It is double breasted with a falling collar.

Complete Guide to Ladies' Garment Cutting, 1883

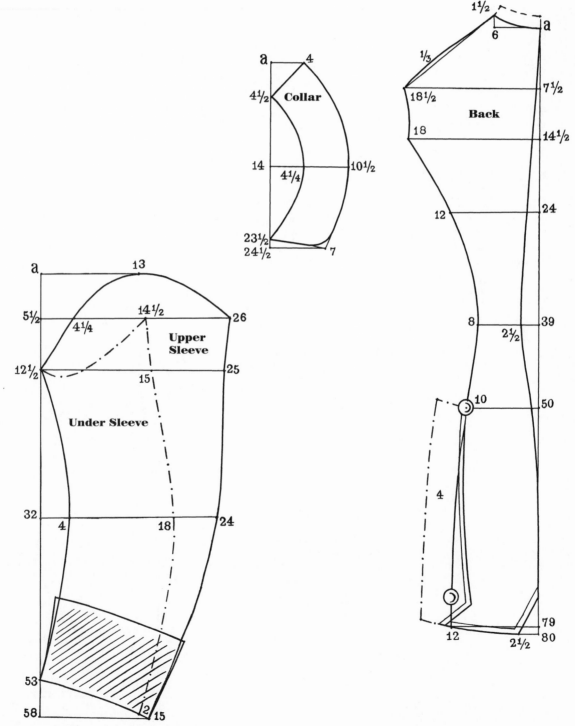

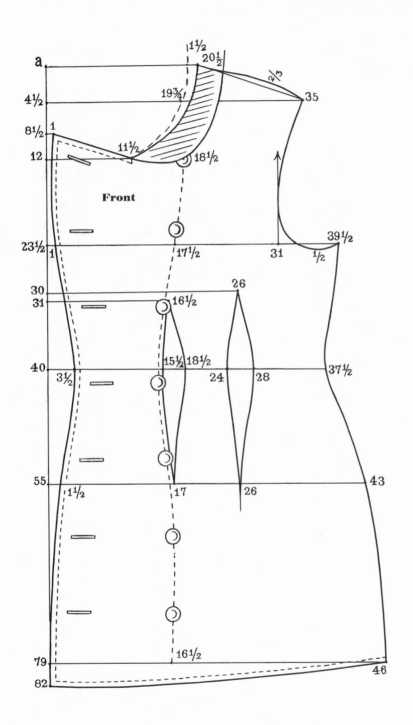

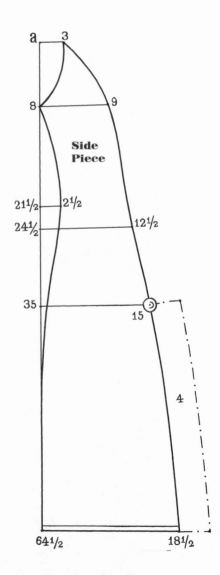

Front

Side Piece

Close-Fitting Coat-Jacket

This jacket with a lengthened waist is drafted with the scale. The front has a straight skirt.

Complete Guide to Ladies' Garment Cutting, 1883

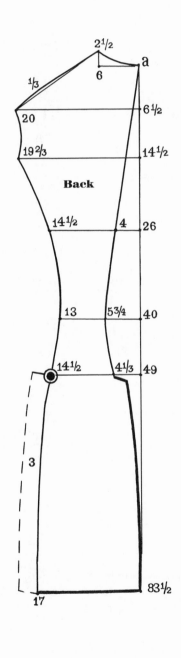

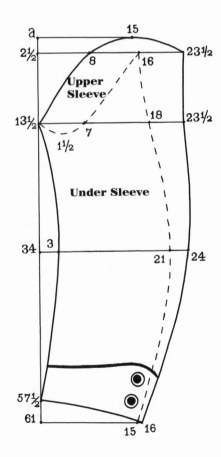

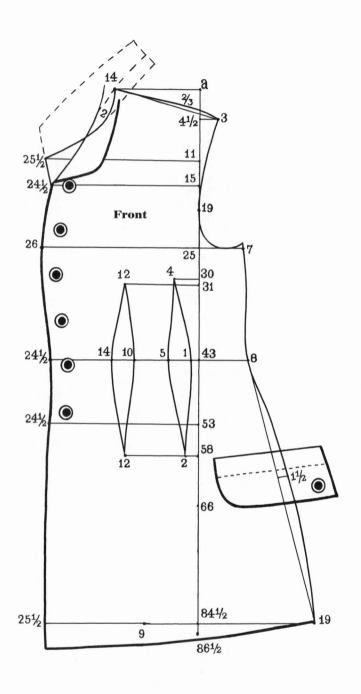

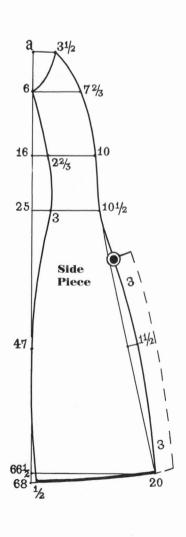

Coat with Shawl Collar

This double-breasted, close-fitting style is decidedly meant for winter. Should it be made with a quilted silk or fur lining, which both add bulk, it is advisable to use a scale 2 cm (13/16 in.) larger.

Complete Guide to Ladies' Garment Cutting, 1883

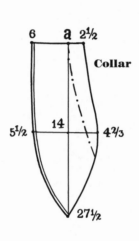

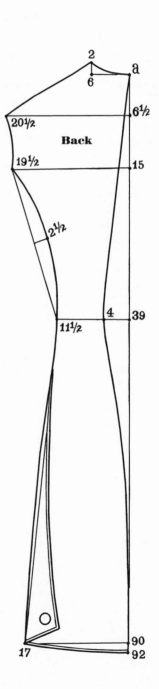

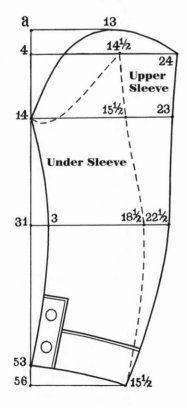

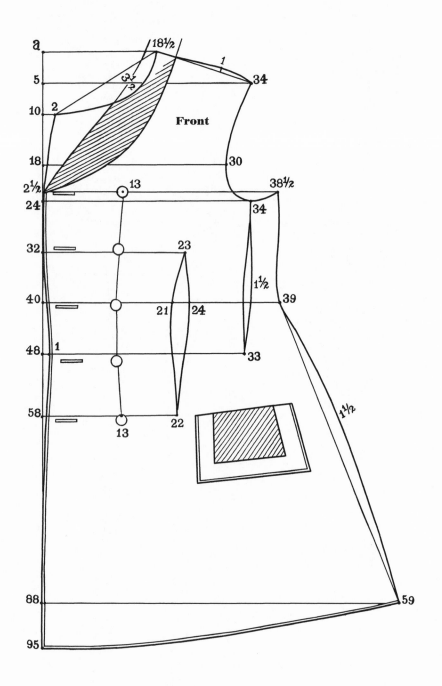

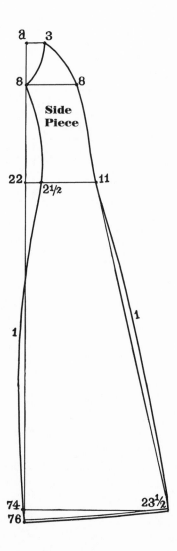

Simple Half-Fitting Coat

This pattern may be used for all kinds of half-fitting
coats for fall and winter. It is drafted with the scale.
Complete Guide to Ladies' Garment Cutting, 1883

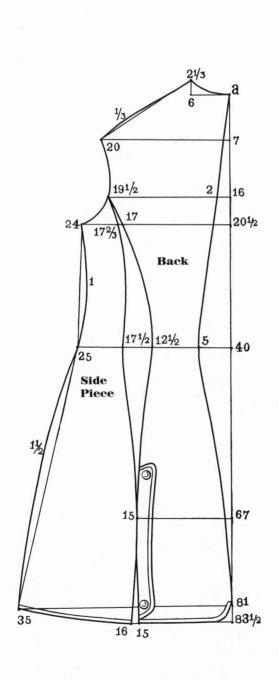

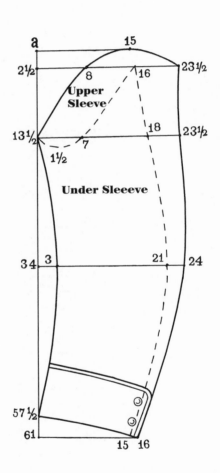

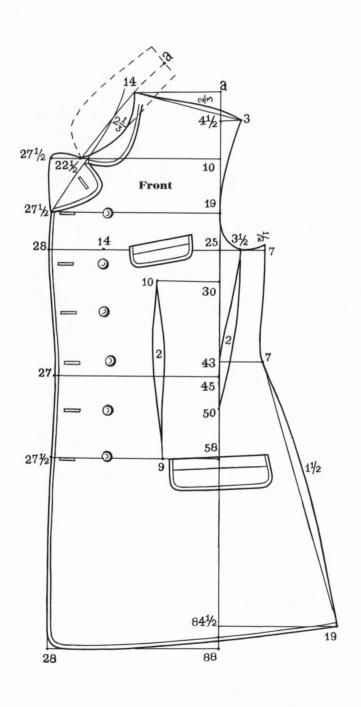

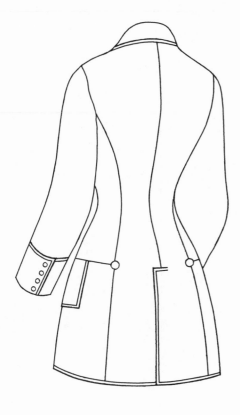

Single-Breasted Coat with Skirt

This coat is drafted using the plain bodice pattern, which is shown by dashed lines. The bodice is lengthened by 14 cm (5 1/2 in.) in back. The coat center back is the same as the bodice's from *A* partway down; but at *C*, the coat is moved out by 1 cm (3/8 in.). The front skirt must be cut and joined separately. Any of the sleeves from "Drafting Sleeves" in chapter 1 may be used.

Complete Guide to Ladies' Garment Cutting, 1883

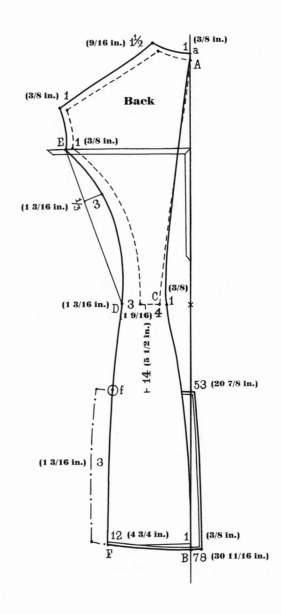

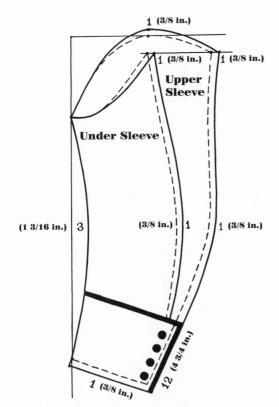

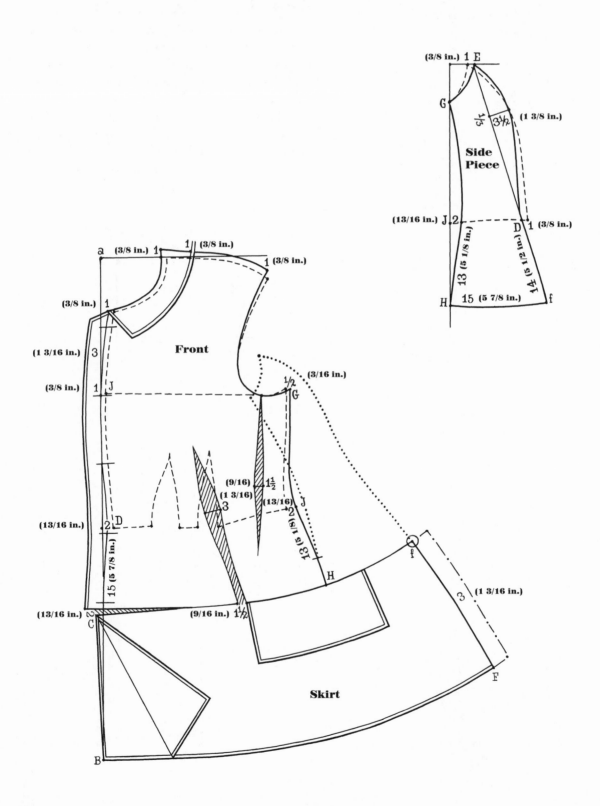

Single-Breasted, Half-Fitting Coat

This pattern is drafted with the scale. It is a jacketlike coat with a skirt. Since the back is cut on the fold, both seams of the side piece must be well stretched at the hollow of the waist. For woolen materials, the back must also be pressed inward well at the waist.

Complete Guide to Ladies' Garment Cutting, 1883

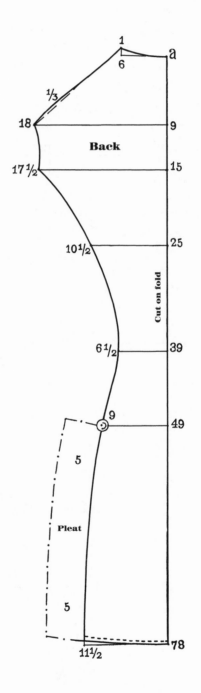

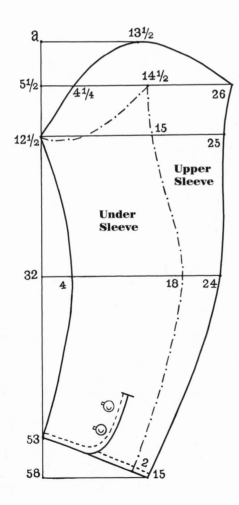

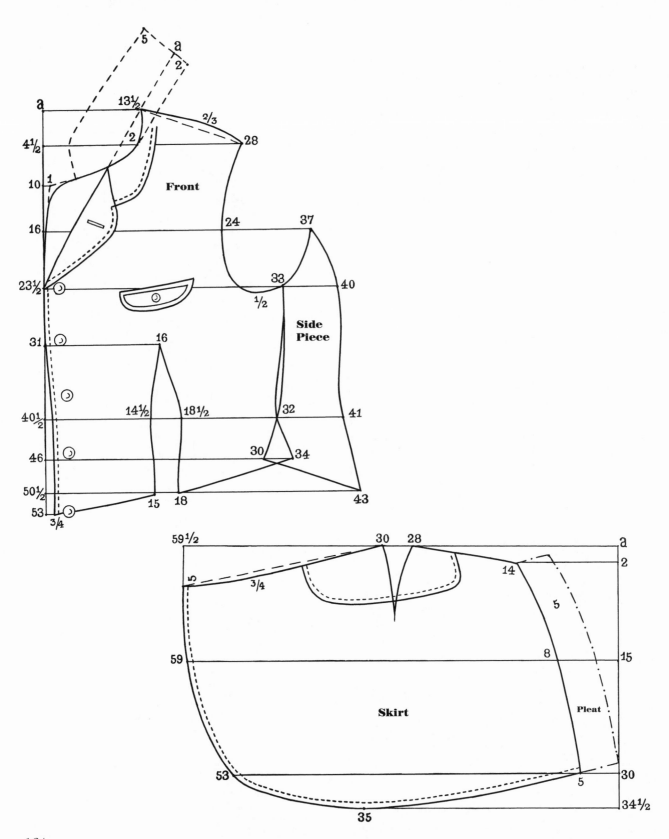

English Surtout

This English surtout may form part of a costume if worn together with a full round skirt. Or it may be made to wear above various dresses as a wrap, or take the place of an Ulster or waterproof. For early spring whole suits will be made of English homespun cloth or other flannel-finished fabrics in livery drab shades, in peacock and navy blue, pheasant brown, and black. For summer traveling, and for mountain and seaside wear, lighter qualities of beige, vigogne, and cashmere will be used. The gray or buff linen, mohair, and India pongee cloaks used for traveling will be made by this design. When the surtout is worn as part of a suit, the skirt may be made of the same material or corduroy.

For the model shown, cut of dark brown cloth two pieces each from the front lap, front, first side piece, second side piece, skirt, pocket flap, back, upper collar, middle collar, lower collar, upper sleeve, and under sleeve. Sew up the darts in the fronts. Join the front lap, front, first side piece, and second side piece according to the corresponding figures.

Cut a slit in the skirt pieces along the narrow line, and join the edges with a pocket. Set the pocket flaps on the skirt according to the corresponding signs. Sew the skirt pieces to the front lap, front, first side piece, and second side piece from *x* to 2 and from 2 to 8. Join the back to the second side piece, the skirt, and to the front at the shoulders according to the corresponding figures. At the waistline fasten *x* on the skirt pieces on ● of the back.

Face the surtout on the front and bottom, including the slit, with a strip of the material. Furnish the right lap of the front with buttonholes. Set on the corresponding buttons along the narrow line of the left front. Baste the collars on the neck of the surtout. Set them together with the neck into a double standing collar 7/8 in. wide.

Sew up the sleeves. Face them at the bottom, including the slit, with a strip of the material 1 3/4 in. wide. Furnish them along the slit with buttons and buttonholes. Set them into the armholes, bringing 18 on 18 of the fronts.

Harper's Bazar, March 1880

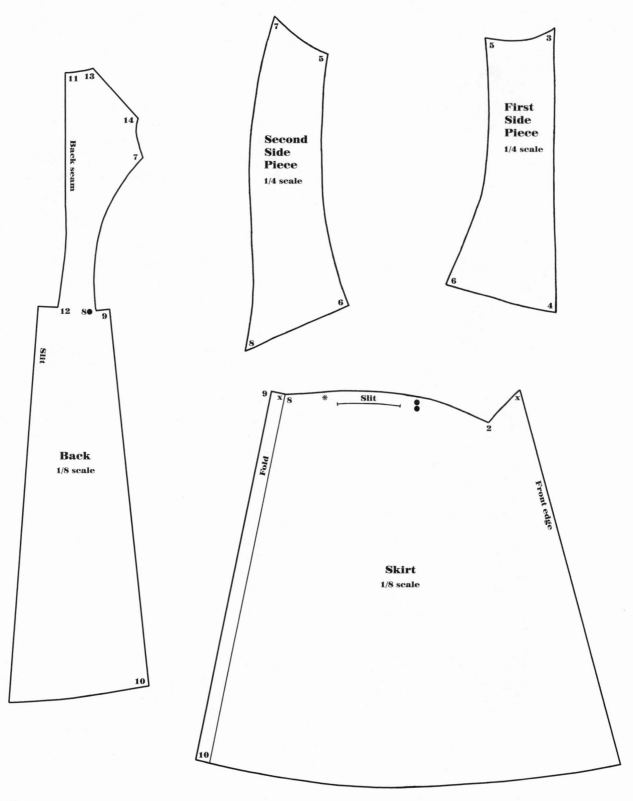

Second Side Piece
1/4 scale

First Side Piece
1/4 scale

Back seam

Slit

Back
1/8 scale

Fold

Slit

Front edge

Skirt
1/8 scale

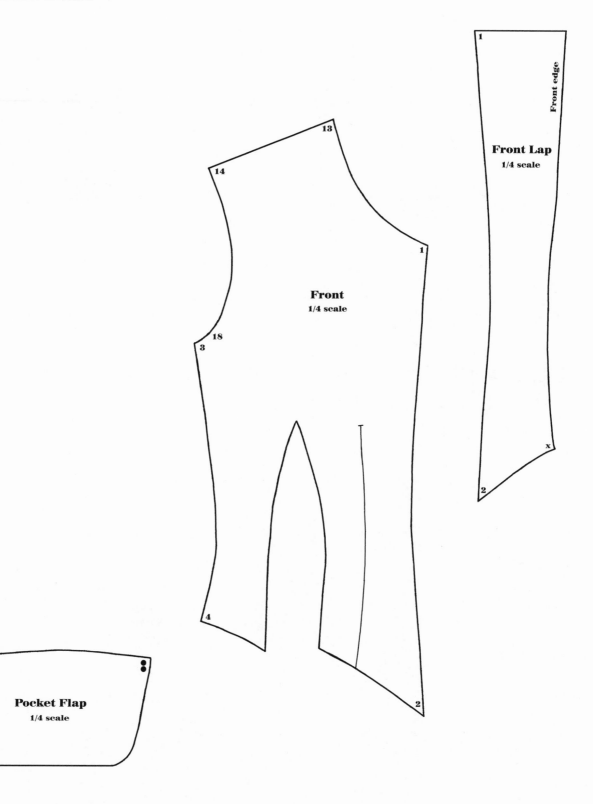

Front Lap
1/4 scale

Front
1/4 scale

Pocket Flap
1/4 scale

167

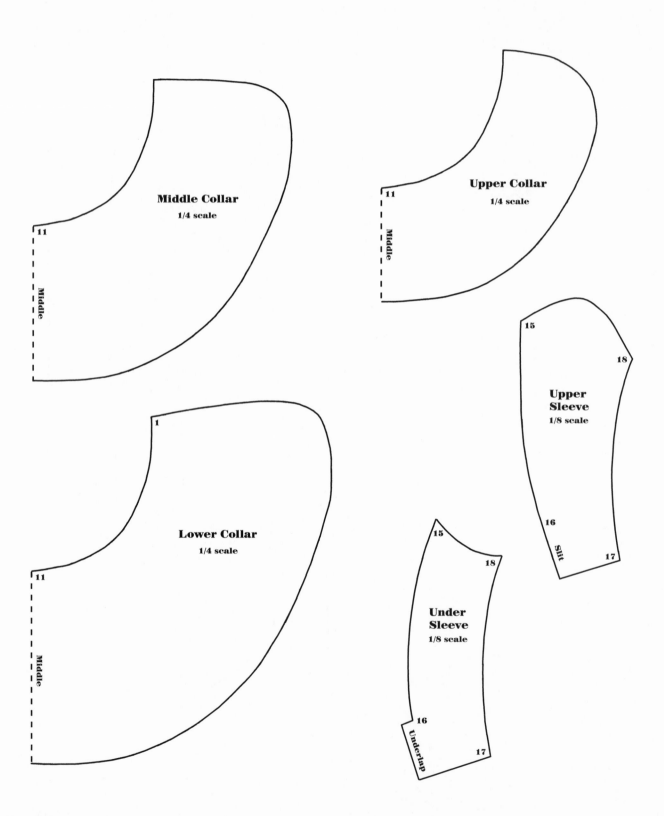

Middle Collar
1/4 scale

11

Middle

Upper Collar
1/4 scale

11

Middle

15

18

Upper
Sleeve
1/8 scale

16

Slit

17

1

Lower Collar
1/4 scale

11

Middle

15

18

Under
Sleeve
1/8 scale

16

Underlap

17

168

Redingote with Revers

This redingote or coat with skirt is drafted with the half breast circumference scale. It is meant only for winter and heavier materials.

Complete Guide to Ladies' Garment Cutting, 1883

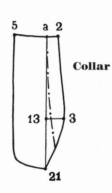

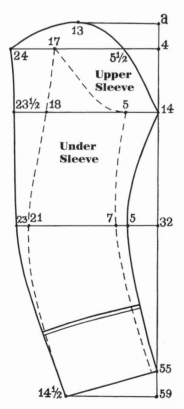

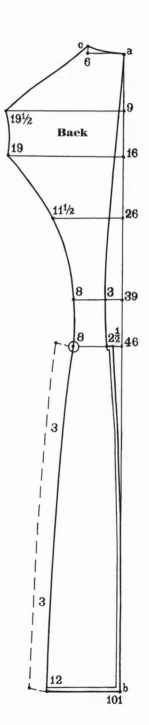

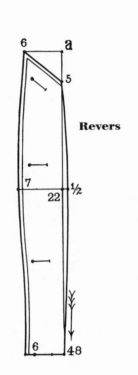

Revers

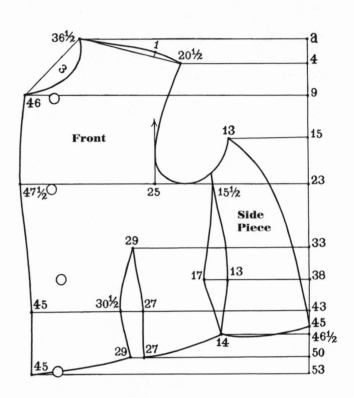

Front

Side Piece

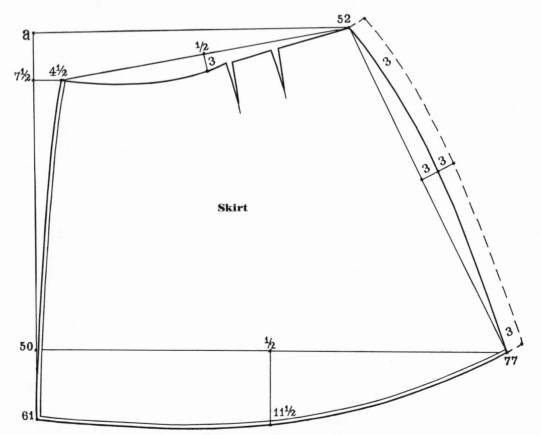

Skirt

Winter Coat

This half-long, double-breasted coat is drafted with
the scale. The pattern may be used for up to 52 cm
(20 1/2 in.) half breast circumferences.

Complete Guide to Ladies' Garment Cutting, 1883

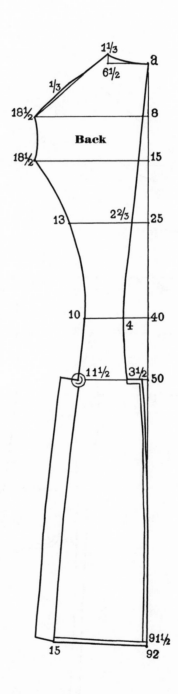

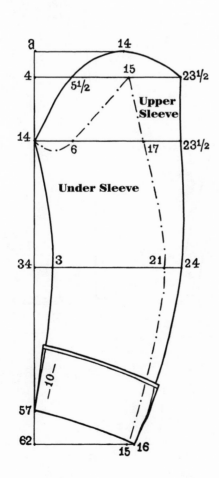

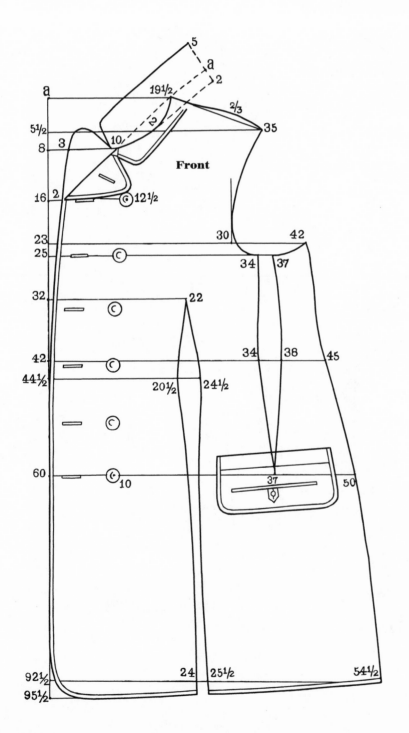

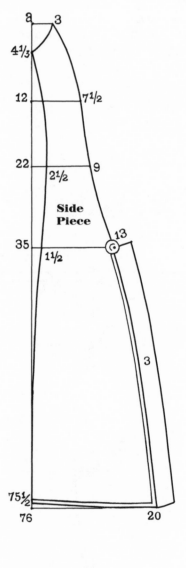

Front

Side Piece

Half-Fitting Coat

Half-Fitting Coat

This coat is drafted using the plain bodice pattern, which is shown by a dashed line. The numbers indicate centimeters. The front is single breasted.

Complete Guide to Ladies' Garment Cutting, 1883

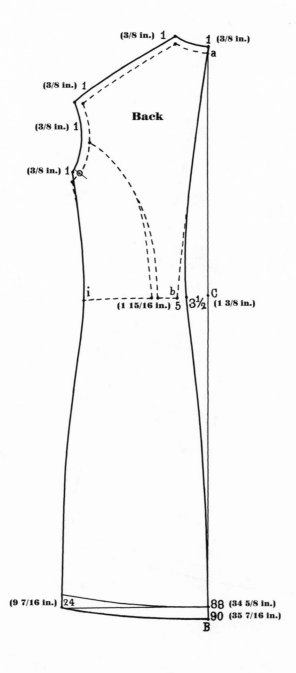

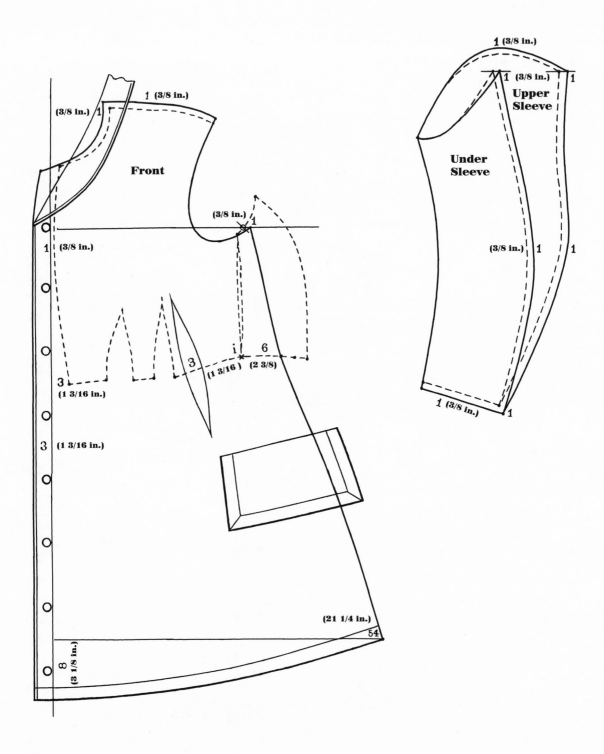

Half-Fitting Coat

This coat is drafted using the plain bodice pattern, which is shown by a dashed line. The numbers indicate centimeters. The front is double breasted.

Complete Guide to Ladies' Garment Cutting, 1883

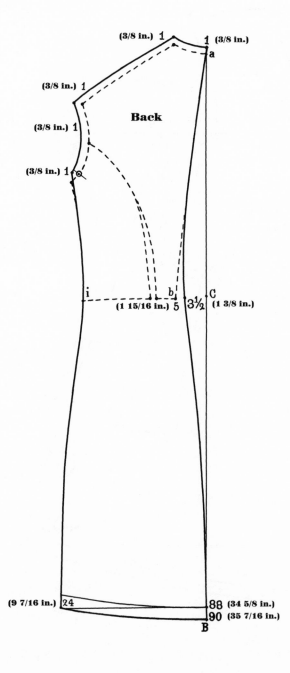

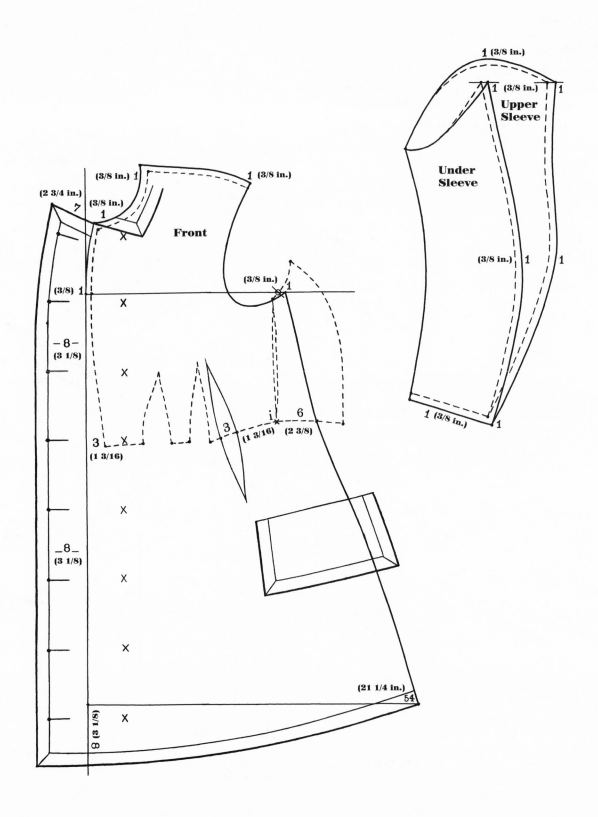

Half-Fitting Coat

This pattern is drafted with the scale. It is suitable for a coat or a waterproof.

Complete Guide to Ladies' Garment Cutting, 1883

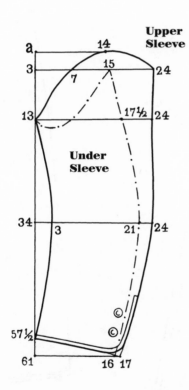

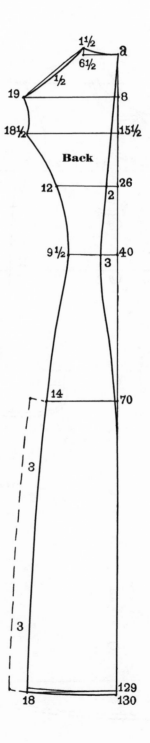

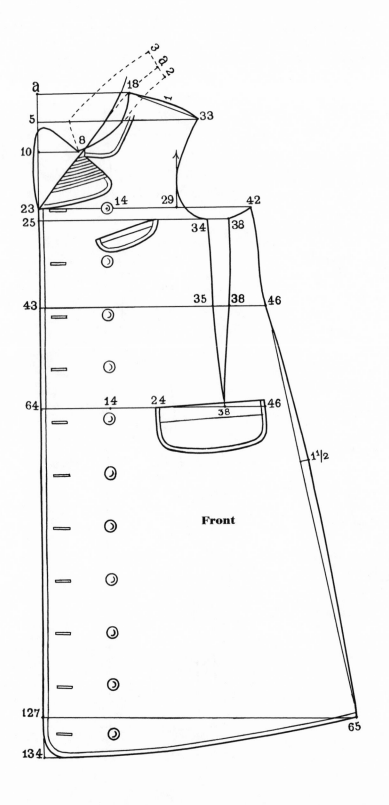

Front

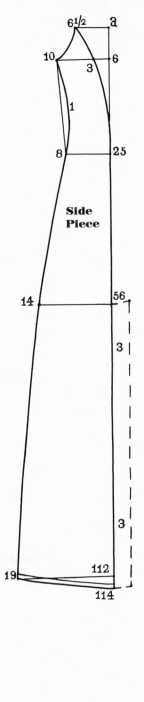

Side
Piece

Half-Fitting Coat

This coat is drafted using the plain bodice pattern, which is shown by a dashed line. The numbers indicate centimeters. The front is double breasted with no bust dart.

Complete Guide to Ladies' Garment Cutting, 1883

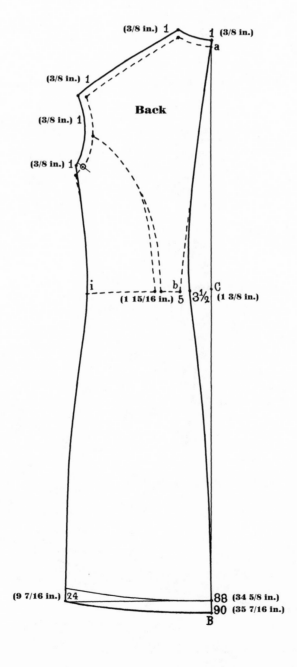

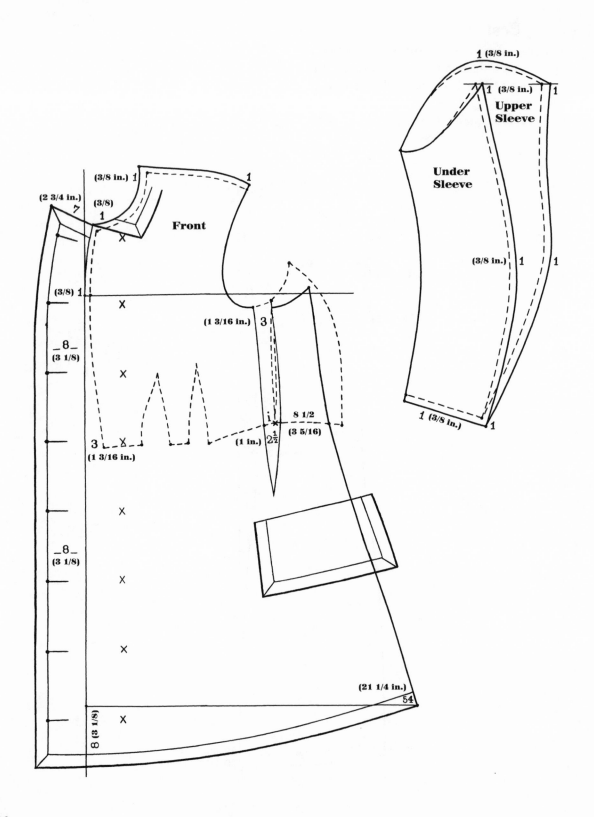

Sacque Coat

This straight coat is drafted using the plain bodice pattern, which is shown by a dashed line. Differences from the bodice pattern are expressed in centimeters. Any of the sleeves from "Drafting Sleeves" in chapter 1 may be used.

Complete Guide to Ladies' Garment Cutting, 1883

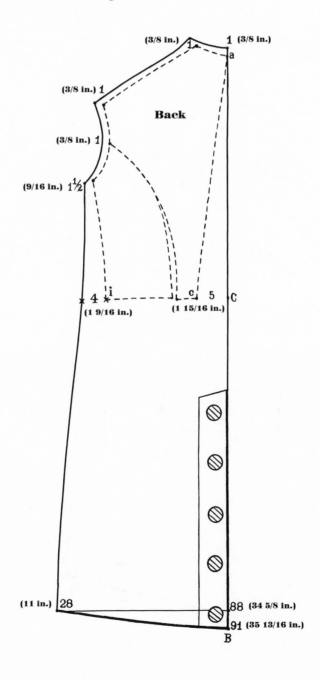

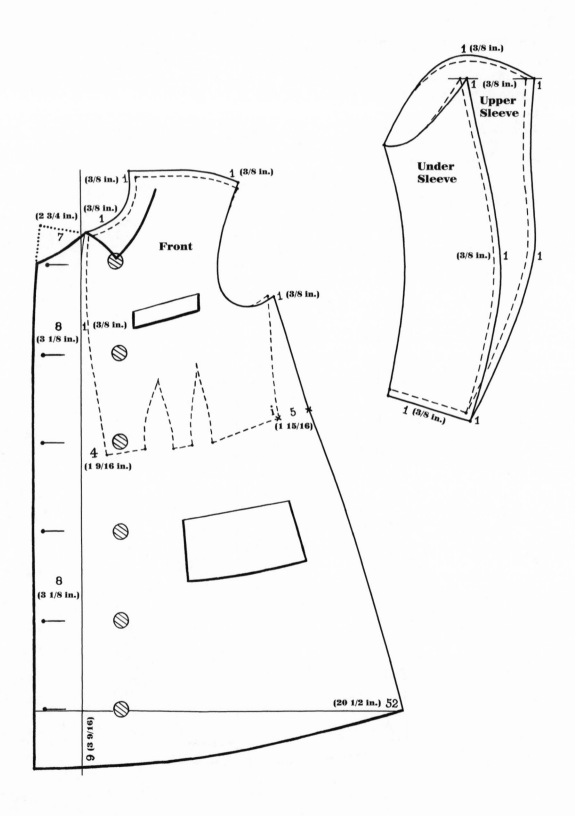

Long, Close-Fitting Waterproof

This pattern, which has been reduced to 1/10 size, is drafted with the scale. It is suitable for all half breast circumferences from 40 to 50 cm (15 3/4 to 19 11/16 in.). The waterproof fits closely without being too tight or pinching. The waist is decidedly emphasized. This pattern may also be used as a princess dress and lengthened in back into a train.

The front is single breasted with a narrow lapel. The skirt, shown drafted smoothly, may be gathered or pleated. For this purpose it must be drafted longer. For a waterproof, a round shoulder collar in pelerine style (not overly wide) may be added.

Complete Guide to Ladies' Garment Cutting, 1883

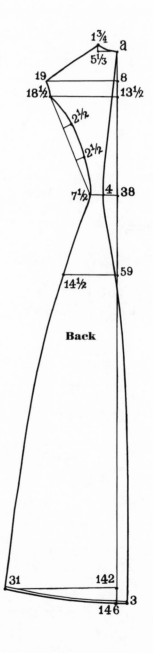

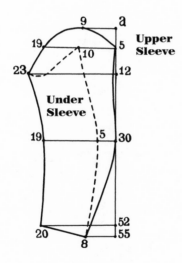

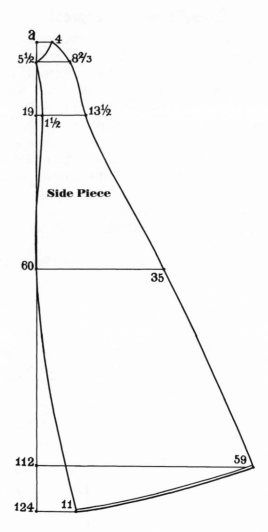

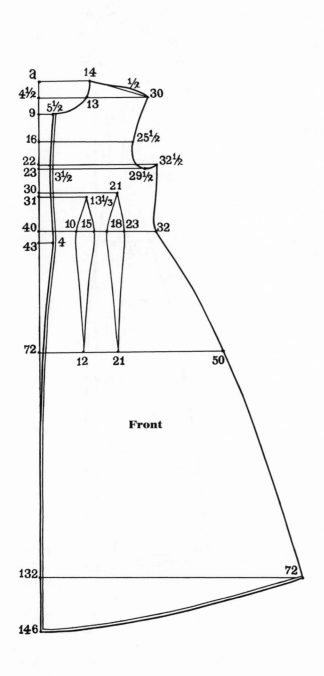

Traveling Mantle or Waterproof

This mantle is drafted using the plain bodice pattern. In back the baseline from *a* to *B* is drawn 120 cm (47 1/4 in.) long, or to measure. The bodice back is laid against the baseline at *A*, and 5 cm (1 15/16 in.) from it at the waist at *C*. The mantle back is 2 cm (13/16 in.) from *C*. At *E* the mantle is 1 cm (3/8 in.) wider, and the same at *F*, as well as widening the back at the top as shown. From *b* to *D*, the lower skirt width is 30 cm (11 13/16 in.). The rest of the back is drafted as shown by the pattern.

For the side piece, the baseline is drawn from *a* to *D* and the first crossline from *a* to *F*. The side of the bodice pattern must touch the baseline and crossline with its points *E* and *F*. The side piece seam from *F* via *E* to *D* is the same length as the side seam of the back piece. At *G* and *H,* the mantle is 1 cm (3/8 in.) wider. The lower skirt width from *D* to *J* is 30 cm (11 13/16 in.).

For the front, the bodice pattern is 1 1/2 cm (9/16 in.) from the baseline at *D,* and 4 cm (1 9/16 in.) from it at *C.* The shoulder is extended at the top by 1 cm (3/8 in.), and widened at the neck opening by 1 cm (3/8 in.). At the side at *G,* 1/2 cm (3/16 in.) is added to the bodice, and 2 cm (13/16 in.) at *H.* The side seam from *G* via *H* to *J* is the same length as the corresponding seam of the side piece. The rest is easy to see on the pattern.

Two choices of sleeve are given. Any of the sleeves from "Drafting Sleeves" in chapter 1 may be used.

Complete Guide to Ladies' Garment Cutting, 1883

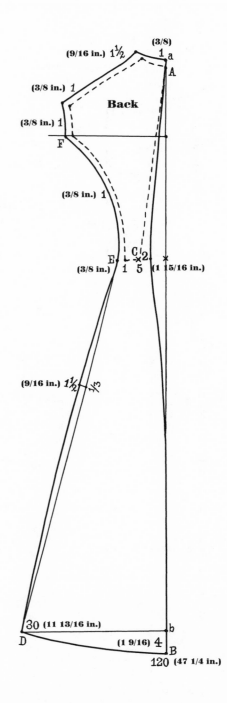

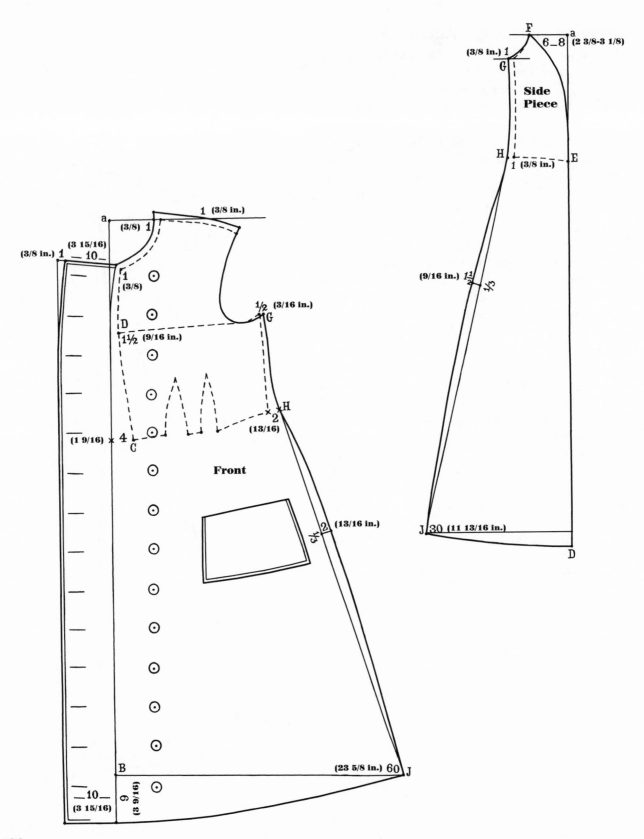

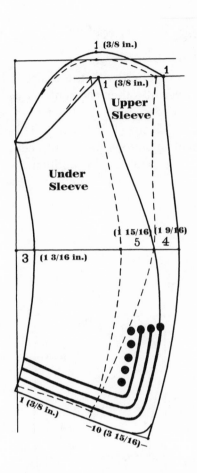

1 (3/8 in.)

1 (3/8 in.)

Upper Sleeve

1

Under Sleeve

(1 15/16)
5

(1 9/16)
4

3 (1 3/16 in.)

1 (3/8 in.)

—10 (3 15/16)—

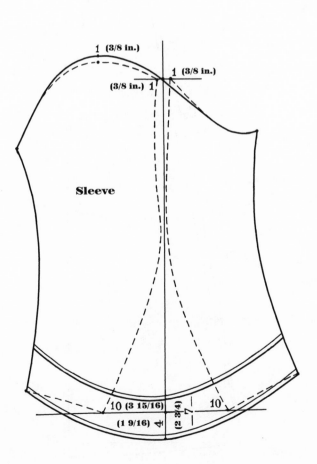

1 (3/8 in.)

1 (3/8 in.)

(3/8 in.) 1

Sleeve

10 (3 15/16)

10

(2 3/4)

(1 9/16) 4

Half-Fitting Waterproof
Or Traveling Mantle

This pattern is drafted with the scale. It is long enough to cover all other garments. If a double-breasted style is preferred, the front overlap must be widened by 5 cm (1 15/16 in.). The sleeves may be made with buttons, instead of a cuff, to keep out dust and rain. The hood is optional.

Complete Guide to Ladies' Garment Cutting, 1883

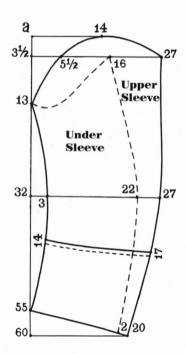

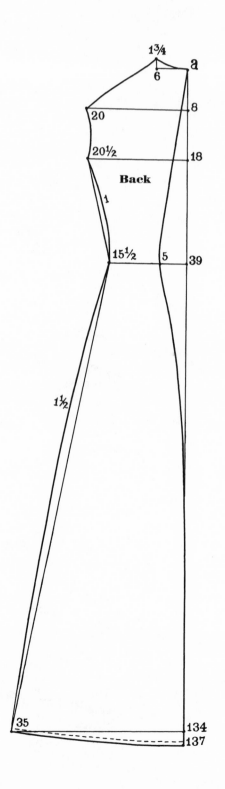

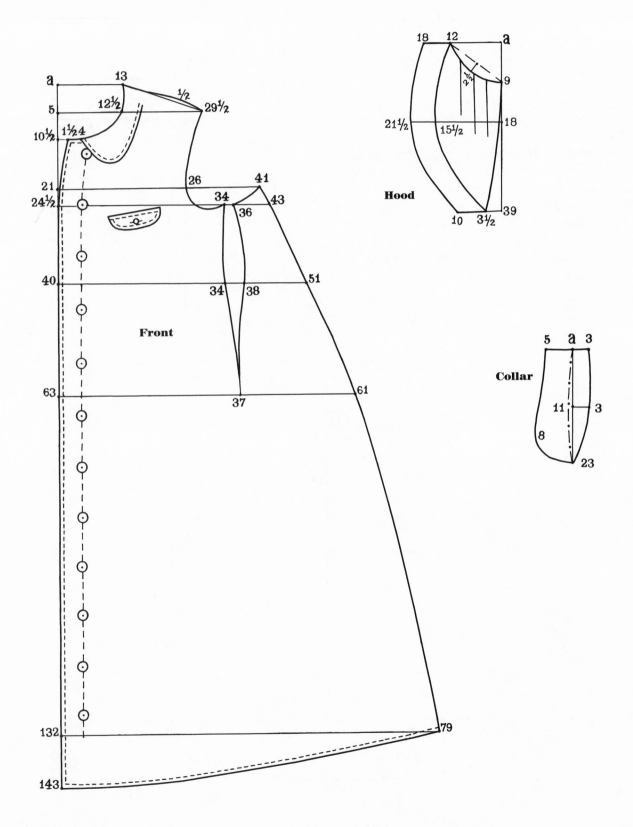

Hood

Collar

Front

Waterproof

This comfortable waterproof has a long pelerine
and a wide falling collar. It may be made without
sleeves, in which case the armhole is cut as shown
by the dashed and dotted line; that is, about 2 to
3 cm (13/16 to 1 3/16 in.) lower. The pelerine will
cover the arms should sleeves not be found necessary. This garment is drafted with the scale.

Complete Guide to Ladies' Garment Cutting, 1883

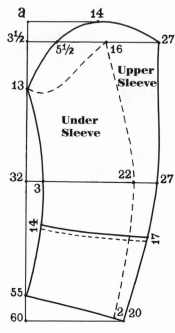

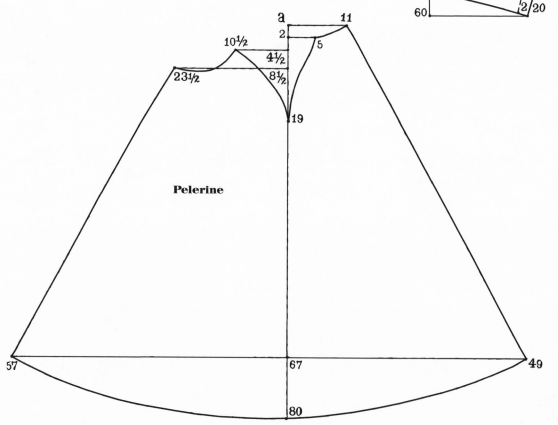

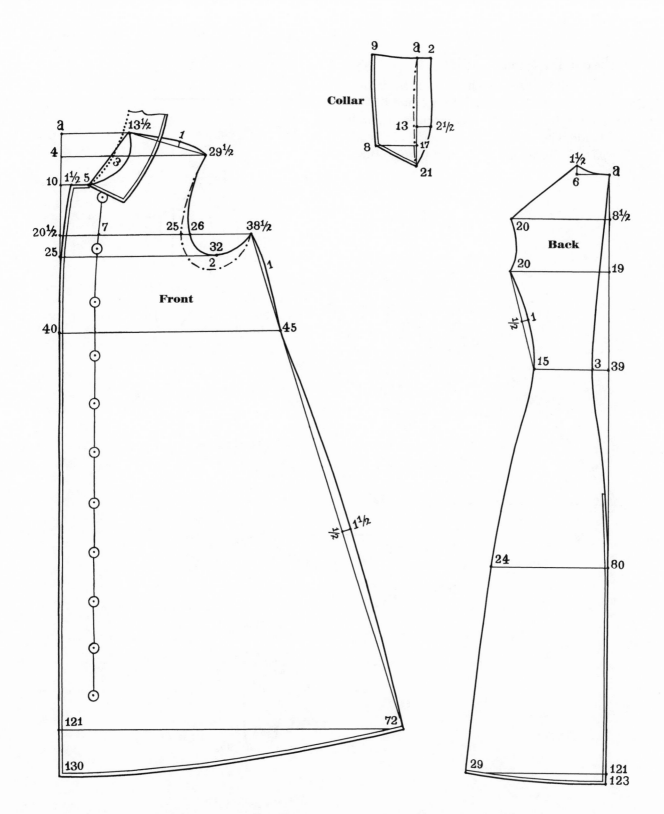

Waterproof for Stout Ladies

This waterproof is drafted with the scale for ladies of 54 to 57 cm (21 1/4 to 22 7/16 in.) half breast circumference. It has a three-quarter pelerine, and may be made with or without the hood.

Complete Guide to Ladies' Garment Cutting, 1883

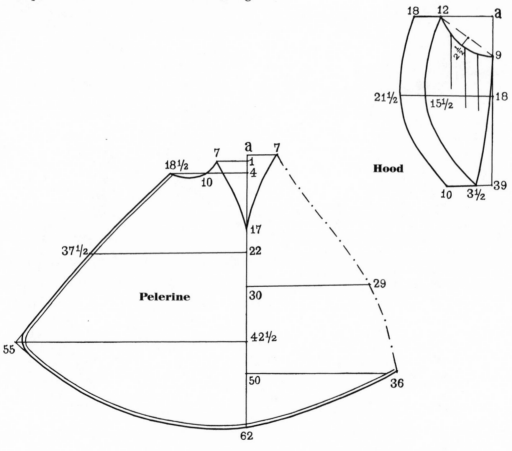

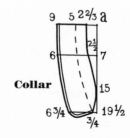

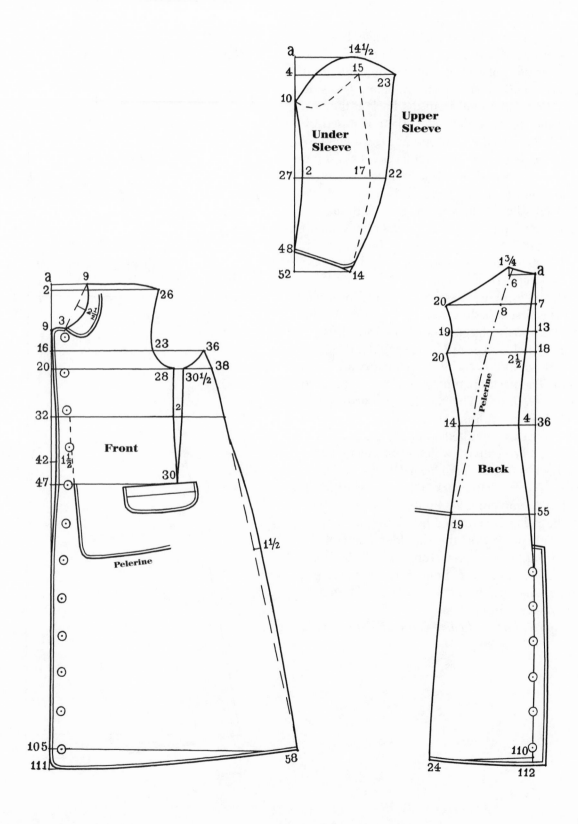

MacFarlane

This pattern is based on the plain bodice. First the back baseline is drawn from *a* to *B*. The back of the bodice pattern is placed on *a* at the top, with point *c* 5 cm (1 15/16 in.) from the baseline. The side piece is 2 cm (13/16 in.) from the back at the bottom. At the top at *A*, the MacFarlane is raised by 1 cm (3/8 in.), and the neck opening is widened by 1 1/2 cm (9/16 in.). At the shoulder point at *f*, 1 cm (3/8 in.) is subtracted. The MacFarlane is widened 1 cm (3/8 in.) at *d* and 5 cm (1 15/16 in.) at the waist. A crossline is drawn 10 cm (3 15/16 in.) below *d*, for marking point *D*. The center back length is 124 cm (48 7/8 in.). The crossline from *b* to *E* is 4 cm (1 9/16 in.) above *B* and marks the lower skirt width of 44 cm (17 5/16 in.).

For the front, the baseline is drawn from *a* to *B* and the first crossline from *a* beyond *M*. The bodice pattern is placed 2 cm (13/16 in.) from *D* and 4 cm (1 9/16 in.) from *E*. The shoulder is lengthened by 1 cm (3/8 in.) while moving forward 1 cm (3/8 in.). The neck opening at *g* is moved forward 1 1/2 cm (9/16 in.). The shoulder is narrowed to 5 cm (1 15/16 in.). A line is drawn 10 cm (3 15/16 in.) below *d*. On this is marked point *D* 3 cm (1 3/16 in.) from the bodice pattern, which must meet point *D* on the back. The side seam from *D* to *E* is the same as the side seam on the back. The lower skirt width from *b* to *E* is 56 cm (22 1/16 in.).

The pelerine is drafted by placing the bodice sleeve with point *f* on the shoulder point of the bodice front. The pelerine runs from *M* by 2 cm (13/16 in.) beyond *f* to *L*. From *M* to *L* is the sleeve length, in this pattern 73 cm (28 3/4 in.). From *M* to *N* is 5 cm (1 15/16 in.) less.

Complete Guide to Ladies' Garment Cutting, 1883

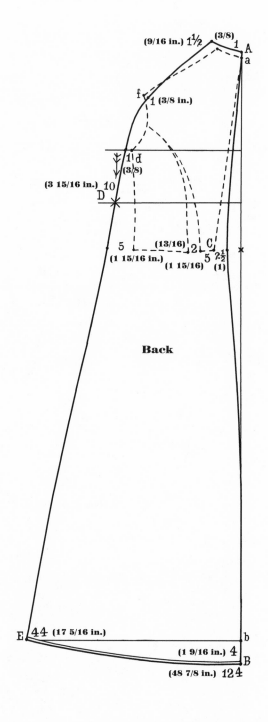

194

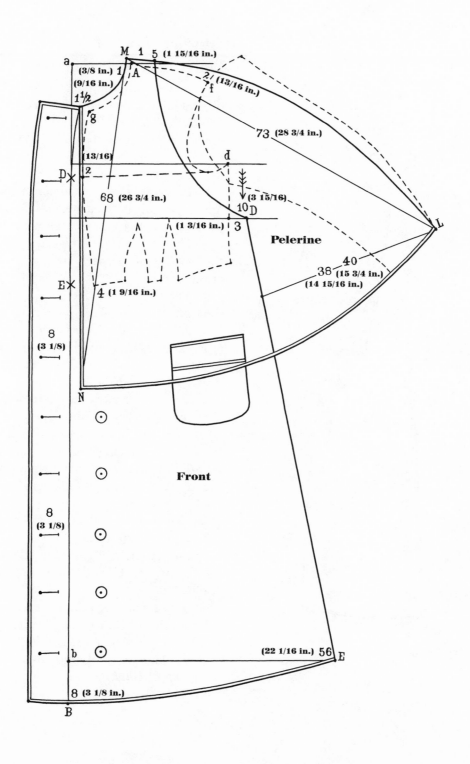

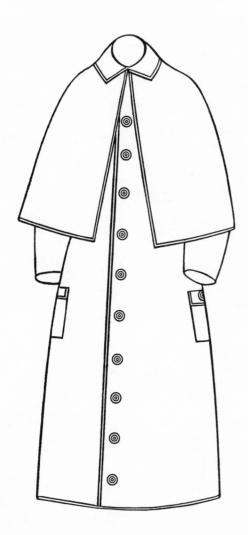

Traveling Coat or Waterproof with Pelerine

This coat is half fitting. The plain bodice is shown by dashed lines in the front and back, and a dotted and dashed line in the pelerine. The outline of the sleeve on the front is meant only to show the pocket position. The numbers refer to centimeters throughout.

Pelerine. Drafting a pelerine requires that the upper part of the coat pattern be used as well as the bodice pattern. The baseline at the left is drawn first. The bodice front is placed 1 cm (3/8 in.) from the baseline at the neck at G, and on the baseline at the bottom.

The back of the bodice is then placed against the front at the shoulders so that the edges are 1 cm (3/8 in.) apart at F. Two and one-half centimeters (1 in.) is measured out from the bottom of the bodice at C. A straight line 51 cm (20 1/16 in.) long is drawn from a to B for the back seam of the pelerine.

The coat front is placed over the bodice pattern lines. The front of the pelerine neckline at G is 1 cm (3/8 in.) down from the coat. The distance from D to E is 2 cm (13/16 in.) more than that from a to B. The distance from G to H, or the front opening, must be at least 1 cm (3/8 in.) shorter than the back length from a to B. Point H lies 6 cm (2 3/8 in.) from the baseline, which means the pelerine will fall open in front. If the edges are to meet or even overlap, the front edge of the coat pattern should be followed. Usually a pelerine falls open somewhat.

Two smaller pelerines are also shown. One is 22 cm (8 11/16 in.) long, the other 30 cm (11 13/16 in.). Another suitable pelerine is shown with the Mantle with Optional Pelerine and Hood.
Complete Guide to Ladies' Garment Cutting, 1883

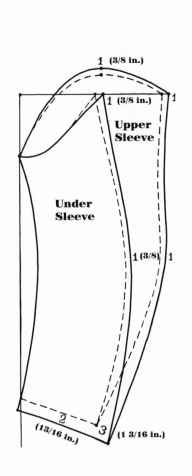

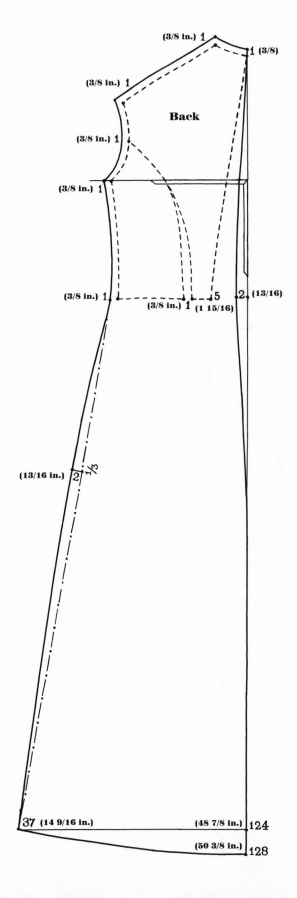

Back

Upper Sleeve

Under Sleeve

(3/8 in.) 1

1 (3/8)

1 (3/8 in.)

1 (3/8 in.) 1

Back

1 (3/8)

(3/8 in.) 1

(3/8 in.) 1

(3/8 in.) 1

(3/8 in.) 1

(3/8 in.) 1

5

2 (13/16)

(1 15/16)

(13/16 in.) 2

1/3

2 (13/16)

3 (1 3/16 in.)

37 (14 9/16 in.)

(48 7/8 in.) 124

(50 3/8 in.) 128

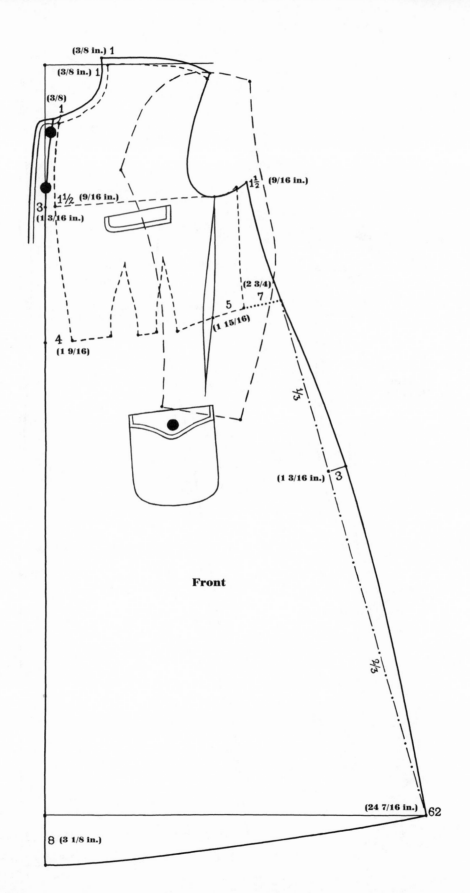

(3/8 in.) 1

(3/8 in.) 1

(3/8)
1

1½ (9/16 in.)

1½ (9/16 in.)

3

(1 3/16 in.)

(2 3/4)

5   7

(1 15/16)

4

(1 9/16)

⅓

(1 3/16 in.) 3

⅔

Front

(24 7/16 in.) 62

8 (3 1/8 in.)

198

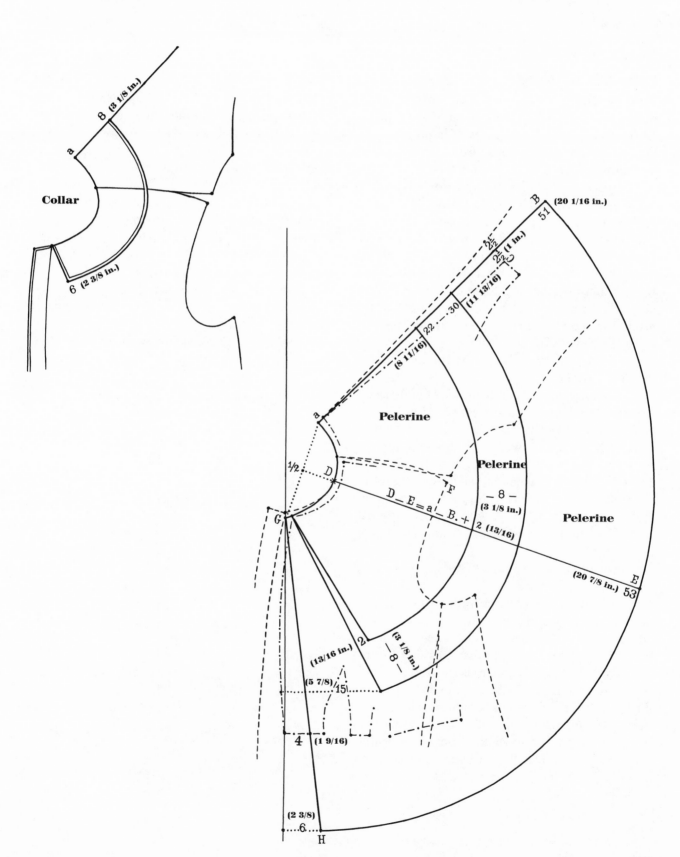

Collar

8 (3 1/8 in.)

a

6 (2 3/8 in.)

B (20 1/16 in.)

51

2½" (1 in.)

2½
(11 13/16)

22 - 30

(8 11/16)

a

Pelerine

½

D

Pelerine

F

— 8 —
(3 1/8 in.)

D _ E = a

B . +

2 (13/16)

G

Pelerine

(20 7/8 in.) E
53

(3 1/8 in.)

2

— 8 —

(13/16 in.)

(5 7/8)

15

4 (1 9/16)

(2 3/8)

6

H

Mantle with Optional Pelerine and Hood

This mantle goes with the pelerine below or the ones given with the Traveling Coat or Waterproof. Also suitable are the two styles of hood given below. All pieces are developed from other patterns, and all numbers indicate centimeters.

The center back length from *a* to *G* is according to measure, here 110 cm (43 1/4 in.). The dashed back of the bodice pattern lies against the center back at *A,* and 6 cm (2 3/8 in.) from it at *L* to *K.* At the neckline, the mantle is 1 cm (3/8 in.) higher than the bodice at *A* and 1 1/2 cm (9/16 in.) wider than the bodice at the shoulder. At the shoulder at *B,* the mantle is 1 cm (3/8 in.) wider. At the armhole at *C,* it is 1/2 cm (3/16 in.) wider, and at *E* 2 cm (13/16 in.). The line from *E* to *G* via *x* forms the side seam. From *F* to *x,* the mantle is 7 cm (2 3/4 in.) wider.

The bodice front is placed 1 1/2 cm (9/16 in.) from the baseline at *D,* and 6 cm (2 3/8 in.) from it at *K.* The shoulder is lengthened from *B* to *A* by 1 cm (3/8 in.), and moved up in the neck opening by 1 cm (3/8 in.). On the side at *e,* the mantle is 1 1/2 cm (9/16 in.) wider and at *F* 6 cm (2 3/8 in.) wider than the bodice. The side seam is drawn from *E* via *x* to *G.* The rest is easy to see from the pattern. The lower skirt widths at *G* are determined by fashion.

Any of the sleeves from "Drafting Sleeves" in chapter 1 may be used.

Pelerine. This pelerine with a shoulder dart must be drafted using the mantle or coat pattern and the plain bodice pattern. The baseline is drawn from *A* down to *F* and the first crossline from *A* across to *F.* The mantle pattern is laid into this angle so that the armhole-shoulder points meet at *G.* In the back at *C,* the dotted back of the bodice pattern must lie 1 cm (3/8 in.) from the first crossline.

Starting from *J* down, the front of the mantle must be laid against the baseline; that is, if the pelerine will close in the front. A rather wide

pelerine is shown by alternating dashes and dots and has a narrower shoulder dart at *M.* The shoulder dart of the half-wide pelerine goes from *D* to *D.* The distance from *B* to *F* is 60 cm (23 5/8 in.), from *D* to *F* in the middle it is 66 cm (26 in.), and from *E* via *J* to *F* 54 cm (21 1/4 in.).

Hood. This hood is drafted using the mantle and bodice patterns. At *H,* the front and back of the mantle are 2 cm (13/16 in.) apart. From *A* to *E* the distance is 16 cm (6 5/16 in.), from *E* to *F* 16 cm (6 5/16 in.), and from *B* to *G* 14 cm (5 1/2 in.). A different style of hood is also given. This is 3 cm (1 3/16 in.) longer in back than the bodice pattern at *C.*

Complete Guide to Ladies' Garment Cutting, 1883

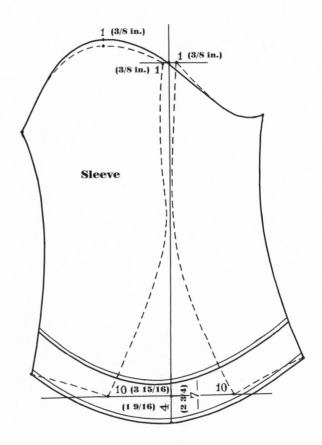

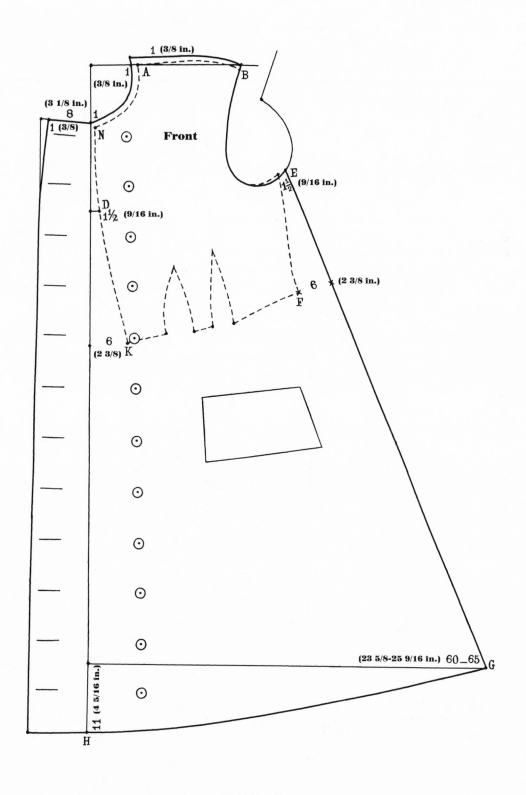

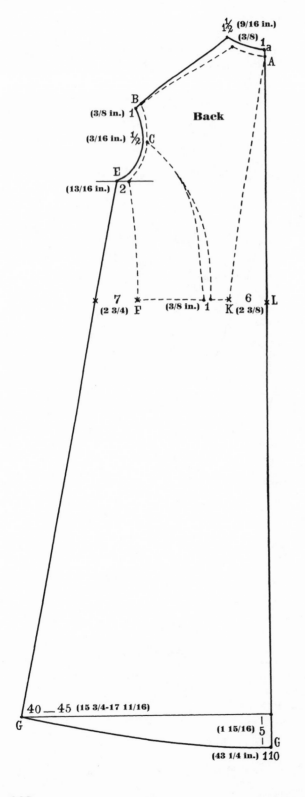

½ (9/16 in.)

(3/8) 1 a

A

B

(3/8 in.) 1

Back

(3/16 in.) ½ C

E

(13/16 in.) 2

7   (3/8 in.) 1   6 L

(2 3/4) F   K (2 3/8)

40 — 45 (15 3/4-17 11/16)

G

(1 15/16) 5

G

(43 1/4 in.) 110

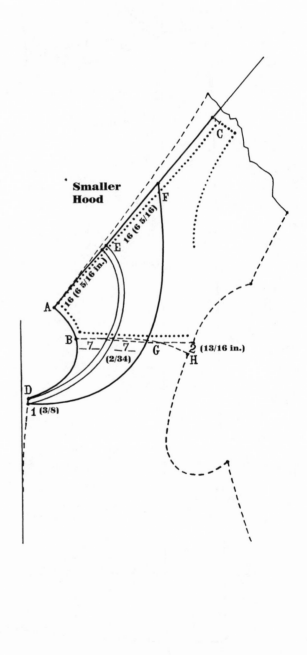

Smaller Hood

C

F

E 16 (6 5/16)

16 (6 5/16 in.)

A

B

—7—   —7—   G   2 (13/16 in.)

(2/34)   H

D

1 (3/8)

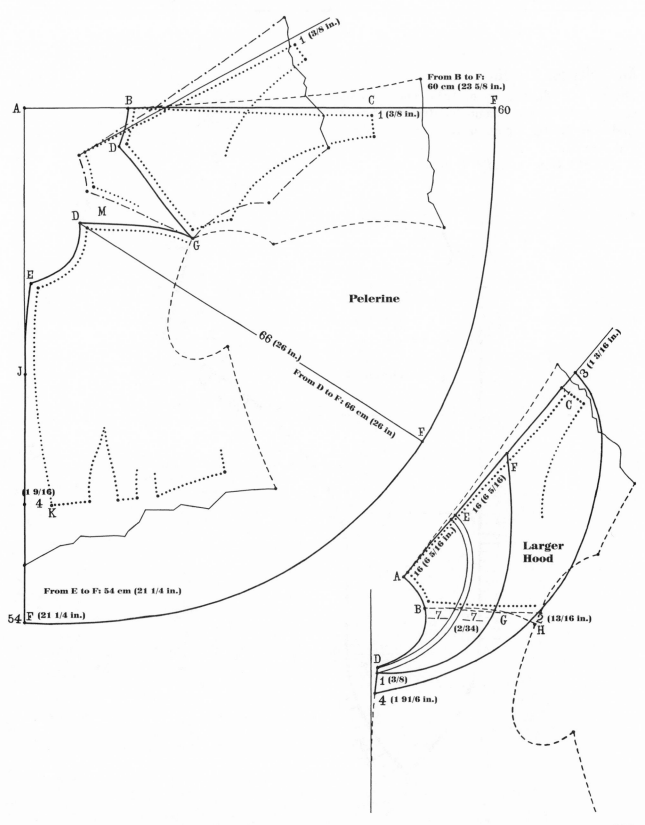

1 (3/8 in.)

From B to F:
60 cm (23 5/8 in.)

A   B   C   F   60

1 (3/8 in.)

D

D   M

G

Pelerine

E

66 (26 in.)

From D to F: 66 cm (26 in)

J

F

(1 9/16)

4
K

3 (1 3/16 in.)

C

F

E 16 (6 5/16)

Larger
Hood

16 (6 5/16 in.)

A

16 (6 5/16 in.)

B   G   2 (13/16 in.)
   7   7   H
     (2/34)

D
1 (3/8)

4 (1 91/6 in.)

From E to F: 54 cm (21 1/4 in.)

54 F (21 1/4 in.)

Mantelet for Evening

This pattern is drafted with the scale. The long ends are tied in front. Any imaginable style may be created from this basic pattern by altering the shape and trimming.

Complete Guide to Ladies' Garment Cutting, 1883

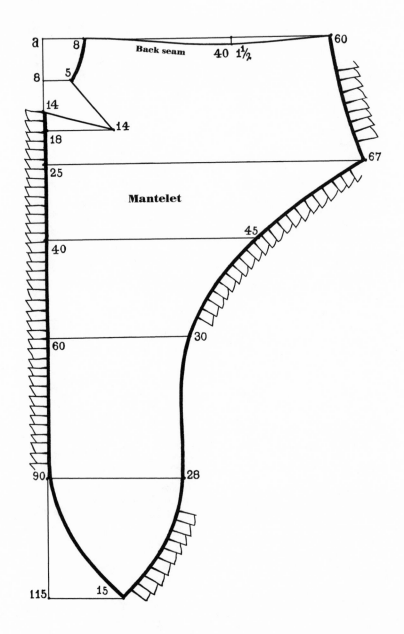

Mantelet for Evening

This pattern is drafted with the scale. The front
edges are closed with invisible hooks and loops.
Any imaginable style may be made from this basic
pattern by varying the shape and trimming.

Complete Guide to Ladies' Garment Cutting, 1883

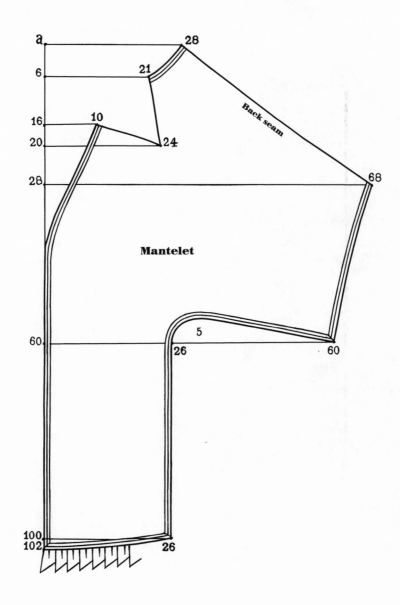

Beaded Tulle Fichu-Mantle

This fichu-mantle is made of polka-dotted tulle, in which the dots are beaded with jet, over a silk lining. Cut one whole piece from the pattern of lining silk. Face the outside from the bottom to the narrow line, and the inside from the top to the narrow line, with tulle. Take up the shoulder darts. Fold the mantle on the outside along the narrow line for the revers. Edge the mantle with a ruffle of Spanish lace. Finish the neck with a box-pleated ruche. Set satin ribbon bows at the neck and shoulder on the left side. Hooks and eyes fasten the front.

Harper's Bazar, July 1882

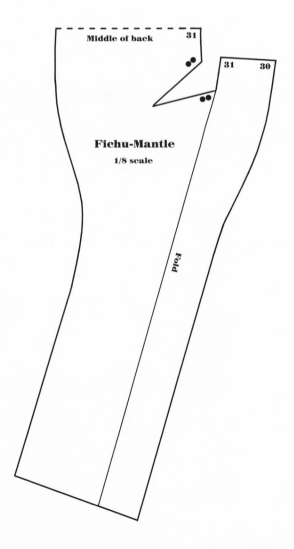

Middle of back   31

31   30

Fichu-Mantle
1/8 scale

Fold

Lace Shawl Worn as a Fichu-Mantilla

This fichu-mantilla is arranged from a three-cornered lace shawl. It is trimmed with bows of black grosgrain ribbon. Transfer the signs and lines on the pattern to the shawl. Fold the middle corner of the shawl on the outside along the narrow line. Pleat the shawl along the fold (which afterwards forms the upper edge of the mantilla) bringing *x* on ●. Fold the middle corner on the outside along the straight line, to form the revers of the hood. Gather the shawl closely along the sloping outline.
Harper's Bazar, June 1878

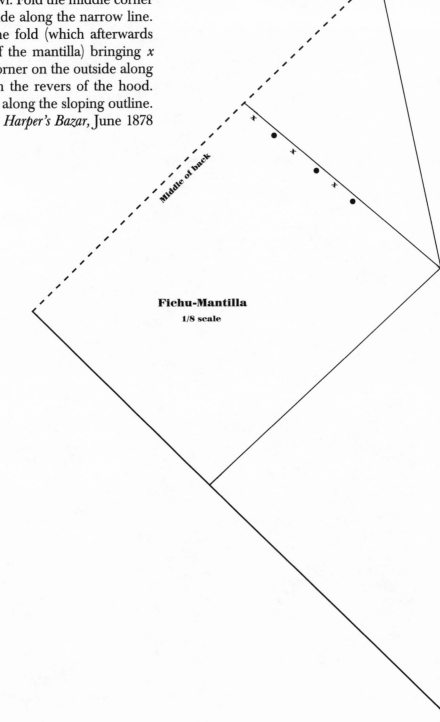

Fichu-Mantilla

1/8 scale

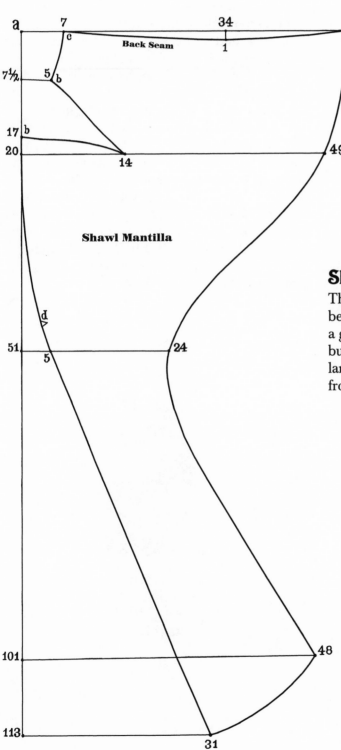

Shawl Mantilla for Evening

This mantilla is drafted with the scale. The dart between *b* and *b* shapes the shoulder and provides a good fit. The long falling collar runs down to the bust. The mantilla may be made without the collar, and trimmed to suit. The long ends are tied in front.

Complete Guide to Ladies' Garment Cutting, 1883

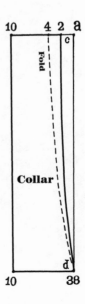

209

Lace Shawl Worn as a Mantle

The illustration shows a three-cornered lace shawl worn as a mantle, which is trimmed with satin ribbon bows and jet buckles. Spread out the shawl, and transfer to it the marks on the diagram, which indicate how the pleats in the drapery are taken up. Run in a white thread for the lines, and define the marks with pins and stitches. Shirr the top of the shawl along the narrow line from 50 to ✳. Set the gathers on a silk neckband cut from the pattern. Pleat the shawl as the marks indicate, bringing x on ●. Sew the xs marked a on ●a. Gather it along the narrow line from ●● to the upper edge. Tack the ●●s in each half to each other so that the folds fall outside. Sew the pleats marked ✳ to the pleats on the middle of the back. Set an inside belt at the waistline in back. Trim the mantle as illustrated with bows of wide black satin ribbon.

Harper's Bazar, July 1882

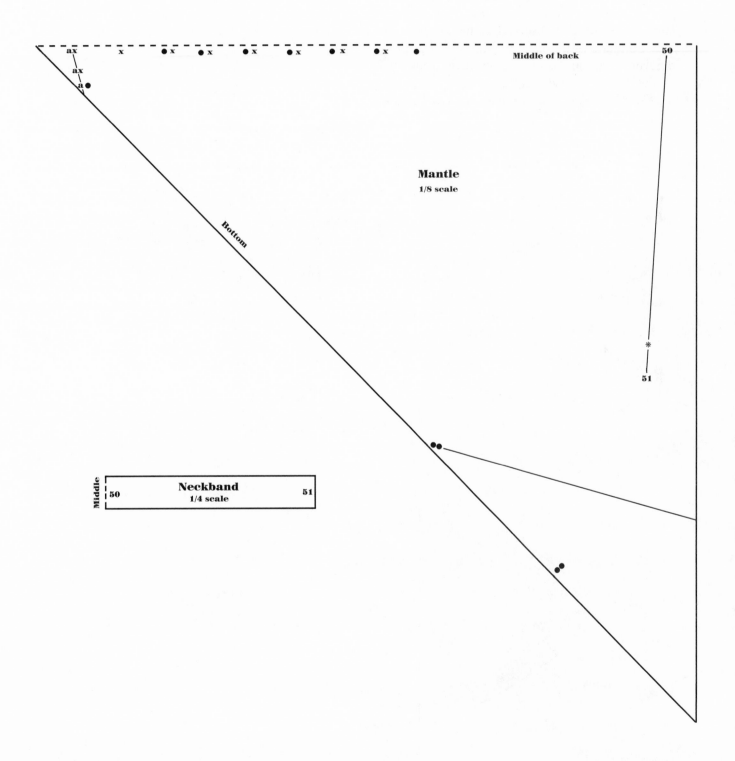

Shoulder Cape for Ball Toilette

This pattern is drafted in centimeters to fit all fully grown ladies. For very stout ladies, the neck circumference must be observed so that an allowance may be made in the back width, as well as down the front. The cape is made from quilted silk, padded and with swansdown trimming.

Complete Guide to Ladies' Garment Cutting, 1883

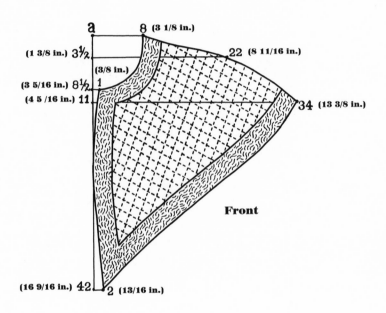

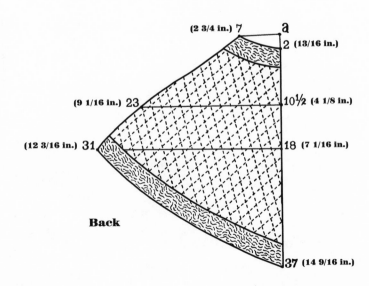

Collar-Shaped Ball Cape

This cape may be worn without the hood, and vice versa. The pattern is drafted in centimeters for all half breast circumferences from 40 to 50 cm (15 3/4 to 19 11/16 in.). It must be adjusted to the lady's neck circumference.

Complete Guide to Ladies' Garment Cutting, 1883

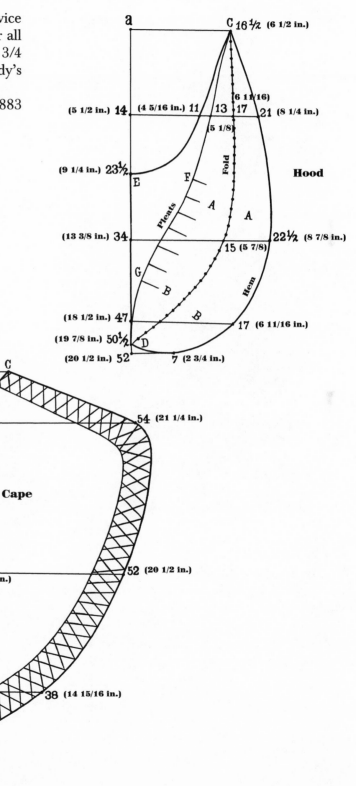

213

India Cashmere Pelerine

This pelerine is made of black India cashmere and lustring lining. Cut the main piece and the collar. Underlay the material with net. Embroider it with chain stitch in the design shown in the small illustration, using coarse black silk and beads. Finish the edge with a grosgrain piping. Edge the standing collar with piping. Set it on the neck. Trim the bottom of the pelerine with a fringe of narrow crimped silk tape 12 1/2 in. deep, which is worked in four graduated rows. On the front edges and the neck set pleated lace 2 1/2 in. wide. Hooks and eyes serve for closing.

Harper's Bazar, September 1878

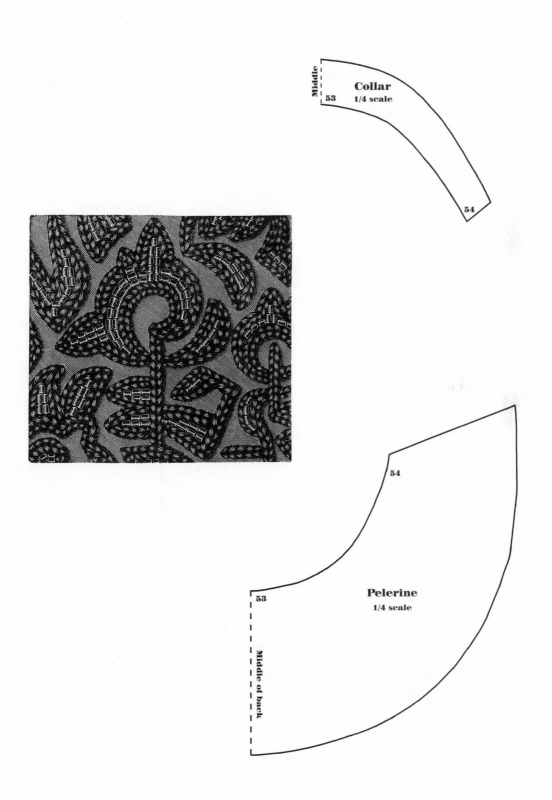

Collar
1/4 scale

Middle

53

54

Pelerine
1/4 scale

53

Middle of back

54

Circular Evening Cloak with Hood

This pattern is drafted in centimeters for a medium
size. The neck must be adjusted to the lady's neck
circumference.

Complete Guide to Ladies' Garment Cutting, 1883

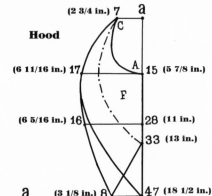

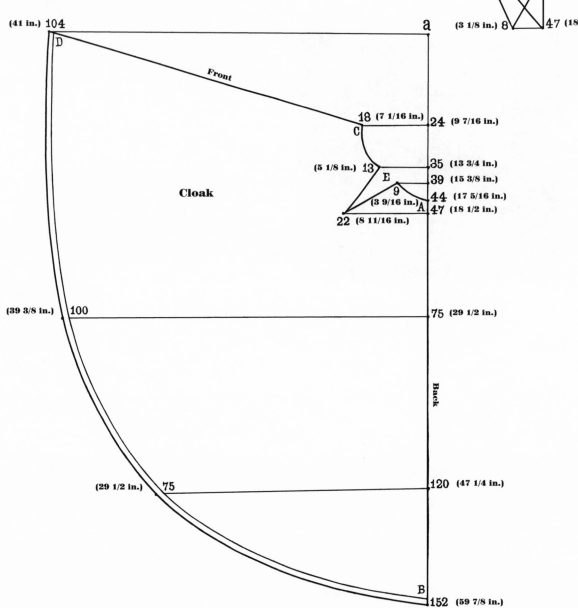

Opera Mantle

This mantle is of cream-colored brocaded satin, lined with quilted scarlet satin. Cut of the material and lining one whole piece from the mantle. Cut of the material only one whole piece from the hood. Take up the shoulder darts in the mantle. Turn in and run together the edges of material and lining. Face the hood with scarlet satin. Pleat it as indicated on the pattern. Join it to the mantle according to the corresponding figures. Trim the mantle with cream-colored chenille fringe.

Harper's Bazar, December 1881

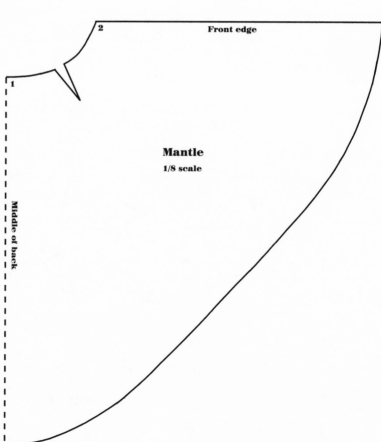

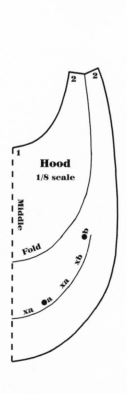

Circular Mantle

This pattern is based on the plain bodice. First the baseline is drafted from *a* to *B* and the crossline from *a* to *F*. The bodice back touches the baseline at *b* and *C*. The bodice front is 1 cm (3/8 in.) from the crossline at *D*, and 4 cm (1 9/16 in.) from it at *E*. Points *G* to *G* at the shoulders are 1 cm (3/8 in.) apart.

As usual, 1 cm (3/8 in.) is added to the neck opening and along the shoulder seam. The length of the mantle back from *A* to *B* is according to the lady's measure; in this pattern, 104 cm (41 in.). The side length from *H* to *J* via *K* is 10 cm (3 15/16 in.) more than in back. The front length from *D* to *F* is 4 cm (1 9/16 in.) less than the back length.

The lower edge of the mantle should be drafted as a smooth curve from *B* to *F* via *J*. The space between points *h* to *H* and *G* to *G* is cut out as a shoulder dart, to be sewn with a seam as invisible as possible. This dart is essential for a good fit on the shoulders.

Three sizes of pelerine-shaped collar are given. If you wish you may instead use a falling collar from one of the other patterns.

Complete Guide to Ladies' Garment Cutting, 1883

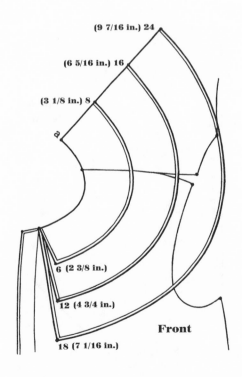

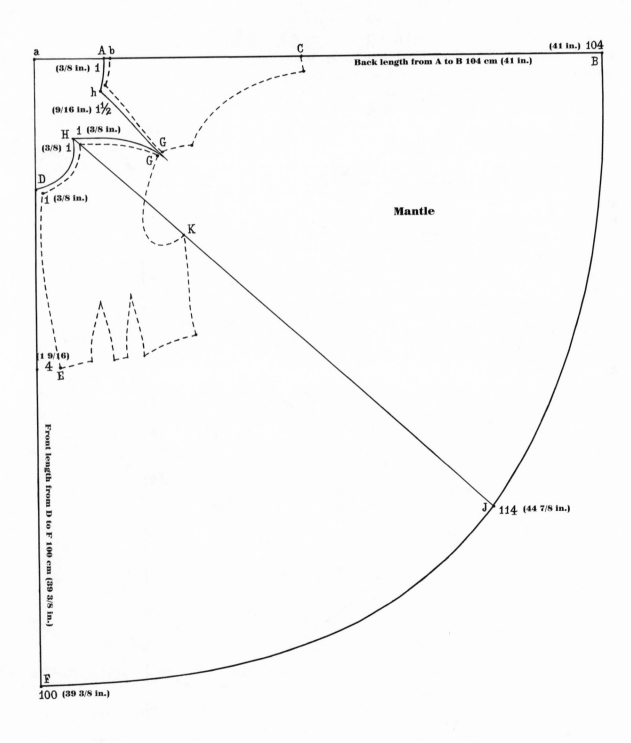

a   A b   C   (41 in.) 104

(3/8 in.) 1   Back length from A to B 104 cm (41 in.)   B

h

(9/16 in.) 1½

H   1 (3/8 in.)

(3/8) 1   G

G

D

1 (3/8 in.)

K

Mantle

A

[1 9/16]
4
E

J   114   (44 7/8 in.)

Front length from D to F 100 cm (39 3/8 in.)

F
100 (39 3/8 in.)

Bedouin for Evening

This pattern is drafted in centimeters to fit all fully
grown ladies. For very tall ladies, the length must
be increased somewhat from *A* to *C* and *D*. From *a*
at the neck vertebra to *C* is the actual back length.
F and *G* are pieces falling loosely in back. The
material must be at least 131 cm (51 5/8 in.) wide
to provide the full length. It is cut double.

Complete Guide to Ladies' Garment Cutting, 1883

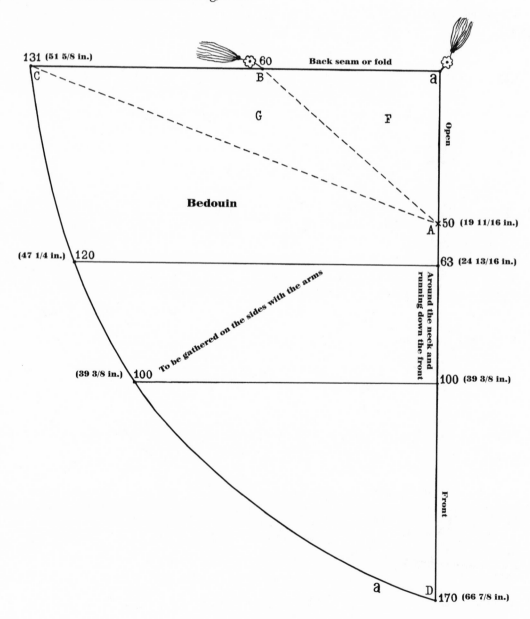

Evening Mantilla for Elderly Ladies

This pattern is drafted with the scale. It is for half the mantilla only. It has short sleeves and two shoulder darts. After the shoulder and back seams are completed, the sleeve is sewn onto the mantilla from *e* to *d* and from *d* to *c;* that is, these letters must meet when the sleeve is inserted. The pleats in the back seam are concealed with a bow.

Complete Guide to Ladies' Garment Cutting, 1883

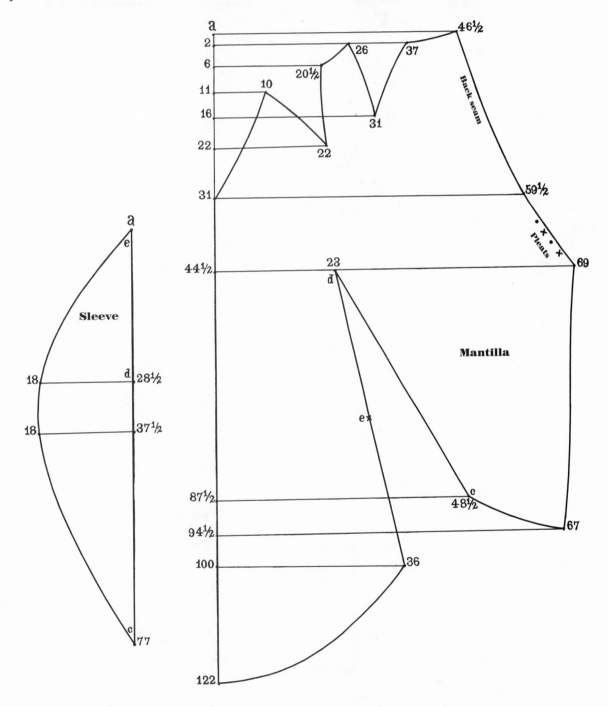

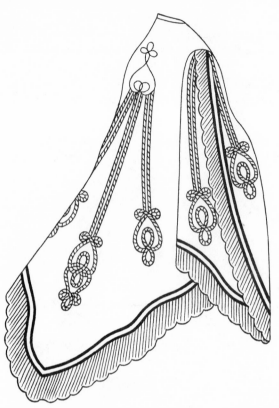

Ball Mantle

This elegant mantle is drafted with the scale. It is of a full cut and may be made longer or shorter, as well as rounded at the bottom or more pointed. It may be trimmed in many different ways with lace or embroidery, depending on fashion or taste.

When it is joined, the sleeve must meet the shoulder seam of the front and back at *a*. Point *xC* must meet point *xC* of the front. Point *B* of the sleeve forms a kind of gusset.

Complete Guide to Ladies' Garment Cutting, 1883

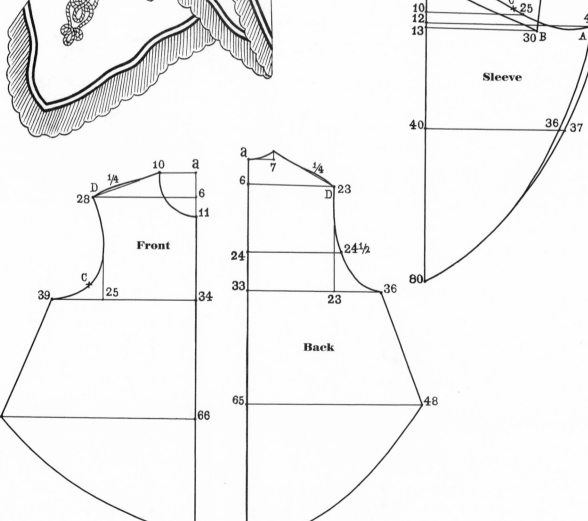

Dolman for Evening

This pattern is drafted with the scale. The end of the sleeve at *h* may be styled square or round, as desired. All the letters from *b* to *g* must meet when joined. The sleeve is gathered and pressed at the shoulder so that the letters *f* and *g* on all three pieces meet. The style of the dolman may vary considerably according to current fashion.

Complete Guide to Ladies' Garment Cutting, 1883

The dolman is a loose wrap, and yet it should give the form of the body. On many a piece of tape is placed inside at the back, to tie around the waist, and hold it close to the body. Yet it must have such a form in back as will retain the peculiar cut, more striking in this than any other garment.

The shoulder, to put the sleeve seam in the proper place, high up, must be cut narrow. This counteracts the tendency of the sloping form of shoulder, more liable to occur on this than any other outside garment.

The sleeve should have just the right proportion of fullness, so that it may hang gracefully without drawing. The front should also be narrow, so that the swing of the sleeve is forward. Although the leading features must take on more or less the same form in each garment, yet there is perhaps none with greater variety of style in the various details as the round and square sleeve.

Dress and Cloak Cutter, 1883

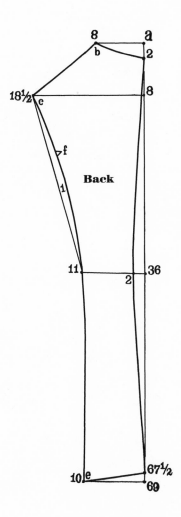

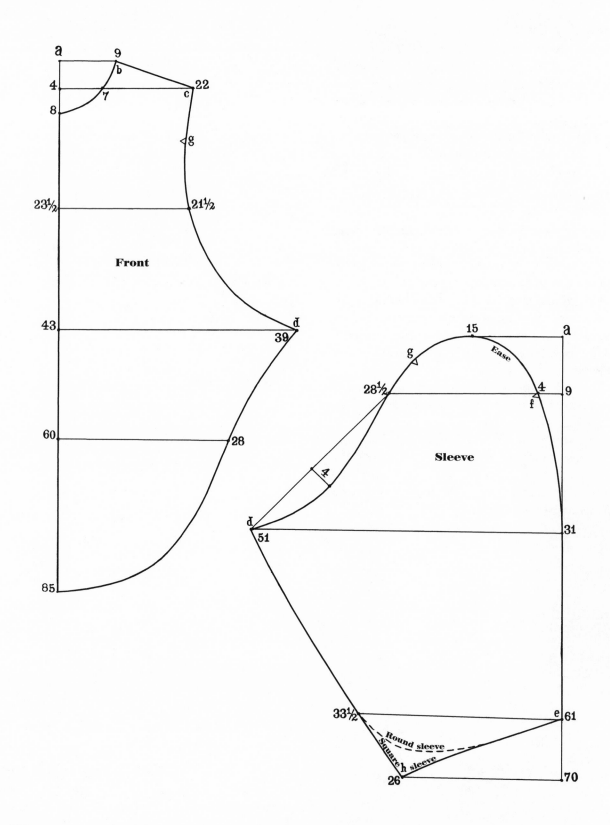

Camel's Hair Opera Cloak

This opera cloak is made of white camel's hair lined with quilted white silk. It requires 2 1/4 yd. of material 48 in. wide. The trimming comprises a bottom border and a collar of white ribbed plush, sleeve borders of pearl embroidery on net, pearl and chenille tassels, and white satin ribbon bows.

Cut of camel's hair and lining two pieces each from the front, back, and sleeve. Join the pieces according to the corresponding figures, pleating the sleeves as indicated on the pattern. Bind the neck with the collar, which is made of ribbed plush and silk lining. Furnish the fronts with a buttonhole fly and buttons. Tack the point of the sleeve marked ✳ to ✳ on the front.

Harper's Bazar, January 1882

14   12

13

Back
1/8 scale

Back seam

15   17

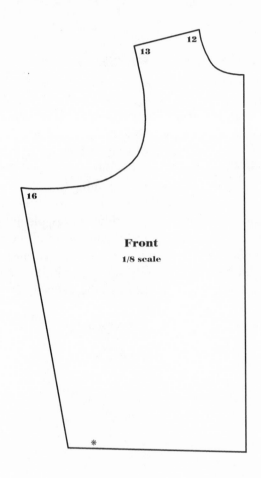

13 12

16

Front
1/8 scale

＊

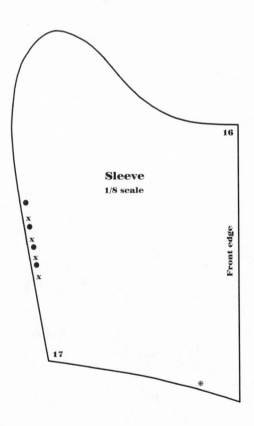

16

Sleeve
1/8 scale

Front edge

x
x
x
x

17

＊

Worth Mantle

This mantle is made of satin, camel's hair, cheviot, and similar materials for general wear. To match costumes it is frequently made of velvet or plush. The illustration shows one of garnet plush lined with old gold quilted satin. It is trimmed with a border of marabou plush, and with passementerie and fringe in silk, chenille, and beads.

Cut two pieces each from the front, back, and sleeve. Join the parts according to the corresponding signs and figures. Finish the neck with a narrow standing collar. Furnish the front with hooks and eyes.

Harper's Bazar, March 1882

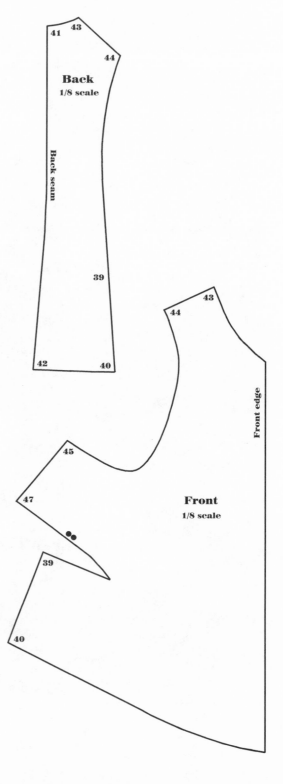

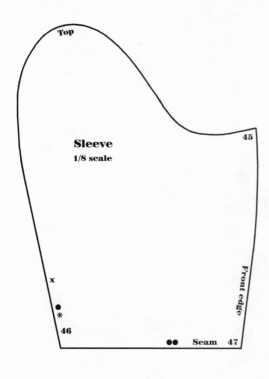

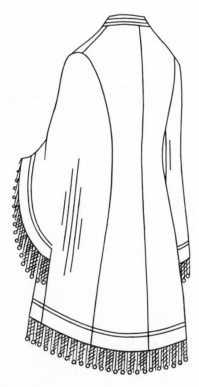

Dolman Mantelet

This pattern is based on the plain bodice. First the back baseline is drawn from *a* to *B*. The back of the bodice pattern is placed against the baseline at *a*, with *C* being 5 cm (1 15/16 in.) from it. An additional point is marked 3 cm (1 3/16 in.) from *C*. The entire back length is 76 cm (29 15/16 in.) in this pattern. The widening of the back on the side from *c* to *x* is 3 cm (1 3/16 in.). Two centimeters (13/16 in.) is taken from the front shoulder by laying it against the back shoulder, as shown, and subtracting 2 cm (13/16 in.) from the neck opening and armhole. Then the back is raised by 1 cm (3/8 in.) at *A,* by 1 1/2 cm (9/16 in.) at the shoulder point of the neck opening, and by 1 cm (3/8 in.) at the highest point of the shoulder. The back width is reduced by 3 cm (1 3/16 in.) at *i.* A line is drawn from *b* to *D* to mark the assumed lower skirt width of 14 cm (5 1/2 in.). Then the draft of the back may be completed.

The under sleeve is placed at the top at *G* with its back seam where the sleeve seam of the bodice pattern would be. In this pattern, this is 8 cm (3 1/8 in.) from *F,* the highest shoulder point. At the bottom at *t,* the sleeve is 34 cm (13 3/8 in.) from the baseline. The upper sleeve is placed with its upper back seam on *G;* the elbow points correspond. At the waist at *e,* the sleeve is 3 cm (1 3/16 in.) from the back. The sleeve head is raised by 2 cm (13/16 in.). The front sleeve seam is drafted from *K* to *L,* staying 2 cm (13/16 in.) from the sleeve of the bodice pattern at the elbow, and 8 cm (3 1/8 in.) from it at the end.

The bodice side piece and front are dotted to the extent possible into the sleeve pattern. The side is 2 cm (13/16 in.) from the back at the bottom, and the front is 12 cm (4 3/4 in.) from the side at the bottom from *H* to *H.* The distance from *H* to *E* is 2 cm (13/16 in.) less than from *e* to *D* on the back, in this pattern 34 cm (13 3/8 in.). The lower notch, which is halfway across the width of the lower sleeve, is 10 cm (3 15/16 in.) long. Then the draft of the sleeve may be finished.

The front is begun by drawing a baseline from *a* to *B.* The bodice pattern will be 2 cm (13/16 in.) from the baseline at *D,* 3 cm (1 3/16 in.) from it at the bottom of the bodice. At the shoulder, the 2 cm (13/16 in.) that were added to the back shoulder must be subtracted. The front shoulder is lengthened by 1 cm (3/8 in.), and the neck opening is enlarged by 1 cm (3/8 in.). It is 8 cm (3 1/8 in.) from *G* to *K,* which determines the high bust width of the mantelet. It is 6 cm (2 3/8 in.) from *H* to *J* at the bodice bottom. From *H* to *E* of the front is as long as *H* to *E* of the sleeve. It is 10 cm (3 15/16 in.) from *F* to *E.*

The sleeve of the bodice pattern is placed with its back point *X,* which is 8 cm (3 1/8 in.) from the back sleeve seam, onto *F,* and with its front sleeve seam onto *K.* Both points *K* must meet when joined. From *K* to *L* is as long as is *K* to *L* on the upper sleeve. The width of the lower sleeve from *F* to *L* is

36 cm (14 3/16 in.). Should the arm need more room to move, the distance may be larger, or in the reverse, smaller.

The lower skirt width of the front is 33 cm (13 in.) in this pattern. The lengthening of the front from *b* down must be left to taste or fashion.

The narrow standing collar is drafted in centimeters.

Complete Guide to Ladies' Garment Cutting, 1883

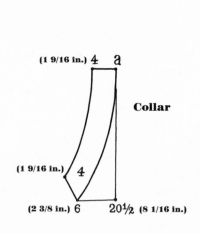

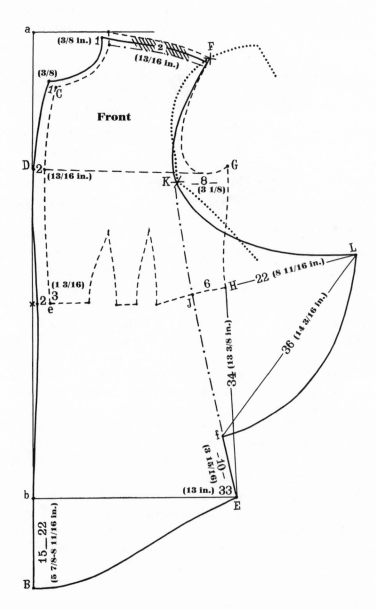

Dolman Mantelet

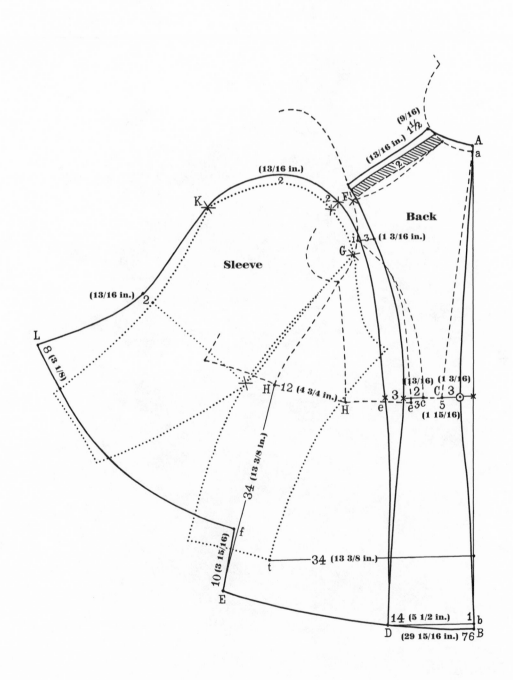

Sleeve

Back

(9/16)

(13/16 in.) 1½

(13/16 in.)
2

K

2

2 F

1 3 (1 3/16 in.)

G

A
a

(13/16 in.)
2

L

8 (3 1/8)

H 12 (4 3/4 in.)

H

3

2
e 3c

(13/16) (1 3/16)

C 3
5
(1 15/16)

34 (13 3/8 in.)

f

10 (3 15/16)

t

34 (13 3/8 in.)

E

14 (5 1/2 in.)

1 b

D

(29 15/16 in.) 76 B

Pannier Mantle

This style is especially used for dressy mantles made of the material of the costume, or else of the rich Oriental fabrics with palm-leaf and arabesque designs and tapestry patterns. These Oriental goods are of silk and wool combined, and have the effect of embroidery. These wraps are so gay and rich

looking that they are confined to carriage use, and are especially liked for day receptions, for opera cloaks, and as *sorties de bal.* They are, however, used for church and for paying visits, where they serve to brighten any dark costume. The trimming is passementerie and deep fringe made of beads of all the colors of the cashmere mingled with chenille; or else the fringe is of tape that is raveled on the edges.

Thick, warm, yet soft cloth of drab and ecru shades is used for cloaks for nice wear made in the pannier shape. These are bordered with fur, and have deep fringe falling below the fur, also passementerie in the back. This pattern will be much in favor for spring wraps, as it is light and graceful, short enough for short skirts, and the pannier fullness makes it suitable for bouffant tournures. Black satin de Lyon garments made by this pattern, and trimmed with passementerie and fringe, will be worn warmly wadded all winter, and the lining will be removed in the spring. For plain velvet, figured velvet, brocaded satin, and plain satin wraps this is the favorite model. Camel's hair mantles in pannier shape are shown in the light shades and in black, trimmed with passementerie and fringe.

The original of this mantle is made of a Turkish shawl. Cut from the shawl two pieces each from the front, back, upper sleeve, and under sleeve. Line the parts with red silk. Join them according to the corresponding figures. Run the material and lining together on the edges. Pleat the upper sleeves as indicated on the pattern. Fold them on the wrong side along the narrow line. Tack the pleats to the back. Fasten the point marked ✳ on the under sleeve to ✳ on the upper sleeve. To the lower corners of the fronts sew silk tapes 1 1/4 in. wide, which are tied in a bow behind underneath the back. Trim the mantle with colored crimped silk fringe 5 1/4 in. deep and a passementerie trimming of cord of the same color.

Harper's Bazar, December 1879

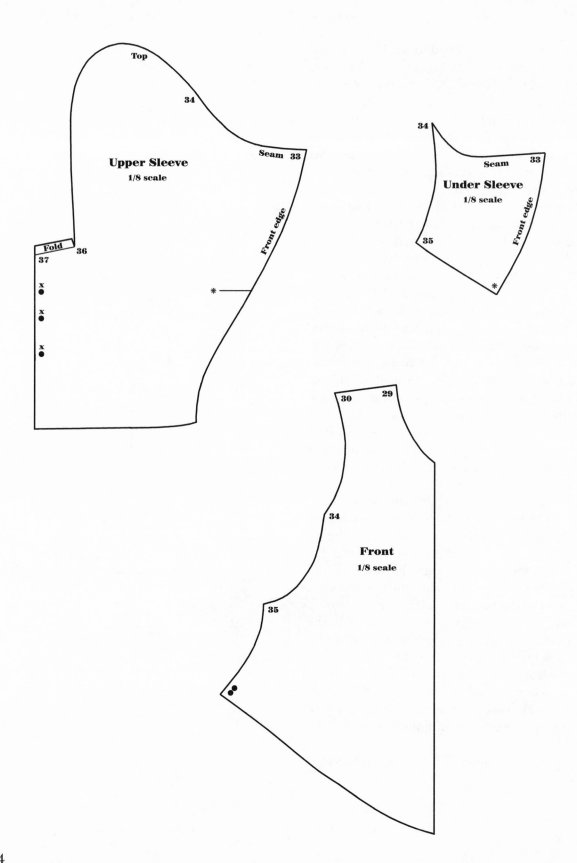

Top

34

Seam 33

Upper Sleeve
1/8 scale

34

Seam 33

Under Sleeve
1/8 scale

35

Front edge

*

Fold 36

37

x ●

x ●

x ●

*

30   29

34

Front
1/8 scale

35

234

Sicilienne Visite

Sicilienne Visite

This visite is made of sicilienne lined with thin silk. It requires 5 1/4 yd. 23 in. wide. It is trimmed with passementerie borders, and silk cord and tassels. Cut two pieces each from the front, back, under sleeve, and collar of sicilienne and lining.

Join the front and back from 8 to 9 and from 12 to 13. Take up the shoulder dart. Join the upper part of the sleeve, which is in one with the back, from 13 to 15 with the front. Join the under part of the sleeve from 14 to 15 and from 8 to 16 with the back. Sew up the back from 10 to 11. Shirr it at intervals of 1/2 in. across the space between 17 and 18, and 19 and 20. Fasten the shirring on the stay according to the corresponding figures. Sew up the collar from 10 to 21. Join it to the neck from 10 to 22. Roll it on the outside along the narrow line.

Passementerie clasps fasten the visite. Borders are on the sleeves and the bottom.

Harper's Bazar, May 1882

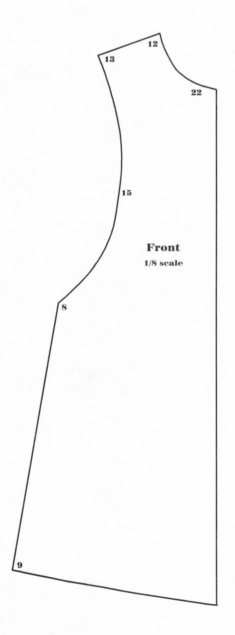

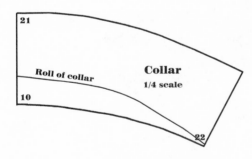

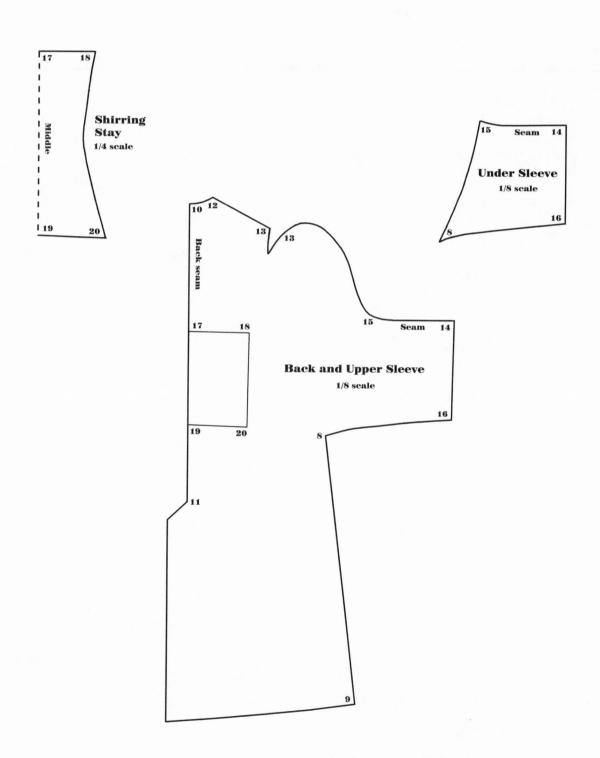

Shirring Stay
1/4 scale

Middle

Under Sleeve
1/8 scale

Back seam

Back and Upper Sleeve
1/8 scale

Seam

237

Dolman Coat

This pattern is based on the plain bodice. First the baseline is drawn from *a* to *B* and the first crossline from *a* to *C*. The back of the bodice pattern is placed on the baseline at the top and about 5 cm (1 15/16 in.) from it at the waistline. The back is raised at *A* by 1 cm (3/8 in). The shoulder is increased by 1 1/2 cm (9/16 in.), and the armhole by 1/2 cm (3/16 in.). The bodice is widened by 3 cm (1 3/16 in.). The coat length from *A* to *B* is as measured; in this pattern it is 88 cm (34 5/8 in.). Point *b* is 8 cm (3 1/8 in.) above *B*. The lower skirt width from *b* to *G* is 18 cm (7 1/16 in.).

The front of the bodice pattern is placed 1 cm (3/8 in.) from *D,* and 4 cm (1 9/16 in.) from *E*. The coat is narrowed by 8 cm (3 1/8 in.) from *K* to *L*, and by 6 cm (2 3/8 in.) at the waistline from *P* to *J*. The side seam is continued from *L* down beyond *J* to *H*.

In the sleeve, the distance from *F* to *H* is 2 cm (13/16 in.) less than from *F* to *G*. In the front sleeve seam, from *H* to *H* is 8 cm (3 1/8 in.), from *J* to *O* 6 cm (2 3/8 in.). In the back sleeve seam, from *G* to *G* is 4 cm (1 9/16 in.), and at the waist 8 cm (3 1/8 in.). The sleeve head is inserted 3 cm (1 3/16 in.) into the front. The rest is easily accomplished by following the pattern.

Complete Guide to Ladies' Garment Cutting, 1883

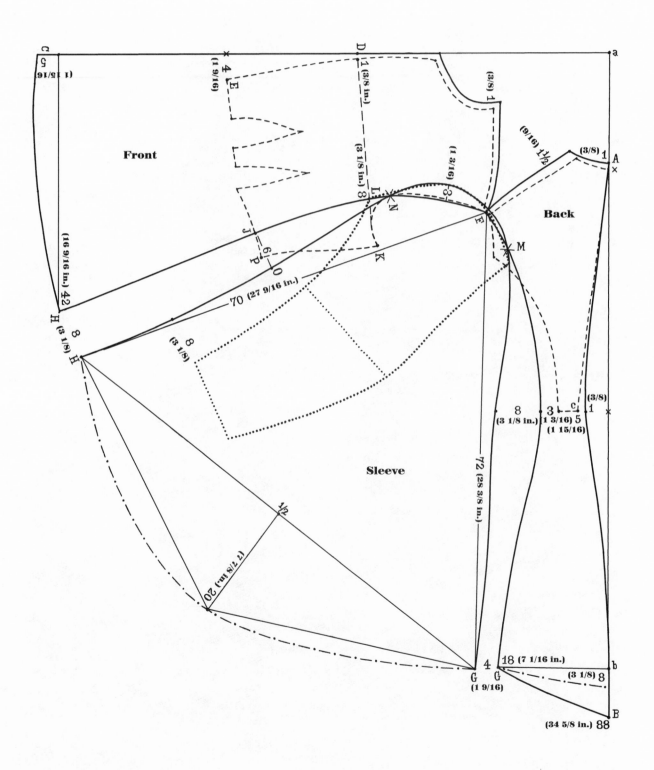

India Shawl Worn as a Cloak

These directions and the accompanying diagram show how to drape a square shawl of average size, to be worn as illustrated, without cutting or otherwise injuring the shawl. Spread out the shawl, and transfer to it all the lines and signs given on the large shawl pattern. Run in white basting cotton for the narrow lines. Mark the *x*s and ●s with black and white pins, and the corresponding figures by corresponding stitches of colored wool or silk.

Pleat one end of the shawl as indicated, bringing *x* on ●. The parallel narrow lines mark the outside folds of the pleats. Tack to each other the two points marked 40 and those marked 41, which will form the sleeves and the pouf on the back. Pleat the rest of the shawl as indicated by the lines and signs. Fasten an inside belt, which is to be hooked in front, along the back at the waistline.

The cloak is finished by a collar and cuffs made of dark-colored or black silk. Cut the collar with silk lining and stiff interlining from the collar pattern, and edge it with fringe. Turn the upper corners of the shawl down on the outside along the narrow line. Join on the collar and roll it on the outside along the narrow line. Cut the cuffs from the cuff pattern, and set them on the sleeves. Provide the front with a broad metal clasp for fastening. Set a silk bow and ends on the pouf as illustrated.

Harper's Bazar, April 1882

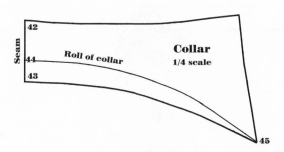

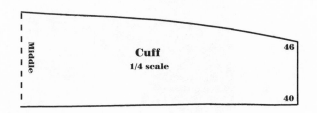

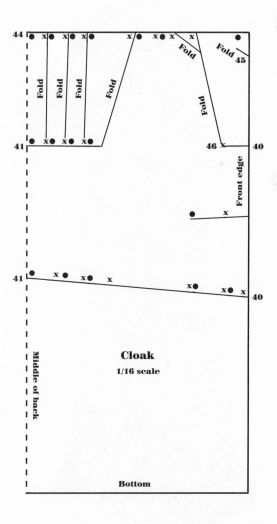

Shirred Mantle

This mantle is of steel blue brocade. The trimming consists of box-pleated frills and bows of satin ribbon in the same shade, and black lace embroidered with blue steel beads. It requires 7 1/8 yd. of brocade and 1 1/8 yd. of satin 24 in. wide.

Cut of brocade two pieces each from the front and the sleeve. Cut of brocade one whole piece from the back. Cut of black surah one whole piece from the back lining.

Line the fronts and sleeves with surah. Shirr the brocade back at regular intervals from the top to the narrow line, and between the two narrow lines at the waist. Baste it on the lining as the figures indicate. Shirr the fronts as indicated on the pattern. Join them to the back. Turn in and run together the material and lining at the front edges. Face the bottom.

Sew up the sleeves from 7 to 8. Fasten *x* on ●. Gather them at the front edge. Set them into the armholes. Edge the neck and sleeves with box-pleated satin ribbon. Trim the mantle, as illustrated, with lace and bows.

Harper's Bazar, April 1881

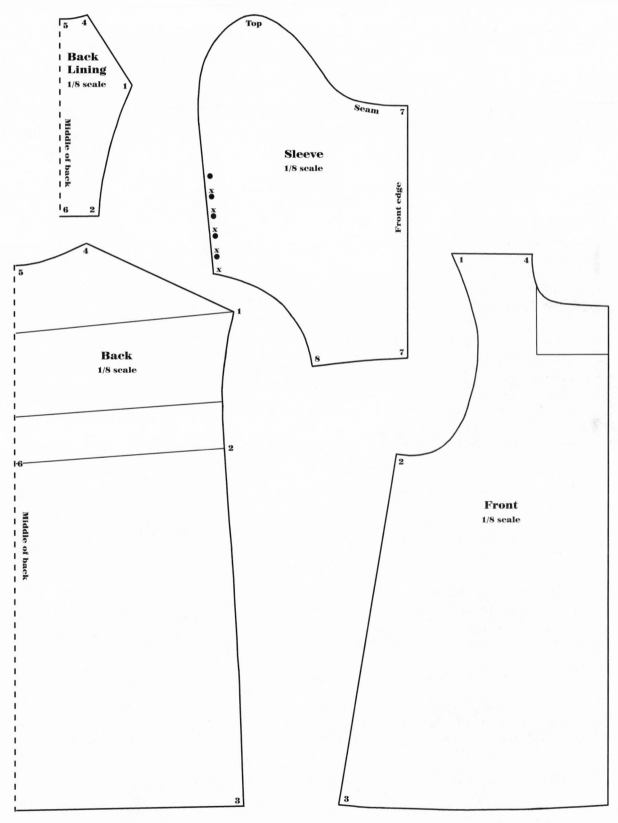

6. Hairstyles, Millinery, and Accessories

White muslin hats with fichus to match are shown, to be worn with any gay short dress as a pretty costume for garden parties and summer fetes. The round hat is of the sheerest organdy muslin, made with a low broad crown and wide brim drawn on wires placed about 1 in. apart. The brim may be turned up on one side, or indented in front a la Marie Stuart, or worn low on the forehead to shade the eyes.

The simple trimming is a ruche of the muslin edged with Breton lace passed around the crown. Or it may be a puff of the sheer lawn, through which pale blue or rose ribbon is drawn. A cluster of red and yellow cherries may be placed under the left side of the brim where it is turned up, or a bunch of field flowers is stuck in the ruche.

Sometimes the hat is drawn down at each side in cabriolet shape. It is held there by ribbon, which forms a bow on top and, passing down the sides, forms strings to tie under the chin.

Harper's Bazar, June 1879

The Langtry hood is a popular part of English costumes. It is made of the dress material, but is laid widely open to show a gay surah lining, which is sometimes striped in contrasting colors. It may be attached to an elbow cape or scarf mantle, but Englishwomen wear it alone over basques or coat-shaped garments. The shape is very simple. It is merely folded double (about 1/2 yd. wide when double), and sewed together at the end. The neck is rounded slightly, and the top is shirred to a standing collar.

Harper's Bazar, July 1880

Ladies are now making themselves throat bows of the double-faced satin ribbons. The fancy is for 1 in. wide ribbons of two or three colors, and for long ends hanging from the throat to the waist. The simple way is to buy 1 1/2 or 2 yd. of satin ribbon, black on one side and cardinal red on the other. Fasten it—with a slender brooch or lace pin—in two long loops and two hanging ends.

Harper's Bazar, January 1878

The new fichu is a Madras foulard in pale or bright shades. It is worn high behind on the neck and low in front.

Fold a square on the cross. Cut through it from point to point, which will give two three-cornered pieces. Neatly hem and border each with lace (fringe is sometimes preferable). Then join the two sides together by their extreme points, leaving a hole in the center for the head to pass through. Make two ribbon bows to match, one for the back and the other for the front. When in this unfinished state, put the fichu on your neck and pin down on each side three folds on the bias. Tack these afterward on the wrong side, but so that they appear laid down only. The points to the right and left in front form revers. You may make a buttonhole through one rever for an artificial bouquet.

Demorest's Mirror of Fashions, June 1877

Very new fichus are mere strips of white gauze, beautifully embroidered in variegated colors. They are outlined to the shape of the neck, the ends descending on the breast, and bordered with a double row of fine old lace.

Another pretty little decoration for the neck consists simply of a handkerchief of very sheer and delicate linen cambric. This is shaped and doubled, and edged with Valenciennes or duchesse lace. The handkerchief is brought close up on the neck, and fastened against the throat with a gold pin. The two ends are fastened on the breast with a second pin, instead of hanging loose.

Demorest's Mirror of Fashions, March 1878

Scarves of fine net edged with Breton lace are used for two purposes. They may be worn as bonnet strings that begin on the crown in a bow or in

pleatings. Or they may serve as a neck scarf to be tied in a large bow at the throat, with the ends folded straight down in front to the waist. They are 2 yd. long, and about 3/8 yd. wide. They are finished across the bottom with a pleated frill of the lace. Ladies sometimes buy 4 or 5 yd. of wide lace, and make the scarf by sewing together the plain edges.

Harper's Bazar, March 1879

The fashion of outside pockets has been the means of introducing a great variety of exquisite little handkerchiefs, Vandyked and edged with borders in solid or mixed colors, and with dainty embroidery. Of course they are not relied on for use, as they are small, fragile, and somewhat expensive. It is the style to have a corner of one visible above the edge of the side pocket. The handkerchief is generally pinned in, and kept there for show, while another is kept in an inside pocket for use.

Demorest's Mirror of Fashions, November 1877

The belt is the objective point to which are attached many pretty things for use or ornament. The fan, the bag, the chatelaine, with watch, tablets, and vinaigrette, are all grouped amid the flowing ribbons that hang from the side. A buckle of cut silver or pearl fastens the wide belt in front, or else there is a mammoth bow.

Harper's Bazar, August 1879

For general wear light-colored leather or morocco belts are used, with bags attached. The favorite is of alligator skin. Belts of medium width are most becoming to the figure, but those 4 in. wide are most fashionable. A more dressy fashion is a wide plain belt and flat square bag or reticule made of the dress trimming material. Thus a costume of dark green silk, trimmed with gay brocaded silk, has a round reticule of brocaded silk suspended from the belt by a cord and tassels of red, green, and old gold.

Harper's Bazar, March 1879

The greatest demand is for plain simply stitched and bound gloves with wrists long enough to be fastened by three or four buttons. Those with six buttons are reserved for more dressy wear, as when used with close coat sleeves they rumple the cuffs in being buttoned, and are really concealed. Black gloves fastened by eight buttons are, however, especially stylish to wear with light suits, and sometimes for dress occasions.

Harper's Bazar, November 1879

Cream and tan gloves remain the popular choice. These are worn with black, white, and colored costumes, without any attempt at matching the gloves to the dress. There are also the various wood colors, mode, drab, slate, mastic, and seal brown shades, as well as straw and pearl tints. The preference is for darker gloves for all occasions, even full dress. Mustard and lichen shades are shown, and as an extreme novelty terracotta.

Harper's Bazar, April 1882

Among the smaller items of the evening toilette are the long mittens of lace—white, black, or tinted blue, cream, or pink to match the dress.

The newest lace fans are merely transparent lace with slender pearl sticks extending to the point, and making the silk mounting unnecessary. Ostrich feather fans with tortoiseshell sticks are very handsome for elderly ladies. Very expensive ones have the sticks of pale amber-colored shell, with a white ostrich feather on each stick. Darker shell sticks have the natural gray feathers, or else black. For very young ladies fans are made of marabou feathers in which are small flowers—forget-me-nots, violets, or rosebuds.

Silk, satin, or velvet reticules or pouches of old-time shape are worn suspended from the side to hold the handkerchief and fan. The flat pockets of lace and flowers are still worn hanging by a chatelaine of ribbons or flowers.

Another pretty fancy is the necklace of lace with drooping pendants in medallion shape. Some ladies fasten a narrow barbe of lace around the neck, like a dog collar, crossing the ends behind, and pinning it with a jeweled brooch, a small bow, or a flower. An ornament worn sometimes in the hair and sometimes at the throat is a bunch of transparent gauzelike leaves of gilt or silver. This is very brilliant in the evening, and is especially handsome in black hair and with dark velvet dresses.

Harper's Bazar, January 1878

The new muffs made of the dress material are in reticule shape, and are trimmed with lace. The muff is nearly flat, and is broader on the lower edge than on top. The velvet, satin, or brocade used for the most conspicuous part of the costume is chosen for the muff. The lining is of silk plush, either white, garnet, or old gold. The open ends are bordered with soft white lace, such as Breton or point d'esprit, very fully gathered to fall in shells.

Harper's Bazar, November 1879

Dealers say that nine-tenths of their hosiery sales are colored stockings. Black silk stockings are the most stylish for the street, and also for full-dress day and evening wear with the lightest dresses, and with white. Terracotta and rose are the new shades this season. There are also very dark garnet, cardinal, and brighter Turkey red, with porcelain blue, tan, drab, ecru, seal brown, navy blue, bronze, and dark green. Solid colors are preferred for general wear, with very light clocking or leaf embroidery up each side. The lacework open designs and hand embroidery of self-color or in contrast are the ornaments for silk or thread stockings to be worn with low slippers. These slippers, most often of black satin, are so very low at the toes that the embroidery on the stockings begins just above the pointed toes, and extends halfway up to the knees. Figured stockings have lengthwise ribbed stripes 1/2 in. wide, in such contrasts as black with white, blue with pink, green with red, olive with ecru, and red with black. The heavier English cotton hosiery for morning wear is in gingham colors, striped around the leg.

Harper's Bazar, April 1882

Figure 1. Coiffure, and front and back of coiffure

Hairstyles

For the coiffure at the left of figure 1, part the hair from ear to ear and the back hair crosswise. Tie a small portion of the upper back hair, and fasten it in a knot on the crown. Divide the remainder of the back hair into two equal parts. Twist the strands loosely together. Arrange them in a loop falling on the neck, and caught with a tortoiseshell band. Comb back the front hair. Arrange the ends in two puffs and a short loop as illustrated.

For the coiffure in the middle and the right of the plate, divide the hair from ear to ear. Pin up the twisted back hair in a knot on the crown. Comb back the waved front hair, and fasten the ends to the knot. Then take a thick strand of hair and divide it in two parts. Twist these loosely together, and arrange them on the crown in a coronet. On the knot of natural hair fasten curls of various lengths. Let the short curls fall to the front and the long ones on the neck, as shown. The short hair on the forehead and neck is curled. A hairnet is drawn over the curls in front to keep them in place, if desired.

Harper's Bazar, April 1878

247

Figure 2. Four coiffures

The coiffure at the top of figure 2 is for an elderly lady. Part the hair from ear to ear and through the middle. Tie the back hair very high. Comb down the waved front hair over the ears and fasten the ends to the back hair. Divide the back hair into two parts. Braid it, and wind it around the head to form a coronet. The headdress is arranged on a stiff lace foundation. It consists of loops of claret-colored satin ribbon 1 1/4 in. wide set in a semicircle, and gathered white lace 2 1/2 in. wide. It is finished with a knot of claret-colored ribbon.

To arrange the coiffure on the left of the plate, part the hair from ear to ear. Tie the back hair. Curl the short front hair. Comb back the front and side hair. Fasten the ends to the back hair, which is arranged in braids as illustrated. Narrow light blue ribbon is wound around the head, and the ends concealed underneath the braids.

The coiffure at the right of the plate is for a young girl. Separate the side hair. Comb it back, and fasten it with side combs of tortoiseshell ornamented with gilt balls. Curl the short locks on the middle of the forehead. Comb back the front hair over the crown, and join it with the rest of the hair. Twist all the hair together, and arrange it in a coil. If the natural hair is insufficient, add a strand of false hair and wind it around the natural coil in the same manner. A tortoiseshell arrow is pushed through the knot.

The coiffure at the bottom of the plate is for a young girl. Comb back the side hair. Tie it together with the back hair, and arrange it in a bow as illustrated. The short front hair is curled. The rest is combed back, passed underneath the bow, and pinned across the middle of the bow, forming a knot. To complete the coiffure fasten a puff on the crown and a tortoiseshell comb with gilt balls. In back, fasten a waved strand falling on the neck.

Harper's Bazar, August 1878

Figure 3. Ball coiffure

Figure 4. Bridal coiffure

Harper's Bazar, January 1879

Figure 5. Chignon

The chignon in figure 5 is composed of two torsades. One is arranged in a diadem. The other forms a knot in the center, and is fastened with a comb ornamented with gold balls.

Figure 6. Chignon

For the chignon in figure 6, divide the hair lengthwise into two parts. Divide each part into two strands, which are twisted together. Pin up one of these twisted strands in a coil. Arrange the second strand around the coil. Fasten three tortoiseshell combs ornamented with gold balls into the chignon as illustrated.

Harper's Bazar, March 1879

Great variety and individuality of tastes is shown in the styles of hairdressing, yet three kinds of coiffure generally prevail. First is the chatelaine of two loops, which is most becoming to slender oval faces. This is made of two very thick braids, plaited each in three tresses, and, after being tied very high, allowed to fall in two loops behind. This is usually accompanied by a waved bang on the forehead. Some ladies find a straight bang, like a fringe, more easy to manage in the hot days of midsummer. A cluster of three to five small puffs, or two long loops of hair, are placed at the top of the chatelaine. To make this coiffure more dressy, a serpentine knot of hair is used instead of the puffs. This is made of a small switch of hair simply tied in a loose knot, and worn directly on top of the head. For variety's sake a bow of hair may be made of this switch, or a gay Alsatian ribbon bow may be used.

Ladies with full round faces use the high coiffure. The back hair is combed straight up from the nape of the neck. That about the temples is carried back to meet it. The whole is massed in two or three long puffs, or in a serpentine knot. Into this a comb, dagger, or trident of tortoiseshell, silver, or gold is thrust so that both ends show. The front hair shows the parting down to the forehead. It falls in crevecoeur half rings on the sides. Or it is parted on the left side, and thrown up in Pompadour fashion in the middle. Gold-headed pins are worn stuck in dark coiffures to the extent of six or eight. There are also many side combs worn. When these are of gold, with beads for heading, they are as often stuck in the front of dark puffs as on the sides. When of shell, they are worn on the sides to keep the hair back. A great deal of bandoline is used to paste down the curves and locks about the temples. Invisible nets are also very useful for both the front and the back hair.

The third fashion is the simple classic coiffure, with the Greek coil very low at the back. It is first braided into a plait of three tresses. This requires very little hair; but the head should be finely shaped, as this severe style discloses its entire outline. The front is plainly parted, and perhaps slightly

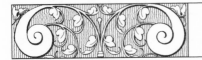 

waved. Or the hair just above the forehead and temples is allowed to fall in short curves. Ladies with blonde hair use dark tortoiseshell pins in star or marguerite shape, while silver ornaments are preferred by brunettes. Flowers, so elaborately worn on ball dresses, are very slightly represented in the coiffure. A small bouquet is stuck on one side, or perhaps on top just in front of the puffs, and a trifle toward the left. If the flowers are artificial, they are sometimes set in a lace rosette; but this must be done carefully, or it will look too much like a cap. Natural flowers are more worn than artificial ones.

Harper's Bazar, August 1879

front hair that is combed back, and the short loose front and side hair, with a curling iron. Pin a waved strand like that shown in figure 15 to the knot on the crown on each side, and let it fall on the shoulder. Shorter strands fall on the neck behind, and are likewise fastened to the knot. Comb out the curled front and side hair. Complete the coiffure with a spray of white roses and leaves, which is fastened on the right side as illustrated.

Figure 8. Coiffure

For the coiffure in figure 8, part the hair from ear to ear. Pin up the back hair in a knot. Then part the front hair in the middle. Comb it back over a crepe, and pin the ends to the knot. On this knot fasten a chignon made of long and short curls. A string of gilt wax beads, a spray of pink and yellow rosebuds, and loops of white satin ribbon complete the coiffure.

Figure 7. Coiffure

For the coiffure in figure 7, part the hair from ear to ear. Pin up the twisted back hair in a knot on the crown. Part the short front hair above the forehead. Comb the back part of the front hair back over a Valois crepe, and pin it to the knot. Curl the

Figure 9. Coiffure

For the coiffure in figure 9, part the hair from ear to ear. Pin up the back hair in a knot. Part the front hair in the middle. Comb it back over a crepe, and fasten it likewise. In the knot fasten a tortoiseshell comb, the middle teeth of which are removed, and to which are attached thick strands of hair. Divide all the hair into three parts. Arrange the hair at the right and left each in a three-strand plait. Carry the plait at the right to the left side and that at the left to the right side in the form of a diadem. Twist the middle part of the hair in a knot, and pin it up on the crown. A tortoiseshell comb completes the coiffure.

Figure 10. Coiffure

For the coiffure in figure 10, part the hair from ear to ear, and the front hair in the middle. Pin up the back hair in a knot. Again divide the front and side hair. Comb back the latter, and fasten the ends to the knot. Comb back the front hair over small crepes, and pin it to the knot. Curl the upper front hair. Next fasten into the knot a small tortoiseshell comb, to which are attached two full crimped strands. Then wind each strand, twist it double, and arrange it in a falling loop. Pin it on the knot, so as to conceal the knot and the ends of the strands. This coiffure is completed by a tortoiseshell comb with silver filigree balls.

Figure 11. Chignon

The chignon in figure 11 consists of long and short curls arranged as illustrated. It is designed to complete the coiffure when the natural hair is not very plentiful.

Figure 12. Outside of chignon

Figure 13. Inside of chignon

For the chignon in figures 12 and 13, divide the hair, which is fastened to a tortoiseshell comb, into three strands. The outer two are twisted and arranged in a falling loop. The middle strand is looped in a knot as illustrated. Pin the knot above the two loops. Carry the remainder of the strand to the right (see figure 13), then underneath the chignon to the outside. Fasten the ends in the knot. A comb with balls of filigree silver is fastened into the chignon.

Figure 14. Frizette

Figure 14 shows frizettes of curled hair arranged on a mull foundation. It is fastened under the natural hair above the forehead.

Figure 15. Waved hair

Figure 15 shows a long waved strand attached to a tortoiseshell pin. This may be arranged in one or several curls, at pleasure.

Figure 17. Coiffure

Figure 16. Finger puff

Figure 16 shows a finger puff attached to a tortoiseshell hairpin. A number of these finger puffs are fastened under the front or back hair to complete the coiffure.

Harper's Bazar, May 1880

Figure 18. Psyche knot of coiffure

Figure 19. Frizette for coiffure

In the coiffure in figure 17 part of the front hair falls in short curls on the forehead. The rest is waved and pinned back. The back hair is tied high on the crown, and arranged in the knot shown in figure 18. The hair is divided into two large strands of equal size and one smaller one. Each large strand is formed in a loop toward the side, and curled at the end. The small one is brought down for a crossing, and likewise curled. When the front hair is too thin to be becomingly arranged, it can be supplemented by the frizette shown in figure 19, which consists of curled hair mounted on a hair tulle foundation.

Long and thick natural hair can be dressed as shown in figure 20. The front hair is parted in the middle, combed back, and added to the back hair. This is then divided into three strands and plaited in one long braid. The loose end of the braid is brought up and looped through a loop of hair at the top, and secured with thick shell pins. The short front hair is curled on the forehead.

Figure 21. Coiffure

For figure 21 the hair is divided front and back. The front hair is parted in the middle, and the back hair is tied as high as possible. If the back hair is thick, the lower half of it is braided and looped up. If not a braided switch is pinned on. The lower part of the front hair is brought back first, and pinned over the braid. Then the waved upper hair is brought back. The ends of it and the rest of the back hair are arranged in puffs as illustrated. The short hair on the forehead is curled.

Harper's Bazar, December 1882

Figure 20. Coiffure

Figure 1. Headdress of forget-me-nots

Hair Ornaments and Headdresses

The headdress in figure 1 is composed of a wreath of forget-me-nots and blue faille ribbon 1 1/4 in. wide. This is wound on stiff lining, and finished with loops and ends of similar ribbon. It is fastened on a hairpin.

Figure 2. Hair bow

The bow in figure 2 is made of loops and ends of pink satin ribbon 1 1/4 in. wide, on which are fastened a hummingbird and Brazilian bugs. A long hairpin is fastened on the wrong side of the bow.

Figure 3. Matching brooch bow

The bow in figure 3 is made of loops of pink satin ribbon 1 1/4 in. wide and Brazilian beetles. It is furnished on the wrong side with a safety pin.

Harper's Bazar, April 1878

Figure 4. Blue reps ribbon hair bow

The bow in figure 4 is made from blue reps ribbon 2 1/2 in. wide. It is raveled out on one side, and laid in double box pleats on the other side. It is set on a stiff lace foundation. The remaining five petals each consist of three pieces of similar ribbon 3 1/4 in. long, which are pointed on one end. They are gathered on the other end from the middle to 7/8 in. from the points, drawn together, and arranged on the foundation as illustrated. The hair bow is finished with gold wheat, mother-of-pearl lilies of the valley, blue and white daisies, and metal grasses. A pin is set on the wrong side.

The hair bow in figure 5 is made of bell-shaped flowers and leaves of pink reps ribbon. The flowers are made of ribbon 2 1/2 in. wide. This is folded double diagonally and fastened to wire. Each leaf requires two pieces of ribbon 3 1/4 in. wide. These are sloped off on the ends and joined on the wrong side. Fasten the ribbons together in the middle, gather the double layer on the inner side, and fasten it to ribbon wire. The bow is trimmed besides with pink daisies, steel- and gold-colored grasses, pearl lilies of the valley, and a bronzed wheat. On the wrong side of the bow is fastened a hairpin.

Harper's Bazar, May 1878

Figure 5. Pink reps ribbon hair bow

Figure 6. Two Spanish combs and a favorite design

Figure 7. Three handsome combs

Combs are much narrower than those worn last season. The latest novelty consists of a tall, narrow design known as the Spanish comb (see figure 6). This has only two strong teeth, which can therefore be inserted with ease between the numerous puffs and braids that are now so fashionable. These combs are made of French shell. They are finished in a superior manner, the teeth being well cut so that they do not catch in the hair. The carvings are so perfected and rounded that it is difficult to distinguish some of them from real shell. Other styles are similar to those in vogue last season (see figure 7).

Demorest's Mirror of Fashions, August 1878

Figures 8 to 15 are all evening coiffures. Figure 8 consists of a cluster of moss rose buds, pink hyacinths, silver and green fern leaves, and red bellflowers, with calyxes formed of white satin beads, set on a bow of pink satin ribbon.

Figure 9. Cluster of flowers and ribbon

Figure 9 is made of pink and blue flowers, bunches of mignonette, and silver hop buds and leaves, fastened with a bow of blue satin ribbon.

Figure 8. Cluster of flowers and ribbon

Figure 10. Velvet, satin, and lace coiffure

Figure 10 is arranged on a stiff lace foundation of leaves of white satin and velvet and black lace 1 3/4 in. wide. It is trimmed with gold cord and white chenille tassels. The ends of the tassels are finished with gold beads.

Figure 11. Spray of flowers and ribbon

Figure 11 is composed of a cluster of pink, red, and garnet fuchsias and metal leaves and

grasses. It is finished with bunches of brown elastic stems tied with blue reps ribbon.

Figure 12. Coiffure of leaves and grasses

Figure 12 consists of a cluster of bronze grasses and dark brown velvet leaves in two shades, several of which are covered with gold dust. This is continued in a trailing branch finished with dark red rosebuds in two shades and brown velvet leaves. This coiffure is trimmed, besides, with tassels of gold bullion.

Figure 13. Coiffure of flowers and ribbon

Figure 13 is formed of silver lilies of the valley, pink rosebuds and brown leaves, and a bow of pink satin ribbon. A branch of leaves connects the coiffure with a spray of rosebuds and leaves tied with pink ribbon.

Figure 14. Wreath of flowers and ribbon

Figure 14 is composed of a wreath of pink auriculas and fern leaves, and of pink bellflowers turned downward, fastened at the back with loops and ends of pink satin ribbon.

Figure 15. Coiffure of flowers and leaves

Figure 15 consists of a coronet of brown velvet auriculas, velvet and satin leaves covered with gold dust, and leaves of fine gold wire and gilt elastic stems laid in loops. It is finished with a bronze beetle.

Harper's Bazar, February 1879

The combs on the left and right of figure 16 are in medium tints. The one in the middle is in dark tints. It is tall and pointed, and the pattern is very open.

Demorest's Mirror of Fashions, July 1879

Figure 16. Three combs

brown and olive green velvet and satin leaves, and oats arranged on elastic stems.

Figure 17. *Touffe* of geranium and oats

Figures 17 and 18 are evening coiffures. Figure 17 is composed of red geranium blossoms,

Figure 18. *Touffe* of roses and ribbon

Figure 18 is composed of pink roses with brown velvet buds, brownish leaves with metallic luster, and loops and ends of flowered brown satin ribbon 7/8 in. wide.

Harper's Bazar, December 1879

The set in figures 21 to 23 is composed of hair and corsage bouquets, and a long garland for the skirt of white roses and foliage. Two tiny glistening birds are secured in the skirt garland, and one a little larger in the corsage bouquet.

Figure 19. Evening coiffure of ribbon, flowers, and lace

Figure 22. Matching corsage bouquet

Figure 20. Evening coiffure of lace, ribbon, and strawberries

Harper's Bazar, January 1880

Figure 21. Hair garniture

Figure 23. Matching skirt garniture

Figure 24. Hair garniture

In figures 24 to 26 a similar set is shown. It is composed of scarlet poppies and buds in satin and velvet and velvet foliage. The sprays are tied with loops of claret chenille.

Figure 26. Matching skirt garniture

Figure 25. Matching corsage bouquet

Figure 27. Bouquet for hair

Figure 27, a bouquet for the hair, is a peony with buds and foliage in plush, with chenille stems.
Harper's Bazar, January 1882

263

Figure 1. Black chip bonnet—front and back

Bonnets and Hats

The black chip bonnet in figure 1 has a moderate crown and narrow turned-down brim. The brim is edged with brown and silver galloon. In front is an arrangement of loops of dark olive green and light platina-colored satin ribbon, which passes around the crown, and is finished with a loop and end. A metal agrafe is set on the loops. A spray of fine grasses and a dark red rose with leaves trim the bonnet, as shown by the back view. A tulle ruche forms the inside trimming.

Harper's Bazar, March 1878

Figure 2. White chip bonnet

The white chip bonnet in figure 2 has a moderate crown and narrow brim turned up in a revers on the left side. This is edged with a piping of blue and old-gold-colored satin and white wax beads. The brim is faced on the inside with shirred blue satin. Around the crown is wound blue satin and gauze of the same color, twisted together. A bow of blue satin ribbon and an olive green shaded bird-of-paradise complete the trimming. On the revers is a spray of forget-me-nots and grasses.

Harper's Bazar, May 1878

Figure 3. Leghorn straw hat

The leghorn hat in figure 3 is trimmed with brown silk gauze and fawn-colored satin ribbon, which are twisted as illustrated. On the left side are loops of brown and fawn-colored satin ribbon finished with long ends. Under the brim in back is a spray of yellow roses, hazelnuts, flowers, and metal grasses.

Harper's Bazar, July 1878

Figure 5. White India muslin garden hat

Figure 4. Brown chip Russian bonnet

Figure 4 shows a brown chip Russian bonnet. The brim is narrow on the left, turned up in a revers on the right, and is faced with shirred beige satin. Beige satin ribbon is wound around the crown, and is finished in back with a rosette composed of loops of similar ribbon. A half wreath of pink roses and mignonette completes the trimming. Strings of beige satin ribbon.

Harper's Bazar, May 1879

Figure 5 shows a white India muslin garden hat. The broad brim is composed of a double layer of muslin shirred at regular intervals on wire, and forming a heading on the outer edge. The crown of stiff lace is covered with double muslin, and joined with the brim. Folds of muslin edged on the sides with pleatings of the same form the trimming. They are held at the right side by a bronze agrafe. A spray of wild roses and wheatears trims the front a little to the right. Under the brim on the right side, toward the back, is a bow of pale pink satin ribbon and a wild rose with dark red velvet calyx.

Harper's Bazar, June 1879

 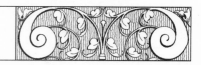

Figure 6. Beaver hat

The hat of cream-colored beaver shown in figure 6 has a high crown, and brim turned up on both sides. Around the crown are laid folds of brown velvet. On the right side is a brown wing and a hummingbird.

Harper's Bazar, January 1880

Figure 7. White chip bonnet

Figure 7 shows a white chip bonnet. The brim is lined with a shirring of ivory silk, finished with a double heading of ivory and black silk under the edge of the brim. A three-cornered plaid silk handkerchief, edged on one corner with round cord, is arranged on the crown in front as illustrated, and the ends tied carelessly behind. Blue cords and pompons of worsted and silk complete the trimming.

Harper's Bazar, July 1880

Figure 8. Two opera bonnets

The small cap-shaped frame of the bonnet on the left of figure 8 is covered with white satin merveilleux, and over this with pearl embroidery on net. Around the edge is a full binding of white satin merveilleux, which, turned inward, forms the facing. Two pink roses and a cluster of three white ostrich tips are set on the left side of the front. The strings, which are 4 in. wide, are of double white satin merveilleux. They are trimmed at the ends with pearl embroidery and fringe.

The bonnet on the right is of shell pink satin, shirred to form narrow full puffs, which are set diagonally on a small close-fitting frame. The front edge is finished with a full binding of garnet velvet, and the back with a double frill of satin. A cluster of dark red plush roses is set on the left side. The strings are made of garnet velvet.

Harper's Bazar, February 1882

Figure 9. Two bonnets

The bonnet on the left of figure 9 is made of Suez blue satin merveilleux. Two double pleated puffs of this material are arranged on the crown, and three similar narrower ones on the brim. Frills of Oriental lace, which is embroidered with light blue silk, are set between the puffs. The back is trimmed with shaded leaves and pendant grasses studded with steel beads. Strings of wide light blue satin ribbon.

The black Spanish lace bonnet on the right has a broad crown and a poke brim. The brim is faced with black velvet, which narrows in back. The crown is covered with full puffs of jetted Spanish net. Similar net is laid smoothly over black satin on the brim. A long scarf of ivory white crimped silk gauze is knotted on the middle of the front, and carried down to the sides, where it forms the strings. A cluster of ivory ostrich tips and an aigrette are on the left side.

Harper's Bazar, April 1882

Figure 10. Two felt hats

On the left of figure 10 is a ficelle gray felt hat. The brim is drooping on the right side, rolled high on the left, and bound and faced with brown ridged plush. Two rows of beaded brown lace are set along the drooping side with a brown velvet fold between them covering the straight edges. A bird with bluish green and brown plumage is at the front. A long brown ostrich plume extends above the revers on the left.

On the right is a Russian green felt hat. The high crown is trimmed with a wide bias scarf of Russian green velvet arranged in folds, and extending around the front and the right side. On the left are two fancy plumes laid one over the other. These are headed by a bird with flame-colored and brown plumage. The wide rolled brim is bound by two velvet folds.

Harper's Bazar, November 1882

Figure 1. Cap with veil

Caps

The cap in figure 1 is set on a stiff lace foundation 1 3/4 in. wide and 23 1/4 in. long. This is edged with wire, and closed in a ring. It is made of figured Swiss muslin underlaid with blue silk. It is furnished in back with a cape of the same materials, which is laid in pleats at the top, and sloped off on the bottom from the middle toward the sides. The cap is edged with Valenciennes lace 2 1/2 in. wide. Blue reps ribbon is wound around the crown, and covers the seam made by setting on the latter. On the right side is a bow of blue reps ribbon 6 7/8 in. wide. Underneath this is fastened a scarf of cream-colored silk gauze 22 1/2 in. wide and 80 in. long, draped as illustrated.

Harper's Bazar, August 1877

The cap in figure 2 is made of a piece of Swiss muslin (cut from its pattern piece), edged with lace 2 1/2 in. wide. This is arranged on a stiff lace foundation so that one corner falls toward the front and the other toward the back. The trimming consists of pink satin ribbon 1 in. wide.

Cut the crown from its pattern piece. Sew up the pleats as indicated on the pattern. Set the front edge into a double binding 7/8 in. wide. The ends of the binding project 2 in. beyond the crown. They are joined by a band 7/8 in. wide and 8 in. long. The band is covered with two rows of ribbon loops 2 in. wide. Similar ribbon is set plain on the binding, and the ends are tied in a bow in back. Arrange the Swiss muslin on the crown as indicated. Trim the cap with the bows.

Harper's Bazar, March 1878

271

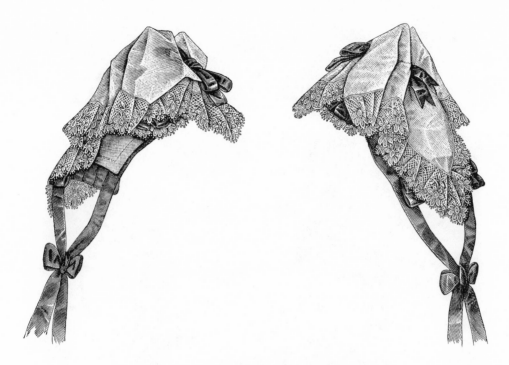

Figure 2. Swiss muslin cap–front and back

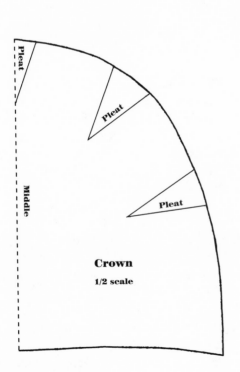

Crown

1/2 scale

Pleat

Pleat

Pleat

Middle

Swiss Muslin Piece

1/4 scale

Figure 3. Cap of crepe lisse and flowers

For the cap in figure 3, arrange of stiff lace a pointed brim 12 in. long. Edge it on both sides with box-pleated white satin ribbon 2 in. wide. The ends are tied in a knot in back. On the brim arrange a piece of crepe lisse, which is bordered with insertion 1 1/2 in. wide and Spanish lace 1 3/4 in. wide, as illustrated. Bows of white satin ribbon and a spray of violets complete the trimming.

Harper's Bazar, October 1878

Figure 4. Cap made of a Madras handkerchief

The cap in figure 4 is made of a figured Madras handkerchief. Fold down the edge on one side 2 7/8 in. deep on the wrong side. Then lay the handkerchief in pleats, turning downward. Arrange it as illustrated, so that one corner falls in the back, while the other corner is used for a knot.

For the bathing cap in figure 6, cut of oiled silk on the bias one piece from the pattern. Set a linen tape on the wrong side for a shirr as indicated on the pattern. Run in an elastic braid. Buttonhole stitch the crown on the back edge with red worsted. Pleat the front edge as indicated on the pattern. Trim it with pieces of oiled silk folded to form leaves and edged with buttonhole stitches.

Figure 5. Cap made of a batiste handkerchief

For the brim of the cap in figure 5, cut of stiff lace a piece 3/4 in. wide and 20 in. long. Join it on the ends. Sew a three-cornered pleat in the middle of the front. Bind the under edge with silk ribbon. On this brim arrange a batiste handkerchief 12 in. square, and bordered with a strip of Pompadour foulard 2 in. wide, as illustrated.

Harper's Bazar, May 1880

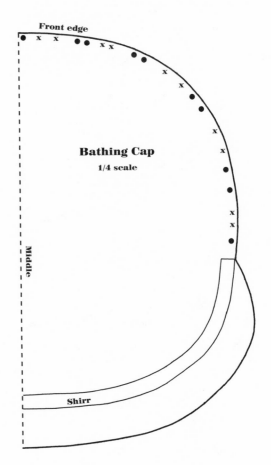

Front edge

Bathing Cap

1/4 scale

Middle

Shirr

Figure 6. Bathing cap trimmed with leaves

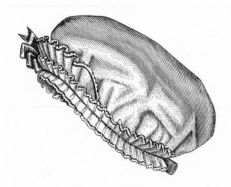

Figure 7. Bathing cap trimmed with ruffle

The cap in figure 7 is cut of oiled silk from the same pattern as the cap in figure 6. Observe that the lower line indicates the back edge. The cap is furnished with a shirr in back, through which are run blue worsted braids crosswise. The trimming consists of a box-pleated ruffle 2 in. wide. This is sloped off toward the ends and pinked on the upper edge. It is trimmed with blue soutache, a ruche of oiled silk 2 in. wide, trimmed in a similar manner, and a bow of blue ribbon 7/8 in. wide.

Harper's Bazar, July 1880

Figure 8. Mull and lace cap

The small turban-shaped frame of the cap in figure 8 consists of a rounded piece of stiff net that measures 10 in. across. This is adjusted by shallow pleats around the edge, wired, and bound with ribbon. It is surrounded by two rows of gathered lace. A folded band of mull is set around the side of the frame, the top of which is covered by a double cascade of lace. An Alsatian bow of figured satin ribbon is on the front.

Harper's Bazar, March 1882

Figure 9. Figured grenadine cap

The turban-shaped cap in figure 9 is of figured light blue silk grenadine, trimmed with white lace and satin ribbon bows. The frame consists of a stiff net brim 1 1/4 in. wide, the ends of which are joined in back. This is wired, and bound with satin ribbon. To complete the frame, a crown made of white foundation is joined to it. The latter is covered with grenadine, a pointed end hanging at the back. Over the rim two pleatings, one of lace and one of ribbon, are set. A second lace pleating covers the edge of the crown, and extends around the ends. A bow of satin ribbon and lace is on the front.

Harper's Bazar, June 1882

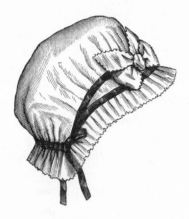

Figure 10. Bathing cap

The bathing cap in figure 10 is cut of oiled silk. Cut one whole piece each from the crown and the front. Pleat the crown as indicated. Join it to the front according to the corresponding figures. Cover the seam with blue or red alpaca braid. Edge the cap with a pleated frill of oiled silk 2 in. wide and notched at the outer edge. This is set on under a row of braid. Set a bow of the oiled silk on the front.

Harper's Bazar, July 1882

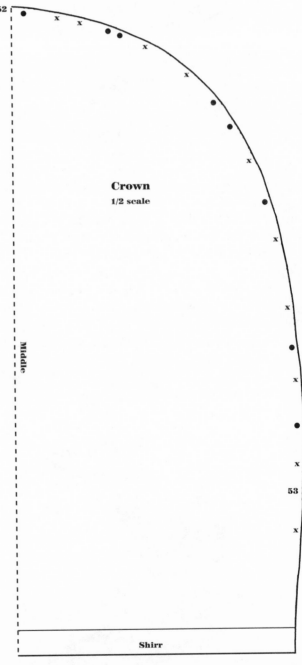

Crown
1/2 scale

52

53

Shirr

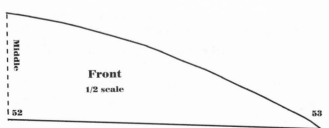

Front
1/2 scale

Middle

52

53

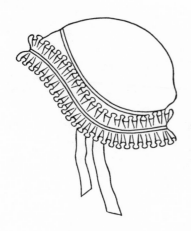

Figure 11. Nightcap

The nightcap in figure 11 is drafted for a medium size in centimeters.

Complete Guide to Ladies' Garment Cutting, 1883

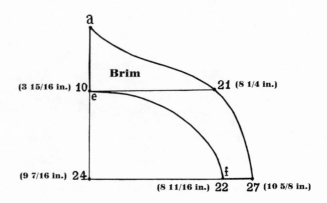

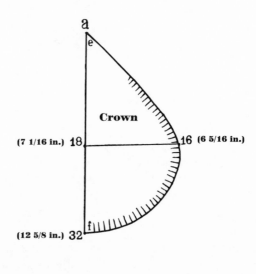

Figure 1. Opera hood

Hoods

Figure 1 shows an opera hood. For the brim cut of double black stiff lace one piece each from the front and the back patterns. Cut the band. Cut the scarf of black tulle. The scarf is embroidered in chain stitch with colored silk.

Join the brim front and back according to the corresponding figures. Wire the brim on the edge and along the joining seam. Join it from 50 to 51 with the band. Arrange the scarf on the band. The trimming consists of loops and ends of black reps ribbon 2 1/2 in. wide, with a colored satin edge. The ends of the scarf are held together in front with a spray of carnations and green leaves.

Harper's Bazar, March 1879

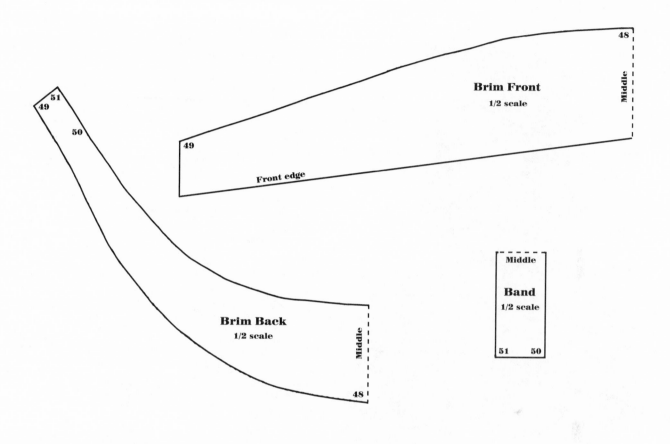

Brim Front
1/2 scale

48

Middle

49

Front edge

51
49
50

Brim Back
1/2 scale

Middle

48

Middle

Band
1/2 scale

51   50

Scarf
1/8 scale

Middle

Sew up the hood from 87 to 88. Turn in and run together the edges of the material and lining in front and at the slit. Roll the front to the outside along the narrow line.

Join the cape and hood according to the corresponding figures. Bind the seam with satin, and trim the hood with satin ribbon. Finally, work a thread loop on the right side at the point of the cape marked ✳. Sew the hook to correspond on the point of the hood.

Figure 2. Cashmere and satin hood

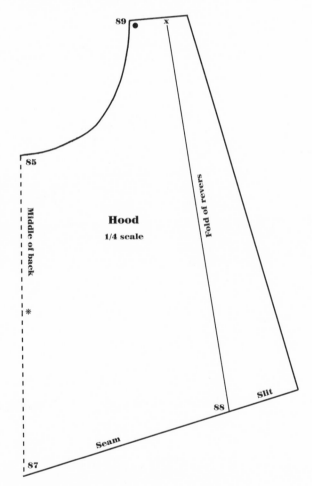

The hood in figure 2 is of white cashmere; it requires 1 1/8 yd. of material 26 in. wide. The hood is lined with Pompadour satin and trimmed with white satin ribbon bows. Strings of similar ribbon serve for closing. Cut of the material and lining two whole pieces from the cape, and one piece from the hood.

Take up the shoulder darts in the halves of the cape. Join the cape from 85 to 86. Cut it in tabs at the bottom, as indicated on the pattern. Edge the fronts and bottom with satin piping. Trim with white silk gimp 3/4 in. wide.

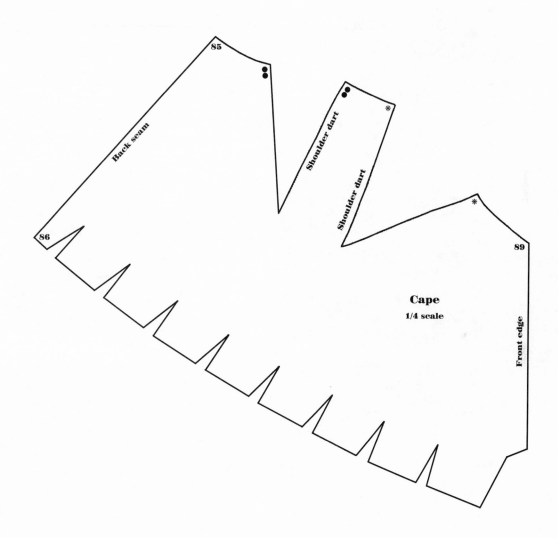

Figure 3. Matelassé hood

The hood in figure 3 requires 3/4 yd. of white woolen matelassé 27 in. wide. Cut one whole piece each from the back and front, and two pieces from the cape. Gather the front from 103 to ✳ at each side. Join it to the back from 103 to 104. Take up the shoulder darts in the cape. Pleat the hood. Join the back, front, and cape according to the corresponding figures. Trim the hood as illustrated with strips of swansdown. Furnish it with satin ribbon strings.

Harper's Bazar, November 1880

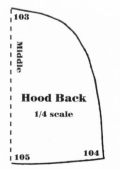

corner at the front, three pleats are laid toward the back. Strings of black satin ribbon 1 1/2 in. wide are fastened thereon on the wrong side. A box pleat 2 in. wide is folded on each side of the middle 14 in. from the corner in the back of the hood, and ornamented with a beetle similar to those in front.

Harper's Bazar, December 1880

Figure 4. Opera hood

Figure 4 shows an opera hood made of a silk handkerchief. A brim is cut of black stiff net. This is 12 in. long and 3 3/4 in. wide, sloped at one edge to form a point in the middle of the front. The brim is then wired and bound with taffeta ribbon.

A surah silk handkerchief 30 in. square, old gold with a black border, is attached on the brim. The handkerchief is lined with foundation, faced 4 in. deep with black satin on the two sides taken toward the front, and edged entirely around with side-pleated black lace. At the corner that forms the middle of the front, three pleats each 1 3/4 in. deep are turned toward the back as illustrated. Then the handkerchief is fastened on the brim.

A beetle is set at each side of the middle of the front, and a bow of black satin ribbon 2 in. wide behind the three pleats. Then, 7 in. from each lower

Figure 5. Gauze hood

283

Figure 5 shows a hood made of a piece of cream-colored gauze 44 in. long and 28 in. wide. It is surrounded with cream lace 4 in. wide. The hood is adjusted with pleats around the front edge and the neck. Bows of cream satin ribbon 2 in. wide and a spray of red chenille flowers compose the trimming.

Harper's Bazar, June 1881

The pattern for this bashlyk (figure 6) is drafted in centimeters for a medium size. Point *A* will be on the forehead when the hood is worn, point *B* under the chin. The long ends are usually carried to the back and fastened with a hook and loop at the back of the neck.

The bashlyk may be either seamed or cut on the fold from *A* to *B*. It is seamed from *A* to *F*. The opening for the face is from *C* to *B*.

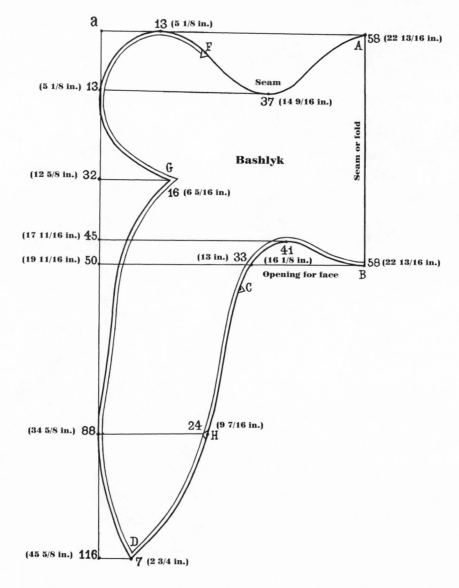

Figure 6. Bashlyk for evening

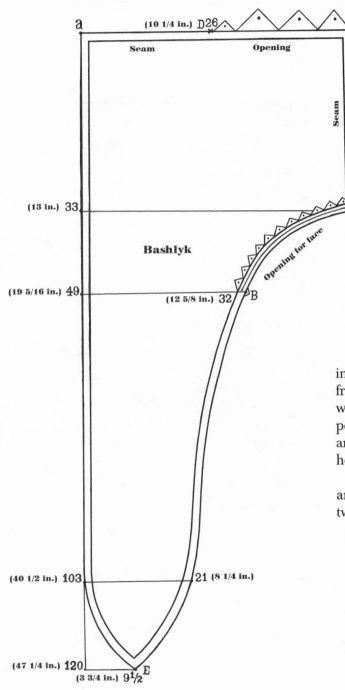

The pattern for this bashlyk (figure 7) is drafted in centimeters for all half breast circumferences from 40 to 50 cm (15 3/4 to 19 11/16 in.). Point *A* will be on the forehead when the hood is worn, point *B* under the chin. The long ends from *B* to *E* are usually carried to the back and fastened with a hook and loop at the back of the neck.

The bashlyk is open from *C* to *D*, tacked at *D*, and seamed from *D* to *a*. The four triangles between *C* and *D* signify trim that falls to the back.

Complete Guide to Ladies' Garment Cutting, 1883

Figure 7. Bashlyk for evening

Collars

The collar in figure 1 is made of black grosgrain and Swiss muslin lining. It is trimmed on the edge with black lace, headed by a border with colored flowers and leaves on a black satin ground. The neck is trimmed with a side-pleated ruffle of white crepe lisse laid in box pleats.

Harper's Bazar, March 1878

Figure 1. Grosgrain and lace collar

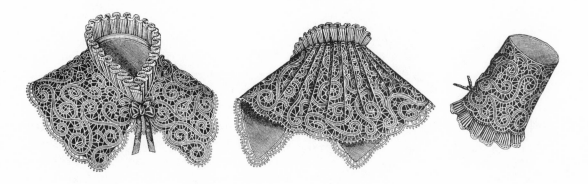

Figure 2. Velvet and lace collar and cuff

Figure 2 shows the front and back of the collar, and the cuff. To make the collar, cut of black velvet, net interlining, and lustring lining one piece from the collar pattern. Run the material and lining together on the edge. Cover the collar with lace, which is pleated on the back of the neck as illustrated. A side-pleated crepe lisse ruche is set in the neck. The cuffs are cut by the cuff pattern and made to match the collar.

Cuff
1/4 scale

Middle

286

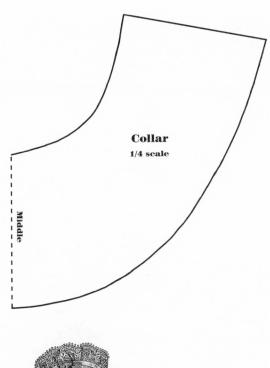

Collar
1/4 scale

Middle

Figure 4. Spanish lace fichu-collar

Figure 3. Linen, insertion, and lace collar and cuff

Figure 3 shows a plastron collar, and cuffs to be worn over the sleeves. They are composed of strips of linen embroidered in satin stitch with white embroidery cotton, and lace insertion 7/8 in. wide. The edge is trimmed with lace 1 3/4 in. wide.

Figure 4 shows a Spanish lace fichu-collar. The foundation consists of a strip of tulle 1 3/4 in. wide and 40 in. long. Into this are sewed three-cornered pleats 4 in. and 18 1/2 in. from each end, to obtain the shape illustrated. On this foundation is set insertion 1 3/4 in. wide. This is run with olive, pink, and blue silk floss. It is bordered on both sides with gathered Spanish lace 1 1/2 in. wide, run with similar silk. A box-pleated crepe lisse ruche is set in the neck. On the left side is a wild rose, mother-of-pearl lilies of the valley, and wild flowers. The fichu-collar is trimmed, besides, with flies of silver wire run with colored silk. The fichu-collar is finished in back with a bow of pale blue satin ribbon 2 in. wide.

Harper's Bazar, May 1878

Figure 5. Collar of Russian braid

Figure 5 gives the pattern and design for a collar in Russian braid. Transfer the design to linen. Run Russian braid along the outlines. The braid is then embroidered with guipure cord. The single figures are joined with twisted bars. For these stretch the thread going forward and wind it going back. Separate the embroidery from the foundation. Edge the collar with picot braid.

Collar

1/2 scale

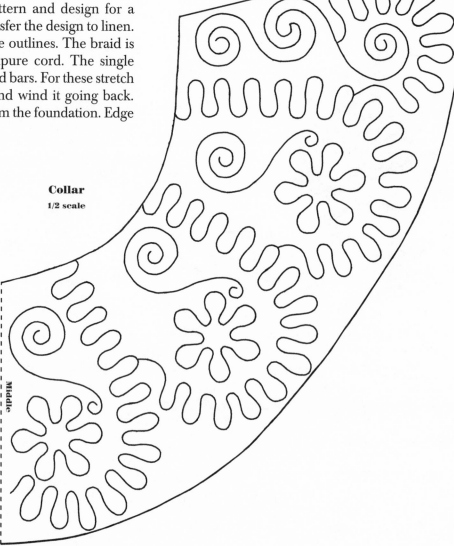

Middle

288

Figure 6. Collar in point lace embroidery

The collar in figures 6 and 7 is made of point lace braid of various widths, which is furnished on both sides with picots. Transfer the design to linen. Run the braid along the outlines. Pleat it in the corners and gather it in the curves. Join it with wheels and twisted bars of fine thread. For the bars, stretch the thread going forward and wind it going back. For the leaf figures in the center of the design, overcast the braid in buttonhole stitch with coarse thread. Ornament it with dots, which are likewise worked in buttonhole stitch.

Harper's Bazar, July 1878

Middle

Collar
1/2 scale

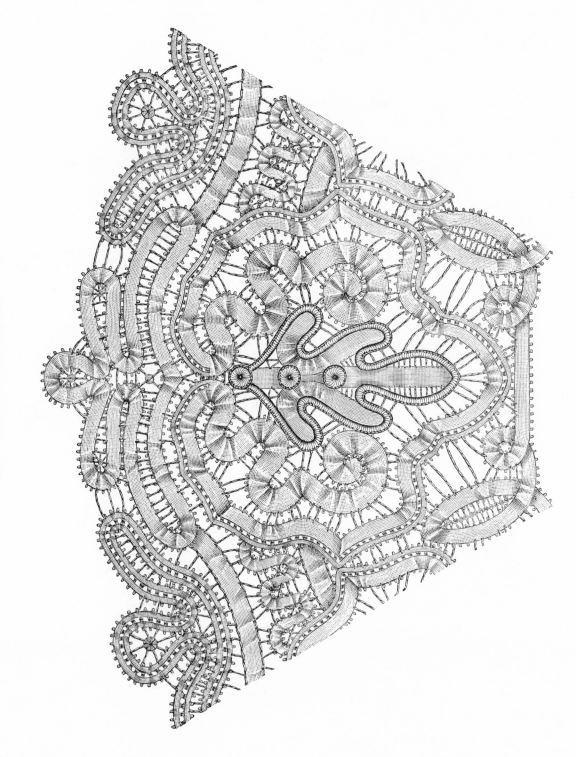

Figure 7. Middle of point lace collar–full size

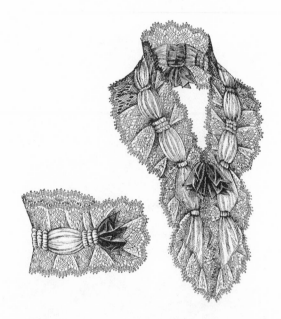

Figure 8. Muslin and lace fichu-collar and cuff

Figure 8 shows a fichu-collar of Swiss muslin and lace. The collar consists of a bias piece of muslin 6 7/8 in. wide and 40 in. long, which is sloped off on the ends. It is trimmed with Spanish lace 2 in. wide. Shirr the fichu at regular intervals as illustrated. Trim it with pale blue grosgrain ribbon 1 1/4 in. wide.

The cuffs are arranged to match the fichu. Each consists of a piece of Swiss muslin 6 7/8 in. wide and 14 in. long.

Harper's Bazar, August 1878

The collar and cuffs in figure 9 are made of white openwork muslin. They are trimmed with gathered lace.

Harper's Bazar, October 1878

Figure 10. Muslin, insertion, and lace fichu-collar

For the fichu-collar in figure 10, cut of Swiss muslin on the bias one piece 46 in. long and 16 in. wide. Round it off on the sides from the middle toward the ends, so that the ends are 8 7/8 in. wide. Fold the piece double lengthwise. Trim the fichu-collar with guipure insertion 3/4 in. wide and with side-pleated guipure lace 3/4 in. and 2 3/4 in. wide. Cut away the Swiss muslin underneath the insertion. Pleat the collar along the fold. Gather it closely 2 1/2 in. from the ends.

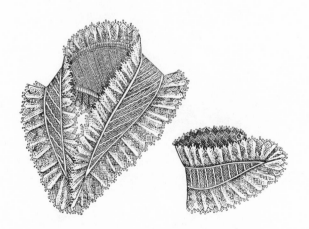

Figure 9. Openwork collar and cuff

Figure 11. Swiss muslin and lace collar with jabot

Figure 12. Darned net edging

The collar in figure 11 consists of a bias pleating of Swiss muslin. This is trimmed on the under edge with side-pleated lace 2 7/8 in. wide. The lace is worked on net with glazed cotton in the design shown by figure 12. The jabot is arranged of similar lace and Swiss muslin.

Harper's Bazar, November 1878

Figure 13. Lace and ribbon collar

For the collar in figure 13, cut of white mull a binding 7/8 in. wide and 17 in. long. On the bottom in the middle of the front fasten a three-cornered foundation of tulle. This should measure 3 3/4 in. on the bias edge, and be sloped out for the neck at the top. Edge this foundation with box-pleated Breton lace 3 1/2 in. wide, which is continued on the free under edge of the binding. On the upper edge of the binding is sewed side-pleated Breton lace 1 1/2 in. wide. Trim the collar with lace 1 1/4 in. and 2 in. wide, and loops and ends of blue satin ribbon with faille face. A bow of similar ribbon finishes the collar in back.

Figure 14. Mull, insertion, and lace fichu-collar and cuffs

The fichu-collar in figure 14 is made of a bias piece of mull 11 1/4 in. wide and 54 in. long. This is rounded off on the bottom from the middle of the back toward the ends. It is edged with lace 2 in. wide, and laid in pleats. Join the upper edge of this part with a collar composed of lace insertion 1 1/4 in. wide, and needlework insertion 1 in. wide, and edged with lace. The ends of the fichu-collar are tied in front. The cuffs, which are worn over the sleeves, are arranged in a similar manner, as illustrated.

Harper's Bazar, August 1879

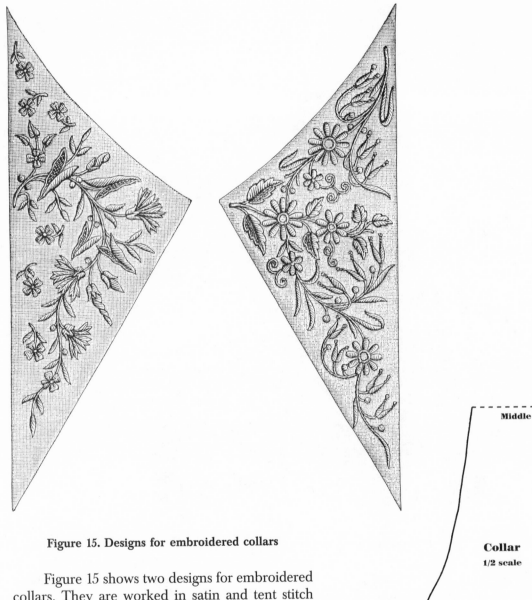

Figure 15. Designs for embroidered collars

Figure 15 shows two designs for embroidered collars. They are worked in satin and tent stitch with fine white embroidery cotton. The pattern piece given is suitable for either design.

Harper's Bazar, October 1879

Middle

Collar
1/2 scale

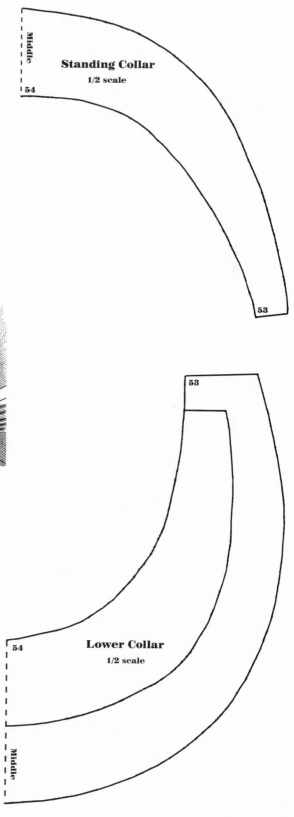

Standing Collar
1/2 scale

Middle
54

53

53

Lower Collar
1/2 scale

54

Middle

Figure 16. Linen and lace collar

To make the collar in figure 16, cut two pieces from the lower collar pattern. Cut one piece full size and the other only to the inner parallel line. Cut the standing collar of double linen from the pattern.

Face the lower parts of the collar 1/2 in. wide with a strip of linen. Join them at the neck with the standing collar. Cover the inner side of the standing collar with gathered ivory lace, which projects 7/8 in. beyond the upper edge, and then turn it to the outer side and tack it down. Edge the lower parts of the collar with lace 2 3/4 in. wide. Set a cravat bow of fine batiste and lace at the throat.

Harper's Bazar, October 1880

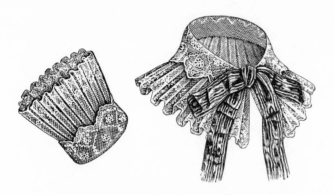

Figure 17. Lace collar and cuff

Figure 19. Embroidered collar and cuff

The collar and cuff in figure 19 are in ecru Venetian embroidery. Trace the design on fine ecru batiste, and baste this on ecru net. Run the design through both materials in coarse ecru cotton. Overcast the edges with finer embroidery cotton. Cut away the batiste from around the edges, leaving the net ground exposed. The collar and cuff are joined to a double batiste band.

Harper's Bazar, May 1882

The collar in figure 17 has a band or standing collar of double stiff white foundation long enough to fit the neck and 1 1/4 in. wide. The band is covered with shell pink watered ribbon, and a row of plain lace is laid smoothly over the ribbon. A row of wide box-pleated lace is joined to the lower edge of the band. The collar is fastened under a watered ribbon bow. The matching cuff is worn outside the sleeve. It is arranged in a corresponding manner on a band 10 in. in circumference.

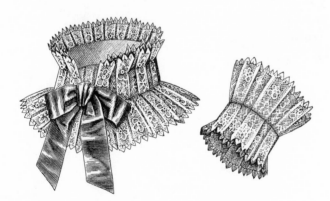

Figure 18. Lace collar and cuff

Figure 20. Lace fichu-collar

The foundation of the collar in figure 18 is a band similar to that for figure 17, but covered with light blue satin ribbon. Two rows of box-pleated lace about 3 in. wide are joined to it underneath the lower edge. One row projects from beneath it. The other is turned up over it on the outside, the pleats being tacked at the upper edge. A satin ribbon bow finishes the front.

Harper's Bazar, April 1882

For the fichu-collar in figure 20, about 4 1/4 yd. of Breton lace 4 in. wide are required. A round foundation collar, which is sloped narrower toward the front, is edged and covered with gathered lace. The rest is gathered, sewed together along the straight edge, and tacked into curves to form the ends. The collar is joined to a foundation band or standing collar. The ends of this cross in front, and it is covered with lace.

Figure 21. Mull and lace fichu-collar

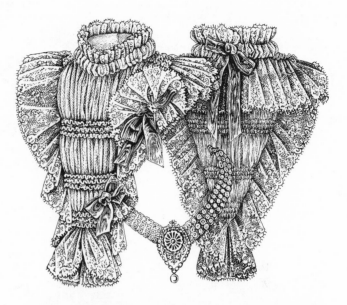

Figure 22. Front and back of fichu-collar, and a girdle

The fichu-collar in figure 21 is made of cream-colored crape mull and cream lace 4 in. wide. It has a foundation standing collar 1 1/4 in. wide. To the ends of this two strips of foundation 11 in. long and 3 in. wide are joined. The strips are sloped along the outer side to 1 in. wide at the top and bottom. They are covered with pieces of crape mull 14 in. wide, the right one 22 in. long, and the left one 12 in. Both are shirred at the top. The former is shirred at the bottom also, where it is edged with lace, and fastened over the end of the left. The collar and the outer edge of the mull are bordered with lace, that around the collar being pleated. A row of plain lace is also folded over the outside of the collar. A clasp at the throat, and a small knot and a clasp at the bottom, complete the collar.

Figure 22 shows a fichu-collar made of tulle and lace, and a silver girdle. The fichu-collar consists of a piece of white tulle about 28 in. square, the upper corners of which are rounded, and which is slanted on the sides to a width of 14 in. on the bottom. At the middle of the top a slit 8 in. long is cut. From the end of the slit to 3 in. from the top the neck is hollowed out. The edges of the upper part where it is not hollowed form the back edges of the collar and are hemmed. The tulle is edged with lace 3 1/2 in. wide, plain on the back and full on the front. It is shirred at intervals in clusters of three rows, each row of shirring forming an erect heading 1/2 in. deep. The full lace is tacked on the front as illustrated, and bows of pink moiré ribbon are fastened among the folds. At the neck the collar is joined to a foundation band. This is edged with a lace frill and covered with puffed tulle over pink ribbon.

The silver girdle is designed to be worn with a pointed bodice. It does not encircle the waist, but is secured by hooks at the ends to loops on the side seams, and hangs in front in medieval fashion. It is composed of small plaques of silvered metal connected by links, and a central rosette with a chain and pendant.

Harper's Bazar, June 1882

Figure 23. Crape and lace collar with jabot

The foundation for the round collar in figure 23 is a stiff net band. This is 1 1/2 in. wide and 18 in. long, and adjusted by a three-cornered pleat in the middle of the back. The foundation is covered with light blue crape. Pleated lace 4 in. wide is joined to the top, and folded down on the outside. A frill of narrower lace is around the top. The jabot consists of a lace-edged loop of folded crape and a slanting end edged with lace and pleated, which are joined under a crape knot.

Harper's Bazar, August 1882

Figure 1. Neck bow

Cravats and Neckties

Figure 1 shows a bow for the neck, arranged out of white muslin with lace ends. The design for the ends is given in figure 2. The design is worked with point lace braid, knotted, overcast, and buttonhole stitch. The bow is then finished off with a metal clasp and dropper.

Englishwoman's Domestic Magazine, February 1877

Figure 2. Design for neck bow

Figure 3. Cravat bow

The cravat bow in figure 3 is made of striped claret-colored silk gauze. This is edged on the bottom and on one side with white Spanish lace 1 1/4 in. wide. Arrange the gauze in a knot on a four-cornered stiff lace foundation. Set on the jabot-shaped part. A bunch of mandarin yellow flowers completes the trimming.

Harper's Bazar, August 1877

Figure 4. Satin ribbon necktie

The necktie in figure 4 is made of claret-colored satin ribbon 4 in. wide. This is edged with Valenciennes lace 2 7/8 in. wide. It is folded so that the lace lies uppermost, and is continued in spirals on the ends of the ribbon. The ends are fastened by a band of claret-colored ribbon held by a bronze buckle.

Figure 5 is composed of a lace cravat. The middle of this is laid in spirals and loops, and arranged on a white stiff lace foundation. The ends of the cravat are tacked together. Sprays of myrtle and seaweed, and colored butterflies of feathers, complete the cravat.

Harper's Bazar, April 1878

Figure 6. Satin and lace cravat

The cravat in figure 6 consists of two straight pieces of pink satin, each 3 1/2 in. long and 13 3/4 in. wide. These are edged on the bottom with white lace 3 1/2 in. wide, sloped off on the top toward one side, and pleated. Set these parts on a pleated satin band, and cover the seam with a broad metal ring. The ends of the band are joined in back.

Harper's Bazar, July 1878

Figure 5. Cravat bow

Figure 7. Design for cravat end

Figure 7 shows a cravat end in English guipure embroidery. It is worked with fine linen braid 1/4 in. wide, very fine guipure cord, and fine thread. To work the embroidery, transfer the design to linen. For the outlines of the design figures and the connecting bars, run on linen braid as illustrated. Fasten the ends of the braid carefully. Work the lace stitches inside the design figures with fine thread as illustrated. These consist of interlaced buttonhole stitches worked more or less close together. In working the close buttonhole stitch always overcast a double guipure cord.

After finishing the embroidery, work the connecting buttonhole stitch bars interspersed with picots, which consist of single loops. Overcast the edges of the braid, the guipure cord that borders the cravat, and the scallops with buttonhole stitches, inserting a piece of guipure cord at the same time.

In embroidering the scallops work in picots as illustrated. For the heavier lines in the design, cover the linen braid with cotton until the figure is raised sufficiently, and overcast the braid as illustrated.

Harper's Bazar, September 1878

Figure 8. Tulle and lace cravat bow

The cravat bow in figure 8 is composed of side-pleated loops of black silk tulle and ends of black guipure interwoven with gold thread. A brooch pin is set on the wrong side of the bow.

Harper's Bazar, October 1878

Figure 9. Handkerchief arranged as a cravat bow

The cravat bow in figure 9 is arranged from a light blue batiste handkerchief bordered with red silk stripes. Three corners of the handkerchief form ends, while the fourth is used for the knot. The bow is fastened on a stiff lace foundation as illustrated.

Harper's Bazar, December 1878

Figure 10. Satin and lace cravat

For the cravat in figure 10, cut of black satin a straight piece 1/2 yd. long and 10 in. wide, which is rounded off on the under end. In the middle of this part cut a slit 11 1/2 in. long from the top, and below this slit shirr it horizontally at regular intervals. Gather both halves of the upper part and fasten them on a binding 1 1/4 in. wide and the requisite length. The trimming is composed of white lace 2 1/2 in. wide, red corals, satin bows, and a spray of flowers.

Harper's Bazar, February 1879

Figure 11. Muslin and lace cravat bow

The bow in figure 11 is made of India muslin and Breton lace 2 in. wide. For one end of the bow this lace is set on in spirals on a stiff lace foundation 1 3/4 in. wide and 3 3/4 in. long. The muslin knot is finished with a bronze agrafe.

The bow in figure 13 is made on a stiff lace foundation 1 3/4 in. deep and 3 3/4 in. wide. On this is set pale blue ribbon shot with silver and embroidered with flowers, and white lace 2 in. wide, on which are embroidered flowers with filling silk of various colors.

Harper's Bazar, April 1879

Figure 12. Crepe de chine and lace cravat bow

To make the bow in figure 12, cut a foundation of stiff lace 1 3/4 in. wide and 3 3/4 in. long. On this set a piece of blue crepe de chine edged with lace 1 3/4 in. wide and loops of the same material, as illustrated. The knot is formed of crepe de chine closely pleated. Clusters of forget-me-nots joined with long silver stems complete the cravat bow.

Figure 14. Cravat in filigree point

Figure 14 shows a cravat in peacock blue satin. The ends are embroidered with fine silk in several colors and real gold thread. Figure 15 shows the design full size. Transfer this to linen, which is underlaid with stiff paper.

Begin the work in the center of the middle leaf, which is filled in filigree work. Lay on a double gold thread, the end of which is tacked to the upper point of the openwork leaf. On this foundation work six buttonhole stitches with golden brown silk, then work the picots as illustrated. In working each picot carry the working thread through the preceding one. On the opposite side of the figure fasten the picots with buttonhole stitches. On this round work over two gold threads one round with light brown silk. Next follow two rounds worked with reseda silk. In the last round lay the upper gold thread in picots as shown. The remaining lancet-shaped leaves are worked in a similar manner. The

Figure 13. Ribbon and lace cravat bow

cloverleaf figures are worked with fine red silk in two shades as illustrated. For the stems, the middle portion of which is formed of picots of a single gold thread, use wood brown and dark green silk.

The finished ends are set on satin ribbon of suitable width.

Harper's Bazar, May 1879

Figure 15. Cravat end

Figure 16. Embroidered necktie

Figure 17. Embroidery design

The necktie in figure 16 is made of a piece of white batiste 42 1/2 in. long and 4 1/2 in. wide. This is embroidered on the ends, and hemmed narrow on the sides. The embroidery is worked as shown by figure 17, with red, blue, and yellow cotton, in satin and tent stitch. The buttonhole stitch scallops are worked alternately with red and blue cotton.

Harper's Bazar, November 1879

Figure 19. Blue brocade necktie

The necktie in figure 19 is made of blue brocade shot with silver threads. It requires a piece of material 40 in. long and 4 in. wide. This is cut in two points on each end, and faced there with light blue faille. Edge the ends with silver cord, and turn them up on the outside in revers. Shirr the brocade 1 in. above the hollow of the point. Border the ends with gathered white lace 4 in. wide.

Harper's Bazar, February 1880

Figure 18. Black satin necktie

The necktie in figure 18 is made of a straight piece of black satin 40 in. long and 4 7/8 in. wide. This is folded on the wrong side on the ends to form a point. Shirr the satin 4 1/2 in. from the point twice at intervals of 1/2 in. Then after an interval of 1 1/4 in. shirr it four times at intervals of 1/2 in. each. Fold the remainder of the satin to a width of 1 7/8 in. Trim the ends with gathered black lace and a spray of flowers.

Figure 20. Satin cravat

The cravat in figure 20 requires a piece of gendarme blue satin 20 in. long and 4 7/8 in. wide, and a piece of white satin of the same size. Join both pieces at one end. Gather the cravat in the middle of the back five times at intervals of 1/2 in. each. Cut the ends pointed. Shirr the cravat five times 14 7/8 in. from each end. Edge the ends with gold lace 3 3/4 in. wide. Besides this, apply a figure of gold lace and edge it with garnet beads. Cut away the material underneath these figures.

Harper's Bazar, March 1880

Figure 21. Cravat bow with Spanish embroidery

Figure 22. Design for embroidery

The cravat bow in figure 21 is made of navy blue velvet ribbon with satin face, 4 in. wide. One of the loops and the ends are trimmed with pieces of Spanish embroidery. The embroidery is worked on fine ecru linen with real gold thread and fine sewing silk in dull tints.

Transfer the design to the material. Edge the outlines of all the design figures with two gold threads, which are fastened on the foundation with long buttonhole stitches of colored silk. In doing this either lay the outer gold thread in loops (as illustrated), forming picots, which are fastened by buttonhole stitches on the opposite figure, or draw it through one of the loops on the opposite figure. For the arabesque figures use reseda, and for the palms blue silk in two shades. Work the corner figures with rose, and the edge with blue silk. The design figures are filled with satin stitch and point Russe with silk of a color to correspond with that of the edge, as illustrated.

Harper's Bazar, July 1880

For the cravat bow in figure 23, a back or foundation 6 1/2 in. long and 2 in. wide is cut of white stiff net and sloped to 1 in. wide at the bottom. On this are arranged, as shown, a bow of pleated lace 2 1/2 in. wide, pleated strips and a crossing of crepe lisse, and red silk cord and tassels.

Harper's Bazar, April 1881

Figure 24. Cravat bow of lace and flowers

The cravat bow in figure 24 requires a stiff net back 1 1/2 in. wide and 9 in. long. On this Breton lace 3 in. wide is arranged in irregular curves and shells. Clusters of rosebuds are fastened here and there among the folds of lace.

Figure 23. Crepe lisse and lace cravat bow

Figure 25. Gauze cravat bow

For the cravat in figure 25, two strips of cream-colored gauze edged with Oriental lace are pleated and mounted on a stiff net back under a gauze knot. A safety pin on the back serves to fasten it on.

Harper's Bazar, March 1882

For the neckband of the cravat in figure 26, a bias strip of white mull is folded around a double foundation band 1 1/2 in. wide, and arranged in soft folds on the outside of it. The cravat bow is mounted on a narrow foundation back and attached to the right end of the band. It consists of strips of white mull 10 in. wide, which are trimmed with Venetian lace, and arranged in loops and knots as illustrated.

Figure 27. Grenadine and lace cravat

The band of the cravat in figure 27 is made of cream-colored silk grenadine. A wide bias strip is laid around a foundation band, and folded on the outside as illustrated. The bow consists of two cream lace ends 24 in. long and 8 in. wide, formed by two rows of lace run together at the straight edge. The ends are gathered at the top, fastened inside the right end of the band, and tied as illustrated.

Harper's Bazar, April 1882

Figure 26. Mull and lace cravat

Figure 1. Tulle and lace scarf

Fichus and Scarves

The scarf in figure 1 is draped about the shoulders, and loosely tied in front as illustrated. It requires a piece of cream white crepe tulle 3 5/8 yd. long and 29 in. wide. The scarf is turned over 14 1/2 in. at the top. It is edged all round with point d'Alençon lace 2 1/4 in. wide. At the middle of the back, and 6 1/2 in. on either side of it, are clusters of shirring.

These extend from the fold at the top to 8 in. below it. Each cluster consists of five closely drawn rows. These are tacked on the wrong side to a piece of yellow satin ribbon 1 1/4 in. wide and 16 in. long. This serves as a stay to the shirring, and falls below the scarf.

Figure 2. Darned net fichu

Fichu
1/4 scale

Middle of back

The fichu in figure 2 is made of white Brussels net; a pattern of the fichu is given. It is ornamented with a border worked with fine linen floss as shown by figure 3. The single figures of the design, as also the foundation figures and sprays, are outlined with coarse linen thread. Fine thread is used for the lace stitches and for the ornamentation in the eyelet holes, which are worked in overcast stitch. The outer edge is finished with buttonhole stitch scallops.

Harper's Bazar, October 1880

Figure 3. Section of design for fichu

Figure 4. Tulle fichu

The fichu in figure 4 is made of a strip of dot-ted tulle 48 in. long and 12 in. wide. This is sloped on both sides from the middle to a point at each end. The fichu is edged all around with lace 2 in. wide, folded over to half the width, and shirred at the middle of the back. When worn the fichu is knotted loosely in front and ornamented with a clus-ter of flowers.

Harper's Bazar, November 1880

Figure 5. Crape and lace fichu

For the fichu in figure 5, a bias strip of ivory white crape 1/2 yd. wide and 1 1/4 yd. long is re-quired. The strip is pointed at one end and cut straight at the other. It is edged with lace 4 in. wide across the pointed end and along the short side edge to 14 in. from the straight end. This scarf is arranged in four upturned folds, which are tacked in place. At the straight end the folds are joined to a piece of foundation 3 in. wide and 5 in. long. This together with the scarf end is turned under, forming a loop.

Figure 6. India mull and lace fichu

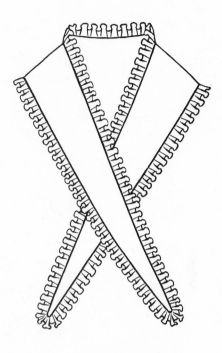

Figure 7. Fichu

The fichu in figure 7 is drafted for a medium size in centimeters.

The fichu in figure 6 is made of a bias piece of cream-colored India mull. This is 1/2 yd. wide and 1 1/4 yd. long, and sloped to a point at the ends. It is surrounded with cream lace. It is folded double, arranged in upturned folds that are tacked in place, and fastened with a lace pin in front as illustrated.

Harper's Bazar, October 1882

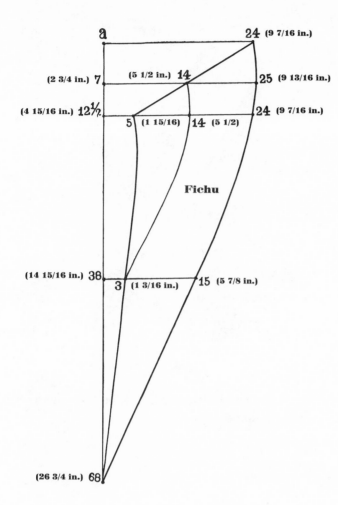

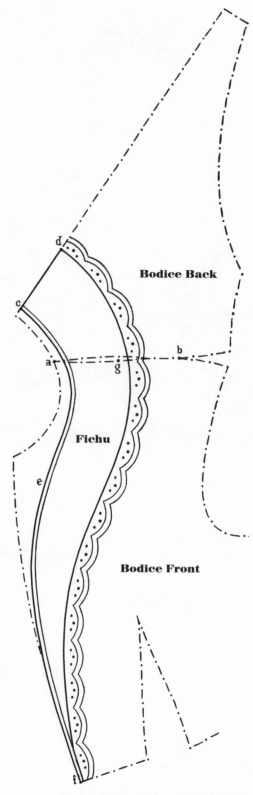

The fichu in figure 8 is drafted using the plain bodice pattern, which is indicated by a dotted and dashed line. The front and back of the bodice are placed at *a* and *b*. The width of the fichu at *g, d,* and *e* may be in any style desired.

Complete Guide to Ladies' Garment Cutting, 1883

Figure 8. Shawl-shaped fichu

Figure 1. Muslin and linen kitchen aprons

Aprons

The apron on the left of figure 1 is made of fine muslin. It is trimmed with folds of the material piped with blue zephyr and braided with blue soutache. It is buttoned on one side, on the shoulder and under the arm, and is trimmed with buttons on the other side. It has a heart-shaped bodice both back and front. Sew up the front, side piece, and back according to the corresponding figures.

315

The right of figure 1 shows an apron of gray linen with a bodice, which finishes with shoulder straps. These are crossed in back and buttoned on the belt. The trimming consists of a side-pleated ruffle headed with a bias strip of linen and buttons.

Harper's Bazar, September 1878

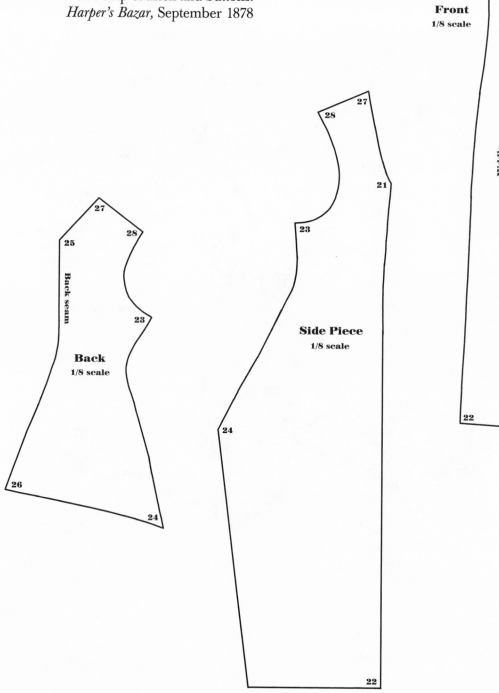

Figure 2. Linen apron

Figure 2 shows a gray linen apron. Pleat the pocket and sew it onto the skirt. Join the bodice with the skirt according to the corresponding figures. The trimming consists of bias strips of white batiste 3/4 in. and 1 in. wide. These are stitched with blue cotton, needlework edging 1/2 in. wide, and a bow of linen and batiste.

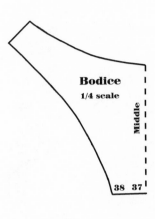

Bodice
1/4 scale
Middle
38 37

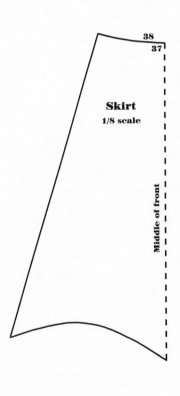

38
37
Skirt
1/8 scale
Middle of front

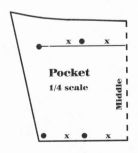

Pocket
1/4 scale
Middle

Figure 3. Embroidered batiste and lace apron

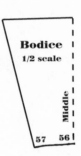

Bodice
1/2 scale

Middle

57   56

57
56

Skirt
1/8 scale

Middle of front

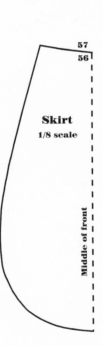

To make the apron in figure 3, cut of batiste one piece each from the skirt and bodice patterns. Trim the skirt in chain stitch embroidery with green and blue cotton. Edge it with white lace 2 1/2 in. wide, which is embroidered with blue cotton, and headed with a bias strip of batiste 3/8 in. wide. Edge the bodice with lace at the top. Sew pieces of similar lace 8 7/8 in. wide on the sides. Join the bodice with the skirt according to the corresponding figures. Furnish the apron with a belt. This is joined with batiste strings 2 in. wide and 21 in. long, trimmed with lace. These are tied in a bow in back.

Harper's Bazar, November 1878

Figure 5. Italian apron

Figure 4. Handkerchief apron

The apron in figure 4 is made of a dark blue cotton handkerchief, bordered 4 1/2 in. wide with red striped with white. It is arranged as illustrated.

Harper's Bazar, January 1881

The apron in figure 5 is made of fine white linen, cut lengthwise, 3/4 yd. long and 24 in. wide, and hemmed on three sides. The upper edge is sloped off about 1 in. toward the middle. It is sewed plainly to a straight waistband, the corners being left loose about 5 in., and cut off about 1/8 yd. from the top. The strings are sewed to the waistband at the sides, and may be of double-faced satin ribbon of any desired color. The trimming is colored embroidery upon the material, in bands 3 in. wide, and at the distance of 1 in. for the lowest row, 1 1/4 yd. for the upper row, from the lower edge. Smyrna lace, embroidered in colors, is sewed on just below the embroidery.

Demorest's Mirror of Fashions, January 1881

Figure 1. Necklace of silver beads

Jewelry

The necklace in figure 1 is made of graduated strings of small silver beads. These are held by a clasp on each side, and form short even rows in back.

Harper's Bazar, March 1877

The exquisite Italian filigree silver jewelry is exceedingly popular. It is unusually well adapted to light evening toilettes worn by young ladies. The brooch in figure 2 represents a butterfly with outstretched wings, while for the earrings dragonflies are selected.

Demorest's Mirror of Fashions, January 1878

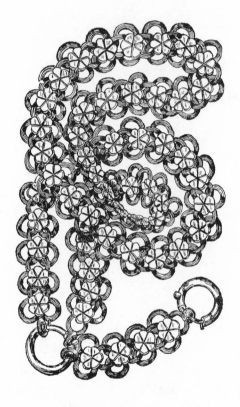

Figure 3. Rolled gold necklace–full size

Figure 3 shows a necklace of rolled gold, designed in a new style, links of gold connecting small flowers of burnished gold.

Demorest's Mirror of Fashions, February 1878

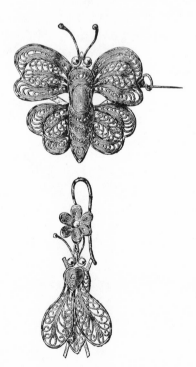

Figure 2. Silver filigree brooch and earring–full size

Figure 4. Imitation point necklace

Figure 5. Medallion—full size

The necklace in figure 4 is composed of single roses in darned net. These are joined in front by three rosettes worked in a similar manner. Transfer the outlines of all the roses and rosettes to linen, observing figure 5, which shows the rose in the center, and figures 4 and 6. Baste Brussels net on the linen.

Run the outlines with fine guipure cord, which is fastened with long half-polka stitches of fine thread. Darn the foundation of the single leaves with similar thread, going back and forth. The veins are run with guipure cord overcast on the foundation with half-polka stitches of fine thread. The lace stitches and wheels are worked with very fine thread as illustrated.

Having finished all the design figures, cut away the projecting net foundation all around, and arrange the necklace as illustrated.

Figure 6. Detail of medallion

Figure 7. Velvet and steel necklace

The necklace in figure 7 is composed of a piece of black velvet ribbon 1 in. wide and 60 in. long. On the middle of this is fastened a tab of black velvet 1 1/2 in. wide and 5 1/4 in. long. The lower end of the tab is pointed, and finished with a steel rosette. Plaques of steel are also set on the necklace.

Harper's Bazar, March 1878

Figure 8. Scarf pin and earrings

The set of scarf pin and earrings in figure 8 is of rolled gold. The body is of dead gold, tastefully ornamented with filigree work, and the raised bars and balls are burnished.

Figure 9. Brooch and earring

The set of brooch and earrings in figure 9 is of rolled gold. It is ornamented with triangles in polished gold filigree at the edges, and raised bars set with turquoise.

Figure 10. Brooch and earring

The set of brooch and earrings in figure 10 is of rolled gold. The body is of dead gold ornamented with filigree. The rings and balls are in polished gold.

Demorest's Mirror of Fashions, June 1878

Figure 11. Four bracelets

The bracelet at the top of figure 11 is in rolled gold, 5/8 in. wide. The body is encrusted, and the design on both sides is engraved, and the front enriched with black enamel. Sold as a pair.

The bracelet on the left is in rolled gold, 1/2 in. wide. It is Etruscan gold entirely satin finished, with scroll on the front in burnished gold. Sold as a pair.

The bracelet on the bottom is in rolled gold, 1 in. wide. The body is encrusted, and beautifully engraved. The design on both sides is alike, and highly burnished. Sold as a pair.

The bracelet on the right is in rolled gold, 5/8 in. wide. It is Etruscan gold entirely satin finished, except for a raised ornament in front, consisting of four rings, linked together, in polished gold. Sold as a pair.

Demorest's Mirror of Fashions, January 1879

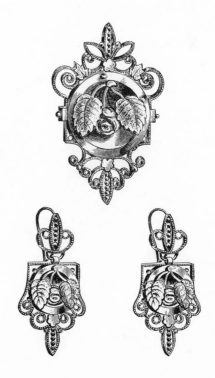

Figure 12. Set of brooch and earrings

Figure 12 shows a brooch and earrings in rolled gold. The body is in burnished gold, and is concave. A rose of real coral and two chased leaves in colored gold are placed in the hollow. The scrollwork at the top and bottom is in filigree Etruscan gold, ornamented with small plates of polished gold.

Demorest's Mirror of Fashions, February 1879

Figure 15. Silk earrings and medallion

Figure 13. Jet necklace

Figure 16. Ear wires and back of medallion

The necklace in figure 13 consists of a jet chain with pendants.

Harper's Bazar, February 1879

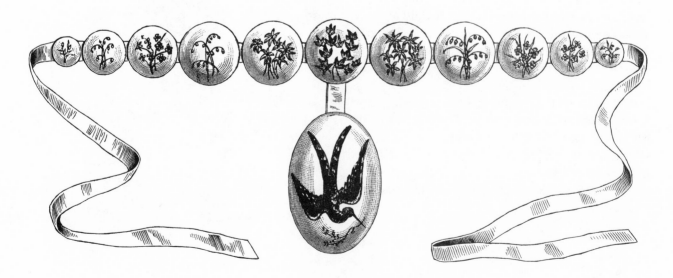

Figure 14. Silk necklace

A new kind of ornament is jewelry made of silk-covered button molds, on which some little floral design is painted. The necklace in figure 14 is the most simple. The materials required are, first, eleven button molds. Five should be about 1 1/4 in. in diameter, two about 1 in., two 3/4 in., and two 1/2 in. It is not necessary to have them of exactly these dimensions, but the grading must be in about that relative proportion. The oval for the center is made of wood, cork, or pasteboard. Also required are some scraps of silk—the exact amount used is 1/8 yd.—and 1 1/2 yd. of narrow ribbon, not over 1/2 in. wide. The best silk on which to paint is a closely woven one without any cord. Satin never looks perfectly smooth, and presents a poor surface for painting.

Cover the molds neatly. To avoid a bunch in back, be careful not to use too large pieces of silk. When covered, sew them on the ribbon, the five larger ones in the middle, the others grading off on each side. Cover the oval very smoothly, and finish the back by covering a smaller oval of stiff paper with silk, and sewing it on the back. But first insert the little bit of ribbon by which the oval is attached to the necklace. Fasten the oval to the necklace by sewing the other end of the ribbon under the center button.

The set of earrings and medallion shown in figure 15 is somewhat more difficult of construction. It requires three button molds, one 1 1/2 in. in diameter and two 1/2 in. Also required are 1/4 yd. of gold wire, which can be bought at any jeweler's, and some bits of silk—about 1/16 yd. is ample. For each earring take 3 in. of the wire and bend into a hook, with a loop at one end, the extremity of the wire projecting the loop being at right angles to the hook. (See the two views in figure 16.) Press the sharp point of the wire into the back of the mold. It is sometimes necessary to bore a little hole first. Then cover with silk, taking care to sew the wire loop to the silk. Finish the back like the oval for the necklace. The pendant is made in the same way, except the wire must be twisted into a ring instead of a hook.

The decorative part requires rather more skill, but ladies who have any taste for art will find little difficulty in copying some pretty design of birds or flowers from gift cards. Paint with ordinary watercolors, using a little gum in the water. Lighten the colors with Chinese white.

Figure 17. Set of brooch and earrings

Figure 17 shows a set of brooch and earrings of rolled gold, set with real cameos. (Amethysts may be furnished instead.) The body is in Etruscan gold. It is enriched with filigree and small plaques and rims of polished gold, while the cameos are mounted in highly burnished gold.

Demorest's Mirror of Fashions, May 1879

Figure 18. Two bracelets

The bracelet on the top of figure 18 is in rolled gold, 3/4 in. wide. The body is in Etruscan gold, satin finished. The ornament in front produces the effect of two oblong flat rings encircling the band, and united by a horizontal bar. Both bar and rings are richly decorated with filigree and small polished plaques. Delicate filigree extends along the entire front, and is finished with a perpendicular bar at each end, embellished like the rings. Sold as a pair.

The bracelet on the bottom is in rolled gold, 3/4 in. wide. The body is in Etruscan gold, having a narrow, raised, burnished band on each edge. The front is ornamented with delicate filigree work, enriched with small plaques of polished gold. This encloses a raised floral design of the reed known as cattail, the leaves in light green gold and the heads in red gold. Sold as a pair.

The bracelet on the bottom is in rolled gold, 7/8 in. wide. The body is in Etruscan gold with embossed edges. In front is a raised bar of frosted gold terminating with scrollwork. In the center and at each end is a medallion of polished gold, on which is a raised concave ornament of filigree, with a highly polished ball in the interior. Sold as a pair.

Figure 20. Two bracelets

The bracelet on the top of figure 20 is in rolled gold, 1/2 in. wide. It is in Roman gold, ornamented with filigree work and small plaques of polished gold. On the front is placed, in relief, a branch of lilies of the valley, with silver bells, gold stems, and colored gold leaves. Sold as a pair.

The bracelet on the bottom is in rolled gold, 3/8 in. wide. The band is delicately chased on a frosted surface, and the edges highly burnished. In front is a narrow raised strap of black enamel and gold, which has the effect of being twisted in the middle around a solid oblong, hexagonal ornament, and the ends passed under bars. On each side of the strap, and curved like it, are slender wires, finished with small knobs. The ornament, wires, and bars are all of highly polished gold. Sold as a pair.

Figure 19. Two bracelets

The massive bracelet on the top of figure 19 is in rolled gold, 1 in. wide. The body is in Etruscan gold, satin finished, enriched with delicate filigree. The center of the front has a raised ornament embellished with two carved rows of polished gold plaques, placed together in reversed position, and the spaces between filled in with filigree. Sold as a pair.

Figure 21. Scarf pin–full size

The scarf pin in figure 21 is of rolled gold. The body is in dead yellow gold, and is ornamented with filigree, and two bars of polished red gold, separated by small balls of dead gold. The center is occupied by a spray of lily of the valley, with dead gold stem, leaves in green frosted gold, and flowers in light-colored gold.

Demorest's Mirror of Fashions, November 1879

Figure 22. Cameo pendant–full size

The pendant in figure 22 is in rolled gold. The cameo is a white head on a black ground. This pendant can be furnished instead with a white head on a pink ground.

Figure 23. Rolled gold and coral pendant–full size

Figure 23 shows a medallion in rolled gold, satin finished, and enriched with fine scrollwork in filigree, and two raised ornaments in polished gold. The center of the front is occupied by a real coral rose between two leaves in frosted green gold. There is a place at the back for a picture. The pendant has a pin so that it may serve as a brooch if desired.

Demorest's Mirror of Fashions, December 1879

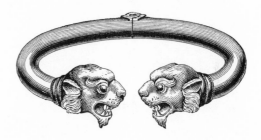

Figure 24. Gold bracelet

Figure 24 shows an elegant solid gold bracelet in colored or Etruscan gold, finished with richly chased heads.

Figure 25. Gold bracelet

Figure 25 shows a solid gold bracelet in colored or Etruscan gold, with delicate tracery in relief.

Figure 26. Bangle ring

Figure 26 shows a dainty bangle ring of solid gold. The two ends are lapped about 1/2 in., like a spiral. They are set with a single real pearl on each end, and a pink conch-shell pearl in the center.

Demorest's Mirror of Fashions, February 1881

Figure 28 shows a lace pin of rolled Roman gold. The center is a ball of burnished gold, ornamented with filigree and plaques of highly polished gold. The round bar is of burnished gold. The ends are covered with filigree work and ornaments of polished gold.

Demorest's Mirror of Fashions, March 1881

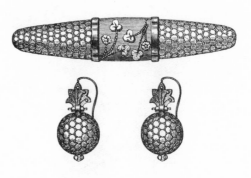

Figure 29. Set of lace pin and earrings

Figure 27. Scarf pin

Figure 27 shows a scarf pin of rolled gold. The head is a ball of burnished Roman gold, with plaques of highly polished gold on four sides. A similar style, which can be had in 2 1/4 or 2 3/4 in. length, is used to secure bonnet strings, jabots, and neckties. It has a plain round head, either polished or dead gold.

Figure 29 shows a lace pin and earrings of rolled gold. The center of the pin is ornamented with raised flowers of copper-colored frosted gold on a satin-finished surface, between two raised vertical bars of highly polished gold. The rest of the pin is covered with filigree representing lace. The earrings match in design, and are swinging balls suspended from shell-shaped ornaments in filigree.

Demorest's Mirror of Fashions, May 1881

Figure 28. Lace pin

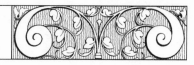
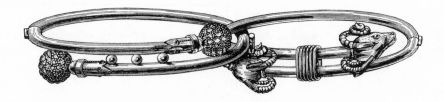

Figure 30. Two rolled gold bracelets

The bracelet on the left of figure 30 is of rolled gold, of highly polished red gold wire with the two ends lapped like a spiral. They terminate in dead gold balls, enriched with lace-patterned filigree. The lapped ends are connected by three tiny gold balls.

On the right is a bangle bracelet of red rolled gold. The ends lap about 1 1/2 in., are connected with a strand of twisted wire, and terminate in rams' heads, with curled horns of wrought yellow gold. The bangle opens with a hinge and a clasp.

Figure 31. Ring

The ring in figure 31 is a heavy circle of solid gold, set with a cameo representing a female head in profile. The setting is a square medallion of polished gold.

Figure 32. Ring

The ring in figure 32 is of solid gold. It is set with a fine, pure, white stone that closely resembles a genuine diamond, and has all the beauty and brilliancy of a real gem. The ring is richly chased, and the stone set in the latest style of diamond setting.

Figure 33. Necklace—full size

The necklace in figure 33 is composed of bar links of dead gold ornamented on the upper surface with filigree scrolls set with an engraved ornament of polished gold. These are alternated with flat circle links of highly polished gold. All the polished gold that is seen is solid. The long chain measures 19 in., and the pendant chain 1 1/2 in.

Demorest's Mirror of Fashions, June 1881

Figure 34. Lace pin—full size

Figure 34 shows a lace pin of rolled gold. It is ornamented with a diamond-shaped medallion in the center set with a garnet. The ends of the pin represent fleurs-de-lis. Tiny plaques and trefoils of polished gold enrich the center of the design.

Figure 36. Necklace or collarette

The necklace in figure 36 consists of two box-pleated satin frills of a color to harmonize with the dress with which it is to be worn. The frills are set, one turned upward and the other downward, on a stiff band 1 in. wide. The band and the edges of the pleatings are covered by a black velvet ribbon, studded with coins and spangles, which is tied in back.

Harper's Bazar, March 1882

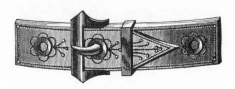

Figure 35. Lace pin—full size

Figure 35 shows a lace pin of rolled gold. The design represents a strap of satin-finished yellow gold, with buckle of highly polished gold and filigree ornaments. All the polished gold that is seen is solid.

Demorest's Mirror of Fashions, September 1881

Figure 1. Leather belt and oxidized silver belt

Belts

The belt on the left of figure 1 is of black leather. It is furnished with a metal clasp and bands. The belt on the right is of openwork oxidized silver. It is joined on the sides with black satin ribbon.

Harper's Bazar, January 1878

Figure 2. Embroidered belt

The belt in figure 2 is made of wide black reps ribbon. It is embroidered in point Russe and in satin and tent stitch, with pink, blue, and white silk floss. The buckle is oxidized silver.

Harper's Bazar, November 1878

Figure 3. Velvet belt

The belt in figure 3 consists of two parts. These are cut of stiff lace, and are covered on the outside with black velvet and on the wrong side with blue lustring. The ends are finished with silver ornaments with rings attached, by which both parts are joined. The wide front is trimmed with a silver ornament. A hook serves for closing.

Harper's Bazar, December 1878

Figure 4. Pompadour belt

The black leather belt in figure 4 is covered on the outside with Pompadour satin ribbon. A bronze buckle closes the belt. It is also furnished with a slide and chain for holding the fan.

Harper's Bazar, March 1880

Figure 1. Bouquet holder with brooch

Chatelaines, Bouquet Holders, And Skirt Supporters

Figure 1 shows a bouquet holder of oxidized silver and bronze. It is furnished with a brooch pin, to fasten the flowers to the bodice. The upper part of the quiver holds the flowers.

Figure 2. Skirt elevator

The skirt elevator in figure 2 consists of two pieces of silver galloon 1/2 in. wide and 2 7/8 in. long. They are joined with silver rings and agrafes. They are furnished on one end with a belt loop and on the other end with pincers. These pieces consist of two pieces of silver joined with a hinge, and covered on the outside with ebony inlaid with silver. On the inside the pincers are furnished with a spring, and are closed with a movable ring.

Harper's Bazar, March 1877

Figure 3. Handkerchief holder

The holder in figure 3 consists of a ring 1/2 in. wide and 12 in. in circumference. It is covered with linen tape overlaid partly with pink and partly with navy blue gathered serge ribbon. This ring has a band in the middle, for which a piece of wire is covered with pink and navy blue serge ribbon to match the ring. A silver chain, which is joined with a belt hook covered with pink ribbon, is fastened on the ring.

The cambric handkerchief, which is drawn through the ring underneath the band, is trimmed with Spanish lace and insertion. Between the lace and insertion is a design resembling mosaic work. It is composed of squares of pink and navy blue serge 1 3/4 in. in size, and squares of insertion.

Harper's Bazar, July 1877

Figure 4. Bouquet brooch

Figures 4 through 7 are used for fastening small corsage bouquets. Figure 4 is a salamander of gilt bronze and black enamel, which rests on two bronze rings, and is furnished with a pin.

Figure 5. Bouquet brooch

Figure 5 holds a spray of violets and lilies of the valley. The stems are run through the brooch of gilt metal in the shape of a serpent.

Figure 6. Bouquet brooch

333

Figure 6 shows a bouquet of rosebuds and leaves. It is clasped by a brooch representing a bronze leaf and vine set with stones and pearls.

Figure 7. Bouquet brooch

The brooch in figure 7 represents a fly of black and white enamel and gilt bronze.

Harper's Bazar, August 1878

Figure 8. Skirt supporter, closed and open

The skirt supporter in figure 8 is made of oxidized metal. The two clamps are furnished on the ends with elastic plates. The train is caught between these, and is kept in place by tightening the screw. The skirt supporter is furnished with thick black silk cord, which passes around the waist.

Figure 9. Skirt supporter, closed and open

The skirt supporter in figure 9 is composed of double loops of steel. These are joined by hinges, and hooked by a spring in adjusting the train. The skirt supporter is furnished with thick black silk cord.

Harper's Bazar, October 1879

Figure 10. Chatelaine fan holder

The fan holders in figures 10 through 12 are made of gilt bronze. They are furnished with swivel hooks for holding the fan, flacon, etc. The fan holder in figure 10 is composed of two shells of different sizes, joined with chain links, and ornamented with blue stones and a pear-shaped Roman pearl.

Figure 11. Chatelaine fan holder

The upper part of the fan holder in figure 11 consists of a medallion in painted porcelain, enclosed in a bronze frame.

335

Figure 12. Chatelaine fan holder

Figure 12 shows another gilt bronze chatelaine fan holder.

Figure 13. Fan-shaped ball tablets

The tablets in figure 13, in the shape of a miniature fan, are of carved ivory. The outer sticks are inlaid with mother-of-pearl, and ornamented with a silver shield, on which a monogram is engraved. The fan is attached to a silver chain finished with a ring.

Figure 15. Brooch with bouquet holder

The brooch with bouquet holder in figure 15 is of silver. It is specially adapted for fastening lace scarves at the throat or on the bodice.

Harper's Bazar, July 1880

Figure 14. Vinaigrette with chatelaine

Figure 14 shows a vinaigrette of cut crystal. It is closed with a bronze stopper with chain attached, which is fastened to a hook on the wrong side of the belt.

Harper's Bazar, January 1880

Figure 1. Embroidered glove

Gloves

Figure 1 shows a long glove embroidered in chain and buttonhole stitch, satin stitch, and point Russe. Olive green, tilleul, brown, and yellow are the colors used.

Englishwoman's Domestic Magazine, August 1877

Figure 2. Gauntlet gloves

The gray kid glove on the left of figure 2 is trimmed with a monogram. This is worked with navy blue and light blue silk in satin and half-polka

stitch. The gauntlet is of blue velvet, slashed at the top, and appears to be laced with light blue braid. Buttons and hooks and eyes close the glove.

The yellow kid glove on the right is trimmed with claret-colored chenille. The gauntlet is of claret-colored velvet. The seam where it is joined to the glove is covered with gathered black lace, which is embroidered with olive green silk. Similar lace borders the top of the gauntlet.

Harper's Bazar, April 1878

Figure 3. Lady's glove

The glove in figure 3 is of dark gray kid. It is trimmed with white lace insertion, beneath which the material is cut away.

Figure 4. Lady's glove

The short glove in figure 4 is of black kid. It is trimmed with a simulated fur border.

Harper's Bazar, February 1879

Figure 6. Kid glove

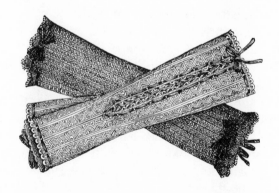

Figure 5. Insertion and lace mitts

The glove in figure 6 is of light blue kid, and is trimmed with puffs of blue satin. The top is bordered with white lace.

Harper's Bazar, January 1880

Figure 7. Knitted and crocheted mitt

The mitt with gauntlet in figure 7 is knitted with white Gobelin worsted, and is trimmed on the front with crochet edging. On the upper side the mitt is embroidered with blue silk in point Russe, and is trimmed with a bow of narrow blue silk ribbon.

The mitt is worked crosswise, beginning on the inside (where the thumb ends) with a foundation of 32 stitches, and working one hundred and thirty-two rounds all knit plain, going back and forth. But in the ninety-sixth round, on the side nearest the front edge of the mitt, cast off 9 stitches. In the following round at the same point cast on anew 5 stitches for the thumb, and knit them off in the following round. From the ninety-eighth round on to the one hundred and thirtieth, in every second following round, on the side nearest the wrist, pass over the last stitch in the preceding round, so that in the one hundred and thirtieth round only 11 stitches are knitted. In the following two rounds work off all the stitches that were left standing, then cast off the stitch. First join the 9 stitches cast off in the ninety-sixth round with the 9 foundation stitches nearest the front edge. Then join the 5 stitches cast on for the thumb with the next 5 stitches cast off after the last round. Finally join the remainder of

the cast-off stitches with the following foundation stitches to the wrist, from the wrong side. Take up the edge stitches at the wrist, then those on the front, and finally the stitches at the thumb on needles. Always going forward work 6 rounds, always alternately 1 purled, 1 knit crossed. To do the knit crossed, insert the needle in the stitch from the wrong side to the front, and knit the stitch plain.

Next work the gauntlet on a foundation of 18 stitches, crosswise, in rounds going back and forth as follows. First round: Slip, 15 knit plain, throw the thread over, 2 knit plain. Second round: Knit 1 crossed, then all knit plain. On the single throw the thread over work 1 stitch. On the double throw the thread over work 2 stitches, 1 knit, 1 purled. All rounds denoted by even numbers are worked in this manner, which will not be referred to further.

Third round: Slip, 16 knit plain, throw the thread over, 2 knit plain. Fifth round: Slip, 17 knit plain, throw the thread over, 2 knit plain. Seventh round: Slip, 12 knit plain, knit 2 together, twice throw the thread over, knit 2 together, 2 knit plain, throw the thread over, 2 knit plain. Ninth round: Slip, 19 knit plain, throw the thread over, 2 knit plain. Eleventh round: Slip, 10 knit plain, knit 2 together, twice throw the thread over, twice knit 2 together, twice throw the thread over, knit 2 together, 2 knit plain, throw the thread over, 2 knit plain. Thirteenth round: Slip, 21 knit plain, throw the thread over, 2 knit plain. Fifteenth round: Slip, 9 knit plain, knit 2 together, twice alternately twice throw the thread over, twice knit 2 together; then twice throw the thread over, knit 2 together, 1 knit plain, throw the thread over, 2 knit plain. Seventeenth round: Slip, 20 knit plain, knit 2 together, throw the thread over, knit 2 together, 1 knit plain. Nineteenth round: Slip, 10 knit plain, knit 2 together, twice throw the thread over, twice knit 2 together, twice throw the thread over, knit 2 together, 1 knit plain, knit 2 together, throw the thread over, knit 2 together, 1 knit plain. Twenty-first round: Slip, 18 knit plain, knit 2 together, throw the thread over, knit 2 together, 1 knit plain. Twenty-third round: Slip, 12 knit plain, knit 2

together, twice throw the thread over, knit 2 together, 1 knit plain, knit 2 together, throw the thread over, knit 2 together, 1 knit plain. Twenty-fifth round: Slip, 16 knit plain, knit 2 together, throw the thread over, knit 2 together, 1 knit plain. Twenty-seventh round: Slip, 15 knit plain, knit 2 together, throw the thread over, knit 2 together, 1 knit plain. Twenty-ninth round: Slip, 14 knit plain, knit 2 together, throw the thread over, knit 2 together, 1 knit plain. Thirty-first round: Slip, 13 knit plain, knit 2 together, throw the thread over, knit 2 together, 1 knit plain. Thirty-second round: Like the second round. Repeat five times the first through the thirty-second rounds.

Overseam the ends of the gauntlet together from the wrong side. Gather the straight edge, and join it with the mitt. Border the mitt with edging as follows. First round: Always alternately 1 double crochet on the next edge stitch, 1 chain stitch, pass over 1 stitch. Second round: Always alternately 1 single crochet on the next chain in the preceding round, one picot (consisting of 4 chain stitches and 1 single crochet) on the first of these.

Harper's Bazar, March 1880

Figure 8. Netted mitt

The mitt in figure 8 is netted with black silk, and ornamented with yellow silk.

Harper's Bazar, July 1880

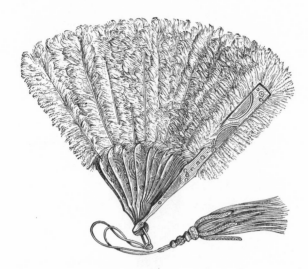

Figure 1. Marabou fan

Fans

The dress fan in figure 1 has ivory sticks, and is covered with white silk. The front is overlaid with white marabou feathers. White silk cord and tassel.

Figure 2. Painted feather fan

The sticks of the dress fan in figure 2 are of carved ivory. They are covered with curled grouse feathers, which are ornamented with a painted spray of flowers in different colors.

Harper's Bazar, March 1877

Figure 3. Evening fan

The fan in figure 3 is made of gray dove's feathers. It is trimmed on the center with a butterfly composed of green and brown changeable feathers. Ivory handle.

Harper's Bazar, March 1878

The sticks of the fan in figure 4 are of mother-of-pearl. The cover is worked in Spanish embroidery on fine ecru linen with real gold thread and gold spangles of various sizes, and fine sewing silk in several dull tints. The flowers are worked with light and dark red silk. The vines, leaves, stems, and calyxes are worked with olive green and brown silk. The crescent figure is worked with violet silk.

After finishing the embroidery, cut away the material between the design figures on the wrong side. Each section of the cover is underlaid with black faille, and fastened separately on the fan. The fan is furnished with silk cords and tassels in the colors of the embroidery.

Harper's Bazar, December 1878

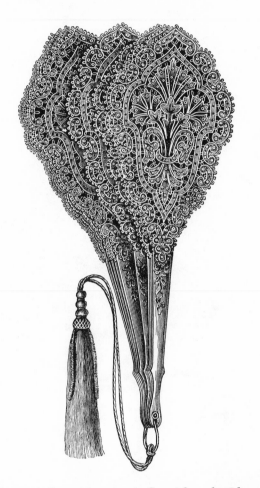

Figure 4. Fan with cover in Spanish embroidery

Figure 5. Point lace fan embroidered with beads

343

The frame of the fan in figure 5 is of carved mother-of-pearl in changeable colors. The cover is of real point lace, with the design figures embroidered with red, green, and pale blue beads. The top is finished with a border of changeable feathers. A white silk cord and tassel completes the fan.

Harper's Bazar, February 1879

Figure 6. Ivory fan

Figure 6 shows an ivory fan ornamented with a tea rose held in place on one of the outer sticks with a silver holder.

Demorest's Mirror of Fashions, August 1879

Figure 7. Cork fan

The frame and the cover of the fan in figure 7 are made of cork, and ornamented with painting. The fan is covered on the wrong side with black silk. It is finished with a cord and tassel.

Harper's Bazar, March 1880

Figure 8. Satin cretonne fan

The fan in figure 8 is of satin cretonne, embroidered with gold thread in an elaborate design. It is mounted upon a frame of ebonized wood with gilt ornaments.

Figure 9. Peacock feather chatelaine fan

Figure 10. Fan, necklace, and bracelet

The fan in figure 9 is composed of peacock eyes, mounted on a handsomely wrought ivory handle. Both sides of the fan are finished alike. The handle is tied with a gold-colored silk cord and tassels, and has a ring at the end by which it may be suspended from a chain or ribbon.

Demorest's Mirror of Fashions, August 1881

The square fan in figure 10 has an ebonized frame with silver ornamentation. The leaf is of pale olive satin, with a spray of flowers in natural colors painted on it, and a pale black satin lining. A silver chain is attached to it.

The necklace is composed of links in combined gold and platina, with a lapis lazuli at the center. The pendant, of gold and lapis lazuli, bears a Roman silver coin. The bangle bracelet consists of fine gold and silver hoops, connected by a bar, from which three owls' heads in silver hang.

Harper's Bazar, November 1882

Figure 1. Navy blue faille parasol

Parasols

Figure 1 shows a parasol of navy blue faille, lined with ivory color. Each section is trimmed with pale blue faille, embroidered with yellow silk of two shades, bows of narrow ribbon the same shade, and fringe to match round the edges. A double piping of the same shade, and all around a flounce of ivory lace. Handsome handle of carved ivory.

Figure 2. Pale blue parasol

Figure 2 shows a parasol of pale blue, not lined. It is trimmed on each section with palms of white gauze plissé, surrounded by lace of the same material broché. All these palms are fastened to the parasol by a blue ribbon. There is a small frill at the end of the parasol. Ribbon of the same shade encircles the handle and forms a bow. The handle is wooden with a gilt end.

Englishwoman's Domestic Magazine, June 1877

Figure 3. Black faille and ecru silk parasols

The parasol on the left of figure 3 is of black faille lined with white lustring. It is edged on the bottom with a double strip of black silk tulle 3 3/4 in. wide. This is darned with gold thread in squares, ornamented with gold spangles, and edged with fringe composed of black silk and gold beads. Stick of carved black stained wood.

On the right is an ecru silk parasol lined with the same material, which is furnished with a printed brown border. The stick is of carved yellowish-brown wood.

Harper's Bazar, June 1878

Figure 4. Embroidered parasol

The black satin parasol in figure 4 is ornamented with a border in Spanish embroidery after the design in figure 5. The piece for each gore of the parasol is worked by itself. The design is first transferred to ecru linen.

Then all the design figures are edged with a double row of gold cord, fastened down with long buttonhole stitches of red or olive silk. Loops or picots are formed at intervals with the outer row of cord. These are either caught down with a buttonhole stitch in the adjacent outline, or lined with one or more adjacent picots. The surface of the design figures is embroidered in herringbone stitch and point Russe with embroidery silk of the color with which it is edged, and with gold or silver bullion. When the embroidery is completed the linen is cut away from around the design figures. Lastly the border is applied on the parasol.

Harper's Bazar, July 1881

Figure 5. Design for parasol

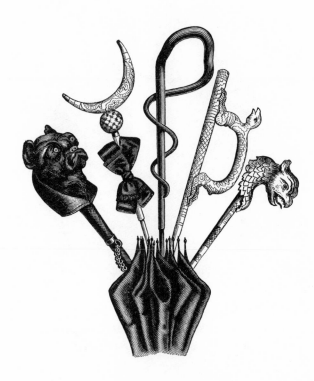

Figure 7. Parasol handles

The group in figure 7 comprises some of the latest styles in parasol handles. The one on the left is of carved, and the one in the middle of twisted, wood. The rest are of ivory.

Harper's Bazar, May 1882

Figure 6. Black satin parasol

Figure 6 shows a black satin parasol lined with Japanese foulard, cream tinted with scarlet figures. The gilt ribs of the frame show outside the lining. The carved wood handle is tied with black and red cord and tassels.

Demorest's Mirror of Fashions, August 1881

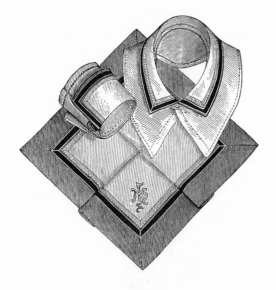

Figure 1. Linen set

Figure 2. Lace handkerchief

Figure 2 shows a handkerchief with a Valenciennes border. It is seldom that duplicates of handsome lace handkerchiefs can be obtained.
Demorest's Mirror of Fashions, December 1878

Handkerchiefs

Figure 1 shows a stylish linen set, comprising collar, cuffs, and handkerchief. It is finished with a dark-colored border.

Figure 3. Border for batiste handkerchief

Figure 3 shows a darned net handkerchief border. It is worked on Brussels net, and edged with buttonhole stitch scallops. The design figures are outlined with coarse thread, as illustrated. They are filled partly with darning stitches of fine thread and partly with lace stitches. The dots are worked in satin stitch, or else darned in point de reprise. Edge the border with buttonhole stitches, cut away the projecting edge of the net, and buttonhole stitch the border on batiste with fine cotton.

Harper's Bazar, May 1880

Figure 5. Ladies' handkerchiefs

The trimming for the batiste handkerchief on the left of figure 5 consists of a border of dark blue figured sateen 1 3/4 in. wide.

The handkerchief on the right is made of batiste. It is trimmed with a figured sateen border, edged with buttonhole stitch points of colored cotton. Overcast stitches of similar cotton cover the joining seam of the foundation and the border.

Harper's Bazar, July 1880

Figure 4. Ladies' handkerchiefs

The white batiste handkerchief on the left of figure 4 is edged with a border of dark dotted blue foulard 2 1/2 in. deep, finished with buttonhole stitch points of cotton in various colors. The border is overseamed on the batiste foundation with colored cotton.

The foundation of the handkerchief on the right is of white foulard. This is hemstitched, and edged with a colored foulard border.

Reticules and Satchels

The bag in figure 1 is designed to hold small articles of fancy work, the handkerchief, etc. It is worn at the belt or carried on the arm. It is made of black satin, and embroidered on the upper side.

The leaves in the spray are worked in satin stitch with shaded yellowish-brown silk. The veins and stems are defined with brown chenille. The knotted stitches inside the leaves are worked with maroon chenille. The flowers are formed of high standing loops of white chenille, and the stamens of smaller loops of maize chenille.

To make the bag, cut of satin and lustring lining two pieces from the pattern. Sew them up on the sides. Cover the seam with silver cord. Furnish the bag at the top with a shirr, into which run black silk tape. The ends of the tape are tied in a bow, and finished with tassels of black silk. The bottom of the bag is trimmed with a tassel of white silk and gold bullion.

Harper's Bazar, September 1879

Figure 1. Embroidered bag

Bag
1/4 scale

Figure 2. Embroidered reticule pocket

To make the pocket in figure 2, cut of black satin and silk two pieces each 7 3/4 in. long and 3 1/4 in. wide. Round off the upper corners. Cut off the lower corners so that the parts measure 3 1/4 in. on the bottom. Embroider the satin for the front, working the leaves and sprays with brown and yellow silk in satin, tent, and herringbone stitch. The flowers are formed of loops of chenille of various colors. Join both parts of the pocket. Gather the upper edge, and set it in a steel binding furnished with a chain.

Harper's Bazar, October 1879

Figure 4. Embroidered reticule

Figure 3. Handkerchief bag

To make the bag in figure 3, take 11 in. of 22 in. satin. Lay the two selvages together, and cut a half round. Then lay the two straight edges together and sew. Turn in the round edge 1 1/2 in. Run it twice, and put in the drawing cord or ribbon. Finish the point with a heavy tassel.

Demorest's Mirror of Fashions, January 1881

The pretty reticule in figure 4 is made of bronze plush lined with bronze satin. Cut two pieces each of plush and satin 9 in. wide and 12 long. Cut one piece for the pocket on the front, which is 4 in. long and 21 wide. Lay the pieces of plush and lining over one another. Round off the lower corners as illustrated. Round off those of the pocket to correspond.

Embroider the top of the bag in the design given in figure 5. Transfer its outlines to the plush. Work the flowers and leaves in satin stitch with old gold silk, and cross them with gold thread. Define the stems and tendrils with fine gold cord, which is sewed down with fine yellow silk.

Join the plush and lining of the pocket along the top. Run them together twice a little below the edge. Draw elastic cord through the shirr thus formed. Pleat this piece along the rounded lower edge. Baste it on the embroidered top of the bag. Sew up the plush, taking the edge of the pocket into the seam. Then sew up the lining, and set it into the bag so that all the seams will be hidden. Run the plush and lining together twice at 1 in. from the top of the bag. Draw brown silk cord finished with tassels at the ends through this shirr. Set a cord bow and tassels on the pocket as illustrated.

Harper's Bazar, April 1882

Design for Reticule

Full size

Figure 5. Embroidery design

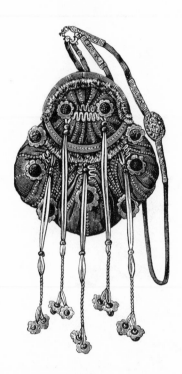

Figure 6. Chamois leather chatelaine bag

Figure 7. Satchel with Spanish embroidery

The bag in figure 6 is an exact copy of an antique *aumônière* in the Munich Museum. It is made of light drab chamois leather, with drab silk chain stitching, silvered metal ornaments, and pendants, the latter hanging by leather ribbons. It has one large and three small pouches. It is attached to a leather girdle with metal mountings.

Harper's Bazar, June 1882

The satchel in figure 7 consists of a maroon satin bag with silk lining, made of a piece 24 in. long and 12 wide. This is folded double, joined at the sides, and closed at the top by a drawstring. The bag is set into a stiff outer case, consisting of maroon velvet with satin lining and cardboard interlining. This is cut in an oblong, with rounded corners, 13 in. long and 11 wide, and folded across the middle.

The velvet for the front is decorated with an appliqué in Spanish embroidery, for which the design is given in figure 8. Trace it onto fine ecru linen. Then outline the design with a double row of fine gold cord sewed down along the lines with rather wide buttonhole stitches in bronze silk, forming the outer cord into loops at regular intervals as illustrated. After the edge is defined, ornament the surfaces of the figures in point Russe and coral or feather stitch with colored silks. Then cut away the linen from around them, and apply the embroidery on the velvet. The outer case is edged with gold lace, and provided with handles.

Harper's Bazar, December 1882

Design for Satchel

Full size

Figure 8. Embroidery design

Figure 1. Satchel with muff

Muffs

The satchel in figure 1 is made of black faille, lined with violet satin, and bordered at the ends with fur. The binding and lock are of oxidized metal. The back of the satchel forms a muff, which is lined with fur.

The muff in figure 2 is made of dark sealskin, and lined with satin. It is suspended round the neck by a thick black silk cord, finished at the ends with metal capsules, and furnished with chains, a swivel hook, and black silk tassels. A black silk ribbon, furnished on one end with a ring and attached to the cord at the other end, is slipped through the muff in adjusting the latter, and is fastened to the swivel hook by the ring. Two metal balls are slipped, also, on the cord, and are held together by a hook and eye.

Harper's Bazar, January 1878

Figure 3. Olga muff

Figure 3 shows a convenient and dressy little arrangement, which serves the double purpose of muff and reticule. It is made of silk, satin, velvet, or plush. It may be made of goods to match the costume, wrap, or bonnet, or an entirely different material. It is trimmed at the sides with lace, and ornamented on the outside with a large bow of satin ribbon.

Figure 2. Muff with guard

Figure 4. Paola muff

The dainty little muff in figure 4 may be made of plush, satin, velvet, or silk. The material may match the costume or bonnet, or differ from both. The muff may be lined with the same or a different material or color. It may be trimmed as shown with a silk cordelière and a bow of satin ribbon, or in some other appropriate manner.

Demorest's Mirror of Fashions, January 1881

Figure 5. Moiré muff

The muff in figure 5 is lined with black satin, and covered with moiré, which is arranged in puffs. Between the middle two puffs the muff is encircled by a jet band. On each side are two frills of double moiré, wired along the edge to keep them extended, and studded with jet beads. The sides are edged with full frills of Spanish lace, and finished with pendant bows of moiré ribbon.

Harper's Bazar, December 1881

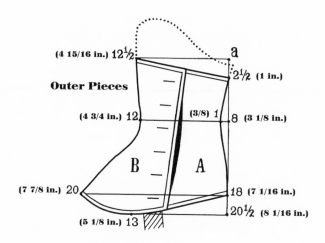

Outer Pieces

(4 15/16 in.) 12½

a

2½ (1 in.)

(4 3/4 in.) 12 (3/8) 1 8 (3 1/8 in.)

B   A

(7 7/8 in.) 20 18 (7 1/16 in.)

20½ (8 1/16 in.)

(5 1/8 in.) 13

Figure 1. Short gaiters

Gaiters

The gaiters in figure 1 have three pieces. Pieces A and B form the outer part. The inside is one piece. Whether the gaiter is lined with canvas, as is customary, will depend on how thick the material is, as well as the season. A 3 cm (1 3/16 in.) wide strip of material must be allowed on piece A as an underlap for the buttons. There will be a seam each in back and front. The seams must be sewn very strong because they receive much wear. They are pressed flat, then sewn to either side. This pattern is drafted in centimeters.

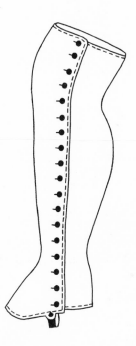

Figure 2. Long gaiters

The gaiters in figure 2 have three pieces. Pieces A and B form the outer part. The inside is one piece. Whether the gaiter is lined with canvas, as is customary, will depend on how thick the material is, as well as the season. A 3 cm (1 3/16 in.) wide strip of material must be allowed on piece A as an underlap for the buttons. There will be a seam each in back and front. The seams must be sewn very strong because they receive much wear. They are pressed flat, then sewn to either side. This pattern is drafted in centimeters.

Complete Guide to Ladies' Garment Cutting, 1883

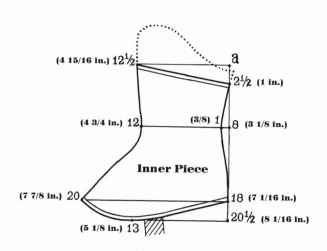

(4 15/16 in.) 12½

a

2½ (1 in.)

(4 3/4 in.) 12 (3/8) 1 8 (3 1/8 in.)

Inner Piece

(7 7/8 in.) 20 18 (7 1/16 in.)

20½ (8 1/16 in.)

(5 1/8 in.) 13

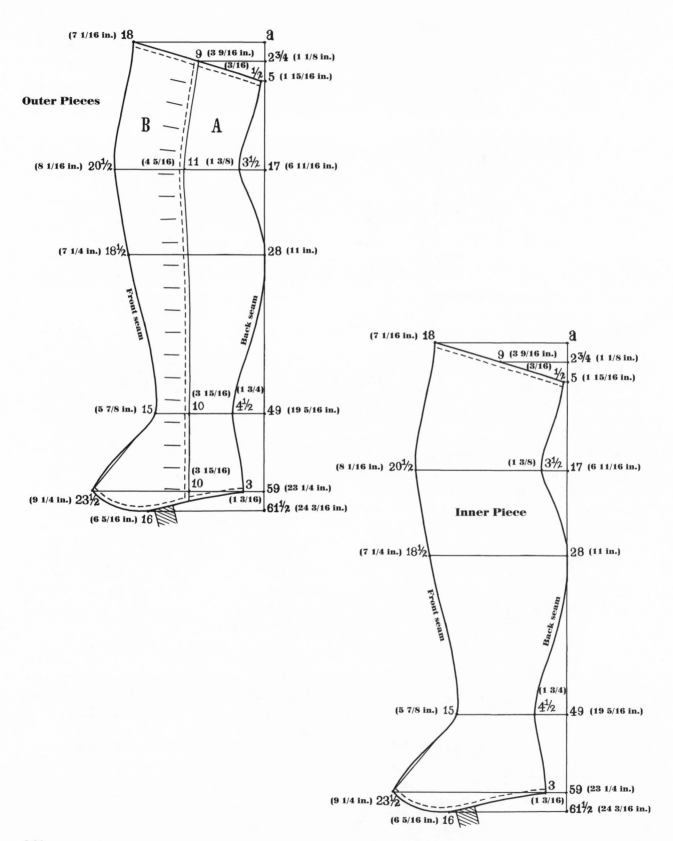

Outer Pieces

(7 1/16 in.) 18   a

9 (3 9/16 in.)   2¾ (1 1/8 in.)

(3/16)   ½   5 (1 15/16 in.)

B   A

(8 1/16 in.) 20½   (4 5/16)   11 (1 3/8)   3½   17 (6 11/16 in.)

Front seam   Back seam

(7 1/4 in.) 18½   28 (11 in.)

(3 15/16)   (1 3/4)

(5 7/8 in.) 15   10   4½   49 (19 5/16 in.)

(3 15/16)   10   3   59 (23 1/4 in.)

(9 1/4 in.) 23½   (1 3/16)   61½ (24 3/16 in.)

(6 5/16 in.) 16

Inner Piece

(7 1/16 in.) 18   a

9 (3 9/16 in.)   2¾ (1 1/8 in.)

(3/16)   ½   5 (1 15/16 in.)

(8 1/16 in.) 20½   (1 3/8)   3½   17 (6 11/16 in.)

Front seam   Back seam

(7 1/4 in.) 18½   28 (11 in.)

(1 3/4)

(5 7/8 in.) 15   4½   49 (19 5/16 in.)

3   59 (23 1/4 in.)

(9 1/4 in.) 23½   (1 3/16)   61½ (24 3/16 in.)

(6 5/16 in.) 16

Figure 1. Garter

Stockings and Garters

Figure 1 shows a garter of honeycomb canvas. It is embroidered in various stitches with coarse black silk and coarse white knitting cotton. It is closed by a crocheted buttonhole tab.

Cut of white honeycomb canvas a straight strip 8 7/8 in. long and 13 stitches (squares) wide. Work the design shown by figure 2. Line the garter with muslin. Bind it with white cotton tape 3/4 in. wide, ornamented with herringbone stitches of black silk. On each end put a linen button embroidered in point Russe and knotted stitch with black silk.

Figure 2. Detail of garter

Next work the buttonhole tab, which is fastened on these two buttons, as follows. Make a foundation of 80 chain stitches. Close the last 20 in a ring for a buttonhole, working on the foundation stitch, going back, 5 single crochet on the next

5 stitches. For four additional buttonholes work three times alternately 10 chain, pass over 10 stitches, 5 single crochet on the next 5 stitches, and then 10 chain and 1 single crochet on the 1st foundation stitch. Then work always going forward the first to third rounds in single crochet, working always 1 single crochet on each stitch, but at both ends widen several stitches so that the work will not draw. The stitch coming on the single crochet of the preceding rounds should always be worked on the upper veins. For the fourth round, always work alternately 1 single crochet on the upper veins of the 2nd following stitch, but at both ends, between 2 single crochet, work a loop of 18 double foundation stitches. On this fasten a white cotton tassel tied with black silk. Edge each buttonhole with single crochet worked with black silk.

Harper's Bazar, February 1877

Figure 3. Fashionable hosiery

For general wear, both in wool and cotton, handsome shades of slate, dark blue, seal brown, and red, relieved by differently colored clocks, are seen. They divide favor with other varieties of hosiery in wool and cotton, which are woven throughout with prettily contrasting hairline stripes (see figure 3). As a novelty of the season, we may note the introduction of woolen hose in pale shades of gray, slate, pink, and blue.

New styles of hosiery in silk, cotton, and wool are shown in combinations of two colors, such as cardinal red with navy blue, seal brown with cardinal red, seal brown with royal blue, slate with pink, etc. The upper half of the stocking is woven in one color, the lower half in the other. Where they join above the ankle a finish is given by the introduction of hairline stripes and embroidery. Besides these novelties, we find checkerboard and crossbarred designs.

Expensive hosiery is wrought in beadwork on a solid foundation, chiefly black. For example, gay floral patterns in red and pink beads are executed on black silk, on the instep rather than the side of the stocking. Another very handsome novelty is "camel's hair embroidery," this being executed chiefly on black silk. It appears on the instep, and derives its name from a resemblance to the work on camel's hair shawls, but it is done in silk.

Light styles of hosiery in lisle thread and silk are openwork throughout. A large pattern is wrought on the upper portion of the stocking, while the lower half shows the same pattern repeated smaller. The colors are charming—pale pink, blue, lilac, cream color, pearl gray, bright cardinal, ruby, and royal blue.

Colored hosiery presents so many advantages over white that it seems hard to believe it will ever be out of vogue. Yet even at present, in order that all tastes may be suited, white hosiery is shown, as well as the unbleached and the standard balbriggan.

Demorest's Mirror of Fashions, February 1878

Figure 4. Woven stocking

The stocking in figure 4 is woven of fine black yarn. It is ornamented on the front with flowers and leaves embroidered in satin and tent stitch with white and yellow filling silk. The stems are worked with fine gold thread in chain and tent stitch.

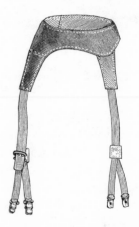

Figure 6. Stocking supporter with belt

The stocking supporter in figure 6 is attached to a sateen belt lined with muslin. The belt closes in front with buttons and buttonholes. The supporters consist of two strips of elastic webbing 5 3/4 in. long, the lower end of which passes through a metal buckle. Attached to the buckle are two ends of elastic webbing 3 in. long, which are provided with clasps to hold the stocking at the lower edge.

Harper's Bazar, July 1881

Figure 5. Woven stocking

The stocking in figure 5 is of cream-colored yarn, with three openwork stripes. It is ornamented with forget-me-nots worked in satin and tent stitch.

Harper's Bazar, September 1879

Figure 1. Fur-lined boot

Figure 2. Embroidered slipper

Shoes

The fine leather boot in figure 1 is lined with fur, and trimmed at the top and along the instep with a fur border. Passemeterie buttons and cord loops with tassels serve for closing.

Harper's Bazar, January 1878

The slipper in figure 2 is made of brown grosgrain, trimmed with application embroidery, and lined with white cashmere. It is furnished with a felt sole, which is covered with cashmere on the inside.

Cut for the front of grosgrain and cashmere one piece each. Transfer the design in figure 3 to the material. Cut the leaves of the pansy of dark brown velvet, and of light and dark brown grosgrain. Apply the pansy to the foundation with buttonhole stitches of brown silk, which are edged with gold cord. Embroider it in point Russe with yellow silk. The calyxes are simulated with gold and wax beads. The vines are worked with brown saddler's silk in herringbone, half-polka, and chain stitch.

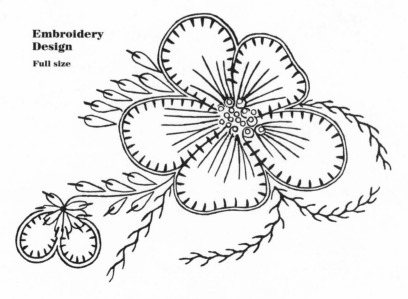

**Embroidery
Design**

Full size

Figure 3. Embroidery design

After finishing the embroidery put in the lining. Join the front with the sole, which is first covered with cashmere and embroidered in satin, half-polka, and herringbone stitch with shaded brown and yellow silk. The front is bordered with a strip of swansdown.

Figure 4. Embroidered slipper

The slipper in figure 4 is made of black woolen reps and white cashmere lining. It is furnished with black satin revers and a felt sole.

Transfer the design in figure 5 to the material. Cut the application of black velvet. Edge it with fine gold cord, and ornament it with large gold beads. The rest of the embroidery is worked in satin and herringbone stitch with yellow silk. The edge of the front and the revers are embroidered with similar stitches.

The felt sole is covered with white cashmere, and embroidered in satin and herringbone stitch with black silk. It is joined to the front, which is furnished with the revers. On the front is a bow of black and yellow grosgrain ribbon 1 1/4 in. wide.

Harper's Bazar, February 1878

Figure 6. Sandal gaiter

Figure 6 shows a sandal gaiter made in fine French kid, with a Louis XV heel. It has velvet bows and steel ornaments.

Embroidery Design

Full size

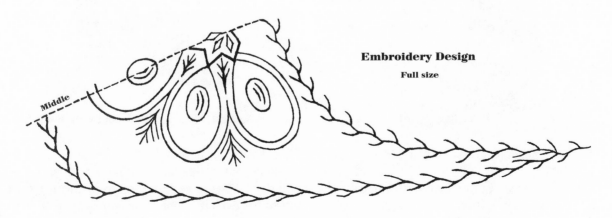

Middle

Figure 5. Embroidery design

Figure 7. Buttoned boot

Figure 7 shows a buttoned boot made in black satin Française. It is embroidered with black silk and jet beads.

Figure 8. Sandal slipper

Figure 8 shows a sandal slipper of French kid. It is fastened with bows of pale blue ribbon.

Figure 9. Sandal slipper

Figure 9 shows a sandal slipper of black velvet. It is laced with ribbon, and has large velvet and steel ornaments.

Demorest's Mirror of Fashions, February 1878

Figure 10. Black patent leather shoe

The front of the shoe in figure 10 is trimmed with a long rosette. This is composed of loops of bronze-colored satin ribbon, and edged with gathered lace of the same color.

Harper's Bazar, April 1879

Figure 11. Patent leather and satin boot

The lower part of the boot in figure 11 is made of black patent leather, trimmed with silver embroidery. The top is of maroon satin, furnished with elastic sides. The heel is ornamented with silver. At the top of the boot are fastened silver cords and tassels as illustrated.

Harper's Bazar, June 1879

Figure 12. Drilling bathing slipper

Figure 13. Embroidered bathing slipper

Figure 12 shows a bathing slipper of gray drilling. It is furnished with a sole of Manila straw, covered on the inside with carriage leather, and lined with gray linen. Patterns for the sole and top are given.

The trimming consists of a bias strip of brown cashmere 3/4 in. wide, which is ornamented with small Venetian shells as illustrated. For the half rosette on the instep take a bias strip of brown cashmere 3 in. wide. Fold it through the middle, lay it in side pleats on one edge, and set it on the slipper as illustrated. A large shell covers the seam of the rosette.

The slipper in figure 13 is made of white frieze, and cut from the same pattern as the slipper in figure 12. It is embroidered with worsted of various colors in satin, tent, and knotted stitch, and in point Russe. It is bound with blue worsted braid, and trimmed with a bow. The cork sole is lined with frieze.

Harper's Bazar, July 1879

Figure 14. Walking shoe

The shoe in figure 14 is of light yellow kid with a high heel covered with black kid. It is finished on the front and top with black patent leather, stitched with white silk. A bow of grosgrain ribbon with a buckle is on the instep.

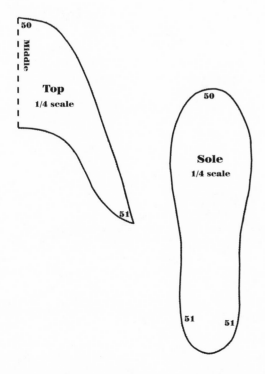

Figure 15. Walking shoe

The shoe in figure 15 is of black kid. It is furnished in front with an inserted piece of gray silk with eyelet holes, through which a cord is run. A chain stitching of white silk, a bow of grosgrain ribbon, and a jet agrafe trim the shoe as illustrated.

Harper's Bazar, September 1879

Figure 16. Velvet house slipper

The slipper in figure 16 is of light olive embossed velvet, on which the ground figures are veined with crystal beads. It is lined with cardinal satin, and has a French heel faced with similar material. The top is finished with narrow chenille and gold thread lace.

Figure 17. Blue satin slipper

The slipper in figure 17 is of light blue satin. It is ornamented with applied embroidery, which is worked with ruby, bronze, and jet beads and chenille on a net ground. The edge is finished with chenille and gold cord. A rosette of blue silk lace is set on the instep. Over the center of it are three leaf-shaped bead ornaments with pendants.

Harper's Bazar, May 1882

Figure 18. Walking boot

The boot in figure 18 is of bronze checked silk foxed with bronze kid. The heel is covered with kid. A brown grosgrain ribbon is set at the top of the boot.

Harper's Bazar, July 1882

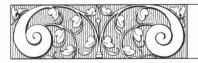 

Figure 19. Half of embroidery design for slipper

The ground for the slipper in figure 19 is Indian red cloth. On this the embroidery is executed in shades of leaf brown and blue split filoselle silk.

Trace the design on the cloth. Work the upper large leaf on the front in three shades of leaf brown, and the lower in similar brown shades, with dark blue for the round disk at the center. On each side is a flower in shades of blue, with French knots in gold-colored silk at the center. The chain stitch arabesques are in light, and the French knots within them are in darker, brown. The leaflets and the vine that extends along the side of the slipper are in three shades of leaf brown. In the narrow border that finishes the upper edge the waved lines are in brown, the straight lines in light blue, and the French knots in dark blue. The veins of the leaves are defined by the ridge of the buttonhole stitch.

Harper's Bazar, August 1882

7. Handmade and Purchased Trimmings

Colored embroidery is the novelty in embroidered underclothing. Gowns, chemises, and petticoats of the nicest French percale have the neck, sleeves, and the frills of skirts needleworked in tiny scallops of three colors. The first scallop is pale blue, the next red, and the third yellow. A delicate vine tracery is then wrought inside in matching colors.

Harper's Bazar, March 1878

Mull muslin, French nainsook, and other sheer lawns that have no starch and are of dull ivory white, are the fabrics used in imported dresses. Embroidery is invariably employed for the trimming. To this is sometimes added some inexpensive trimming lace, or perhaps a little real Mechlin, or Valenciennes in the new designs that have small figures with feathery edges, and show a great deal of foundation mesh work.

The embroidery is most effectively used as scant flounces for the skirt, trimming it sometimes in many rows up the front, with three rows extending all around it, and ample back drapery to cover the plain part of the back. Other dresses have three or four embroidered flounces, so wide that they cover all the skirt but a short space for hip drapery.

The open designs for such work have been most in favor. But there are also many flounces of the thicker work that can scarcely be detected from needlework. For simple dresses this work is done in patterns of dots scattered about, or else in scalloped rows near the edge, and is very effective. For more elaborate dresses there are larger flower, leaf, and vine patterns, and some blocks, Greek squares, and involved geometrical designs.

Harper's Bazar, June 1882

Cotton laces in showy effective patterns are much used for trimming muslin and cambric dresses. Byzantine point is liked as it washes well, and imitates the rich designs of antique laces.

Russian laces in braidlike patterns are still popular. Point Raguse lace is used on bonnets as well as dresses. This has the fine irregular meshes of thread lace, with the pattern applied and held by buttonhole stitching; the designs are like those of point appliqué lace. This lace and Breton are preferred for trimming very nice dresses of white muslin or white gauze bunting.

The black French laces known as imitations of thread laces are now given what dealers call the thread finish, by weaving them in irregular meshes that can scarcely be distinguished from those of handmade laces. These are to be laid in knife pleatings. The designs are mostly with reference to this, having a space between the wrought figures, which are narrow and lengthwise. The trimming widths vary from 1 1/2 to 5 in. Black Breton lace is shown in similar patterns. It is very stylish for edging veils and neckties, and for trimming bonnets.

Beaded laces brighten up black chip or tulle bonnets. Both jet and gold beads are used to outline the design.

Harper's Bazar, June 1879

Among the new black laces for trimming outside garments, gold threads are introduced most effectively. Others have masses of glittering tinsel—silver, gold, and copper red tints combined in most effective ways. Black torchon laces have leaves of gilt threads. Black Spanish laces have the large leaf designs entirely of gilt. White Spanish lace has gilt or silver threads, and is beautifully beaded with pearl and opal cut beads. Black Brussels net beaded with jet in foliage designs and in stripes, also in passementerie patterns, is largely imported for trimming black silk dresses. For evening dresses the same designs are repeated on white net with white jet and iridescent opal beads.

New white laces for trimming lingerie are also shown. The point fleurette is especially pretty for trimming mull fichus and collarettes. It is on the

same fine-meshed net used for Languedoc and point d'esprit. But instead of the large figures of Languedoc, or the pin dots of point d'esprit, it has tiny detached flowers wrought upon it in rows, and is then finished with small points or scallops. Vermicelli lace is also new, and is made by drawing cordlike threads through its serpentine designs. New appliqué laces have large artistic designs made of mull muslin applied on Brussels net, with buttonhole stitching on the edges. These should be put on plain without gathers, in the way Russian laces are used. There are also several laces made in the designs of round point, some of which are called Alençon, and others point de Brabant lace. Languedoc laces remain in favor.

Harper's Bazar, October 1880

A more summery trimming seen on wraps of black wool or silk is pleated French lace in three or four rows that touch each other without lapping. Instead of sewing this lace on the thick goods of the mantle, it is sewed on strong black net, and the net is then sewed to the edge of the mantle. This makes the several rows of pleating hang as gracefully and softly as fringes. It is also a good way to enlarge mantles left over from past seasons. Jet ornaments in oval shapes, with pendants like tassels, are put down the back, on the shoulders, down the front, or on the square sleeves of wraps.

Harper's Bazar, March 1879

A great deal of black French lace imitating thread lace patterns is used as a rival to the black Spanish lace, which must be all silk to be handsome. There is also much of the ficelle guipure or twine lace in antique designs, called Medici lace, for trimming light dresses. Black lace and black open silk embroidery are very effectively used on colored dresses, especially on olive and bronze green silks and on ecru dresses. Whole dresses are made of cream-colored antique lace over dark blue or black satin surah.

Heavy rich jetted passementeries in feather and leaf patterns are used on black dresses. There are also many jet edgings in place of cords and pipings. There are whole tabliers, panniers, vests, and collars made of appliquéd jetted gimps. Drop

trimmings are much used in large jet beads, and in satin drops with cords of satin forming the lacelike passementerie from which they depend.

Colored velvet ribbon with satin on the wrong side is used for bows on dresses of contrasting colors, such as maroon velvet on olive green, or sapphire blue velvet ribbon on pale salmon color.

Harper's Bazar, May 1882

The new passementeries represent the fashionable soutache braiding. They are made of mohair or silk braid laid in knife edge shape in the familiar braiding designs. These come in wheels, stars, leaves, and geometrical or architectural patterns. They can be had only 2 in. wide for edging collars and cuffs, and they can be had in borders 1/2 yd. wide, to take the place of a flounce on a dress skirt. These come in patterns 2 1/6 yd. long. This is just enough to go around a dress skirt, or else it may be cut in two pieces for panels down the sides, or for two rows across the front and side breadths. Satin cords, softly stuffed and pliable, are arranged in similar designs.

A great deal of chenille is found in new arrangements in the passementeries, such as loops, drops, rings linked in other rings like a chain, and as covering for flat disks and for drooping balls, some of which are like large marbles. Much chenille is also in the new fringes, both in the small, sleek, rattail chenille and in thicker strands twisted like cords. These are so thickly inserted that they may be used either as a marabou (or ruche), or else as drooping fringe. There are also tabliers of chenille netted in squares with a disk of satin or jet in each mesh, and tips to match are on each pendant of the fringe.

Jet passementeries are of solid jet representing flowers, leaves, grapes, berries, and other small fruits. Soutache sets of passementeries for sleeves, bust, and the back of a bodice are largely imported. There are many fourragères—loops of braid with ornamental rosettes or drooping balls—for the front of a dress or jacket. Flowers in relief made of silken cords are on many of the passementeries mixed with chenille. Many of the wide passementeries with drops are made in designs that may be cut apart,

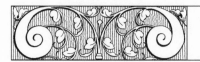 

and each figure used to ornament a different part of a cloak. Special ornaments made of great knotted ropes of chenille, or of satin cords with drooping balls, are large enough to cover the upper part of a wrap. There are rolling collars made entirely of chenille, jet, or cord passementerie.

The richest new trimming, however, is velvet embroidered in open designs with silk. It is sold by the yard in widths varying from 3 in. to 3/8 yd. This comes in black and all the stylish dark colors. It is scalloped on the lower edge, and is to be sewed on by the plain upper edge.

The newest silk embroidery or cashmere has large bold figures, such as daisies, roses, dahlias, wheels, circles, and balls, done in thick raised work with neatly scalloped edges. This is always wrought in self-colors. There are cashmeres for overdresses that have the wheels or balls wrought at intervals all over the ground. These are accompanied by bands that have scalloped edges and two, three, or four rows of the figure, of graduated sizes, for trimming different parts of the garment. These come in all colors, and will be made up with velvet skirts for visiting costumes, church dresses, and brides' traveling dresses.

Feather trimmings of cock's plumes and of marabou feathers will be much used.

Crocheted, metal, and pearl buttons, or combinations of metal and pearl in tints like colored silver, are largely imported. Small ball-shaped crocheted buttons and wooden molds covered with velvet are used for the bodices of house dresses. For outside garments there are two or three larger sizes of buttons. Some are balls as large as marbles, made of horn that looks like tortoiseshell, or else they are flat buttons of colored metals. Small horseshoe-shaped metal buttons, cup shapes holding beads, and balls on which are figures in relief, are the novelties in metal buttons. Jet buttons are flat, and might be thought to represent crushed blackberries.

Harper's Bazar, September 1882

Illuminated beads of dark rich colors are on dresses of various kinds, such as black silks, camel's hairs, gray cloths, and louisines of varied colors.

Jet beads are also largely used, and many opaque white beads, also amber. Fewer of the clair de lune beads are imported than last year. Fringes are made up of linked loops of these beads, with many large pear-shaped pendants. There are many silk galloons of open designs, in which they are introduced, while others are entirely of strung beads.

Thick yet narrow braids of colored wool or black are also shown for trimmings. There are many cords and braids *laminé,* or with silver and gold threads wrought in them. Trimmings cut from the piece are mostly of satin, though plain faille and watered silk are also used.

Above everything else, embroidery is chosen for French dresses, from the simplest gingham or lawn up to the richest silks. For the latter, colored beads are worked in the figures. For simple wash dresses the embroidery is mostly Hamburg work. But the designs are so elaborate, and include so many colors in each pattern, that it seems at first glance to be the most artistic handwork.

Very few silk buttons are seen, but occasionally small satin buttons are used. The preference, for wool suits of the nicest quality, is for exquisitely shaded pearl buttons, for those richly carved, or else tinted to match the dress. And finally, for the substantial horn and wooden buttons 1 in. in diameter, quite thick and heavy looking, with eyes sunken in the center.

Harper's Bazar, March 1878

Pearl beads in passementerie and fringe are much used for trimming white satin wedding dresses. A pyramid of the fringe is on the skirt front. The neck and edges of the basque are finished with it. Perhaps there are panels of pearls on the side pieces. The sleeves are made to look like a network of pearls, as they are made of lengthwise strips of the passementerie. Pearl-embroidered skirt fronts and embroidered vests for the bodice are imported ready for use. The beads are iridescent pearls, showing opal tints. They are strung on threads, and wrought in loops and branches in the needlework.

Sometimes lace is used for the transparent sleeves instead of the pearl trimming. Handsome laces are especially desirable now for arranging in

rows across the front and sides of the satin dress, or in jabots and panels on the sides. Wide lace flounces at the foot are festooned at intervals with small bouquets and satin ribbon loops. When lace is used on the train, it is not as flounces, but in lengthwise designs.

Small bouquets set at intervals down the front amid rows of lace, or else clusters for the front and back of the panniers, are the favorite styles of garniture. Some sets of orange blossoms outline the pannier on the hips. Others form a curve around a tablier, and still others are massed as panels on the side. White lilies, jasmine, or clematis are mixed with orange blossoms.

Harper's Bazar, May 1879

Epaulets of flowers are the novelty on French evening toilettes. A small branch or garland of roses passes around the armhole of the short puffed sleeve, making it look still higher. Elbow sleeves, and others that are not puffed, have only an epaulet bouquet set on one or both sleeves. There is then another bouquet stuck in the belt or in the left side of the corsage at the waist.

There is no definite arrangement for the flowers on skirts, as skirts are made in various styles, each of which requires a special design. It is best, however, to place the flowers on the left side, as they will be better seen there than on the right, where the escort walks. Crushed roses without foliage are massed together to form a cordon, or else broader panels down each side of the skirt. When there are draped scarves or a regular apron, a fringe of flowers is used on the edges, such as drooping fuschias or blue harebells. Seaweed is the delicate garniture for tulle dresses.

Silk embroidery on tulle represents flowers so perfectly, and is so beautiful, that many ladies prefer it to flowers for giving a touch of color to plain silk evening dresses. This is used in bands for heading lace or fringe. When appliquéd neatly it looks as if the needlework was done directly on the dress. Vines of olive and moss green leaves are especially liked in this embroidery. These are usually brightened by cardinal flowers, rich damask roses, violets, or yellow buttercups. Foliage plants in all their

high colors are favorite designs for these bands. Some are shaded in the delicate Pompadour tints. There are also rich tabliers and scarves for drapery made of China crape or tulle, and embroidered in patterns like those on the bands. Chenille embroidery is very effectively used in this way.

Harper's Bazar, January 1878

The most useful addition to the toilette a lady can have is one or two complete sets of ribbon garnitures that can be taken off, and put on evening or dinner dresses at pleasure.

Demorest's Mirror of Fashions, September 1877

A new style of kilting for trimming skirts is made of a straight band of silk about 6 in. deep, and lined with thin muslin. It is then cut in scallops 1/4 yd. broad, and reaching up half the depth of the flounce. Each scallop is formed into 12 small pleats, all turned one way and pressed flat. The pleating is often headed with a band of 3 in. galloon, or with a crossband of brocade, above which is an upright pleating. The edge of this is sometimes hemmed plain, and sometimes scalloped on a narrower scale than the kilting below.

Demorest's Mirror of Fashions, February 1877

Fur borders for dresses are more used than ever. They are no longer restricted to the overdress and wrap, but are now seen in a single broad band near the foot of the lower skirt, or as panels down each side. A single wide border is more stylish than two or more narrow ones. Beaver furs are the favorite trimmings. Chinchilla is equally fashionable, but is used in narrower widths, on account of its deep fleece; 3 to 5 in. is preferred for chinchilla bands. Gray lynx bands are beautiful on gray cloths. Natural raccoon skins make a very effective trimming for light cloth.

The black hare borders are of excellent jet black and fine luster for trimming black cloth and other dark stuffs. Glossy black fox bands are used for satin and velvet costumes and wraps. Black marten trimmings are excellent for black cloth suits. Stone marten tails are again used for trimmings.

Harper's Bazar, November 1881

Figure 1. Woven braid and crocheted trimming

Trimmings for Drawers

The trimming in figure 1 is composed of insertion and edging. It is worked with woven braid and crochet cotton no. 80. For the insertion, crochet on both sides of the braid two rounds as follows. First round: Always alternately 1 single crochet on the next loop, 5 chain stitches. Second round: Always alternately 1 single crochet on the middle of the next 5 chain stitches in the preceding round, 2 chain stitches.

For the edging, crochet on one side of the braid the first round as follows. ✳ Work 1 single crochet on the next loop, nine times alternately 5 chain stitches, 1 single crochet on the next loop. Then 4 chain stitches, 1 single crochet on the following loop, 3 chain stitches, 4 single crochet on the next four loops, 3 chain stitches, 1 single crochet on the following loop, 3 chain stitches, 4 single crochet on the next four loops, 3 chain stitches, 1 single crochet on the following loop. Fasten to the 4th of the 4 chain stitches worked previously. (To do this, drop

the stitch from the needle, insert the needle in the corresponding stitch, and draw the dropped stitch through.) Then 4 chain stitches, and repeat from ✳.

Second round: ✳ Nine times 4 chain stitches separated each by 3 chain stitches on the next 5 chain stitches in the preceding round. Then twice 2 single crochet separated each by 3 chain stitches on the next 4 chain stitches. Repeat from ✳.

The third round is worked on the other side of the braid as follows. Work 1 single crochet on the loop above the hollow, 5 chain stitches, 1 single crochet on the following loop, 4 chain stitches, 2 short treble crochet, the upper veins of which are worked off together on the same loop on which the last single crochet was worked, five times alternately 1 chain stitch, 3 short treble crochet, the upper veins of which are worked off together on the second following loop, but with the middle of these 3 short treble crochet fasten together three loops. Then 1 chain stitch, 2 short treble crochet, the upper veins of which are worked off together on the second following loop, 12 chain stitches, fasten to the 4th of the 4 chain stitches worked last, six times 2 single crochet on the chain stitch before the next 3 short treble crochet (catching the 12 chain stitches worked previously at the same time), 1 slip stitch on the last 2 short treble crochet which were worked off together. Turn the work on the wrong side. Work 4 chain stitches, 2 short treble crochet, the upper veins of which are worked off together on both sides of the middle 3 short treble crochet, catching the single crochet there at the same time, 4 chain stitches, 1 slip stitch on the stitch on which the last fastening was done, 9 chain stitches. Turn the work. Work 1 slip stitch on the slip stitch before the last, 9 chain stitches, fasten to the slip stitch before the last, 1 single crochet, 1 short double crochet, 13 double crochet, 1 short double crochet, 1 single crochet on the last 9 chain stitches and on the 9 chain stitches before the last, catching both together, 1 slip stitch on the last 2 short treble crochet worked on a loop, 4 chain stitches, 1 single crochet on the same loop on which the last 2 short treble crochet were worked, 5 chain stitches. Repeat from ✳.

Fourth round: ✳ Work 6 single crochet on the next 5 chain stitches in the preceding round, 8 chain stitches, 1 single crochet on the middle of the next 13 double crochet, 8 chain stitches, 6 single crochet on the following 5 chain stitches. Repeat from ✳.

Fifth round: Always alternately 1 double crochet on the next stitch in the preceding round, 2 chain stitches, and pass over 2 stitches.

Harper's Bazar, April 1878

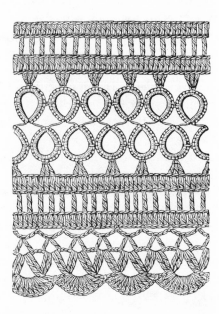

Figure 2. Tatted and crocheted edging

The edging in figure 2 is worked with fine cotton in tatting and crochet. ✳ With one shuttle work one ring of 26 double stitches (the double stitch consists of 1 stitch right and 1 stitch left). Between the 13th and 14th and between the 19th and 20th double stitches work 1 picot each. Turn the work, and after a thread interval of 1/4 in. work one ring as before. Turn the work, and after a thread interval of 1/4 in. repeat from ✳. But in every repetition fasten each ring, after working the 7th double stitch, to the 2nd picot of the corresponding ring in the preceding pattern figure.

Having in this manner tatted a piece of suitable length, crochet on each side four rounds, as follows. First round: Always alternately 3 double

crochet on the picot of the next ring, 3 chain stitches. Second round: Work 1 double crochet on each stitch in the preceding round. Third round: Always alternately 1 short treble crochet on the 2nd following stitch in the preceding round, 1 chain stitch. Fourth round: Like the second round.

On one side work for the bottom of the edging four rounds as follows. Fifth round: Always alternately 1 single crochet on the upper veins of the next stitch in the preceding round, 5 chain stitches, pass over 4 stitches. Sixth round: Always alternately 2 double crochet separated by 3 chain stitches on the middle of the next 5 chain stitches in the preceding round, 1 chain stitch. Seventh round: Work 2 short treble crochet on the next 3 chain stitches in the preceding round, working off the upper veins together, ✳ 4 chain stitches, 2 short treble crochet on the 3 chain stitches on which the preceding 2 short treble crochet were not worked, not working off the upper veins for the present, 2 short treble crochet on the following 3 chain stitches, working off the upper veins together with those of the preceding 2 short treble crochet. Repeat from ✳. Eighth round: Always alternately 1 single crochet on the next 4 chain stitches, 11 double crochet on the following 4 chain stitches.

Figure 3. Serpentine braid and crocheted edging

The edging in figure 3 is worked with fine cotton. Take a piece of serpentine braid, and on one side crochet the first round as follows. ✻ Work 4 double crochet on the middle of the next scallop (working them close together), 5 chain stitches, after an interval of 1/2 in. work 1 double crochet on the braid, 2 chain stitches, 1 double crochet 1/4 in. from the preceding double crochet (so that it comes before the hollow), not working off the upper veins, after an interval of 1/4 in. work 1 double crochet on the braid (on the other side of the hollow), working off the upper veins together with those of the preceding double crochet, 2 chain stitches, after an interval of 1/4 in. work 1 double crochet on the braid, 5 chain stitches. Repeat from ✻.

Second round: Work 6 double crochet on the next 6 stitches in the preceding round, ✻ 3 chain stitches, for 1 cross double crochet work 1 short treble crochet on the next 2 chain stitches between 2 double crochet, working off only the lower vein, 1 double crochet on the following 2 chain stitches, then work off the upper veins of the short treble crochet, 1 chain stitch, 1 double crochet on the middle vein of the short treble crochet, then 3 chain stitches, pass over 3 of the next 5 chain stitches, 8 double crochet on the next 8 stitches, so that the middle 4 double crochet come on the 4 double crochet of the preceding round. Repeat from ✻.

Third round: ✻ Work 4 double crochet on the next 4 stitches in the preceding round, 6 chain stitches, 1 double crochet on the single chain stitch in the next cross double crochet, 6 chain stitches, pass over 6 stitches. Repeat from ✻.

Fourth round: Always 1 double crochet on each stitch in the preceding round.

Fifth round: Always alternately one pointed bar figure (for this work 1 short treble crochet on the following stitch, working off only the lower vein, 2 double crochet on the next 2 stitches, working off the upper veins together with the middle vein of the short treble crochet, then work off the upper veins of the short treble crochet), 3 chain stitches, and pass over 1 stitch.

Sixth and seventh rounds: Work the same as the preceding round (the middle stitch of every 3 chain stitches in the preceding round should be passed over).

Eighth round: Work like the fourth round.

Ninth round: Always alternately 1 double crochet on the 2nd following stitch, 1 chain stitch.

Tenth round: On the other side of the braid work always alternately 9 single crochet separated each by one picot (composed of 4 chain stitches and 1 single crochet on the last single crochet), at regular intervals on the next scallop, 2 chain stitches, pass over 1/4 in. in the next hollow.

Harper's Bazar, May 1879

Figure 1. Chemise with Russian embroidery

Chemise Yokes and Sleeves

The embroidery on the chemise in figure 1 is
worked as shown in figure 2, in satin, overcast, and
knotted stitch, with red and blue thread.

Englishwoman's Domestic Magazine, January 1877

Figure 2. Detail of embroidery

377

Figure 3. Chemise for heart-shaped dresses

Figure 3 shows a fine linen chemise. The trimming consists of bias strips of the material, lace insertion, needlework insertion and edging, and gathered lace.

Harper's Bazar, April 1878

Figure 4. Lace chemise yoke

Figure 4 shows a fine linen chemise set on a lace yoke. The yoke is composed of Breton lace insertion 1 1/4 in. wide, batiste insertion 1 in. wide, and pieces of needlework batiste. It is edged with

Breton lace 1 1/4 in. wide. The joining seams are covered with narrow bias strips of batiste embroidered in knotted stitch and stitched on. The sleeves are trimmed with insertion, lace, and bias strips of batiste.

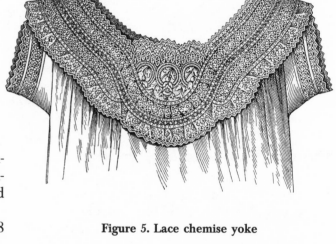

Figure 5. Lace chemise yoke

Figure 5 shows a fine linen chemise set on a lace yoke. The yoke is composed of needlework batiste, Breton lace insertion 1 1/4 in. wide, and batiste insertion 1/2 in. wide. It is edged with Breton lace 1 1/4 in. wide. The joining seams are covered with narrow bias strips of batiste, which are embroidered in knotted stitch with fine cotton.

Harper's Bazar, June 1879

Figure 6. Crocheted chemise yoke

The chemise in figure 6 is made of fine linen, and set on a crocheted yoke. Work with cotton no. 25, on a foundation of suitable length, divisible by 12, the first round as follows. ✳ Work 2 chain stitches, 4 short treble crochet separated each by 2 chain stitches (the middle 2 by 3 chain stitches), on the 5th following stitch 2 chain stitches, 1 single crochet on the 5th following stitch. Repeat from ✳. The second round is worked on the other side of the foundation and is like the preceding round.

Work a new foundation, which should be 96 stitches shorter than the first, as each of the four corners in the chemise requires two pattern figures less. Crochet thereon the third and fourth rounds, like the first and second rounds. But in the fourth round always fasten the middle of the 3 chain stitches to the corresponding stitch in the first round. In each corner, fasten the figure there to the next three figures in the first round.

Fifth round: Always alternately 1 single crochet on the middle of the next 3 chain stitches in the third round, 10 chain stitches, but in each corner twice instead of 10 chain stitches work 13 chain stitches. Sixth round: Work 1 double crochet on the 1st stitch, then always alternately 1 chain stitch, 1 double crochet on the 2nd following stitch (in each corner in this and the next three rounds pass over several stitches more). Seventh round: Always alternately 2 double crochet on the next 2 stitches in the preceding round, 4 chain stitches, pass over 4 stitches. Eighth round: Like the sixth round. Ninth round: ✳ Work 2 double crochet separated by 3 chain stitches on the 3rd following stitch, 3 chain stitches, 1 single crochet on the 3rd following stitch, 3 chain stitches. Repeat from ✳.

The tenth through twelfth rounds are done on the other side of the work. They are like the sixth through eighth rounds, but in each corner work several stitches more.

This completes the yoke. The trimming on the front slit and the sleeves is worked in the same manner.

Harper's Bazar, September 1879

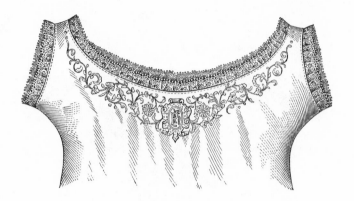

Figure 7. Embroidered chemise

Figure 8. Center of embroidery

Embroidery Design
Full size

Harper's Bazar, February 1882

Figure 9. Embroidery pattern

Figure 1. Corset cover, closed on the side

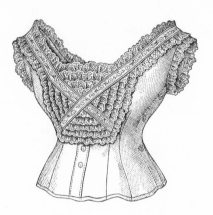

Figure 2. Corset cover, closed on the side

Trimmings for Corset Covers

Harper's Bazar, March 1877

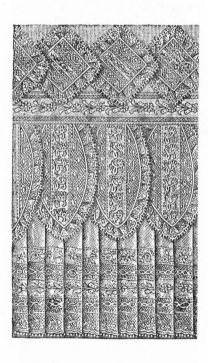

Figure 1. Edging for underskirt

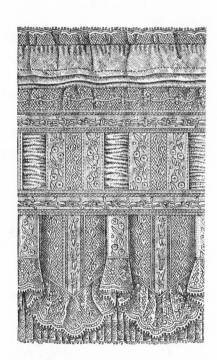

Figure 2. Edging for underskirt

Trimmings for Petticoats

The trimming in figure 1 consists of squares and narrow ovals of lace with a band of insertion. At the lower edge is a pleated frill of muslin, edged with lace.

Figure 2 shows a pleated frill of cambric, edged with Valenciennes lace, beneath a Vandyked flounce with insertion.

Englishwoman's Domestic Magazine, October 1877

Figure 3. Trimming for petticoat

Figure 4. Trimming for petticoat

The trimmings in figures 3 and 4 are set on the petticoat in lieu of flounces. For the trimming in figure 3, edge a strip of batiste, which is run in five narrow tucks on the bottom, with lace insertion 2 in. wide. To this insertion join a strip composed of needlework and lace insertion 2 in. wide, and edged on the bottom with needlework 4 in. wide. Cover the joining seams with narrow bias strips of batiste stitched on. A gathered row of lace 2 1/4 in. wide, headed with a needlework border 1/2 in. wide, completes this trimming.

For the trimming in figure 4, form a strip 4 7/8 in. wide, of needlework insertion 1 3/4 in. wide, and lace insertion 1 1/2 in. wide. Edge it at the top with needlework insertion. On the latter join a strip of batiste run into narrow tucks on the bottom. On the under edge of the strip arranged of insertions, set a strip of batiste 4 1/2 in. wide. This is run in narrow tucks and edged with lace insertion, underneath which the material is cut away, and finished with lace 2 in. wide. A similar row of lace completes the trimming.

Harper's Bazar, August 1878

Figure 1. Insertion

Trimmings for Dressing Sacques And Nightdresses

The trimmings in figures 1 and 2 are worked on batiste, nainsook, or linen in satin, tent, back, and buttonhole stitch with white embroidery cotton. They are ornamented with lace stitches and wheels of fine cotton. After finishing the embroidery, cut away the material between the design figures.

Figure 2. Border

Harper's Bazar, November 1878

Figure 1. White embroidery border

Trimmings for Lingerie

The border in figure 1 is worked on batiste or linen with fine embroidery cotton. The stitches are satin, half-polka, knotted, and overcast stitch. It is finished on the edge with buttonhole stitch scallops.

Harper's Bazar, July 1877

Figure 2. Knitted insertion

The insertion in figure 2 is worked with crochet cotton no. 25, and fine steel knitting needles, crosswise, in rounds going back and forth. Make a foundation of 24 stitches, and knit on them as follows. First round: Slip, knit 1 stitch crossed, knit 2 together crossed, four times alternately twice throw the thread over, twice knit 2 together crossed; then twice throw the thread over, knit 2 together crossed, knit 2 crossed. Second round: All knit plain, but on the double throw the thread over work always 1 knit, 1 purled. Third and fourth rounds: Like the first and second rounds. Fifth round: Slip, knit 3 crossed, knit 2 together crossed, three times alternately twice throw the thread over, twice knit 2 together crossed; then twice throw the thread over, knit 2 together crossed, knit 4 crossed. Sixth round: Like the second round. Seventh and eighth rounds: Like the fifth and sixth rounds. Repeat always the first through the eighth rounds until the insertion is the length desired.

Harper's Bazar, March 1878

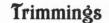

Figure 3. Mignardise and crochet insertion

The insertion in figure 3 is worked in two parts, with mignardise and crochet cotton no. 60. For one part take two pieces of mignardise and work the first round. ✱ Twice alternately 1 single crochet on the third following loop on the first piece of mignardise, 3 chain stitches, 1 single crochet on the third following loop on the second piece of mignardise, 3 chain stitches. Then 1 single crochet on the third following loop on the first piece of mignardise, 3 chain stitches, pass over two loops on the second piece of mignardise, and with 1 single crochet fasten together the next four loops, 3 chain stitches, 1 single crochet on the same loop of the first piece of mignardise on which 1 single crochet was worked last, twice alternately 3 chain stitches, 1 single crochet on the third following loop on the second piece of mignardise, 3 chain stitches, 1 single crochet on the third following loop on the first piece of mignardise. Then three chain stitches, 1 single crochet on the third following loop on the second piece of mignardise, 3 chain stitches, pass over two loops of the first piece of mignardise, and with 1 single crochet fasten together the following four loops, 3 chain stitches, 1 single crochet on the same loop of the second piece of mignardise on which 1 single crochet was worked last, 3 chain stitches. Repeat from ✱.

The second round is worked on one side of the crochet work. ✱ With 1 single crochet fasten together the middle four loops in the next hollow, four times alternately 1 chain stitch, 1 single crochet on the next loop. Then for one figure work 9 chain stitches, 1 slip stitch on the 1st of these, 11 single crochet on the 9 chain stitches, 1 slip stitch on the same stitch on which the preceding slip stitch was worked, 1 single crochet on the next loop, eight times alternately 1 chain stitch, 1 single crochet on the following loop. Then one figure as before, four times alternately 1 single crochet on the next loop, 1 chain stitch. Repeat from ✱. But in every repetition fasten the 6th single crochet of the first figure to the 6th single crochet of the second figure in the preceding pattern figure. To do this drop the stitch from the needle, insert the needle in the corresponding stitch, and draw the dropped stitch through.

For the third round work 1 single crochet on the 6th single crochet of the next figure in the preceding round, ✱ 8 chain stitches, 1 single crochet on the next point, 8 chain stitches, 1 single crochet on the vein between the next two figures. Repeat from ✱.

For the fourth round work always alternately 1 double crochet on the next stitch in the preceding round, 1 chain stitch, pass over 1 stitch.

The fifth round is worked on the other side of the work. ✱ Fasten together the middle four loops in the next hollow with 1 single crochet, four times alternately 1 chain stitch, 1 single crochet on the next loop. Then for a four-leaved figure work 9 chain stitches, 1 slip stitch on the 1st of these, 5 single crochet on the next 1 of the 9 chain stitches, + 9 chain stitches, 1 slip stitch on the 1st of these, 11 single crochet on the 9 chain stitches, 1 single crochet on the stitch on which the last slip stitch was worked. Repeat twice from +. Then 5 single crochet on the free stitch of the first 9 chain stitches in this figure, 1 slip stitch on the stitch on which the 1st slip stitch in this figure was worked. This completes one figure. Next work thirteen times alternately 1 single crochet on the next loop, 1 chain stitch, and repeat from ✱. But in every repetition,

after the 5th single crochet in the second leaflet of the four-leaved figure, work 1 single crochet on the chain stitch between the 9th and 10th of the following 13 single crochet separated each by 1 chain stitch in the preceding pattern figure. This completes the first part of the insertion.

The second part is worked in a similar manner. But in the fifth round, instead of the four-leaved figure, work 1 single crochet on one of the free leaflets in the next four-leaved figure in the first part of the insertion, and join the next free leaflet of the same figure to the second part at the corresponding point in a similar manner. Besides this fasten each point to the corresponding point of the first part of the insertion with a single crochet stitch.

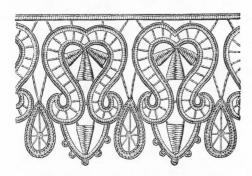

Figure 4. Wrought guipure border

Transfer the design on figure 4 to thick cardboard. Baste Swiss muslin on the latter. Run the outlines of the design figures with hemp thread, no. 90. For the connecting bars stretch the thread going forward and wind it going back. Darn the pointed figures in point de reprise. Edge all the design figures partly in simple and partly in interlaced buttonhole stitch. For the latter first overcast the outline on one side in buttonhole stitch with thread no. 130. Then work a second row in the opposite direction, always inserting the needle between the next 2 stitches of the first row. The buttonhole stitches on the outer edge are partly interspersed with picots. After finishing the embroidery, cut away the material between the design figures.

Harper's Bazar, July 1878

Figure 5. Point lace embroidery on net border

For the border in figure 5 transfer the design to linen, on which baste Brussels net. Along the outlines run different kinds of point lace braid. These are laid in pleats on the corners and gathered in the curves. Stitch the braid on the foundation with fine thread. Darn the net inside the design figures as illustrated. Finish the border on the outer edge with picot braid.

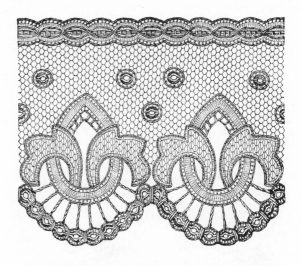

Figure 6. Point lace embroidery on net border

For the border in figure 6 transfer the design to linen, on which baste Brussels net. Run on plain and medallion point lace braid. Run the leaves with medium-sized thread, and edge them with buttonhole stitches. For the dots sew on single medallions of the braid with fine thread. Stitch the braid on the foundation with similar thread. Work the lace stitches and twisted bars. Darn the net as illustrated.

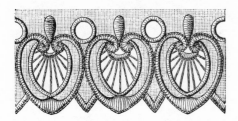

Figure 7. White embroidery border

The border in figure 7 is worked on nainsook or linen in satin, overcast, and buttonhole stitch. Work the twisted bars with fine thread. Cut away the material underneath.

Harper's Bazar, September 1878

Figure 8. Woven braid and crocheted edging

The edging in figure 8 is worked with woven braid composed of single figures, and with crochet cotton no. 60. The figures are joined with cords 1/2 in. long, and are furnished on each side with six loops.

First round: ✳ Work 6 double crochet separated each by 3 chain stitches on the six loops of the next figure on one side of the braid, 3 chain stitches, 2 double crochet separated by 3 chain stitches on the next cord, 3 chain stitches, 3 double crochet separated each by 3 chain stitches on the next three loops in the following figure, 8 chain stitches, with 1 single crochet fasten together the next two loops, 7 chain stitches, fasten the middle of these to the 4th of the 8 chain stitches worked previously (to do this drop the stitch from the needle, insert the needle into the corresponding stitch, and draw the dropped stitch through), 1 single crochet on the next loop, 7 chain stitches, but fasten the middle of these to the middle of the 7 chain stitches worked previously, pass over the next loop in the following figure, twice alternately with 1 single crochet fasten together the next two loops, 7 chain stitches, fasten the middle of these to the middle of the preceding 7 chain stitches, then 1 single crochet on the first loop of the following figure, 7 chain stitches, fasten the middle of these to the middle of the preceding 7 chain stitches, with 1 single crochet fasten together the next two loops, 3 chain stitches, fasten to the middle of the preceding 7 chain stitches, fasten to the 3rd of the 8 chain stitches worked previously, 2 chain stitches, 3 double crochet separated each by 3 chain stitches on the next three loops, 3 chain stitches, 2 double crochet separated by 3 chain stitches on the next cord, 3 chain stitches. Repeat from ✳.

Second round: ✳ Work 1 single crochet on the next 3 chain stitches in the preceding round, eight times alternately one picot (which consists of 5 chain stitches and 1 double crochet on the 1st of these), 1 single crochet on the next 3 chain stitches; then 3 chain stitches, 1 single crochet on the following 3 chain stitches, 1 single crochet on the 3 chain stitches corresponding to those before

indicated, 3 chain stitches, four times alternately 1 single crochet on the next 3 chain stitches, one picot. Repeat from ✳.

Third round: Work on the other side of the braid ✳ 6 double crochet separated each by 3 chain stitches on the six loops of the figure in the next hollow of the edging, 5 chain stitches, 1 double crochet on the middle of the next cord, 9 chain stitches, 1 single crochet on the first loop of the next figure, 8 chain stitches, + with 1 single crochet fasten together the next two loops, 7 chain stitches, fasten the middle of these to the 4th of the 8 chain stitches worked previously, with 1 single crochet fasten together the next two loops, 7 chain stitches, fasten to the middle of the 7 chain stitches worked previously, pass over the last loop in this and the first loop in the following figure. Repeat twice from +. But in the last repetition, instead of the last 7 chain stitches, crochet 8 chain stitches, the 4th of which is fastened to the middle of the preceding 7 chain stitches, and the 5th to the 3rd of the 8 chain stitches worked previously. Instead of passing over two loops, work 1 single crochet on the last loop of this figure, 9 chain stitches, fasten the middle of these to the middle of the corresponding 9 chain stitches, 1 double crochet on the middle of the next cord, 5 chain stitches. Repeat from ✳.

Fourth round: ✳ Work 1 single crochet on the middle of the 3 chain stitches between the 2nd and 3rd of the next 6 double crochet in the preceding round, twice alternately 3 chain stitches, 1 single crochet on the middle of the next 3 chain stitches, then 6 chain stitches, 3 treble crochet on the middle of the next 5 chain stitches, not working off the upper veins, 3 treble crochet on the middle of the corresponding 5 chain stitches, working off the upper veins together with the preceding 3 treble crochet, 6 chain stitches. Repeat from ✳.

Fifth round: Always alternately 1 double crochet on the 2nd following stitch in the preceding round, 1 chain stitch.

Sixth round: Always alternately 1 cross double crochet, for which work 1 treble crochet on the next double crochet in the preceding round, working off only the lower vein, 1 double crochet on the next double crochet, work off the upper veins of the treble crochet, 1 chain stitch, and 1 double crochet on the middle vein of the treble crochet, 1 chain stitch.

Seventh round: Like the fifth round.
Harper's Bazar, October 1878

Figure 9. Crocheted edging

The edging in figure 9 is worked with crochet cotton no. 40. First round: ✳ Work 15 chain stitches, 1 slip stitch on the 1st of these, 27 single crochet on the ring, 1 slip stitch on the 1st of the 27 single crochet, 13 single crochet on the next 13 single crochet. Repeat from ✳.

Second round: This is worked on one side of the first round on which only one row of single crochet has been worked. Work 1 double crochet on the 2nd following 1 of the 12 single crochet, ✳ three times alternately 5 chain stitches, 1 double crochet on the 3rd following stitch, not working off the upper veins of the last double crochet, 1 double crochet on the 2nd single crochet of the following ring, working off the upper veins together with those of the preceding double crochet. Repeat from ✳.

Third round: Always alternately 1 double crochet on the middle of the next 5 chain stitches in the preceding round, 4 chain stitches.

Fourth round: Work 5 single crochet on every 4 chain stitches in the preceding round.
Harper's Bazar, November 1878

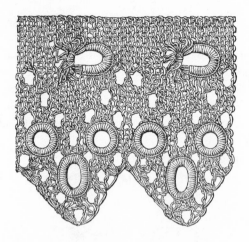

Figure 10. Knitted and buttonhole-stitched edging

The edging in figure 10 is knitted with cotton no. 25, and ornamented with buttonhole stitching worked with white glazed cotton. To work the edging make a foundation of 17 stitches. Going back and forth on these, knit in rounds as follows. First round: All knit plain. Second round: Slip, 4 knit plain, knit 2 stitches together, twice alternately throw the thread over, twice knit 2 together; then twice throw the thread over, knit 2 together. Third to fifth rounds: All knit plain. But before beginning the first and last of these three rounds throw the thread over, and in the following round knit off this thread. On each double thread thrown over work 1 knit, 1 purled. Sixth round: Like the second round. But at the beginning, instead of 4 knit stitches work 6 knit stitches. Seventh to ninth rounds: Like the third to fifth rounds. Tenth round: Slip, 2 knit plain, knit 2 together, twice throw the thread over, knit 2 together, 2 knit plain, knit 2 together, twice alternately twice throw the thread over, twice knit 2 together; then twice throw the thread over, knit 2 together. Eleventh to thirteenth rounds: Like the third to fifth rounds. Fourteenth round: Like the second round. But at the beginning, instead of 4 knit stitches work 10 knit stitches. Fifteenth to seventeenth rounds: All knit plain. But at the end of the second of these three rounds knit 2 together. Eighteenth round: Like the second round. But at the beginning, instead of 4 knit stitches

work 8 knit stitches. At the end, instead of 2, knit 3 together. Nineteenth round: Slip, 14 knit stitches, rip the next 2 stitches in the preceding round, and from these twice take up 1 stitch, knit off the latter (first take up 1 stitch and knit it off, then take up the 2nd stitch and likewise knit it off), 4 knit stitches. Twentieth and twenty-first rounds: All knit plain. But at the end of the twentieth round knit 2 together. Twenty-second round: Like the eighteenth round. But at the beginning, instead of 8 knit stitches work 6 knit stitches. Twenty-third to twenty-fifth rounds: Like the fifteenth to seventeenth rounds. Twenty-sixth round: Like the eighteenth round. But at the beginning, instead of 8 knit stitches work 4 knit stitches. Twenty-seventh to twenty-ninth rounds: All knit plain. Repeat constantly the second through twenty-ninth rounds.

Figure 11. Border of point lace embroidery on net

For figures 11 to 13, transfer the designs to linen. Baste thereon Brussels net, and overcast the various kinds of point lace braid on the foundation. The design figures of the border in figure 11 are overcast on the edges. The ground is darned with fine thread, with which are also worked the lace stitches. Cut away the net beneath the lace stitches. Edge the border with buttonhole stitch scallops.

Figure 12. Border of point lace embroidery on net

The sprays in the border in figure 12 are worked partly of medallion braid, and partly are edged with glazed cotton and darned with fine thread. The holes inside the flowers are edged with buttonhole stitches. The border is finished with picot braid on the edge.

Figure 13. Border of point lace embroidery on net

For the border in figure 13, darn the net for the flowers and leaves. For the connecting bars, stretch the working thread going forward and wind it going back. Edge the design figures with

buttonhole stitches of similar thread. The stems are worked in dovetailed buttonhole stitch. Inside the design figures, darn the net partly with glazed cotton and partly with fine thread. Work the lace stitches with similar thread. Cut away the net beneath the bars after finishing the embroidery. Edge the border with picot braid.

Harper's Bazar, March 1879

Figure 14. White embroidery border

The border in figure 14 is worked on batiste or fine linen with fine white embroidery cotton. The stitches used are satin and tent stitch. The foundation is cut away between the bars and leaves.

Harper's Bazar, May 1879

Figure 15. White embroidery border

The border in figure 15 is worked on batiste or fine linen with fine white embroidery cotton. The stitches used are satin, tent, and lace stitch.

Harper's Bazar, June 1879

Figure 16. Renaissance embroidery border

For the border in figure 16, transfer the outlines of the design to linen. Run them with embroidery cotton. For the connecting bars, stretch the thread going forward and overcast it going back with buttonhole stitches interspersed with picots. Edge all the design figures with buttonhole stitches. Work the eyelet holes and single bars in tent stitch. Cut away the material between the design figures.
Harper's Bazar, November 1879

The border in figure 17 is worked on batiste or linen with fine white embroidery cotton. The stitches used are satin, tent, and buttonhole stitch. The openwork medallions are filled with wheels and lace stitches.
Harper's Bazar, January 1880

Figure 18. White embroidery border

The border in figure 18 is worked on cambric or muslin with fine white embroidery cotton. The stitches used are overcast and buttonhole stitch.
Harper's Bazar, May 1882

Figure 17. White embroidery border

Figure 1. Satin dress and lace bertha

Berthas

The dress in figure 1 is of garnet satin cut square in
the neck in front and pointed in back. The bertha
is of white lace 4 1/2 in. wide. It is trimmed on the
neck with a roll of red velvet and a crepe lisse pleating. A spray of colored flowers is fastened on the
right side by an agrafe in the shape of a salamander.

Figure 2. Damassé dress and silk gauze bertha

Figure 2 shows a low-necked dress with short
sleeves, made of pale pink damassé. The bertha is
made of pink silk striped gauze on a Swiss muslin
foundation. It is trimmed with white lace 3 in. wide
and loops and ends of pink satin ribbon 2 in. wide.

Figure 3. Faille dress and blonde bertha

The pale blue faille dress in figure 3 is trimmed with white blonde and bows of satin ribbon. For the bertha, cut of white stiff lace one piece from the pattern. Sew it up according to the corresponding figures. Cover the foundation with pleated blonde 3 in. wide as illustrated. Trim the bertha with puffings of pale blue satin.

Harper's Bazar, February 1879

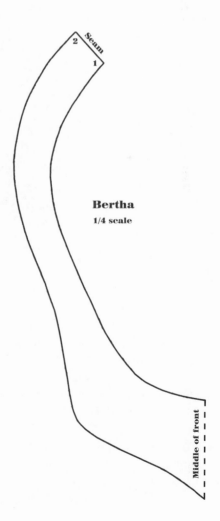

Bertha
1/4 scale

Figure 4. Silk tulle bertha

The bertha in figure 4 is finished with a plastron. For the foundation of the latter cut of stiff lace a three-cornered piece 12 in. high and 9 3/4 in. wide at the top. Cut for the bertha a piece 3/4 in. wide and 1 yd. long.

The plastron is joined with the bertha, and covered with puffs of white silk tulle. It is trimmed with ruches of tulle. These are continued on the outer edge of the plastron and on the bertha, at the same time heading a row of white blonde 3 1/4 in. wide.

Harper's Bazar, March 1879

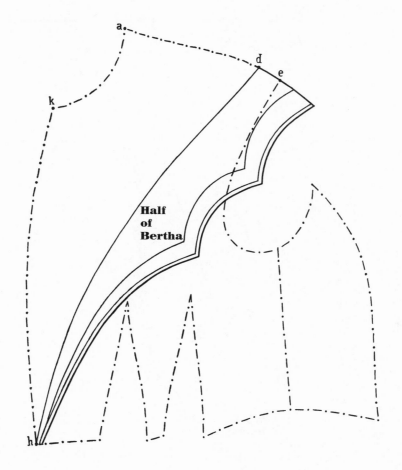

Figure 5. Bertha

    The bertha in figure 5 is drafted using the plain bodice pattern, which is shown by a dotted and dashed line.

The bertha in figure 6 is drafted using the plain bodice pattern, which is indicated by a dotted and dashed line. The front and back of the bodice are placed at *a* and *b*. The width of the bertha and the length of the back end from *e* to *f* may be in any style desired.

Complete Guide to Ladies' Garment Cutting, 1883

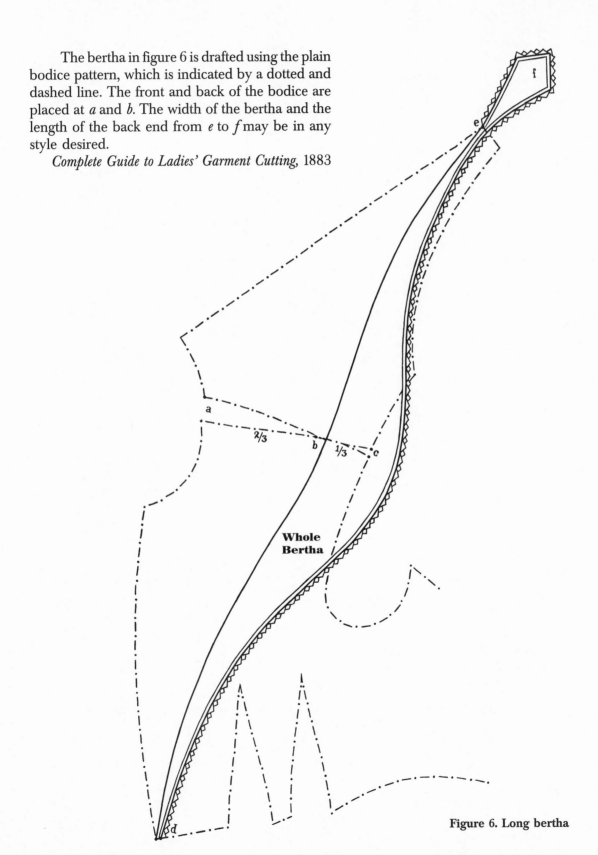

Figure 6. Long bertha

Figure 1. Brocade dress sleeve

Figure 3. Dress sleeve

Trimmings for Dress Sleeves

The sleeve in figure 1 is made of brocaded silk, and is trimmed with dark grosgrain and with bows of the latter material.

Figure 2. Snowflake cloth dress sleeve

The sleeve of snowflake cloth in figure 2 is joined with a triple cuff. The upper and lower cuffs are of snowflake cloth; the middle one is of dark grosgrain. A binding of dark grosgrain finishes the cuffs.

Harper's Bazar, May 1878

Figure 4. Dress sleeve

Harper's Bazar, April 1879

Figure 5. Faille dress sleeve

The sleeve of light gray faille in figure 5 is trimmed with shirring of the material headed with folds. These are edged with lace on one side.

399

Figure 6. Poplin dress sleeve

The trimming for the gray poplin sleeve in figure 6 consists of rolls and a cuff of the same material. This is scalloped and bound on the edges, bordered with lace, and simulates buttoning on the sleeve.

Figure 7. Cachemire des Indes dress sleeve

The sleeve in figure 7 is made of gendarme blue cachemire des Indes. It is trimmed with satin ribbon of the same color with a moiré face.

Figure 8. Beige dress sleeve

The beige sleeve in figure 8 is trimmed with narrow satin ribbon, a fold of the material piped with satin, and a bow of satin ribbon.

Harper's Bazar, May 1879

Figure 9. Sleeve trimming

The sleeve trimming in figure 9 is composed of two pleatings of the dress material, which is the darker of the two shades. The lower pleating edges the sleeve. The upper is laid in broader pleats, and turned in the opposite direction. Set between the two is a brocade cuff in the lighter shade that is used for trimming, which is bound with satin of the same shade. The pleatings are bound with similar satin.

Figure 10. Sleeve trimming

Figure 10 shows the sleeve trimming of a cashmere and satin dress. Two satin pleatings are set on the sleeve. One is an edging and the other turned upward. Between the two is a cashmere drapery, the pleated ends of which are held together under a bronze ornament.

Harper's Bazar, March 1882

Figure 12. Dress sleeve

The sleeve in figure 12 is that of a figured cotton sateen dress. On an ordinary coat sleeve lining, the under part is covered with plain sateen. The upper part is covered with sateen laid in four deep side pleats, which are closer together at the wrist than at the shoulder. The bottom of the sleeve is finished with a cuff of Irish point embroidery and narrow muslin frills.

Harper's Bazar, July 1882

Figure 11. Dress sleeve

The dress sleeve in figure 11 is of cream-colored foulard, figured with dark blue. It is an elbow sleeve bordered with an upturned narrow cuff of cream guipure lace underlaid with blue satin ribbon, and lengthened by a puff of guipure net or piece lace. The latter is made of a piece 8 in. long and 1/2 yd. wide. This is gathered top and bottom, joined to the sleeve, and finished at the wrist with a lace frill headed by folded blue satin ribbon and a bow. A similar bow is on the lace cuff.

Figure 2. Openwork passementerie

The trimming in figure 2 is of silk cord, with fringe in tassels. It is suitable to a nice silk dress.

Figure 1. Cocarde of passementerie

Trimmings for Dresses

The trimming in figure 1 is composed of roses, in thick silk cord. There is a ball of satin in the center, from which descend ends of chenille, with satin balls. This style is useful for trimming dresses or confections.

402

Figure 3. Passementerie tassel

The upper part of figure 3, resembling an acorn, is of satin. It is surrounded at the top with cord, and terminated by pendants of satin balls. This trimming is charming placed *en echelle* on the front of a dress.

Englishwoman's Domestic Magazine, June 1877

Figure 4. Chain stitch embroidery

The design in figure 4 is embroidered on a white ground with split blue and green shaded filoselle.

Figure 6. Border of colored embroidery on batiste

Figures 6 to 8 are worked on batiste with white and colored cotton. Transfer the design to the material. Run all the design figures with white cotton. Work the edge in buttonhole stitch with similar cotton. The rest of the embroidery is worked in chain, half-polka, and herringbone stitch, and in point Russe with blue and red cotton. Work the wheels with fine white thread. Cut away the material between the design figures.

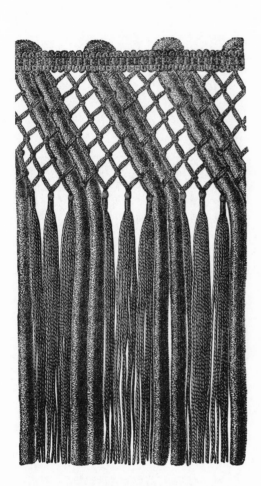

Figure 5. Netted fringe

Figure 7. Border of colored embroidery on batiste

The original of figure 5 is netted over a narrow mesh with a fourfold strand of black silk. After six rows of plain netting, sew a braid like the one illustrated over the foundation stitches. Finish off the lower edge with tassels of silk and chenille, threading the latter aslant through every third and fourth row of the netting.

Englishwoman's Domestic Magazine, September 1877

Figure 8. Border of colored embroidery on batiste

Harper's Bazar, April 1878

Figure 10. Chain stitch border

Figure 9. Border for ball and evening dresses

For the border in figure 9, darn white silk net with white silk floss in point Russe as illustrated. Sew on wax beads in various sizes.

The border in figure 10 is worked on dark brown velvet underlaid with net, in chain stitch, with gold thread and with purled and shaded silk floss. For the scallops and three-figured leaves use red, white, blue, and yellow purled silk. For the leaf figures use bronze, yellow, and red purled silk. The figures inside the leaves are worked alternately with olive, bronze, and peacock blue shaded silk floss, and are edged with a chain stitching of gold thread. Besides this, on the leaf figures set bronze-colored cut glass beads, and define the veins by twisted bars of gold thread. On the four-cornered figures sew garnet-colored beads.

After finishing the embroidery, coat the wrong side of the work with fluid gum arabic. When dry, cut away the projecting material at the top and bottom, and also between the tabs.

Harper's Bazar, April 1880

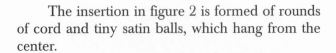

The insertion in figure 2 is formed of rounds of cord and tiny satin balls, which hang from the center.

Figure 3. Fringe

Figure 3 shows a fall of silk cord, which makes a pretty fringe. On it fall ends of chenille trimming in satin balls.

Figure 1. Fringe with border

Trimmings for Dresses or Wrappings

The fringe in figure 1 is composed of silk tassels, headed and separated by satin balls. This style is used for a polonaise or a mantle, rather long.

Figure 4. Small passementerie and fringe

Figure 4 is formed of a lattice of silk cord, with small tassels.

Figure 2. Passementerie insertion

Figure 5. Rose appliqué

Figure 5 shows a rich rose appliqué, with pendants and balls of satin, of which the center one terminates in a silk tassel. Two tiny roses form a finish, with small satin balls.

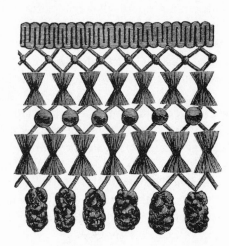

Figure 6. Openwork passementerie with thistles

In figure 6, the openwork in silk cord is mixed with satin balls, and terminated by the thistles.
Englishwoman's Domestic Magazine, June 1877

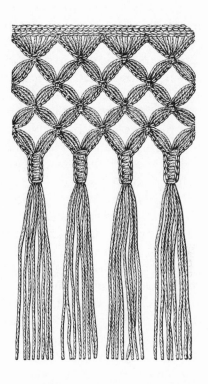

Figure 7. Crocheted fringe

The fringe in figure 7 is worked with split zephyr worsted of various colors, or else with silk or cotton, according to the purpose for which it is designed. First round: ✳ Work 2 chain stitches, draw out the last of these in a loop 5 3/4 in. long, insert the needle in the 1st chain stitch, and repeat from ✳. Second round: Close beneath the preceding round catch each thread of the loops with 1 slip stitch, in doing which the working thread should lie on the wrong side. Third round: Turn the work. On the wrong side of the preceding round, which forms the right side of the fringe, work the same as in the preceding round. Cut through all the loops in the middle. Fourth round: Work 1 single crochet on the next slip stitch in the preceding round, ✳ 5 chain stitches, catch the next eight threads together with 1 slip stitch as illustrated, 5 chain stitches, 1 single crochet on the vein of the slip stitch worked before the next thread in the preceding round. Repeat from ✳. Fifth round: Work 1 chain stitch, with 1 slip stitch fasten together the first four

Trimmings

of the next eight threads caught together in the preceding round after an interval of 1/2 in., ✳ 5 chain stitches, 1 single crochet on the slip stitch with which the next eight threads were caught together, 5 chain stitches, with 1 slip stitch fasten together the next eight threads. Repeat from ✳. Sixth and seventh rounds: Like the preceding round, but the design should always come transposed. Eighth round: Work 1 single crochet on the slip stitch with which the next eight threads of the preceding round were caught together, 5 chain stitches, 4 single crochet on the next eight threads as illustrated, with 1 slip stitch fasten together the same eight threads, going back on the lower veins of the 4 single crochet worked previously, crochet 4 single crochet on the same eight threads, but so that the upper veins of the first 4 single crochet remain free, and always 1 single crochet worked back succeeds 1 single crochet worked forward, 5 chain stitches. Repeat from ✳. After finishing this round cut the ends even, which completes the fringe.

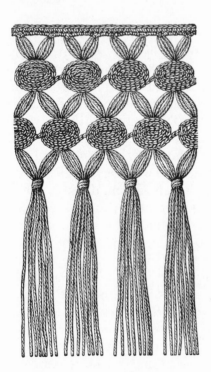

Figure 8. Crocheted fringe

The fringe in figure 8 is worked with split zephyr worsted of various colors, or else with silk or cotton, according to the purpose for which it is designed. First round: ✳ Work 4 chain stitches, draw the last out to a length of 6 in. and drop it from the needle, from the 3rd of the 4 chain stitches take up 1 stitch, 1 chain stitch, draw this out in a loop 6 in. long and drop it from the needle, take up 1 stitch from the 3rd of the 4 chain stitches. Repeat from ✳. Second round: Always 4 single crochet on the next chain stitch between two loops in the preceding round. Third round: Always 1 single crochet on the upper veins of the next stitch in the preceding round. Fourth round: Cut through all stitches drawn out in loops 6 in. long, in the middle, ✳ 4 chain stitches, for a figure worked going forward, after a thread interval of 7/8 in., work as follows, observing the illustration + with 1 slip stitch fasten together the next four threads, and then with 1 slip stitch catch the following four threads, 3 chain stitches, with 2 slip stitches catch together the last and then the first threads fastened together, 3 chain stitches, fastening the middle chain stitch to the 4th of the 4 chain stitches worked previously. Repeat twice from +; but the number of chain stitches between the slip snitches should be increased by 2 stitches at each repetition, and the middle of the chain stitches between the slip stitches should always be fastened to the middle of the chain stitches below; then 2 slip stitches on the ends which have already been caught together three times, 4 chain stitches, fasten to the middle of the next 7 chain stitches. Repeat from ✳. Fifth round: Like the preceding round, but the design should come transposed. Tie every eight ends together in a knot. Cut the fringe even on the under edge.

Harper's Bazar, August 1877

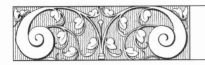

Figure 9. Border in application and embroidery

Figure 9 shows a border in application and point Russe embroidery. Sew black ribbon on a gray cloth foundation in curves, as illustrated. Edge the velvet ribbon with gold soutache overcast on the foundation with black silk. Inside the curves apply leaves of black velvet with point Russe stitches of olive green and red saddler's silk. The colors can be varied to suit the garment.

The fringe in the original of figure 10 is worked with coarse blue and brown saddler's silk and fine gold cord in knotting. Work on a double foundation thread (on one end is fastened a knotting end of gold cord and of brown and blue silk) as follows. With the gold cord work 1 buttonhole stitch loop on the foundation thread. Close to this work with brown silk 1 tatting knot (for this work 1 buttonhole stitch loop downward on the foundation thread and a similar loop upward), * with the gold cord work 1 buttonhole stitch loop, with blue silk 4 tatting knots, with gold cord, after an interval of 1 1/2 in., 1 buttonhole stitch loop close to the last tatting knot, with brown silk, after an interval of 1 1/2 in., 1 tatting knot. Repeat from *. In each loop formed of gold cord and brown silk fasten a strand of blue silk 6 1/2 in. long, laid double, in doing which turn the loop of gold cord in the middle once, as illustrated.

Harper's Bazar, March 1878

Figure 10. Knotted fringe

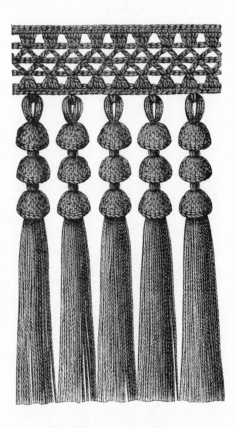

Figure 11. Crocheted fringe

409

The fringe in figure 11 is worked with black saddler's silk. Cut a number of strands 7 1/4 in. long and 20 threads thick, which are laid double. First round: ✽ Work 6 chain stitches, with 1 single crochet catch the next strand at the middle, draw out the stitch 1/2 in. long, and after this interval + work 5 chain stitches, with these catch the strand, and with 1 slip stitch on the 1st of the 5 chain stitches close these in a ring, then 4 chain stitches, which count as 1st short treble crochet, 17 short treble crochet on the 5 chain stitches worked previously, 1 slip stitch on the 4th of the 4 chain stitches counting as the 1st short treble crochet. Repeat twice from +, observing the illustration. But in every repetition instead of the 5 chain stitches work 7 chain stitches, the first 2 of which connect the finished figure to the following figure. Fasten the thread and cut it off. Repeat from ✽, but in every repetition, before working the first 6 chain stitches, crochet 1 slip stitch on the 1st single crochet in the preceding pattern figure and work in the end of the working thread with the following stitch.

Second round: Always 1 single crochet on each stitch in the preceding round. Third round: Always alternately 3 double crochet on the next 3 stitches in the preceding round, working off the upper veins together, 3 chain stitches, pass over 1 stitch. Fourth round: ✽ Work 1 double crochet on the stitch with which the next 3 stitches in the preceding round were worked off, not working off the upper veins, 1 double crochet on the next stitch with which 3 double crochet were worked off, working off the upper veins together with the preceding double crochet, 3 chain stitches. Repeat from ✽, but in every repetition work the next double crochet on the stitch on which the last double crochet was crocheted. Fifth round: Like the preceding round. Sixth round: Always alternately 3 double crochet on the next 2 double crochet which were worked off together in the preceding round, 1 chain stitch. Seventh round: Always 1 single crochet on each stitch in the preceding round.

Figure 12. Crocheted fringe

The fringe in figure 12 is worked with black saddler's silk. First round: ✽ Work 3 chain stitches, 13 double crochet on the 1st of these, 1 slip stitch on the 3rd of the 3 chain stitches worked previously, 7 chain stitches, close the last 3 of these in a ring with 1 slip stitch on the 4th of the 7 chain stitches, 3 chain stitches, which count as 1st double crochet, 7 double crochet on the ring, fasten to the 1st of the 7 chain stitches (to do this drop the stitch from the needle, insert the needle in the corresponding stitch, and draw the dropped stitch through) and work 9 double crochet on the ring, 1 slip stitch on the 3rd of the 3 chain stitches counting as 1st double crochet, 8 chain stitches, close the last 3 of these in a ring with 1 slip stitch on the 5th chain stitch, 4 chain stitches, which count as 1st short treble crochet, 11 short treble crochet on the ring, fasten to the 1st of the 8 chain stitches worked previously, 12 short treble crochet on the ring, 1 slip stitch on the 4th of the 4 chain stitches counting as

410

1st short treble crochet. Turn the work on the wrong side, which now forms the right side. Crochet 8 chain stitches, 1 single crochet on the 3rd following short treble crochet, 18 chain stitches, close the last 6 of these in a ring with 1 slip stitch on the 12th chain stitch, 11 single crochet on the ring, 3 chain stitches, fasten to the upper veins of the 4th short treble crochet before the short treble crochet on which the last single crochet was worked, 9 chain stitches. Cut off the thread and work it in afterward. Repeat from ✳. But in every repetition fasten the 10th of the 18 chain stitches to the 6th short treble crochet of the preceding pattern figure. After the last 9 chain stitches work 1 single crochet on the stitch on which the slip stitch following the 23rd short treble crochet in the preceding pattern figure was worked.

Second round: ✳ Work 13 single crochet on the next 8 chain stitches in the preceding round, 1 single crochet on the next single crochet, 5 chain stitches, for 1 cross double crochet work 1 short treble crochet on the 5th of the next 18 chain stitches, working off only the lower veins, 1 double crochet on the 6th of the next 9 chain stitches (the last 9 chain stitches of this pattern figure in the preceding round), work off the upper veins of the short treble crochet, 3 chain stitches, 1 double crochet on the middle vein of the short treble crochet worked previously (this completes the cross double crochet), 5 chain stitches, 1 single crochet on the stitch on which the next single crochet in the preceding round was worked. Repeat from ✳.

Third round: ✳ Work 1 single crochet on the middle of the next 13 single crochet in the preceding round, 9 chain stitches, 1 single crochet on the middle of the 3 chain stitches in the next cross double crochet, 9 chain stitches. Repeat from ✳. Fourth round: Always 15 single crochet on the next 9 chain stitches in the preceding round. Fifth round: Always alternately 1 single crochet on the middle of the next 15 single crochet in the preceding round, 5 chain stitches. Sixth round: Always alternately 7 double crochet on the next single crochet in the preceding round, 1 single crochet on the middle of the next 5 chain stitches.

Having finished the crochet work, furnish it on the under edge with long and short tassels. These consist of strands 20 threads thick and 6 1/2 and 4 7/8 in. long. The strands are laid double, and are tied with similar cotton.

Figure 13. Crocheted fringe

The fringe in figure 13 may be worked with silk or crochet cotton. It consists of rosettes, which are fastened together, bordered at the top with three rounds worked lengthwise, and finished with strands of fringe knotted into the under edge. Take a wooden knitting needle. Wind it twenty times with the working thread. Slip the threads from the needle, holding them between the thumb and forefinger. Work thereon 1 single crochet and 2 chain stitches, which count as 1st short treble crochet, 31 short treble crochet on the threads, and finally 1 slip stitch on the 2nd of the 2 chain stitches counting as 1st short treble crochet in this round.

Second round: Work 6 chain stitches, 1 single crochet on the 3rd following stitch, twice alternately 5 chain stitches, 1 single crochet on the 3rd following stitch in the preceding round; then three times alternately 5 chain stitches, 1 single crochet on the 3rd following stitch; then twice alternately 5 chain stitches, 1 single crochet on the 3rd following stitch; then 6 chain stitches, 1 single crochet on the 3rd following stitch. Fasten the thread and cut it off.

This completes one rosette. Each following rosette is worked in the same manner. But fasten the first two chain stitch scallops in the second round to the last two chain stitch scallops in the preceding rosette. To do this drop the stitch from the needle, insert the needle in the corresponding stitch, and draw the dropped stitch through.

On the top of the rosette work as follows. First round: ✳ Work 1 single crochet on the chain stitch before the last in the last chain stitch scallop of the next rosette, twice alternately 5 chain stitches, 1 single crochet on the 3rd following short treble crochet, then 5 chain stitches, 1 single crochet on the 2nd chain stitch of the first chain stitch scallop in the same rosette, 5 chain stitches. Repeat from ✳.

Second round: Always alternately 1 single crochet on the middle of the next 3 chain stitches in the preceding round, 3 chain stitches. Third round: Always alternately 1 double crochet on the 2nd following stitch in the preceding round, 1 chain stitch.

Into each chain stitch scallop on the bottom of the rosettes, fasten a strand 6 threads thick and 5 3/4 in. long, which is laid double.

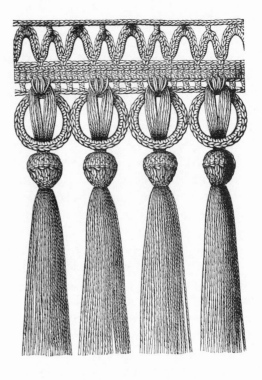

Figure 14. Crocheted fringe

The fringe in figure 14 may be worked with silk or crochet cotton. Work the tassels first, as follows. Take a strand 25 threads thick and 7 1/4 in. long, and lay it double. Catch it with 1 single crochet 7/8 in. from the top, so that it forms a loop. Then crochet 5 chain stitches, which are closed in a ring around the strand with 1 slip stitch, and work 3 chain stitches, which count as 1st double crochet, 15 double crochet on the ring, 1 slip stitch on the 3rd of the 3 chain stitches counting as 1st double crochet, then 4 chain stitches, seven times alternately 1 double crochet on the 2nd following double crochet, 1 chain stitch; finally, 1 slip stitch on the 3rd of the 4 chain stitches worked previously.

Cut off the thread after an interval of 8 in. After turning the figure on the wrong side, run the thread through the edge stitches with a sewing needle, draw it tight around the strand, and fasten with several stitches. This completes one tassel.

Having worked the requisite number of tassels, crochet as follows. First round: ✳ Work 24 chain stitches, 1 slip stitch on the 8th of these to

form a ring, 33 single crochet on the ring, 3 slip stitches on the next 3 of the 33 single crochet. Repeat from ✳. But at every repetition, fasten the 23rd single crochet to the 10th single crochet of the preceding ring. Second round: Always alternately 1 double crochet on the next stitch in the preceding round, 1 chain stitch, and pass over 1 stitch. Third round: Always alternately 7 double crochet on the next 7 stitches in the preceding round, 3 double crochet on the next 3 stitches, but with each double crochet catch the next tassel before working off the stitch. Fourth round: Always alternately 1 single crochet on the next stitch in the preceding round. Fifth round: Work 1 single crochet on the next single crochet in the preceding round, ✳ 7 chain stitches, pass over 3 stitches, 1 single crochet on the next stitch, 9 chain stitches, 1 single crochet on the 5th following stitch. Repeat from ✳. Sixth round: ✳ Work 11 single crochet on the next 7 chain stitches in the preceding round, not working off the last single crochet, 15 single crochet on the next 9 chain stitches, working off the 1st of these together with the last of the 11 single crochet worked previously, and the last of the 15 single crochet together with the 1st single crochet of the next pattern figure. Repeat from ✳. Seventh round: Work 1 double crochet on the middle of the next 11 single crochet in the preceding round, 5 chain stitches, 1 single crochet on the middle of the next 15 chain stitches. Repeat from ✳.

Harper's Bazar, September 1878

Figure 15 shows a border in buttonhole and chain stitch embroidery. It is worked on a foundation of moss green cloth. The leaves are worked with olive green silk in several shades in diagonal buttonhole stitch. The veins and stems are worked in chain stitch with bronze silk. For the flowers in satin stitch use alternately pink, blue, and yellow silk. The winding rows of chain stitching are worked with pale blue and pale pink silk, and the knotted stitches with yellow silk.

Harper's Bazar, November 1878

Figure 16. Passementerie border–full size

The border in figure 16 is made of coarse black silk cord and sewn together in diagonal rows. These are joined by small rosettes arranged of fine black silk cord.

Figure 15. Embroidered border

Figure 17. Passementerie border–full size

The border in figure 17 is made of fine black silk cord, ornamented with black jet beads as illustrated.

Figure 20. Passementerie border–half size

Figures 20 through 22 show some of the new designs in satin cord and jet passementerie. Single figures of such borders as figures 20 and 21 are often placed between the box pleats of black lace frills, and among the folds of the jabot on the front of the garment.

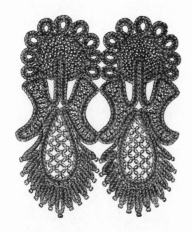

Figure 18. Passementerie border–half size

The border in figure 18 is composed of fine black silk cord and black jet beads. These are sewn in circles on the upper rosettes, and are set in the leaf figures to form a net. Single beads finish the points of the leaves.

Figure 19. Passementerie border–two-thirds size

The border in figure 19 is made of fine black silk cord. The design figures are filled with black jet beads.

Harper's Bazar, November 1879

Figure 21. Passementerie border–half size

Figure 22. Passementerie border–half size

Harper's Bazar, May 1882

Figure 1. Cloak agrafe–half size

Clasps, Pins, and Buttons

Figure 1 shows a cloak agrafe in oxidized metal.

Figure 2. Agrafe–half size

Figure 2 shows an agrafe that has a Japanese design in silver and gilt.

Figure 3. Agrafe–half size

Figure 3 shows a Japanese agrafe in silver and gilt.

Figure 4. Agrafe–half size

Figure 4 shows a Japanese agrafe in silver and gilt on a dark ground.

Demorest's Mirror of Fashions, January 1878

Figure 5. Bonnet pin

The bonnet pin in figure 5 represents a miniature whip. The end is ornamented with steel plates and the handle with jet.

Figure 6. Bonnet pin

The bonnet pin in figure 6 is made of gold bronze in filigree work.

Figure 7. Bonnet pin

The bonnet pin in figure 7 is in the shape of a curved band of gold bronze. It is finished on the ends with black balls, around which is coiled a bronze serpent.

Harper's Bazar, November 1878

Figure 8. Painted mother-of-pearl button

Figure 8 shows a button of smoked mother-of-pearl with painting in a Chinese design.

Figure 9. Painted mother-of-pearl button

Figure 9 shows a button of smoked mother-of-pearl with painting in a Chinese design.

Figure 10. Mother-of-pearl button

The oblong button in figure 10 is of white pearl. It is ornamented with a plate of cut smoked pearl.

Figure 11. Bronze button

The button in figure 11 is of bronze with colored enameling in a mosaic pattern.

Figure 12. Passementerie button

For the button in figure 12, take a four-cornered mold. Cover it with single crochet in black silk.

Figure 13. Passementerie button

For the button in figure 13, cover a six-cornered mold with single crochet in black silk.

Harper's Bazar, November 1879

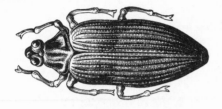

Figure 14. Agrafe for bonnet

The agrafe in figure 14, in the form of a beetle, is of black jet and silver. It is designed for trimming bonnets.

Harper's Bazar, March 1880

Figure 15. Agrafe

The pretty gilt agrafes in figures 15 and 16 are designed for trimming bonnets, for fastening lace scarves or small bouquets, etc.

Figure 16. Agrafe

Harper's Bazar, July 1880

Figure 17. Two buckles

Figures 17 and 18 show various gilt and steel buckles. These are used to confine the folds of tunic and scarf draperies on dresses.

Figure 18. Two buckles

Harper's Bazar, April 1882

Figure 19. Bonnet clasps–half size

Harper's Bazar, May 1882

8. Dressmaking and Millinery

Fashion, like the law, is equal for all women. Some copy it in material costing ten dollars a yard. Others copy it in goods of one dollar a yard, but of the same color as the former, and cut in the same style as the richest garments.

Planning the Garment

Color, design, and shape are the foundations of a systematic and artistic toilette. Complexion and figure must be taken into consideration when deciding on the color and shape of a costume. After that you are able to select the style of pattern. Choose first the color, second the material, third the shape, and fourth the quantity of material and trimming.

Designing Dresses for More Than One Occasion. If the dress is to be employed for many different occasions, for day as well as evening wear, for in and out of doors, it is necessary to select a quiet, close design, one that will be proper for the street, and relieve it, for occasions of more ceremony, by the addition of a handsome collar and cuffs, or a pretty lace fichu.

If the dress is to be reserved for indoor wear, the cut of the bodice and sleeves should be more dressy. The bodice should be open or square, and the sleeves half short, reaching only just below the elbow.

Ladies who cannot afford a great variety in their wardrobe, and yet have to go considerably into society, often make up their one handsome dress with two basques, and two pairs of sleeves. The elbow sleeves may be of lace, gathered full upon the arm, and finished with a double ruffle below the elbow.

Altering Styles. There are many ways in which patterns may be used, so the same one will suit different requirements. It is always easy to cut a garment a little longer or shorter than illustrated,

and still retain the design. With few exceptions, all fitted garments can be arranged to fasten either in front or in back, whichever is preferred, by simply allowing the lap at the desired place for fastening. The addition or omission of one or more slashes in a garment does not alter the cut. By leaving the front darts out of a three-fourths or half-fitting garment, a loose front may be obtained, and the back can be held in position by a belt underneath. The looping of overskirts and polonaises may be varied indefinitely, and still the cut will be the same.

The princess polonaise is merely a princess dress gathered up at the back, or the breadths (some cut longer than the others) pleated into each other; arranged, in fact, in any style. Very pretty morning dresses, as well as dressing gowns and wrappers, are made from the princess pattern. The only alteration needed is to make it rather looser, particularly at the waist. The Watteau fold is especially suitable and becoming for a garment of this character.

Copying Designs. By a little thought and care, the most accurate copy of the most complicated fashion plate can be read and reproduced, where two sides are shown. Use a pencil and notebook to accurately note the number of seams, their style, the neck style and finish, the sleeve style and finish, the body of the garment (whether plain, pleated, scalloped, draped, etc.), the skirt (trimming, drapery, etc.), the tailor finishings, etc., and last but not least, the combinations of materials, colors, etc.

Measure the entire size or height of the figure on the plate. From this, fix a scale on which to base your measurements of the depths, in the measurement of trains, draperies, points, shirrings, pleatings, angles of slopes, vests, lapels, etc.

Suppose the figure on the plate is 4 in. high, from the skirt bottom to the neck. A point of drapery, at the side, is shown at a depth below the waist,

at a point which is one-quarter of the entire figure, or 1 in. from the skirt bottom. Now find the sum of the front height, plus the front waist depth, plus the skirt depth of the wearer. Take one-quarter of this distance, then drape so the point hangs exactly that distance from the skirt bottom.

Proceed by the same principle when imitating the widths of vests, lapels, pleats, etc.; basing the ratio of proportion sought, on the measure of the form for which it is intended. Then transfer the style thus copied to the draft of the correct fit.

Calculating Materials. In selecting materials and trying the necessary quantities, bear in mind the different widths of the various textures, and find out before you enter the shop exactly the quantity of material you wish to purchase. Suppose, for instance, that you want to make yourself a jacket. The material is to be serge, which is 32 in. wide. You fancy that it will take 3 yd.–from that to 4.

Clear a strip of the floor, about 4 yd. by 32 in. Mark it out distinctly on the carpet with white chalk. Then lay the different parts of your pattern on it. Turn and twist them till they lie in the smallest possible compass. Be sure to allow for a right and wrong side, should there be a difference, and that the grain or nap of the material is the same up and down. Measure exactly the length taken by them on the carpet. Give yourself two minutes to thinking it all over, and satisfying yourself that there is no mistake, such as forgetting a sleeve, or having arranged the two fronts for the same side. Before taking the pieces up make a little sketch on paper of the way in which they are arranged, lest you should forget.

It is a good plan, when you are going to buy materials, to keep in the pocketbook a little table of the widths of different materials and the respective quantities required. Thus, 14 yd. of serge 32 in. wide are equal to 8 yd. of tweed at 52 in. Sixteen yards of silk, 24 in. wide, equal 14 yd. at 27 in. wide.

It is almost impossible to give minute directions as to the quantities required for a dress, jacket, tablier, or bodice. Much depends on the size of the wearer, and much on the quantities of trimming. A perfectly plain dress (an untrimmed skirt, tablier-overskirt, and jacket bodice) for a figure of medium size requires 12 yd. of material 32 in. wide. To make a short jacket takes about 1 1/4 yd. of tweed, according to the size of the wearer. In linsey or serge it takes about 3 yd. In Irish frieze, which is somewhat narrower, it takes 3 1/4 yd. For a tablier-overskirt and bodice, of double-width material such as merino, a little under 3 1/4 yd. will suffice. If the serge be single width, 5 yd. is required; if narrower still, say 27 in., then 5 3/4. Frieze, although narrower, will take less, on account of the extra thickness of the material. This is all reckoned without allowance for trimming.

Certain materials require to be made up with the nap running up; of these are sealskin and velveteen. If the nap brushes downward, they will look very badly. There will be a dusty-looking white sheen on them, instead of a rich gloss.

The nap must be allowed for in calculating the quantities of material. For instance, in cutting gored skirt pieces, it will not do to make two gores out of one breadth, as may be done in ordinary plain materials. That would necessitate turning one of them down and the other up. In goring velveteen it is well to cut off the unnecessary portion in a way that will enable you to utilize it for some other part of the dress, such as the under part of the sleeve, the cuff, or the pocket.

Calculating the quantities is rather more difficult for trimmings than for the plain dress. A rough guess may be made by allowing three times the length of the part to be trimmed for kilt pleating, or close pleating as it is sometimes called. Suppose the skirt measures 4 yd. around; you must allow 12 yd. of material cut to the right width for the pleating. If the pleating is to be 7 in. deep, you must cut strips of material of that width till you have 12 yd. For flounces or frills that are simply gathered or pleated, it will be sufficient to allow twice the length of the part to be trimmed. For bias strips it is very easy to calculate. A yard of material, if cut exactly

on the bias and carefully managed, will give the same length in bias strips that it would if cut into straight strips.

Such small matters as collars, cuffs, piping, etc., need not be calculated for in purchasing a dress. These can always be got out of the cuttings. Sometimes the cuff of the coat sleeve is very elaborately trimmed, and in this case the necessary material must be calculated.

Linings, tape, ribbon, braid, buttons, hooks and eyes, and whalebone must not be forgotten. For bodice and sleeves 3 yd. of lining will be sufficient. Properly speaking, sleeves should always be lined with silk. It is more comfortable than linen or cambric, and gives the sleeves a better set. For the skirt, 1 1/2 yd. of lining will suffice, unless the skirt is to be lined throughout. This is not often done now, though it is advisable with the skirts of thin dresses, such as tussah, thin silk, lawns of the lighter kind, and black silks when done up afresh. The lining not only keeps the dress cleaner, but protects it from wear and tear, or such accidents as may befall when the dress gets trodden upon.

Always buy the best braid for putting round the hem. If the dress be 4 yd. round, 4 1/2 of braid should be allowed. It should be put on without the slightest stretching. Otherwise it will not serve its purpose, that of protecting the dress from injury and soil.

Calculating Materials by the English and French Rules. The English rule for ascertaining the quantity of material after it is made up is as follows. Find the width of the material used in the makeup of the garment. If it is 24 in. wide, cut a piece of paper or muslin 24 by 36 in., or equal to 1 yd. of the material–or better, 2 or 3 yd. Then measure the garment, piece by piece. Mark off on the paper a space equal to the size and shape of each piece. Remember that pieces will be cut twice. Then add 7 1/2 percent for waste. It is astonishing how correctly the quantity can be ascertained in the most complicated garment.

The French rule for ascertaining the quantity of material after it is made up is more mathematical. First find the number of square inches in each piece of the garment. At first sight this may seem difficult, especially when ruffles and pleatings are much used. But the process is in fact very simple, and may be accurately done by anyone who can take correct measurements and understands the simple rules of arithmetic.

Measure by inches the length of each piece, and then the width. Then multiply the one by the other. The figure produced will be the number of square inches in the piece. For a ruffle, calculate from two to four times the skirt circumference according to the fullness of the pleating. Say a skirt measures 4 yd. around, and the ruffle requires three times that length of material, or 12 yd. It is 6 in. deep, with a 3/4 in. hem and a 1/4 in. seam, making a total of 7 in. Multiply 12 yd. (432 in.) by 7, and you have 3,024 sq. in.

When you have found the number of square inches in each piece, add them all together, and reduce the total to yards. It is necessary that you first find the width of the material used. Suppose you find your garment calls for a total of 16,416 sq. in., and the material used measures 24 in. wide. Multiply 24 by 36 to find the square inches in the yard, which is 864. Divide the square inches in the garment (16,416) by the square inches in the yard (864) and you find that the garment contains 19 yd. of material. Add 5 percent, or 1 yd. in 20 for waste, and you arrive at the result, namely, that the garment requires 20 yd. Bows and small bias pieces must be calculated as near as possible.

If the material is expensive, a yard or so of material over and above the amount required by the pattern is a prudent investment. It is almost impossible exactly to match a thing a year or so after it is bought, and good material will always bear making over.

Planning the Garment

Garment	Style/Size	Yards/Width	Yards/Width
Basque	9 in. long with sleeve	2 1/4 yd./27 in.	3 yd./24 in.
Basque	9 in. long with sleeve	2 yd./silesia	
Basque	9 in. long with sleeve	2 yd./muslin	
Bodice	Round	2 yd./27 in.	2 1/2 yd./24 in.
Sleeve	Coat, 1 pair	3/4 yd./silesia	
Sleeve	Coat, 1 pair	1 1/4 yd./drilling	
Sleeve	Coat, 1 pair	1 1/4 yd./24 in.	
Skirt	Walking, 40 in. front, 42 in. back	4 yd./ 27 in.	4 1/2 yd./24 in.
Skirt	Walking, 40 in. front, 9 in. train	4 1/2 yd./ 27 in.	5 yd./24 in.
Skirt	Train, 15 in. train	5 yd./27 in.	5 1/2 yd./24 in.
Skirt	Train, 20 in. train	5 1/2 yd./27 in.	6 yd./24 in.
Skirt	Train, 35 in. train	7 1/2 yd./27 in.	8 yd./24 in.
Polonaise	Plain draped	7 yd./27 in.	8 yd./24 in.
Princess	Short walking	8 yd./27 in.	9 yd./24 in.
Princess	18 in. train	9 yd./27 in.	10 yd./24 in.
Princess	27 in. train	10 yd./27 in.	11 yd./24 in.
Sacque	Street, 36 in. long	4 yd./27 in.	4 3/4 yd./24 in.
Sacque	Street, 50 in. long	5 yd./27 in.	6 yd./24 in.
Waterproof	Sacque and cape	4 1/2 yd./54 in.	
Waterproof	Circular	3 3/4 yd./54 in.	
Dolman	Light wrap	1 7/8 yd./54 in.	
Mantelet	Medium size	1 yd./54 in.	
Chemise	Plain	2 1/2 yd./36 in.	
Chemise	4 in. ruffle on bottom	3 yd./36 in.	
Drawers	Plain	1 3/4 yd./36 in.	
Nightdress	Plain	5 yd./36 in.	
Dressing sacque	Ordinary	2 1/4 yd./36 in.	
Wrapper	French sacque	5 yd./36 in.	8 yd./27 in.
Apron	Plain	3/4 yd./27 in.	
Ruffle	Bias, 2 1/2 in. wide for 2 yd. skirt	1/2 yd./27 in.	3/4 yd./24 in.
Ruffle	Bias, 5 in. wide for 3 yd. skirt	3/4 yd./27 in.	1 yd./24 in.
Ruffle	Bias, 10 in. wide for 3 yd. skirt	1 3/4 yd./27 in.	2 yd./24 in.

Table 1. Yardage required from different material widths

 **Dressmaking and Millinery**

Material	Widths in Inches		
Alpaca, 1st quality	30	36	54
Alpaca, 2nd quality	24	36	
Barathea	42		
Batiste	27	30	
Beige	25	28	
Black silk	21	27	
Cashmere	23	46	
Challis	28		
Cloth	28	54	60
Colored silk	22	26	
Crape	23	42	
Crepe de chine	24		
Damask	24		
Foulard	24		
Gauze	44		
Grenadine	18	26	
India silks	32	34	
Janus cord	28	32	
Merino	45	46	
Mousseline de laine	26		
Muslin	33		
Ottoman and turquoise silks	18	20	
Paramatta	42		
Percales	33		
Piqués	33		
Plush	16	21	24
Plush (seal)	54		
Poplin	30	32	
Prints	33		
Rep	30	32	
Sateen	24	27	30
Satin	18	27	
Serge	28	32	
Tweed	28	54	60
Velvet	16	20	22
Velveteen	27	28	
Vigogne	27		
Woolen materials (average)	27	44	

Table 2. Material widths

Material	Widths in Inches					
Alpaca	27					
Armure silk	24	26				
Barege	27					
Black silk	21	22	22 1/2	24	26	60
Bombazine	39					
Brocade silk	21	24				
Brussels net	27	36				
Calico	27	31				
Cambric, colored	26					
Cambric, white	36					
Camel's hair	27	44				
Cashmere	36	40	42	44	46	48
Checked silk	18					
Cloth	27	45	54			
Colored silk	18	20	22	24		
Crepe	27	72				
Crepe cloth	27	44				
Crepe lisse	25	30				
Delaine, all wool	24					
Delaine, mixed	24					
Drap d'été	36	54				
Drilling	27					
Empress	27					
Flannel, opera	27	34	36			
Foulard silk	24					
Grenadine	22	24	50			
Henrietta cloth	39					
Illusion	27	72	98			
Linen	36					
Marseilles	27					
Matelassé	24	26	54			
Merino	36	42	45			
Mohair	27					
Moiré antique	25					
Nainsook	36					
Organdy	66					
Paper cambric	26					
Paper muslin	36					

Table 3. Widths of standard dress goods

Material	Widths in Inches					
Piqué	27					
Poplin, French	24	27				
Poplin, Irish	18	24	27			
Quilted lining silk	25					
Satin	21	22				
Sicilian silk	23	24	26	54		
Silesia	36					
Striped silk	18					
Swiss	33	44				
Tarlatan	44	72				
Velvet	16	18	20	27	28	36
Watered silk	25					
Waterproof	54					
Wigan	27					

Table 3. Widths of standard dress goods continued

Choosing Linings. It is money well invested to purchase the best quality of dress lining. It should combine the properties of strength, firmness, and pliability. Among the standards we place the best drilling, the firmest and best brands of Prussian silesia, the double-faced silesias, and the best quality of foulard silks and cambrics. The sleeve lining should be silk, or some soft material.

Twill, a somewhat stiff and thick cotton material, is the favorite lining of the ordinary dressmaker. But this does not adapt itself readily to the figure, and shows through the least thin or broken place in the outer material. White linen, which is frequently used, is too stiff and unyielding.

Comparing Widths of Dress Materials. As materials for dresses vary so much in width, tables 2 and 3 give some of the standards. Fancy names are often given by drapers to certain fancy materials, each season. In many cases the same material is sold under four or five different names. Special makes, too, in silks and cashmeres, present other difficulties in classification. Yet there are certain time-honored dress materials, the widths of which are fixed by standard looms, and which are

unchanged from year to year. As they are also the most durable and useful in dressmaking, we will only tabulate these.

Taking Measures. Before taking the measures, see that the skirt bands do not increase the waist size or shorten the length of the underarm and back measures. Also ascertain if the lady is wearing the same shaped corset and the same weight undergarments that are to be worn under the finished garment, as a change in these makes quite a difference in the fit. Take all the measures from the form, and not from the seams of the garment worn (unless it be a perfect fit). Take all measures smooth except where the words "tight" or "loose" are used.

To prepare to take measures, tie a cord tightly around the smallest part of the waist. Tie another cord around the largest part of the bust and well up under the arms. Make a cross with chalk or pins just over the point of the shoulder bone (or shoulder seam) and about 1 in. back of the top of the shoulder.

Take the *neck measure* following line *A* in figure 1, around the neck at the smallest point above the dress collar.

424

Planning the Garment

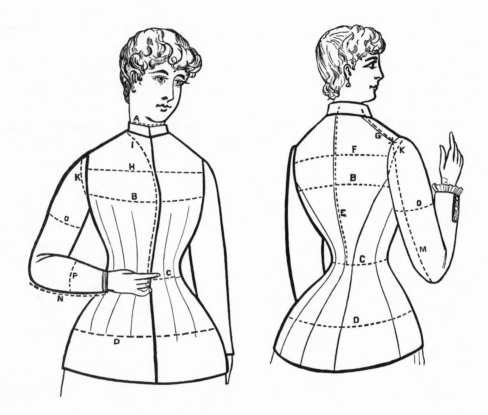

Figure 1. Taking the measures in front and back

Take the *bust measure* following line *B*, around the largest part of the bust over the cord and square across the back.

Take the *waist measure* following line *C*, tightly around the smallest part of the waist, over the cord.

Take the *hip measure* following line *D*, around the hips 6 in. below the waist cord.

Take the *high bust width* following line *H*, across the chest from arm to arm about 2 in. above the bust cord.

Take the *front waist length* following line *I*. This is taken from the socket bone (or most prominent bone in the back of the neck) straight down over the bust to the cord at the front waist.

Take the *back waist length* following line *E*. This is taken from the socket bone straight down to the cord at the back waist.

Take the *back width* following line *F*. This is taken across the back over the shoulder blades from arm to arm.

Take the *underarm measure* from the bust cord (well up under the arm) straight down to the waist cord (well down around the waist).

Take the *shoulder measure* following line *G*. This is taken from the side of the neck (where it joins onto the body) out to the point of the shoulder bone (or cross mark).

Take the *armhole measure* following line *K*. This is taken tightly around the arm, 1 in. below the point of the shoulder bone.

Take the sleeve measures with the hand resting on the center of the front waist as shown. The first is the *shoulder-to-elbow measure*. This is taken following line *M*, from the point of the shoulder bone (or cross mark) down the outside of the arm to the point of the elbow.

The second is the *shoulder-to-wrist measure*. This is taken following lines *M* and *N*, from the same point of the shoulder around the point of the elbow to the wrist bone.

The third is the *upper arm measure.* This is taken following line *O,* around the arm, halfway between the shoulder and elbow.

The fourth is the *elbow measure.* It is taken around the point of the elbow.

The fifth is the *lower arm measure.* This is taken following line *P,* around the arm, halfway between the elbow and wrist.

The sixth is the *wrist measure.* It is taken around the wrist.

For loose-fitting sleeves, the third and fifth measures may be omitted.

In addition to the regular sleeve measures, there are four for dolman sleeves. The first is taken loosely from the junction of lines *E* and *F,* over the arm just below *K* in the back illustration, across *K* to the armhole seam in the front illustration, just below line *H.*

The second is taken loosely from a little below the junction of lines *B* and *E,* over the arm a little above line *O* in the back illustration, to the armhole seam in the front illustration, a little below line *B.*

The third is taken from the cross mark in the front illustration, over the top of the shoulder and down the inside of the arm to the hollow of the elbow.

The fourth is taken from the hollow of the elbow to the wrist.

All other measures for dolmans, wraps, and cloaks are taken the same as for basques; except for all outside garments the neck, bust, waist, hip, and armhole measures are taken about 1 in. larger than for a tight-fitting basque.

For capes and circulars, measure around the form over the arms, 6 in. below the point of the shoulder bone. Take the neck, shoulder, and length measures (only), the same as for wraps.

Take the skirt length measure from the waist cord in front straight down to the length desired.

Understanding Basic Techniques

It will repay you for any inconvenience or trouble to have a well-lighted sewing room where you need not be disturbed or have to clear up and remove unfinished work. This should be furnished with a long table of convenient height, with deep drawers, a low straight-back chair, a footstool, also a high stool for sitting at the table when basting. One drawer should contain all kinds of bits of muslin, dress materials, braids, linings, etc. The room should also be furnished with a line of tape to throw the large pieces of work over at night; a press board, a lap board, and a skirt board for trimming skirts; and a dummy or figure for draperies and hanging the skirts, etc. You should have an easy-running sewing machine. Your tools should include a pair of strong sharp shears, a pair of scissors, a buttonhole cutter, a penknife for ripping, a bodkin, a piece of beeswax, a piece of glue for preparing buttonholes in material that frays, a tape measure, a good assortment of pins and needles, a box of different-colored silk thread, a box of cotton for both sewing and basting, and a box of different-sized and -colored cord.

Working Stitches. In any class of stitch whatever care should be taken that the stitches are even and placed at equal distances. According to the texture of the work they can be near or far apart, so can the work be finely or coarsely done. When working on fine linen the necessary regularity can be obtained by counting the threads.

Running stitch, A (see figure 2). The running stitch is used for seaming skirts, putting on trimmings, and in connection with stitching, for sleeve seams and French seams. This stitch is done by constantly running the needle into the material in front of the stitch just formed. Several stitches may be taken on the needle at the same time before drawing the cotton through.

Simple as it is, the running stitch requires considerable care in taking the exact number of threads up at each entry of the needle. This applies particularly to the running together of silk breadths for skirts, and to grenadines and similar materials. Care must be taken to draw the thread tightly to avoid all puckering or drawing up of the material. When working on dress skirts, an occasional backstitch is necessary to strengthen the seam.

Basting, or *tacking,* is running upon an exaggerated scale, introducing stitches from 2 to 3 in. apart.

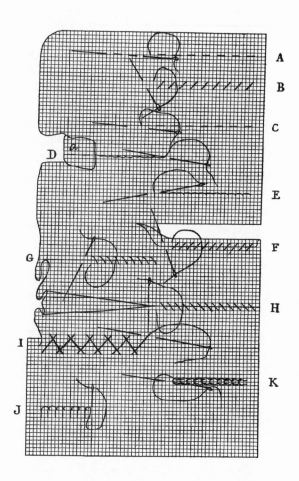

Figure 2. Basic hand stitches

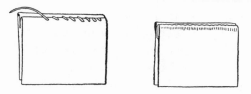

Figure 3. Slip stitch in progress and finished

Slip stitch, so called because the needle must slip under the right side of the material without getting through it. The work is held as for a hem or seam, but the way of inserting the needle resembles a long overcasting stitch. The slip stitch is much used in dressmaking to fix down linings and to put on made trimmings. In plain sewing, the stitches are worked smaller and closer together, as shown in figure 3. When the stitches must be invisible on both sides, the needle is inserted so that the stitches are quite upright. The cotton is drawn as tight as possible without puckering the material.

English stitch, B (see figure 2). For this, the needle is inserted in an upward direction on the cross, for which reason it is much stronger than any other.

Backstitch, C. This is done in two directions. First, going from right to left, the needle stitched into the work behind where it has been drawn out, in order to take a stitch of the same size in front. Passing from left to right, the needle is inserted in front of the stitch just formed. The stitch looks like a running stitch on the reverse side. For this reason, it is frequently used for turned-down seams.

Stem stitch, D. This is a sort of backstitch in which the stitches overlap. It is taken from left to right, and forms a neat finish for the right side of a hem.

Stitching, E is used for all bodice seams (see also figure 7). It is composed of a row of backstitches without any interval between them. The needle is at once inserted backward into the stitch just made, to be drawn out an equal distance in front of the stitch that has to be formed. Extreme regularity must be observed. This is obtained by counting the threads of material for each stitch, according to the required size of the stitches. Stitching is facilitated by drawing a thread or making a fold where the work is intended to be. If it must be done on the cross or in some material besides calico, it is advisable to make a tacking with some bright-colored cotton to guide the needle.

In stitching the fronts and the side pieces to the back, the same number of threads must be taken up each time on the needle to produce the pearl-like appearance so remarkable in the work of good dressmakers. For stitching bodice seams, the stitches may be less carefully executed, but no careless work is allowable.

Hemstitch, F. This stitch is employed to fit a hem in any material. The needle is placed under the material, and drawn out about two threads above the edge.

Side stitch, G. By the help of this stitch the folded edges of two pieces of material are joined. The stitch is made slantingly in the side opposite that which is held toward the worker.

Sewing stitch, also called *oversewing* or *overseaming, H.* This is employed to join two edges of material. It is always required to join two selvages of calico or other material. Place the two selvages side by side. Insert the needle at the far side of the seam on the extreme right. Draw it through, then reinsert it close to the stitch already made, working from right to left. A depth of some threads must be observed.

If the two pieces to be united have not selvages, fold each inward. When the oversewing has been done, make a small double hem on the wrong side, to conceal and secure the raw edges.

Overcasting is sewing with very wide stitches to prevent the edges of the material raveling out. Seams of bodices are usually stitched and overcast. The stitch is taken from left to right, instead of right to left, as in ordinary sewing. It is also taken much deeper into the material (see figure 4).

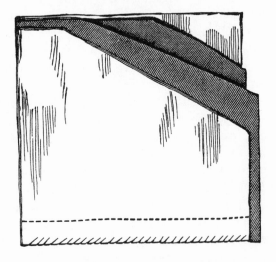

Figure 4. Bodice seam with overcasting

Herringbone or *cross-stitch, I* (see figure 2). This is used to join two edges of material. These, instead of being folded together, are laid one over the other and worked from left to right, making a stitch alternately below and one above. The cross-stitch is made by the thread being drawn out each time above the stitch that has just been done. This stitch is used particularly for flannel garments.

Buttonhole stitch, J. A straight slit is cut for the buttonhole. It is of advantage to strengthen the work by running two threads, one below and one above the hole. Then the stitches are taken from left to right in the slit, to be drawn out behind the tracing at the upper end, making the thread form a species of knot. This is done either by holding it with the thumb below the needle, or in casting it upward. The thread is drawn out gently toward the slit upon the edges of which the knots ought to be formed. It is important to remember to place some stitches across each end of the hole, to give it a nice appearance and ensure its wearing well. There is a difference in the appearance of the front and back of the buttonhole.

The buttonhole stitch is also used for making eyelets. The eyelet is a round hole pierced with a stiletto. It is prepared for working by running a thread around the hole to strengthen the work and guide the stitch.

Chain stitch, K. The needle is held straight, and always placed in the last ring or stitch, to be drawn out an equal distance to the length of the following ring. The cotton is held below the needle.

Sewing Seams. The *flat seam* is used for making garments (see figure 5). After the two pieces of material are joined, whether by a running stitch or a backstitch, they are opened and laid on an ironing board, and a hot iron is passed quickly over them. Then the edges of the seams are fixed to the garment in various ways (see figure 6). It is best to use a cross-stitch, or to run them down, taking care that the stitches do not go through to the right side of the garment.

428

Figure 5. Flat seam—right side

Figure 6. Flat seam—wrong side

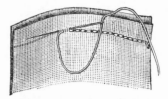

Figure 7. Stitched seam

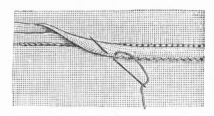

Figure 8. Felled seam

Sometimes the seam edges are covered by a narrow ribbon. To do this, after ironing the seam bring the edges together and bind the ribbon down over them. This is frequently done for unlined jackets. Sometimes the edges are kept in their places by a ribbon sewn over the seam itself. This is useful for seams on the cross.

The *felled seam* is made by means of a stitched seam and a hem. First lay the two materials together with the under edge extended 1/5 in. beyond the upper one. Stitch the seam as shown by figure 7. Open out the material, flatten the seam from the right side, and roll both edges of the seam inward, so that the narrower edge lies within the other. Then hem the edges down as shown by figure 8.

To make the hem even, it is better to roll in only a little at once, and then to hem it down immediately. A good felled seam must be perfectly smooth and flat on the right side, and round like a cord on the wrong side.

The *French seam* or *bag seam* is used for clear, transparent materials, and for unlined materials. It is useful whenever it is desirable to have the inside as neatly finished as the outside. On the right side of the material, run the seam as close as possible to the edge (see figure 9). Turn the seam over, and stitch on the wrong side, just below the turned-in portion (see figure 10).

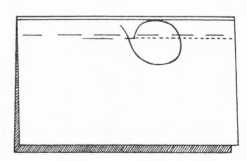

Figure 9. French seam—wrong sides together

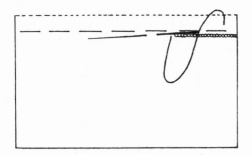

Figure 10. French seam–right sides together

The French seam is often used in making up lace, net, etc. This is not a good practice. As lace and net are frequently worn over colored silks, it is most important to secure an almost invisible seam. The best modistes stitch net and lace materials, then cut the edges close and overcast into every hole of the net or lace. The seam is then scarcely visible.

The *mantua-maker's seam* or *hem* is employed where the ridge formed will be of no consequence, while speed in finishing is an object. It may be suitably used for sleeves, pockets, bags, or skirts. Lay the two pieces of material together, the raw edge of the nearest to you a little below that of the other piece (see figure 11). Turn the upper edge over the lower. Then fold both together over as in ordinary hemming. Fell through the double fold of material, so as to leave a projecting seam, forming a ridge, instead of a flat one (see figure 12).

Wrong Side

Figure 11. Mantua-maker's seam–material arranged

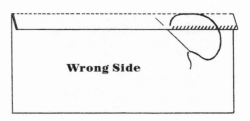

Wrong Side

Figure 12. Mantua-maker's seam–material hemmed

The *double seam* is very useful where strength is required. Lay the upper edge of the material 1/3 in. from the edge of the under piece, with both right sides together. Stitch a seam close to the edge of the upper material. Then lay it over and stitch it down beyond the first seam, where only two thicknesses of the material come together (see figure 13).

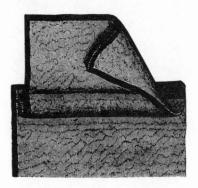

Figure 13. Double seam

The *cord seam* is both useful and decorative. It lies perfectly flat on the wrong side, and imitates a cord on the right side (see figure 14). Leaving the under piece straight, fold the upper inward. Stitch it down to the under part, the width of a small cord from the edge (see figure 15). This stitching must be perfectly even, or the effect will be spoiled.

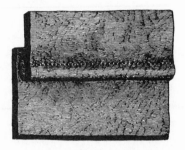

Figure 14. Cord seam

Figure 15. Making cord seam

The *invisible cloth seam* is used for piecing on both heavy and transparent materials. Hold the pieces flat, close together, and sew on the wrong side with very fine overseam stitches, only taking up half of each side of the cloth (see figure 16). The thread must be drawn firmly with each stitch. The right side will only show a delicate line to mark the seam.

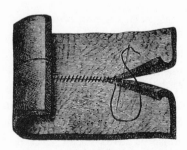

Figure 16. Invisible seam

Putting in Gussets. There are two kinds of *gussets*. One is a square piece of material let in to give more fullness to a sleeve or other part of a garment. It is joined on one side to the upper end of one side of the sleeve by a felled seam. The other side of the sleeve is afterwards joined onto the gusset and remaining part of the first side in one seam, felled like the first. The gusset thus appears cornerwise in the upper part of the sleeve.

The other kind of gusset is always small and cut square or three-cornered (a square cut in two). It is placed in the opening of a sleeve, of a nightgown, blouse, etc., to prevent the seam tearing open. (See figure 17.) When the gusset is not cut square, the edges are turned in on all four sides. Then the gusset is folded in two, to form a three-cornered piece. This is sewed in place with overcast stitch, the needle taking together, at each stitch, both turnings-in of the gusset and the side of the opening.

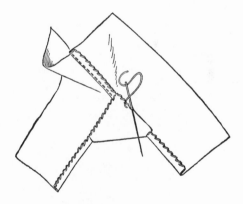

Figure 17. Putting in small gusset

If the gusset has been cut three-cornered, turnings-in are also folded down on all sides of it. The corner that forms a straight angle is sewed in, in overcast stitch, halfway up each side of the gusset. The remaining part is then folded down on the wrong side of the garment and hemmed round neatly.

Tucking Material. *Tucks* are parallel folds of material lying either horizontally or vertically on any article of dress. They are used for shortening a garment or for ornamentation. They are sometimes

431

graduated, when several follow each other successively. At other times they are made of respectively differing sizes.

First measure the material accurately to ascertain how many tucks of a given size may be made. Fold it from selvage to selvage, following a single thread to ensure perfect straightness. Press the fold firmly enough to form a crease. Turn down the folded portion to the depth desired. Then make a very close and delicate running or stitching along the double inner fold. Do not take more than three stitches at a time on the needle. When many parallel tucks are to be made, measure with a piece of cardboard cut exactly the right width. Correct any unevenness in the folds before making the runnings.

To measure the distance exactly, it is best to make a notch in a piece of card to mark the distance from the top of one tuck to the bottom of the other. Figure 18 shows one tuck completed, one in the course of the work, and one in the process of folding.

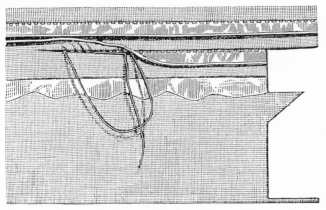

Figure 18. Folding and running tucks

Gathering or Gauging Garments. *Gathering* is required in many parts of dressmaking. Formerly, all dresses were gathered, before the great pleats came in; and many dresses are now gauged at the back pleat. Gathering is employed for drawn sleeves, bouillons, and for all gathered flounces. It is much used for children's dresses and for pelisses.

The mode of gathering used in plain sewing is thus. Fold a piece of material in half, and then into quarters, placing pins at the measurements so made. Do the same with the piece of material on which the gathered portion of material is to be sewn. Place them together, pin to pin. Take upon the needle the same number of threads as are left under at each stitch (see figure 19). In each row, take up the same threads as in the preceding row. Only one needleful of thread is used to make a gathering; it is never broken off until the running is finished.

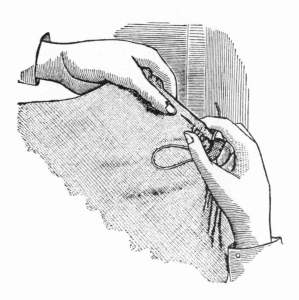

Figure 19. Gathering

When a quarter is completed, draw the material up to within the given space. Stroke down each gather with a large needle, to make them lie evenly together (see figure 20). Place a pin firmly in the material. Wind the cord under and over this pin to secure the work for sewing into the band.

Sew on the gathers, each fold independently of the others. Slope the needle to make the thread slant and slip between the gathers (see figure 21).

The *gathered bouillon* is the reverse of the usual procedure. Gather the top first. Next gather the lower edge, by arranging the stitches to take up all

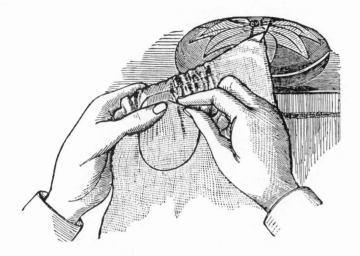

Figure 20. Stroking down gathers

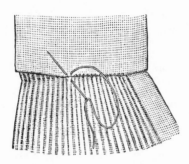

Figure 21. Sewing on gathers

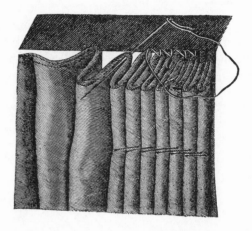

Figure 22. Sewing skirt gathers to waistband

Cutting Bias Strips. To cut *bias strips,* place the material, with the selvage to your front, along the edge of the cutting table. Raise the corner and fold it to the top or upper selvage, so as to place the straight cut end of the material along the selvage (see figure 23). Pin this carefully down, and crease the material where the natural fold occurs. This is the exact cross of the material. This fold is cut through, leaving a half square piece (which is laid aside), and a true bias, or crosscut line, on the material.

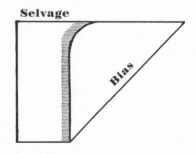

Figure 23. Preparing to cut bias strips

the intervals, or intervening spaces, in the first gathering. To this secret nearly all the beauty of the bouillon is due.

When a skirt is gathered in dressmaking, the gathers are not run through. The fullness of the material is properly portioned on the band and held by pins. The thumb of the left hand pushes up the material to form pleats more or less deep, according to the quantity of material to be gathered in a given space (see figure 22). A double overcasting stitch fixes each pleat in place. About 1 to 1 1/2 in. from the top, the gathers are firmly caught down with slip stitches. This gives great solidity to the work.

The width of the bias pieces is next ascertained. If a 6 in. bias is required, measure 6 in. at both selvages. Turn one selvage down, and pin firmly. Then fold the other selvage down 6 in., and pin the material as before, cutting on the bias line (see figure 24). Repeat this as many times as the number of pieces needed to equal the desired

length. Measure each piece exactly, and independently of the others. Using the first by which to cut the second, etc., is not accurate, and causes the bias to be untrue, and consequently not to hang well.

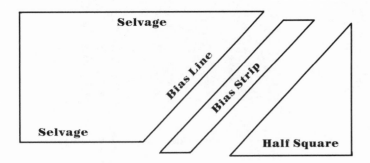

Figure 24. Cutting bias strips

One point to remember is that if you require a 6 in. wide flounce, you must cut your bias pieces 8 in. If you measure 6 in. on the selvages, your flounce will measure about 4 in. only.

Experienced cutters take the material thus: At first cut a very straight line at the edge of the material. A perfect bias line is made by folding up the corner as described above. Mark off the required width with chalk on each side of the selvage. Rapid folding and cutting follows, for as all the measures are exactly and carefully marked, very little delay occurs with the rest of the work.

Great care is required in cutting bias on twilled materials. Place the material, right side down, on the table, and the left-hand corner turned over. This brings the right side uppermost, and the lines of the twill appear perpendicular. The same rule applies to cutting bias on crape.

Hemming Dresses and Trimmings. Cloth and thick materials are often finished by being turned over and stitched down. If hand stitched, this *simple hem* need not be basted, but for sewing machine work it is best to do so.

Turn in the raw edge of the material with a double fold-over. Insert the needle, and secure the thread under the edge of the fold (see figure 25). Directing the needle in a slanting position leftward,

take up two or three strands of the material of single portion, below the fold, bringing the needle through the edge of the fold likewise. Make a continuous succession of fine regular stitches, which will confine the fold closely to the rest of the material.

Figure 25. Simple hem

The *French half-hem* is used for holding dress linings in position. The stitches are taken very far apart, and the needle inserted slanting, so as to take up the least piece at a time, in order not to show on the right side. This is easy enough on thick materials, such as cloth, serge, rep, and poplin. It becomes very difficult on thin silks, when, as it is impossible to keep the stitches from showing on the right side, they are set much closer together and at exactly even distances.

The *stitched hem* is very pretty for muslin dresses, and light summer materials. For children's dresses, it is often worked with a silk contrasting in color, which gives the effect of a Russian braid. Tarlatan ball dress flounces stitched with white or colored silks look admirably; and they are thus neatly trimmed at a trifling expense. The sewing machine can be used to advantage here; being aided and improved by the different sizes of hemmers.

Lay the material over 1/2 in. on the wrong side, and stitch it on the right side. In light materials a second turning is first made to finish the raw edge, but not in heavy materials, which do not ravel easily (see figure 26).

The *rolled hem* is made in fine linen, light materials, etc. (see figure 27). The hem is prepared as required–that is, by rolling the edge of the material between the fingers while sewing.

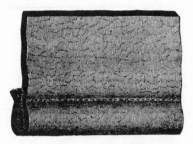

Figure 26. Stitched hem in heavy material

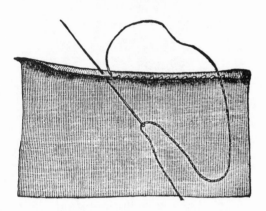

Figure 27. Rolled hem

The *whipped scroll* is prepared like the rolled hem. The difference exists in working the needle over the edge to take several stitches at the same time. This whipping is generally used to make tiny frills as the thread, if taken loosely, can be drawn up to form a gathering (see figure 28).

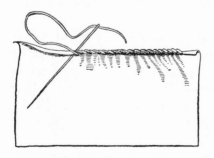

Figure 28. Whipping

The *invisible hem* is very useful. The strip that forms the binding is laid on the outside of the material and run down as far from the edge as the binding should be wide (see figure 29). Then lay it over on the under side, and sew it down so the stitches are not visible (see figure 30). For making this hem take a few threads of the material on the needle, and then run it through the strip.

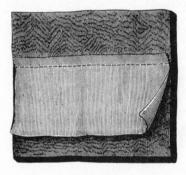

Figure 29. Binding–right side

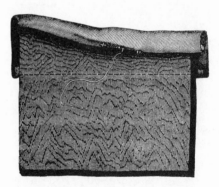

Figure 30. Binding–wrong side

The *false hem* is so called because it appears to be what it is not–part of the dress turned under and hemmed up. It is added to the edges of dresses, and used in many other ways. In figure 31 *A* is the dress; *B,* the lining of the false hem; *C* the false or additional hem. The false hem is stitched to the lining. The lining and false hem are pieces of material run on the right side of the skirt edge, turned over to the wrong side, and lightly hemmed down by slip stitches.

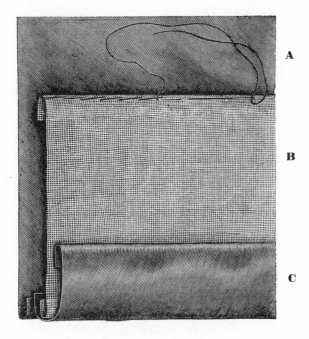

Figure 31. False hem

Figure 32. Buttonhole strip

Various materials are employed for false hems. When economy is no object the dress material is used, or a poor silk or sarcenet matching in color. It is lined or not with muslin, according to the requirements of the dress material. If lined with muslin, it is usually cut the selvage way, to secure long pieces, and small pleats are laid where requisite. The more careful dressmaker cuts her lining exactly shaped to the dress, and we need not say the effect is better.

Dressmakers, as a rule, do not hem the lining up when the skirt is trimmed. The firm work used to keep the trimming in place also keeps the lining in position. The edge of the lining is nicked with the scissors in points, like pinking, to prevent fraying. But this must be cut carefully in neat zigzags. If carelessly cut, it looks very untidy.

Working Buttonholes. In ladies' garments, custom fixes the position of the buttonholes in the right front, when the garment is upon the form. The opposite is true of gentlemen's garments. Figure 32 shows buttonholes worked on a ribbon, or on a piece of the dress material which is sewn under the front of the dress, and when fastened completely conceals the buttons.

The easiest way of placing buttons and buttonholes even, is this. Pin your tape measure down one of the fronts, putting in a pin 1 1/2 in. from the top of the center front line, and add pins at the same interval all the way down. Repeat this on the other side. Naturally the distance between buttonholes depends on the size of the buttons, small round buttons being placed less than 1 in. apart. On a bodice 1 1/2 in. is the greatest distance buttonholes can possibly be apart. The buttonholes come from within the center front line.

When you have finished measuring, compare your two fronts by laying them edge to edge, and shift your pins a trifle to make them correspond. The buttonhole side is generally a trifle longer than the other, so that when laid together that side is a little looser when the pins are made to meet each other.

Never work a buttonhole on one thickness of material. It will invariably break, and pull out. When it is not desired to line the garment, a piece

436

of strong linen 1/2 in. wider than the buttonholes should be basted between the hem, and then the buttonholes cut.

Cut the buttonhole exactly true with the material; in other words, on a horizontal line with the bodice. The strain of the buttonhole must be on the lengthwise. A width of 3/8 or 1/4 in., in front of the center front line, gives sufficient strength.

The first buttonhole should be cut carefully and the button passed through. Then the measure for the size of the rest should be marked with chalk, and cut with buttonhole scissors, if at hand. If not, be careful not to cut the hole too large. It is better to cut buttonholes one at a time and work each one before cutting another. Otherwise they are apt to fray out.

In working the buttonhole, use the best quality of tailor's buttonhole twist. Always use twist that is much coarser than the thread of the material, as the buttonhole shows better and is firmer. It is a good plan to encircle the buttonhole before cutting it. This is done by a double line of running. Two threads of material are usually left between the two stitchings, where the buttonhole is cut.

Always work the buttonhole from left to right. Keep the eye of the needle very near it. The point should be below the outside row of stitches. Close the stitch very closely to the cut edges. To accomplish this, turn the twist around the needle, pulling it out, and then drawing it upward. Each stitch should be taken along the same line of the material.

A short bar is worked across the end, when one side of the buttonhole is completed. This bridges the edges, and gives strength to the buttonhole. Four stitches usually complete the bar. It, of course, reaches entirely across the width of the buttonhole. Then work these stitches back, again using the buttonhole stitch. Work the other side in the same manner as the first. When the side is completed, cross-bar the other end of the buttonhole, then complete the process in buttonhole stitch. Finally, securely fasten the twist, insert the needle, and draw the twist underneath the work, hiding the end.

To begin the *plain buttonhole*, encircle the space to be cut by double stitching. Cut the buttonhole and bar at once, before the threads can become displaced. In some materials it is a good plan to bar the buttonhole before cutting. Work the buttonhole stitches closely and evenly, so that the barring will be completely hidden (see figure 33). At the ends, work directly across. Secure the twist, hiding the end.

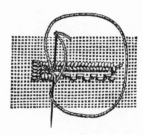

Figure 33. Working plain buttonhole

The ends of the *round buttonhole* are barred in a curved form instead of directly across. It can be worked like the plain buttonhole, but in the main the chain stitch is used (see figure 34). This is positively necessary in heavy materials, and whenever the buttonhole should have a heavy or raised appearance.

Figure 34. Barring round buttonhole

The *double-stitch buttonhole* shown in figure 35 is made as follows. First run the double stitching around the cut and bar it. Work the ordinary buttonhole stitch all around it. Then work the diagonal stitch over all. This is made by taking short diagonal stitches from left to right, throwing the loop and drawing the twist at the top (see figure 36).

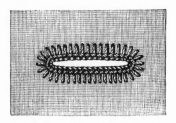

Figure 35. Buttonhole in double buttonhole stitch

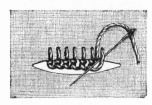

Figure 38. Making knotted buttonhole stitch–enlarged

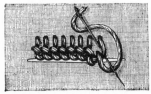

Figure 36. Making double buttonhole stitch–enlarged

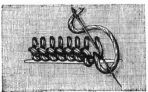

Figure 39. Making knot for buttonhole

The *knotted buttonhole* shown in figure 37 is worked in the knotted stitch. It is first worked like the plain buttonhole. Upon this foundation the twist is laid upward, and drawn through again, underneath the twist of the original work (see figure 38). This is then ornamented with a row of knots (see figure 39). The knot is made as follows. Pass the twist twice around the needle. Put it back through the same insertion into the material. When it is drawn it forms the knot. This is repeated until the work is completed.

Begin the *tatted buttonhole* shown in figure 40 by laying a cord under instead of barring. Cut the buttonhole. Sew the cord around the edge, using fine overcast stitches. Then work using the tatted buttonhole stitch shown in figure 41.

Figure 40. Buttonhole in tatted buttonhole stitch

Figure 37. Buttonhole in knotted stitch

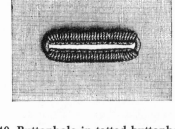

Figure 41. Making tatted buttonhole stitch–enlarged

Cut and bar the *pointed buttonhole,* shown in figure 42, as usual. Then work with ordinary buttonhole stitch, setting the stitches so that they form points (see figure 43). Each stitch is worked off with a second stitch that is shorter than the first. It is, of course, worked from left to right.

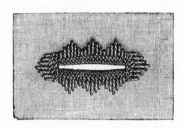

Figure 42. Buttonhole in pointed buttonhole stitch

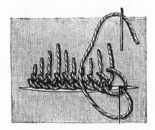

Figure 43. Making pointed buttonhole stitch–enlarged

The *herringbone buttonhole* shown in figure 44 should consist of diagonal buttonhole stitches, one setting the needle from above to below, and the other in the opposite direction (see figure 45). After you have completed this herringbone stitch, work the inside edges nearest the cut a second time with buttonhole stitch.

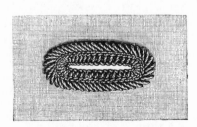

Figure 44. Buttonhole in herringbone stitch

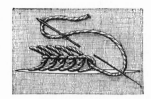

Figure 45. Making herringbone buttonhole stitch– enlarged

For the *twisted stitch buttonhole,* shown in figure 46, insert the needle through the material very close to the edge, then up through the cut. Wind the twist seven times around the needle, and draw the thread and needle through said windings (see figure 47). To do this nicely may require a little experience. Slightly press the windings down when you pull the needle up. This holds them down on the material. Then put the needle through exactly where it was inserted for the last stitch, and draw it through the material to the side underneath. Work the successive stitches in the same manner.

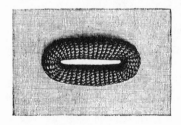

Figure 46. Buttonhole in twisted stitch

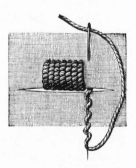

Figure 47. Making twisted buttonhole stitch–enlarged

The *piped buttonhole* shown in figure 48 is made on heavy materials and where very large buttons are used. It is simply a buttonhole bound with piping (see figure 49).

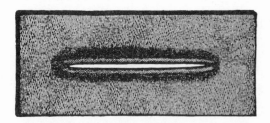

Figure 48. Piped buttonhole

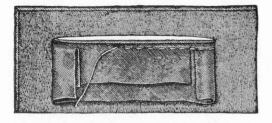

Figure 49. Making piped buttonhole

Sewing on Buttons. The buttons should be sewn on exactly opposite the buttonholes. The best way to be sure of that is to work the buttonholes and sew the buttons on before the garment is sewn together. The buttonholes should be worked first. The upper edge of the bodice should be laid smoothly over the under edge, and pins stuck along directly in the center of the buttonhole. Then there should be a line of basting where the pins were stuck, put in with a cross-stitch exactly where the button is to be sewn.

On soft or unlined material, strengthen the places where the buttons are to be sewn. Cut out from two thicknesses of strong linen circular disks about the size of a wafer. Lightly hem them around onto the bodice under the places where the buttons are to go. Then sew on the buttons. By this means the buttons are held firmly.

The needle should be passed up through the material, through the proper place in the button, then down again. Care should be taken to take as large a hold on the button, if a silk one, as possible; and as small a circumference as can be on the dress.

A *flat button* requires that the thread be wound around the base several times, then fastened underneath by five or six stitches all taken in different directions. If it is not well fastened it soon works loose, and hangs loosely, giving a slovenly look to the bodice.

For the *shank button,* knot your thread or twist. Put the needle through the material, concealing the knot by the work. Two stitches should be given first, to secure the twist. Then insert the needle and twist through the shank seven times. Do not wind the twist around the stitches, but secure it on the wrong side with three stitches.

To attach the *covered button,* make a cover of twist on the under side. Give 1/16 in. space on the material. Knot your thread or twist, and place the knot on the right side exactly under the neck of the button. Take two stitches from right to left. Now put the needle through the material and the crossed threads at the underside of the button. Bring it through the material, close by the first insertion of the needle. Continue this process seven times. Do not draw the twist too closely. Then wind the twist seven times around the stitches. Secure the work on the wrong side with three stitches. Be careful not to draw the material.

The *linen button* is begun like the covered button. First knot the thread or twist, and hide the knot directly under the neck of the button. Take two stitches from right to left. Then placing the needle up, in the center of the button, arrange the stitches to cross on the bottom side. Repeat the stitch seven times. Wind the twist several times around the stitches, between the button and the material. Secure the work on the wrong side with three stitches.

This method is illustrated in figure 50, but also another mode that is more secure and less likely to tear away any portion of the button.

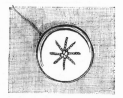 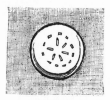

Figure 50. Sewing on linen button

The *eye button* is attached like the linen button, only inserting the needle through the eye.

For the *woven button,* stitch through the material from the right side, through to the wrong side, and draw the knot exactly underneath the center of the button. This is done by two repeated stitches. Using short backstitches, form a circular chain underneath the button. The circle should not exceed 1/16 in. in diameter. Insert the needle, and draw the twist out between the material and the button. Wind the twist seven times around. Secure the work on the wrong side with three stitches.

Attaching Hooks and Eyes. *Hooks* when on a dress should be placed about 1 in., or a little more, inside the edge of the bodice. They should be sewn on by taking stitches in the bows, and again across the bill to hold them flat (see figure 51). Be careful that the stitches are taken no deeper than the lining, and that the thread does not draw too tightly. The hook should be held slightly loose so that it rests on the lining, rather than sinking in and showing on the outer side.

Figure 51. Sewing on hook and eye

The *eyes* should be placed exactly opposite, the most careful measure being taken. A deviation of 1/16 in. will cause them to pull and wrinkle the edges of the garment. They should be set near the edge of the garment, with the loop projecting slightly. The eyes should be sewn in four places, the bows and a few stitches on each side of the loops

to hold them firm. The thread should be carried from one to the other without cutting off until it is finished; and then start on the last one and carry the thread on as before. This is simply to give a better finish.

Making Thread Loops. *Loops* may be manufactured by the seamstress to form an attachment for a small button or hook, by means of three or four threads (see figure 52). Secure the thread to a spot a little within the edge of the side opposite to that of the button. Take up a stitch, leaving a loop long enough to pass freely over the button. Take another stitch at the spot where the thread was first drawn out. Continue to multiply the loops of thread until they are strong enough. Then proceed to form a covering over all the strands, which will connect them together into one cord. This is done by passing the needle round them, and through the thread below it, in a firm buttonhole stitch, securing the thread well at the other end of the loop, on the wrong side of the material.

Figure 52. Making a loop

Sewing on Tape. To sew *tape* on a hem, first stitch the tape close under the hem, taking the stitches from the right side. The end of the tape must lie over the hem as shown by figure 53. Lay the tape over so that it extends beyond the edge. Cover the end of the tape. Stitch it down on the hem again from the right side as shown by figure 54. The other end of the tape is hemmed with a narrow hem, or worked in buttonhole stitch.

Figure 53. Sewing tape on hem—wrong side

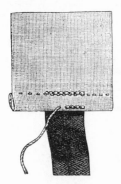

Figure 54. Sewing tape on hem—right side

To sew tape on cloth, first backstitch it down on the material (see figure 53). Then lay the tape over, and stitch it down along the edges and the end, as shown by figure 55.

Figure 55. Sewing tape on cloth

For the sake of distinctness, the illustrations show the tape darker than the material. However, white tape must always be used on white material and vice versa.

Boning a Bodice. Whalebones in dresses are generally used in the two front pieces, and at the side seams; but this is at the option of the maker. They should reach to one-third of the hip depth below the waist, and half the waist depth above. Both ends should be rounded and scraped down to the thickness of a knife blade. The tapes may be ordinary stay binding or fancy ribbon.

Slovenly dressmakers secure the tapes by machine stitching each edge of the tape to one side of the seam. This is not a good method, and if you have sewn your open seam down to the lining with the herringbone stitch, it is out of the question without showing the machine stitch outside the waist. Machine stitching does not answer, as the tape must be eased on each seam to enable a greater length of whalebone to be introduced, thus ensuring greater smoothness to the bodice. The tapes must not be too much puckered or the bones strain the material too much, and have a tendency to protrude the edge of the basque apart from the body. Therefore the tape should be eased and hemmed to the open seam (see figure 56).

Whalebones can be inserted by two methods. For the first, the lower end is rolled in tape, and is passed to the lower end of the casing which is closed by stitches. The upper end of the bone is pierced with a small hole by which is it secured to the casing (see figure 57). For the second method, a hole is pierced in each end of the bone, the lower edge being finished like the upper. Press the bone into the eased casing, so that it stretches out smoothly.

Encasing the Bones in Tapes. The casings are best made of two pieces of tape sewed together and the bone run inside. The ends of the tapes can then be turned over and the needle passed through the ends of the bones and tape several times. The taped bones are then sewed to the seams which should be laid open, taking about six or eight

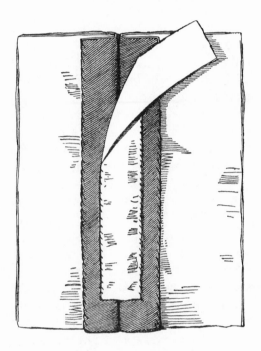

Figure 56. Whalebone casing

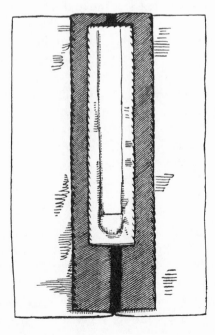

Figure 57. Casing with whalebone inserted

stitches to the inch. This is both a saving of labor and a great advantage in the fit and stability of the bodice.

Omitting Boning. Many persons still cling to whalebones in the bodice of a dress (especially stout people). But these are very undesirable, as, besides giving a stiff look to the figure, and preventing the dress from adjusting itself to its motions, they wear unsightly holes in the material. A disagreeable part of the work, too, is avoided by not being obliged to sew on bone casings and cut the whalebones to fit them.

Padding a Bodice. Few are perfect in form. Better to improve an imperfect form by padding, than to try and fit it by cutting. When taking measures, note the points to be padded and allow for pads in the measures.

For uneven shoulders, pad the lower. For a hollow chest, pad across the chest from arm to arm, a little off from the armhole seam. For low armpits, pad from the back seam of the underarm piece, around the front armhole a little off from the seam, and as far up toward the neck as required.

Cut pads the shape and thickness desired. Tack them on the lining between the cloth and lining. Cut or pull out the edges so they will lay smooth and flat to avoid a break on the outside, which would show the dress to be padded. The edges should taper down gradually to the thickness of a sheet of letter paper. The pads may be made separately and worn under the dress. But if much padding is required, it is better to sew it inside the lining. Pads properly made and sewed onto the lining give a soft and smooth appearance.

For a hollow chest, low armpits, and small flat bust, pad from the back seam of the underarm piece, around the armhole, over the chest and bust down to the top of the darts. Lay on a layer of wadding from the bust up to the shoulder (see figure 58). Lay three or four thicknesses about the upper part of the darts. Sew one thickness in with the dart seam for 1 in. or so at the top. Fasten all the others to it.

443

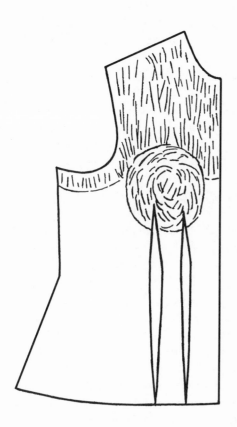

Figure 58. Padding for a thin figure

If the outside is a thin or soft quality of silk, in addition use wadding through the entire waist. For a thin arm, wad the sleeve from the top to the elbow.

Altering Patterns

Suppose you want to make a polonaise. First compare the pattern measures to your own (see figure 59). The back piece is 16 in. from the neck to the bottom of the waist, and your measure is 15 1/2 in. Even though the difference is only 1/2 in., you should make it correct. It is much quicker to alter in the pattern than in the material. Cut through the pattern 1 in. from the bottom of the waist (see figure 60), then lap it 1/2 in.

A quicker way, however, is not to cut the pattern, but first mark out the upper part. To shorten, raise the pattern after the upper part has been drawn. To lengthen, drop the pattern the length required.

The pattern gives but half the back. Starting from the lower point of the armhole and measuring straight across, the width is 7 1/2 in. This would make the entire back 15 in. Your back width measure is 13 in., so you must make the pattern narrower. The present fashion calls for a short shoulder. Thus you may easily preserve the armhole curve by taking 1 in. from it all around the back, which takes 1 in. from the shoulder length as well as 1 in. from the back width. The side piece will fit in the back the same way as before the alteration.

On the front piece, the underarm measure on the pattern is 7 1/2 in., and yours is 8 in. Alter this as for the back length, cutting through it 1 in. above the bottom of the waist and lapping it 1/2 in.

Your measure across the bust is 22 in. Consequently the pattern of one front should be 11 in. Measuring from the straight edge across the bust, just beneath the armhole, you find it is too wide. Mark with your pencil at 11 in., then move the ruler up to get the high bust width. It is 9 in., and you must make it 7 1/2. Mark again at the right point. Because you took 1 in. from the shoulder length in back, you must do the same to the front. Sketching from 1 in. up on the shoulder to the mark indicating the high bust width, and from there to the bust mark, you keep the same curve around the armhole.

Measure the length under the arm on the side piece. Finding it is 1/2 in. too long, cut the waist entirely through and lap it up 1/2 in. the same way as for the waist length of the other pieces. Be careful to keep the front edge even, letting whatever will project of the skirt come out at the underarm edge.

Now get the waist measure. Lay the back and side pieces together and measure across both. Then measure from the straight edge of the front to the first dart, then between the darts, and from the back dart to the underarm edge. The pattern measure on these is 13 in., and you want it to be 12. You must take 1 in. from the waist, and 1 1/2 in. from the bust. Take 1/2 in. from the side piece at the armhole, and 1 in. from the front at the armhole.

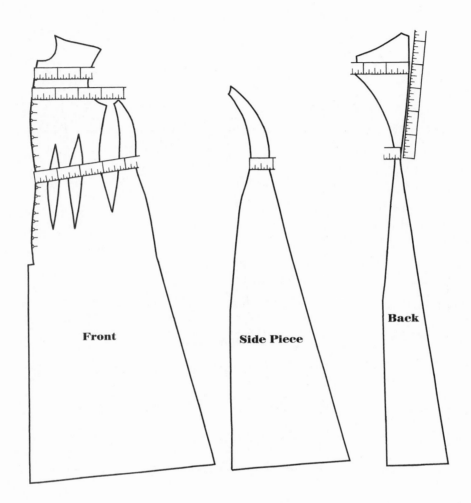

Figure 59. Measuring the pattern

The pattern sleeve measures are 16 and 24 in. They should be 15 1/2 and 22. Since the sleeve is only 1 in. too long on the inside, you will shorten it from the bottom.

Fitting a Muslin

Always prove your draft before tracing any part of it onto the lining or material. Carefully measure the parts that represent the fit upon the high bust, bust, waist, and hips. If you have made a mistake, rectify it in an equal division at the seams on said line or lines.

Basting the Model Bodice or Bodice Lining. Place the various pieces together, so that the construction and waist lines, traced across the pieces at the waist, are exactly even. All the pieces should be pinned very carefully and accurately into position, at intervals along the seams, each way from the waist. Baste up and down, in each direction from said lines, beginning at the waist. Run a single stitch at a time, locating the stitches 1/4 in. apart.

Commence with the back and side pieces, holding the back toward you. Baste it a little full, and stretch the rounded edge of the side pieces. Hold the back toward you, in basting the shoulder seams. Stretch the front shoulder seam until it is even with that of the back. Baste the darts very carefully, upon the trace marks, holding them and basting as described for basting the curved seams at the back.

445

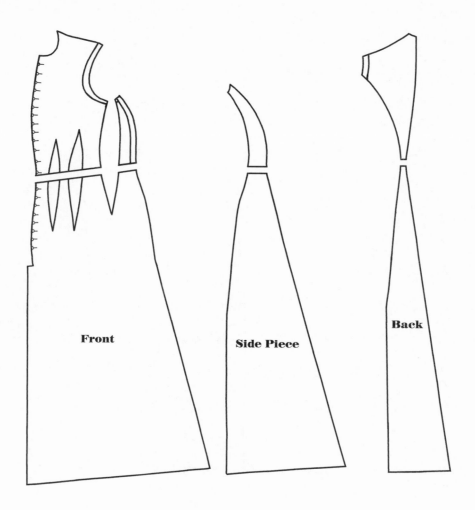

Figure 60. Altering the pattern

Marking Alterations. It is important that the person to be fitted wear the same corset and undergarments that are to be worn after the garment is made. A thick flannel undergarment, or an ill-shaped corset, will make quite a difference in the appearance and fit of the dress. Fit on the model bodice over the dress skirt. Fasten exactly in the center front with pins, 2 in. apart.

If you find the neck is too low, or the shoulder too short, pin a piece of muslin to the part deficient, and cut to the size required. This piece should remain on the model bodice, firmly secured with pins. All other parts requiring additional material should be done in the same way.

Figure 61 represents a model bodice that fits perfectly. When the model bodice is properly fitted it should be removed, with all the pins left in except in front. See that every alteration is distinctly marked. Mark where the lap in front is to be turned in. Rip all the seams apart without stretching. Crease the edge of the model bodice as close to the seam or basting stitches as possible with both hands, between the forefinger and thumb. Where alterations are made, crease exactly where the pins are placed.

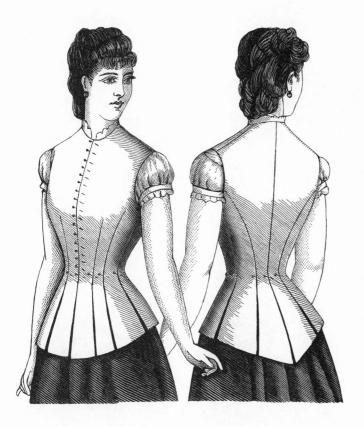

Figure 61. Perfectly fitting model bodice

Fitting for a Bouffant Skirt. In figure 62 the skirt is bouffant; consequently the back of the basque requires to be fuller. The back and side piece below the waist are too small, and must be enlarged as shown. Mark the front with a pencil exactly where the two edges meet.

Figure 62. Fitting over bouffant skirt

Fitting for Large Hips with Small Waist.
Figure 63 shows the fit of a model bodice with the correct bust measure, but which binds in the hips, causing wrinkles to appear above the waist.

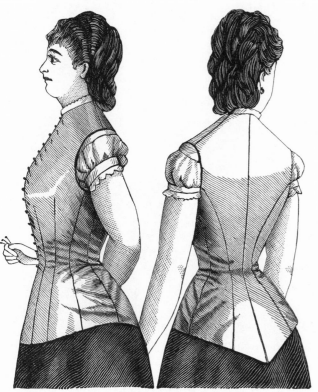

Figure 63. Bodice too small in hips

To fit this model bodice, rip the two seams under the arm from the waist down. Allow the skirt to fall naturally over the hips. The side seams will spread apart (see figure 64). Fill up the gap with muslin pinned to each side. It is important that not only the width but the proper shape be given to the side pieces. The back and front pieces are too full, and must be pinned down to give the proper shape.

Figure 64. Correction for large hips

Fitting Basque for Tight Waist. Figure 65 represents an ill-fitting basque. The wrinkles are caused by either too much taken out of the darts, or the front is too narrow.

Figure 65. Basque with overly tight waist

Figure 66. Model bodice let out in front

To ascertain the cause, unbutton the front from the point where the wrinkles commence, to the bottom of the basque. The front will naturally fall toward the back. The basque will be too loose at the sides and too tight at the front. To remedy this add from 1/2 to 1 in. in front from *A* to *B*, and take up the surplus material at the sides (see figure 66). For stout ladies it is sometimes necessary to place a whalebone in front, directly under the buttons. As this interferes with buttoning the bodice, it is seldom done.

If the basque is made up and finished these alterations can only be made at the expense of a new bodice. A more simple way is to put on a vest front, as seen in figure 67.

Figure 67. Basque with vest front

Fitting Jacket for Tight Waist. Figure 68 shows a perfectly fitting jacket. Figure 69 shows the same jacket too tight below the waist. Add 1/2 in. to each seam at *A*, *B*, and *C*. This will give the necessary spring over the hips.

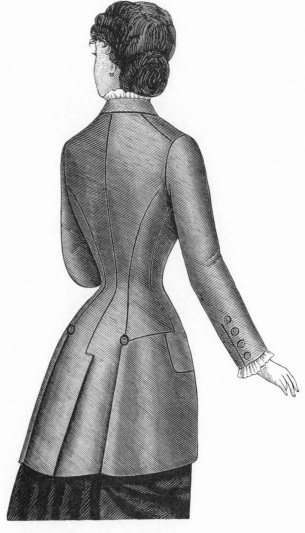

Figure 68. Perfectly fitted jacket

450

Figure 69. Alteration areas for tight waist

sleeve at *F* is cut too long and basted even with the top of the upper sleeve, it will throw the forearm seam at *H* too far over on the top. To prevent this, baste the upper and under part of the sleeve perfectly plain, except at the elbow. If the under part is too long, cut it off at the top at *F,* tapering it gradually toward the forearm seam.

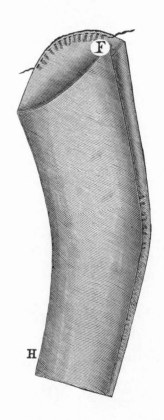

Figure 70. Sleeve ready for fitting

Fitting the Sleeves. When the model bodice is fitted, and before it is removed, fit a model sleeve. In basting the sleeve, place the construction line across the same at the elbow, exactly even, which should bring it even at the front. Place the upper and under sleeve even at each end. Bring any fullness allowed, equidistant each way, from the construction line across the sleeve at the elbow.

Figure 70 represents a sleeve with seams sewed ready for fitting. When the forearm seam at the wrist turns round toward the top, it is caused by bad basting. When the upper point of the under

Pin the top of the sleeve to the armhole with the pins 1 in. apart, as seen in figure 71. If the sleeve is too wide, take in the front or back seam by pinning all the way down. See that the elbow is in the right place. Raise the arm, and bend it forward. If the sleeve draws at the elbow or wrinkles unnaturally, change the position of the sleeve at the top until it fits perfectly. When the sleeve draws at the top near the armhole, it is caused by the forearm seam being too high or too low in the armhole, or the top of the sleeve not rounding enough.

Figure 72. Badly fitting sleeve

Figure 73 represents the same sleeve ripped at the top, showing where the alterations are to be made. From 1 to 1 1/2 in. must be added to the top at the most rounding part, running to nothing at the back and forearm seam.

Figure 71. Sleeve pinned into armhole

Figure 72 shows a badly fitting sleeve. All that is wanted to make this sleeve fit, is to rip the top and allow the sleeve to fall from the shoulder in its natural position on the arm. The top of the sleeve should be more rounding.

Figure 73. Sleeve alterations

In fitting a sleeve over a plump, round arm, carry the fullness further back over the rounding part at the top. Stretch the space between C and P about 1/2 in. or more (see figure 74). If the arm is above the average size, stretch from C 2 in. above the point at P.

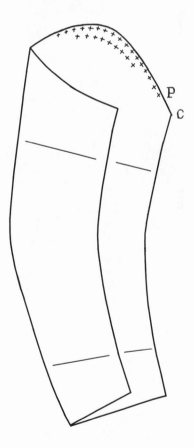

Figure 74. Diagram of upper and under sleeve

Dressmaking and Millinery

Figure 75 shows wrinkles at the top near the back armhole. These are usually unavoidable except in a tight-fitting sleeve. When the sleeve is tight fitting back and front, from shoulder to cuff, the arm cannot be raised above a level. When the sleeve is made to allow the hand to be raised above the head, more or less fullness will appear at the back near the armhole. It is no fault in a sleeve to have a little fullness at the back.

Figure 75. Well-fitting sleeve with arm raised

When the sleeve fits properly, cut a notch in the armhole of the model bodice where each seam of the sleeve is placed. Cut two notches at the top to show where the fullness is placed.

Before the garment is completed–before the seams under the arms are sewed, the buttonholes cut, or the sleeves sewed in–it should be refitted as described for the model bodice.

Cutting Out a Dress

In cutting out a bodice, whatever be its shape, certain rules are always followed. The pattern is first cut out in lining, and then in the material. It is well to pin every part of the pattern in position before cutting out any piece, or to chalk the outline as is done by tailors.

Pin a smooth cloth tightly across the table, on which to fasten the work when necessary. Spread the material on top of it. Lay the patterns on the material in various positions, so as to utilize every spare corner. Lay each piece the right way of the grain. Leave the seam allowances sufficiently deep not only to allow for the stitching, but for enlarging the article if necessary. Tack the pattern pieces to the material and then cut out. If the material be doubled, the two sides may be cut out simultaneously.

Cutting Out the Lining. All linings should be cut out first. If about to prepare a bodice, for example, lay the rolled lining on the table in front of you, the cut end toward you (see figure 76). Along the selvage on the left side place the right front of the pattern (the side with the buttonholes or eyes), and pin along the edge of the pattern parallel with the selvage, allowing 1 1/2 in. for turning in. The whole pattern must be smoothed out well, and pinned down. Then place the left side (where the buttons will be) on the opposite side of the lining. Pin it down likewise at the selvage, running or tacking down the whole model on the lining, following the outline throughout. Then the two backs should be laid upon the lining, the centers parallel with the selvages, 1 in. allowed from them. Pin them down and tack the outlines. For the side and back pieces, be careful to lay the line of the waist exactly parallel with the grain. The bodice will be drawn aside if the cutting be at all on the bias. The shoulder pieces and arm pieces, which stand in lieu of sleeves on mantles such as dolmans, should be cut with the bias down the middle.

Cut out each outlined piece 1/2 in. beyond the outline, to allow for turning in; but the fronts must be left uncut to preserve the selvage edges.

Figure 76. Bodice layout

The lining should be held 1/2 in. full on the material, at and near the waist. For this reason it should always be cut 1/2 in. longer than the outside.

Sleeve linings are cut from silk or some soft material that will yield to the movement of the arm. The sleeves must be turned so that the upper part in front is straight with the material, which will throw the under portion a little on the bias. Figure 77 shows how to place the sleeve on double material. Place each part of the sleeve so that the two points $N N$ touch the selvage. If the material is striped the two edges on the back arm $O O$ should run even with the stripe, regardless of the points at $N N$.

The top of the sleeve should be cut about 1 1/2 in. larger than the armhole. If the garment is made from heavy material, very little fullness will be required. Cashmere and alpaca require more fullness at the top than silk, and beaver cloth least of all. The sleeve seams on the back arm should be 1 in., or large enough for alterations if need be. This is particularly necessary for a tight sleeve.

For a tight sleeve, if the arm is thin cut a separate interlining from alpaca, on the bias. Sew this between the lining and material. One or two thicknesses of wadding can be placed between the interlining and the lining. The wadding should be tacked with stitches 1 in. apart. If the interlining is not wanted the wadding may be tacked on the lining.

After the pieces are cut chalk, or run in cotton, the letters R and L on the right and left sides of the bodice, and also the two sleeves, adding a T to distinguish the sleeve top.

Cutting Out the Material. After cutting out the lining, the material itself is laid out smoothly, pinned down, tacked to the lining, and cut out. No incision should be made until every portion of the pattern is laid in its proper place.

If the material be striped or plaid, the matching of the different pieces should be carefully attended to. In cutting striped materials try to have a perfect stripe down the middle of the bodice front, and down the back also, if there is no seam. Should there be a floral design, make sure it is not turned

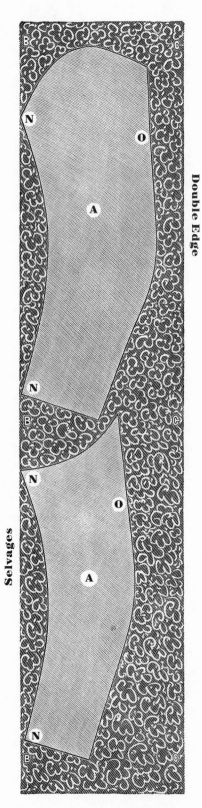

Double Edge

Selvages

Figure 77. Sleeve layout

upside down on any of the pieces. Materials having a nap or pile need careful attention. The portions of the material should be cut to lie in the same direction—whichever way may be preferred, provided that uniformity be observed. As sealskin, which supplied the original idea of plush, is always laid with the fur lying upward, it is usually thought that velvet looks more rich when laid thus.

The widths of materials vary—some velvets being 18 in. wide only, while cashmere, merino, and many mixed goods are 40 in. wide. When the material folded in half is too narrow to cut both bodice fronts, each front must be cut separately. Side pieces, sleeve parts, or backs may, by a little management, be cut out of the piece remaining.

In cutting out on narrow materials, it is necessary to add to the gores of dresses. Figure 78 shows the mode of cutting the additional piece *A* which is run on the gore at the selvages, marked by a dashed line. It also shows the mode of placing the front of a princess dress on the material.

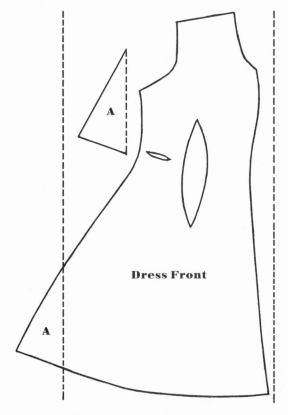

Dress Front

Figure 78. Piecing material

Silk materials are sometimes too narrow for a large sleeve to be cut from one breadth. Joining two selvages is advisable, making the union underneath the sleeve. Cut the parts of the sleeves above the elbow the straight way of the goods, so that if they are at all curved the bias part will come at the wrist. Sleeves that have no seams down the back may be cut either straight or bias down the back, but they are usually cut straight.

When cutting any piece of material on the bias, such as trimmings, flounces, etc., it should be correctly done, otherwise the work will be drawn awry.

If there is a seam down the middle of the back of a polonaise bodice, and the skirt is full, avoid one, if possible, down the middle of the skirt back. This can be done by laying the edge of the pattern for the back part of the skirt to a fold of the material. The same rule applies to a basque with a pleated postilion.

The method of cutting out a bodice has been given first because it is more complicated than cutting out a skirt. The general rules of tacking on the pattern, then cutting out the lining, and then the material, apply equally to the bodice and skirt. It is

Figure 79. Lining pinned to material

457

usual, however, to cut out the skirt first, then the polonaise or bodice and overskirt if there be one. If there is a scarcity of material, the sleeves might be made up of joinings underneath. Small pieces may be added under the arms. The fronts may be faced, or a false hem added, instead of turning down the hems. Often both fronts of a bodice may thus be obtained from one breadth. Trimmings should be left to the last, as scraps might be utilized for them.

Jackets are cut as jacket bodices, but differ usually in size and trimming.

Basting a Bodice

In correctly basting the material upon the linings, and then said parts into the whole, lies the grand secret of garment making.

Place the lining on the material. Do not cut the material close to the edge of the lining; block it out roughly as represented in figure 79. Mark with a tracing wheel where the seams are to be sewed; mark through the two thicknesses of lining.

When cut, pin each part, lining and material, together. Roll each part up separately, ready for basting. In this way there will be no danger of cutting two pieces for one side, or having the pieces mixed or changed.

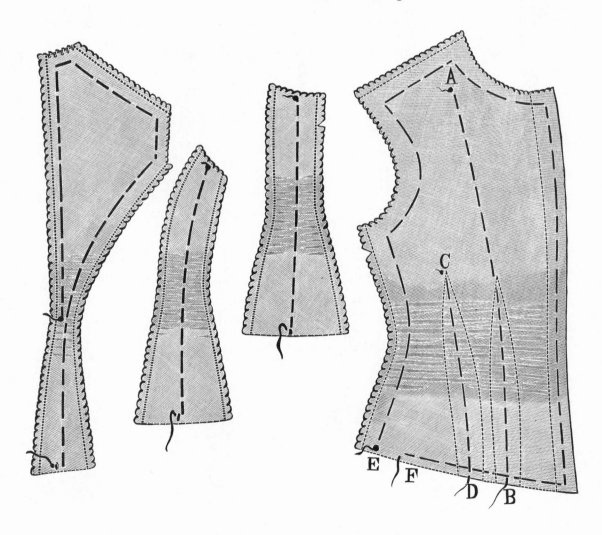

Figure 80. Lining basted to material

458

Basting the Lining to the Material. Place the material on the table, with the wrong side up, and with the wrinkles neatly smoothed out. Begin with the front. Carefully place the lining upon the material. Baste over the knee with the lining on top. Use a long basting needle and basting thread, black on white, or white on other colors. Take one stitch at a time, 1/2 in. apart. Neatly fasten the basting thread, where you begin and quit, on all the pieces. All the pieces should be carefully handled, so as not to stretch the seams.

When each piece is basted, trim the edge and overcast. The overcast stitch should not be drawn tight.

Begin at the top of the front at *A* (see figure 80). Baste in a direct line down to the top of the front dart. Continue to baste through the center of the dart to the bottom.

Hold the lining 1/2 in. full at the waist. This may be done with a slight upward movement of the thimble of the left hand at each stitch. This is done on all parts of the garment, around the entire waistline. It should at least extend, or be distributed, over a space of 3 in. above and 3 in. below the waist. It is the sovereign remedy for inelegance of fit at the waist, and for wrinkles in the outside material. The linings in adjusting themselves to the form stretch the outside material and hold it in this position.

Baste the second dart, beginning at the top at *C* and basting down to the bottom.

Baste all round the edge of the front, about 1 in. from the edge. Baste from *F* to *E* (for the left side, which is illustrated in figure 80) or from *E* to *F* (for the right side).

Baste the lining on the back. Begin at the waist, 1 in. from the seam at the center of the back. Baste like the front, from the waist toward the top; around, and within 1 in. of the edge, down to the waist; from thence, through the center of the piece, to the bottom.

Begin at the top of the side pieces, 1 in. from the edge, and at the center. Baste down through the center to the bottom.

When the lining and material are basted together, and the edges overcast, baste the seams.

Basting the Seams. A dress bodice is cut plain, as if to fit a flat surface. To fit the body some of the seams must be cut rounding, others curved; some must be stretched and others held full. The letters and stars on figure 81 show where each seam and each part of the seam is to be treated.

Before basting, each seam should be fastened with pins 3 in. apart. Remove the pins as you baste. Baste exactly on the trace marks for the seam lines. If the pieces are not cut even, let them run over at the bottom, never at the top.

Begin in front with the dart seams. These should be basted perfectly plain from the top to the bottom, four stitches to the inch. Be careful that you do not allow a fold or crease to appear above the dart.

Next is the piece under the arm. Before basting, the two seams at *E* and *F* must each be stretched about 1/2 in. directly opposite the stars, or 3 in. above the waist; this will prevent wrinkles at these points. Lay the piece so the construction and waist lines are exactly even, and pin them. Start basting this piece at the top.

In basting the side seams, the curved edge opposite the small dots at *G* must be basted easy, but not full, to within 1 1/2 in. of the top. On the side piece, baste the seam perfectly plain below the dots. Always baste the seam with the back next you; baste the right side first, starting at the top. Pin and baste the left side like the right.

In basting the shoulder seam, stretch the front between *A* and *A* 3/4 in., or hold the back marked by the dots at *H* full on the front. The front should be even at the neck and armhole with the back. In pressing the seam, the fullness will all disappear. The object is to prevent wrinkles in front between the neck and shoulder.

In cutting a tight-fitting garment, make the armhole as small as possible, but not to bind. The armhole round the stars at *J* should be stretched until the edge turns over. This will prevent wrinkles in front of the armhole. Care should be taken not

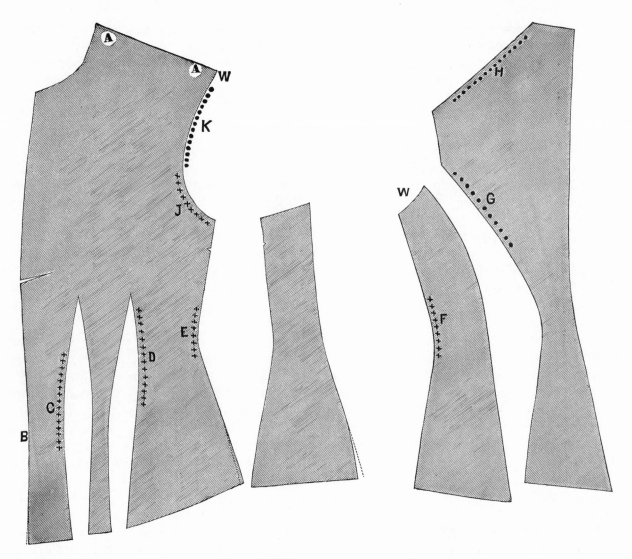

Figure 81. Where seams are treated

to stretch above or below this point. The edge at *W W* is liable to stretch in sewing in the sleeve. To prevent this, run a thread near the edge; make a running stitch very close, say 10 stitches to 1 in. The dots at *K* mark where the sleeve is sewed full into the armhole.

If the seam at center back is stretched during basting, sewing, or pressing, it will materially affect the appearance and fit of the dress.

For the sleeve, any fullness at the elbow should be gathered evenly between the notches and the point of the elbow, exactly at the center of the fullness.

Before the sleeve is basted into position, both lining and material should be overcast neatly. The stitches should be 1/8 in. apart, and the top should be gathered with a running or overcast stitch. Baste the sleeve into the armhole with the fullest or highest part of the top of the sleeve exactly at the top or highest part of the shoulder. The back seam of the sleeve should be turned toward the under part, and fastened to the lining. In heavy materials, the seams should be pressed open.

460

Baste sacques, coats, paletots, and dolman-sleeved wraps per the instructions for close-fitting garments. Press out very carefully, all fullness allowed upon the linings everywhere.

Putting Pleats in the Lining. Several pleats are made in the lining only, to prevent wrinkles in the outer material. Two little pleats are made at the top of the bodice in front. A similar pleat is made at the armhole. Another, lengthwise pleat is made in the waistline of a basque.

Assembling a Bodice

The first note of importance, for sewing and finishing a bodice, is to see that the sewing machine is in perfect order. The needle must have a sharp point, also it is necessary to use a rather fine needle. For very nice materials, always use silk for stitching the seams.

Sewing the Seams. Always begin the stitching of darts and joins at the top and work downward. Stitch the darts closely, holding both edges with equal firmness. Try on the garment before cutting off the dart seams.

Next stitch the central back seam by machine or a close backstitch, exactly on the outlined thread. The two halves of the back with their tacked turning are naturally laid face to face.

If there are two or more side pieces, attach these next the back by stitching the edges together on the inside. Where there is only one on each side, the edge of each is sometimes folded down, basted, and sewn from the outside very near the edge. This depends on whether the taste of the day is to make the seams conspicuous, or as little observable as possible. When outside stitching is in fashion, use very fine sewing silk. Let it be one or two shades darker than the material, as it will always stitch in lighter.

Stitch a line on the outline thread of the left front, but do not turn in the 1 1/2 in. allowed, as it forms a flap to conceal any white the buttonholes may chance to show.

The backs and fronts are joined, by evenly basted seams, at the shoulders and under the arms. The shoulder seam is not placed directly on top of the shoulder, but rather toward the back.

The bodice is then tried on to see what alterations are needed. A second basting should be done if necessary; the bodice should never be sewn till the proper fit is secured.

After sewing the seams, clip the seams under the arms just at the waist to give sufficient spring for the hips.

The underarm seams are sewn next. Shave off any ravelings at the bottom of the bodice. Then oversew the outside material and lining together on either side of the seam, and press them open.

Run the tapes for the whalebones down the opened and pressed seams, at the darts, and under the arms (they should not reach the armhole by 2 1/2 in.). Leave the tops of the tapes open for the insertion of the bones after everything else has been done; it is easier to stitch the sleeves in if the bodice is limp.

The shoulder seams follow the underarm seams. They are not opened. The four layers are oversewn together and turned toward the back. (The ends are confined when the sleeves and neckband are added.) With a clear bodice, such as Swiss, book, or organdy muslin, join the shoulders by a mantua-maker's seam, if both fronts and back be plain. If the fronts be full and the back plain, tack a piping cord, laid in a bias casing, on the back and attach the fronts to it.

When a very thick cording is laid up all the bodice seams, to act as a trimming, cut away the end of the cord when it reaches the seam into which it will be stitched. Cut until only enough of its center remains to be held securely in the stitching. If thick cording is used for the backs of bodices in which there are side pieces that run into the shoulder seam, the shoulder seam is turned forward when the collar and sleeve are put in.

Adding Fasteners. When the seams of the dress are finished, the most important part is making the buttonholes and sewing on the buttons. This is sometimes done before the fronts and backs are joined, as the bodice can then be tried on to better advantage. The buttons and buttonholes fix the front hems, the turnings of which are not actually hemmed down.

Buttonholes with bar ends are the nicest for silk, washing, and thin soft dresses. Real cloth ought to have proper tailor's buttonholes. If the buttonholes are too small for the buttons, it will be very disagreeable work to fasten them. If too large, the effect is slovenly. The distance between them should be carefully measured. The buttons, being sewn on the left side, are placed at about the middle of the hem. The middle of the buttonhole is in the middle of the corresponding hem on the right. It is important that one buttonhole come exactly at the waistline.

A disposition to gap apart and show white underneath is easily remedied by sewing on the wrong side of the button front a piece of the outside material, or ribbon matching in color. It is not at all necessary that this should be new.

A bodice fastened at the back is made in the same manner. The only difference is that the fronts are sewn together, leaving an allowance at the back for hooks or eyelets, if the bodice is to be laced.

A bodice or low bodice without sleeves, or only having small shoulder straps, is fastened under the arms by buttons or laces. The front and back are made in two pieces, and the extra material allowed for fastening is left at the sides.

Polonaises, dressing gowns, mantles, and suchlike long garments are frequently made to meet, but not lap, at the front. Use hooks and eyes to connect them, placing a hook and an eye alternately on either side, to prevent their coming undone. Then lay a sarcenet ribbon over the shanks, leaving only the ends of the hooks and two-thirds of the eyes exposed.

Adding Trimmings. If there should be any trimming over the shoulders or down the fronts, ending at the basque edge, waistband, or throat, it must now be put on, so that the ends may be enclosed. When these parts are finished off, put on the bodice, button it up, and place a tacking thread where the trimming is to go. It is almost impossible to obtain a correct square, equidistant bretelles, etc. by sight alone, when the bodice is in the hand. It is quite easy to mark trimmings by standing before a mirror, placing pins where the trimming is

to be, and winding the cotton from one pin to another. The back, being a flat surface, can be marked for the trimming when the bodice is taken off.

Binding the Neck. While the bodice is on, see that the neck is the right height, particularly where the shoulder seams end, and quite at the back, for if at all too high there it will drag into creases. Put the neckband on next. If a straight one of even height, cut it from the straight of the material, about 1 1/2 in. wide, and use it double. Stitch one edge on at the right side. Cut the turning-in quite within 1/4 in. of the stitches. Turn the band over and hem down on the wrong side.

If the material is very stout or rough, it must be of one thickness for the outside. A strip of silk is run to the top edge and felled down on the inside, over the stitching made by the exterior of the band. Should the neckband be one of those that stand out from the throat, and are deeper in back than in front, cut it that shape in book muslin (used as a stiffener). Cut the muslin, the material, and its inner lining with the direct cross of the material in the center.

The band is generally finished with a collar of the material. Always have the collar lining on exactly the same grain of the material as the outside. Baste the collar on, commencing in the center of the back. Baste the right half on first, always leaving enough material projecting beyond the collar to provide for the lap.

Making the Sleeves. Baste the pieces together. It is well to fit the sleeve to the wearer's arm. Then stitch the sleeves up, and overcast the seams.

A neater way, in which the seams are hidden altogether, is this. Lay the right sides of the linings together. Place this on top of the exterior material, which is also put face to face. Stitch through all four together. Insert the hand between the two linings, so as to draw the sleeve through. Thus turn the top layer of lining over to the under side of the material. The sleeve, though inside out, will be completely lined, and the raw edges hidden under the lining. This method also works for transparent

materials, such as gauze and grenadine, when lined. This finish can sometimes be used to advantage on other parts of the garment.

If the coat sleeve is so tight as to require pleats at the elbow, the linings should be tacked to the material, and the halves stitched together and oversewn. The allowance beyond the joining should not be more than 1/3 in. Care must be taken not to leave the lining in the least degree loose, or the strain put on the outside material will make it ravel out at the seams.

When the sleeves are made from cloth or any heavy material, the seams should be pressed open with a hot iron. When made from silk, cashmere, or any thin material, the seams should not be pressed. The edge should be overcast, under and upper part together. The back arm seam should be turned toward the under part, and fastened to the lining. The seams may be pressed to one side provided it can be done without showing the marks of the seam on the outside. The seams in velvet sleeves should be pressed open, by rubbing the velvet on the iron, instead of the iron on the velvet.

While the sleeve is making, overcast the top, material and lining, together. This keeps the edge from raveling. When the sleeve is finished and before it is sewed in, gather the top or rounding part with short running stitches, eight to the inch. The top when gathered should be the exact size of the armhole; care must be taken to have the fullness in the right place. If the sleeve is tight fitting the top should be stretched a full 1/2 in., between the forearm seam, and 2 in. above. This will prevent wrinkles across the sleeve; these are usually seen at or near the forearm seam running toward the back.

The edge of the lower part of the sleeve is hemmed or has a facing of the material, or silk of the same color. The facing should always be of soft material. Turn down the outside of the facing a little way in, forming a fold, so the facing does not show. Facings for coat sleeves are from 3 to 4 in. deep, and should be cut from the wrist end of the sleeve pattern on the bias.

While the sleeve is inside out, run the facing on the edge of the sleeve, by putting the facing against its right side, and so farthest from you. Begin it at the inner seam of the arm. On reaching the outer one, ease in the facing a little. When again arrived at the inner seam, fasten off. Then turn the facing down on the sleeve lining. Fell it there, before closing the opening at the seam with blind or slip stitches.

When a sleeve is to be trimmed by straight rows of braid, leave the inner seam undone till the last, so as to lay the sleeve out flat for trimming. When the seam is closed, stitch in the ends of the braid.

The sleeve can have a piping similar to that round the armhole. The sleeve can be made large enough at the wrist to slip over the hand. Or it can be made with an opening at the inner seam, which can be fastened by buttons similar to those on the bodice front (though not so large).

The parement, or cuff, can be really added to the sleeve, or merely simulated by the trimming. A separate cuff should be finished and trimmed before it is sewed on the sleeve. All cuffs should be made on book muslin, whether deep and plain, ornamental, or only a band dividing two frills.

When a cuff is to be used, the facing should be laid on and felled to the lining side, leaving the bottom edge unfinished. Turn the cuff wrong side out and the sleeve right side. Join them at the bottom with the seam on the right side. When the cuff is turned back, the seam will be concealed. Fasten the cuff up on the sleeve by either sewing a button or bow through both, or slip stitch it a little below the top on the underside of the cuff.

Sleeves such as those in vogue for dinner dress, etc., are made after the above directions, but are cut at or a little below the elbow. These are generally trimmed with a pleating of silk the same as the dress, and a puffing of lace or tulle below it. A band, or fold of the dress material, which is usually cut on the cross, is generally placed at the top of the pleating. This, when fastened with a bow, gives a pretty and elegant appearance.

Trimming Fancy Sleeves. Sleeves that are in puffs downward take the same extra length as puffs that go round. That is, about half as much again for opaque materials. Net or tulle requires rather more, and these filmy tissues are made on a foundation of the same, to keep the puffs in place. Begin the runnings at the shoulder end, commencing at the middle (where the elbow seam is) and bring the rest nearer together toward the wrist, so the puffs will be smaller there than at the top. Secure all with pins to regulate the fullness, and run down with fine cotton. For puffs that go round the arm run a cord at the required distances, for a thread alone does not give sufficient support. The same rule applies to muslin, gauze, or grenadine, when puffed longitudinally without a foundation. To prevent their falling to the wrist when the sleeves are gathered across, and are unlined, sew a cord, the length of the arm, from running to running, at the seam. Put a second cord in more immediately under the arm. With net or tulle, whether the puffs go up or round makes no difference to the lay of the material; they must be laid in the direction of the selvage from shoulder to hand.

For long hanging sleeves cut the longest part on the straight way of the material. Transparent bodices with low linings have long transparent sleeves over short thick ones. The edge is piped, and short and long sleeves are tacked together and attached to the armhole by one stitching. The stitching must be done firmly with stout thread, and the raw edges should be sewn over.

Inserting the Sleeves. When the dress is in the process of making, overcast the armhole, outside and lining together, with four stitches to the inch. This keeps the material from raveling. When the dress is finished, and before the sleeves are sewed in, stretch the armhole in front about 2 in. below and 2 in. above the notch for the sleeve seam. This should be done with a hot iron. Stretch lining and material together until the edge turns completely over; this prevents wrinkles in front of the armhole.

When no cording is put round the armholes, they should be stayed with a thin narrow silk or cotton tape. The tape should be of the precise width to allow of hemming each edge on the line of stitches made by putting in the sleeve. Sew the tape, lining, and material together with a running stitch, four to the inch. Hold the tape loose in front, plain on the top where the sleeve is gathered, and tight on the back. The sleeve should be sewed through the tapes.

If you desire to cord the armholes, lay the cord in the center of a 3/4 in. bias casing and tack it there, so as to use the cording ready-made round the armhole, instead of embedding it while tacking it into the dress. Commence directly under the arm, not at the seam, and cross the beginning and ending of the cord.

Pin the sleeve into position, starting with the front and back arm seam, then have the wearer try on the bodice. Sleeves will scarcely vary from the rule of placing the top seam from 2 1/2 to 3 in. back of the shoulder seam, while the under seam is about 2 in. in front of the seam under the arm. The object is to have the longest part of the sleeve loose on the top of the shoulder, where length is most needed. Any disposition to fullness is to be brought under the arm, as the slightest visible gather spoils the look of the sleeve; but it is still worse for the armhole to gather.

In sewing, hold the sleeve toward you. The back seam should be sewed by hand, as the machine is liable to leave its mark where alterations are made. When the sleeve is sewed in, bind the seam with silk or narrow tape.

Finishing the Bodice. The bodice is finished by basques, if a jacket; by a cord if a round bodice; and by a band if a waistband or sash will be worn. In finishing the bottom of a basque or polonaise, be very particular that the two sides are exactly alike. Seam should be laid to seam, and the tape measure brought into requisition before the final trimming off is done.

A basque should be corded or faced on the inside, but must never be itself hemmed up. Cut the facing on the cross, 1 1/2 in. wide. Pull the

bottom edge to make it take a better curve when run on. In this way the top edge can be hemmed flat, without any pleats (unless the basque is pointed, deeper in the middle than the sides, or vice versa). Place the facing with its right side on that of the basque and run it about 1/3 in. from the edge. Turn it over to the inside and hem it up. If the bodice has long tabs and open seams, the entire tab should be faced.

A tape is run on the inside to tie round the waist, or a ribbon band with hooks and eyes, which is still neater.

A belt (that is, waistband) bodice should finish at the proper waistline, with the band set upon the waist. If the waist opens in back, the band will finish even with the backs of the waist. If the bodice opens in front, let the right side of the band project some inches beyond the bodice front, far enough to reach the opening in the side of the skirt. Cut the band 2 1/2 in. wide. Turn in 1/2 in. on each side and baste down with a short stitch. Cut a band lining for the inside.

Now baste the outer band upon the bodice. Leave the lower edge to come a trifle below the waist, so that when it is basted against the lining it will just cover the bottom of the bodice. This will make a neat edge for sewing on the skirt. Then lay the lining on the underside of the band. After stitching through, turn the free edge down. Turn the lining up on the lower edge against the outside band. Now baste them together with a fine cotton or silk that need not be removed after the skirt is sewed on. Always put the band on a little tight.

Making a Bodice with Concealed Seams. After the muslin is fitted, transfer the impression to a thin soft French cambric which should be used as an interlining. The interlining should be as thin as possible. From this interlining cut out the lining. The lining should be made from very thin material, such as muslin or light silk; it is merely a covering for the inside of the bodice.

Mark exactly where the seams are to be sewed, for the lining is to be sewed separately, not with the material. From the interlining cut the material.

Allow a good 1 in. for seams everywhere except round the armholes and neck, which should be cut as they are intended to fit.

Baste the interlining and material together. Then sew all seams in the bodice; the interlining should be sewed in with each seam. Press all the seams open with a moderately hot iron. For whalebone cases, cut a strip of muslin 1 in. wide. Baste it on each seam where whalebones are to be placed. The whalebone should fit tightly in the casing and directly over the seam, fastened at both ends. Sew on the collar, work the buttonholes, cord the edges, and finish the postilion before the lining is sewed in.

Then sew up all the seams of the lining except the shoulder seams. Baste the lining to the bodice with the seams facing each other, beginning at center back. The lining should be basted a little loose, especially at the waist. Fasten the lining to the back seam and underarm seam. Turn in the edges and sew neatly with a fell stitch. In this way the seams are covered, giving the bodice a more finished appearance.

All bodices may be treated in this way except velvet, cloth, and grenadine. In heavy materials the upper part of the interlining should be cut away.

Making Blouse and Yoke Bodices

The blouse, or French bodice, is liked both for thick and thin materials, the former with, and the latter without a lining. Plain materials and narrow stripes are very suitable.

Either large or small pleats are laid, both in the back and front of a blouse bodice. (See figure 82.) Three large pleats, or five smaller ones, are sufficient. The best way is to make them in the straight material before it is laid on the pattern, the length of the bodice having first been cut off. When the material is narrow, it can be joined under a pleat without showing. When cutting the blouse by a plain bodice pattern, it is only necessary, in place of darts, to narrow it suitably under the waist by slanting toward the seams under the arms.

Figure 82. Blouse bodice with small pleats

When a lining is used, it is cut after the pattern of the plain bodice. The pleats are taken only in the outside material.

Another style of bodice has a yoke. The yoke and its lining (if there is one) are put together. The lower part is gathered and sewn in between them. A narrow ruffle, or some other trimming, is frequently placed on the seam. Pleats are often substituted for gathers in flannel and other thick materials. These bodices, like the blouses, are finished with a band.

The appropriate sleeve for blouse and yoke bodices is a full sleeve, or the ordinary shirt sleeve; but a plain one is often used.

Making Low Bodices and Ball Dresses

The low bodice can be cut from a high bodice pattern. All the beauty of a ball dress depends on the cut of the neckline; therefore no pains should be spared to perfect it. The lowness of the neck depends entirely on the figure. As crepe lisse and lace tuckers are always added, if the line is too high it appears to cut the figure, while if too low it is as immodest as it is vulgar.

The neckline should be cut fully 1 1/2 in. higher than it is intended to be when completed. The pattern should be placed upon the lining, which for ball dresses is usually fine lawn, which is soft, yet strong enough to bear the strain of lacing. When the lining has been cut, basted, and accurately fitted to the figure, the upper part is turned down outside the dress, and creased at the line where it is to be corded.

A low bodice may be finished at the neck in two ways. Sometimes the edge is turned down, and a 1/2 in. wide sarcenet ribbon hemmed over it on the inside. The ribbon is used as a runner for a silk lace to draw the top to the figure. The other plan is to cord the edge with a fine piping cord, as the neck can be drawn in a little when this is being done. Square necks should be piped, and sharp turning at the corners is essential. The casing of the piping must be snipped in a precise line with the corner, quite up to the cord itself.

If a low bodice fastens behind and has a seam up the front, place a bone up the join, from its extreme end to within 2 in. of the top. Put a bone in every seam, but do not carry it high, for if so all the tops of the bones will press outward and push through. The seams of most low bodices are so shallow that they do not need opening, but will in themselves act as bone cases.

Ball dress bodices are made pointed back and front; with a round waist; with basques of various shapes, cut in one with the bodice; and with front basque and pointed back.

The pointed bodice is usually very becoming. The front points vary in length with the figure, and are kept stiff with whalebone in cases. The edges of the bodice are corded with single or double cording. The sleeves are also corded at the edges, and the top is corded to match. Eyelets are worked on the inside of the back whalebones. They are worked in white silk, in close overcast, not buttonhole, stitch. Dresses are laced from top to edge, therefore the silk lace is put in at the top left-hand eyelet.

Round-waisted bodices are cut off at the waistline and corded. The skirt is then firmly sewn under the cord. A sash is always worn with these simple but pretty bodices.

Ball dress bodices with basques are cut like high bodices as far as the lower part of the basque is concerned. The edges are hemmed or corded, according to the nature of the garniture. Colored

silk cordings are extremely fashionable at the edges of basques. The cording may be either single or double. Turn the peak point well. Take two or three secure stitches when the center is reached; that is, after going down one side, before turning the piping to go up the other. Do not allow any easiness in the piping at the bend, or it will not be a sharp turn. These bodices are laced up the back like the pointed bodice.

A low bodice with front basques and pointed back is extremely becoming. It is made by a union of the first and third styles described.

A low bodice is trimmed with folds of silk tulle or lace, arranged in various forms, and termed a "bertha." The bertha is made on a shape cut from not very stiff net or tulle, and on a tarlatan foundation taken double. The experienced dressmaker will fold the bertha on a paper pattern, running the folds in place and trimming with lace. This has a good and light effect. A bouillonné bertha demands a foundation of stiff net or tarlatan. The bouillonnés are usually finished by lace or a frilling of the material.

The sleeves of ball dresses are always trimmed to match the bertha. They often consist of puffs of tulle, a frill of crepe lisse, or froufrou with velvet run in, being tacked inside the corded edge. A crepe lisse or froufrou tucker is run inside the cording of the neck. Whatever is chosen as the neck tucker must be repeated on the sleeves.

For short sleeves for ball dresses, cut the deepest part directly on the cross of the lining. When covered by a little puff, make this by a bias strip, and pleat fully as long again as the lining. Single puff it rather than gather, doing the top edge first in small single pleats all turned one way. Then do the lower edge, but turn the pleats there in the opposite direction to those at the top. The mouth of the sleeve may be faced with a narrow ribbon, or corded.

Ball dresses are worn over "slips," or petticoats of silk. Or they consist of rich silk or faille trimmed with tulle, net, blonde, crepe de chine, and other diaphanous materials. Nearly all kinds of trimmings are employed for ball dresses. Ball dress skirts and slips are made with long trains. The prevailing characteristics of walking and visiting toilettes will be found repeated in gauzy materials for the ball dress.

Making Skirts

According to the width of the material a greater or less quantity is required in the skirt. A gored skirt is one in which the breadths are much narrower at the top than at the bottom; indeed, according to the present fashion nearly tight to the figure. A gored skirt can be made almost any width, and any length.

Cutting the Gores. The material must be divided into breadths, and then for the gores the breadths must be folded and cut more or less on the cross (see figure 83). The front breadth ought to remain whole, or it can be slightly sloped at the sides (see figure 84). A plan very generally in use is to have a plain breadth in back. Seams in the middle of either the front or back of a skirt should be avoided.

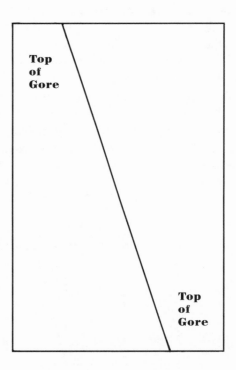

Figure 83. How to cut the gores

The back is first cut to the desired length, likely in these days of trains to be very long. If at all possible, avoid a seam down the middle, by placing the middle to a fold of the goods. Then three more breadths of the material must be cut off, all the same length as the back. These, folded and cut on the cross, will form six gores, three on either side of the skirt. (Four gores may instead be cut if the material is wide and the gores cut large.) It is a good plan, when the first gores are cut, to take one as a pattern and pin it carefully to the breadth that must be cut next, and so on. This ensures all the gores being of equal size.

When the material has a right and a wrong side, lay one pattern of each gore on it. Cut them out, and then fold the cut gores over onto the material, to cut the others. The gores must be either face to face or back to back. When they are taken apart it will be found that there is one of each for either side.

In cutting the gores where there is an up-and-down pattern, they must of course be cut one beyond the other. The parts left may be used for the back, side pieces, sleeves, cuffs, false hem for the skirt, etc. This rule applies to velvet, velveteen, and all fabrics that must be made with the pile brushed in one direction.

Care must be taken, in the case of Indian materials, grenadines, or muslin, that sufficient is allowed for a hem. In other materials, such as woolen materials, silk, velvet, etc., it is usual to make a false hem of lining or alpaca. In this case 1 in. at both top and bottom will suffice for turnings.

The strips of lining for a false hem are better cut in the length of the material than the width. The hem sets better, while numerous joins are avoided. It is well to tack the false hem on the inner side before sewing it, so as to arrange the pleats regularly. These pleats (which may be from 4 to 8 in. deep) arise from the bottom of the skirt being wider than the part higher up.

When the gores are cut very much on the cross, it is well to cut each band of the hem the same shape as the part of the gore it is intended to line. A facing 12 to 14 in. deep can be cut by each gore and basted on the bottom before the skirt is run up, leaving one edge of the facing free on each side to be hemmed down afterward, to cover the raw edges.

Joining the Breadths. All the gores and the two plain breadths must be joined together, beginning at the top and keeping the pieces quite level, so as to have the top of the skirt quite straight. (See figure 84.) It is necessary to tack the gores together before sewing them, taking care not to draw them too tightly. The straight side, *a,* of one gore is sewn to the slanted side, *b,* of the other. The slanted side should be turned to the back. All material when on the cross is apt to stretch when running the seam. It is best to have the gored side opposite to the worker.

Begin by uniting the gores on either side nearest the front breadth, then the next gores to those right and left, and so on to the back. Stitch the seams from the top to the bottom. Cut off any unevenness there.

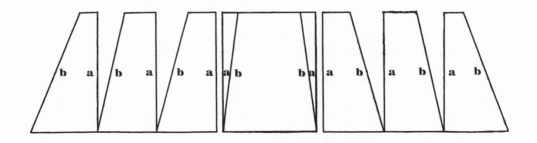

Figure 84. Joining the front and side gores

468

Leave a hole for the pocket between the first and second gores, about 2 or 3 in. below the waist. Make the pocket from the same material as the bodice lining, the sides sloped off to a point at the top. Face the opening for the hand with dress material. Put a strip of the same on the inside of the pocket opposite the opening, so as not to show the white lining when the pocket hole bulges. Dot the edge of the pocket with a mantua-maker's hem. Or stitch it on the inside close to the edges, turn it inside out, and stitch it round again, to enclose the raw turnings.

The opening, or placket hole, may be left at the top of the back or left side, as preferred. It should measure from 9 to 12 in. for a person of ordinary size. The placket hole needs a facing on the right-hand side, and a false hem on the left, when the placket fastens behind. Cut the facing and the false hem on the bias or the straight, according to the breadth to which they are attached. The false hem ought to be quite 1 1/2 in. wide.

The stitching of the gores should be 1/2 in. from the edges. If the dress be unlined, sew over each edge of the seams separately, using fine cotton. Do not work too closely, nor pull the thread tightly. Cotton and other washing skirts do not need the turnings quite so wide, and the two edges are sewn over together instead of being opened. Gauze, thin barege, or any yielding, flimsy material is usually joined by a mantua-maker's seam. Whenever possible, the selvage is used for the turning that is hemmed down, thus saving an extra fold of the material.

When all the seams are oversewn, press open the joins with an iron. Lay a wooden roller longwise underneath the joins, on the right side of the dress. A broom handle is the best roller, with two or three layers of ironing cloth sewn round it. Iron up the center of the separated edges on the wrong side. The heater will only press on the actual stitching, and not on the turnings, the marks of which would otherwise show through on the right side.

Very stout or springing materials need a damp cloth laid over the seam to be pressed. With silk it is better to lay a dry cloth over the seam, instead of rubbing the heater immediately upon the silk. Very delicately tinted silks, such as French gray, dove, and lavender, must not have a very hot iron applied. It is better not to rest the seam on a roller, but to get two persons to hold the seam at the top and bottom, pulling firmly, while a third passes the iron up and down the parted edges of the join.

Finishing the Hem. Supposing that the skirt is to be very long, the train effect is obtained by cutting away the lower part of the gores, from the front to the back. (See figure 85. The cut-off pieces can be used for trimmings.) The length of the front breadth must be taken from the waist of the wearer to the ground. It is very important to make the skirt quite even on both sides. It is therefore advisable, after cutting half the bottom (say from the center of the front breadth to the center of the back) to double the skirt, fit the side now sloped onto the other, and cut the latter by the former. It is well also to pin both sides of the top evenly and firmly together.

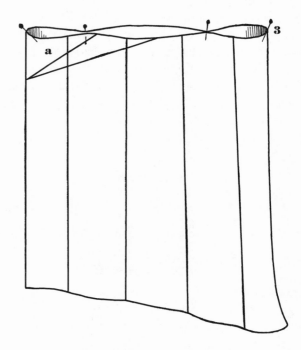

Figure 85. Sloping a trained skirt

Sometimes skirts must be sloped in front to fit comfortably. This is done by cutting to a greater or less depth in the center of the front breadth, turning it in until it suits the figure.

The edge of the skirt is faced with muslin. This is stitched 1 in. from the edge, which is then folded over 1 in. and tacked with very long stitches. The muslin is smoothly laid over the skirt. It is well to baste the edge before hemming it, as little pleats must be put in, and the basting shows exactly where the pleats will fall. The muslin is hemmed at a distance of from 3 to 4 in. This hemming is very slightly taken, in order not to be seen on the right side.

With petticoats or round skirts that are but little gored, it is quicker not to stitch up the hem after the facing is tacked in. Place the right side of the facing against the right side of the skirt, projecting beyond it as much as the hem of material which has been accounted for. Run the dress material against the facing, 1/4 in. within the edge. Then turn the facing over to the inside of the skirt, and hem down the upper edge. Pull the lining up a little higher than the actual depth of the hem, so as to make the extreme edge of the dress of double material.

Bind the skirt bottom with woolen or silk braid, which has been thoroughly immersed in hot water to shrink it. This must be stitched down along the right side (see figure 86) and then hemmed down on the wrong side (see figure 87). It may instead be faced, leaving, in the latter case, one edge in sight below the edge of the dress.

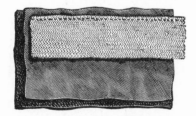

Figure 86. Sewing on braid–right side

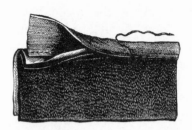

Figure 87. Sewing on braid–wrong side

Whatever trimming, in the way of flounces, etc., has been prepared is now put on the skirt, first being fixed with pins. With horizontal trimming begin with the bottom row. Have the hem, not the waist, of the skirt over the left arm while the running is executed. Work diagonal and longitudinal puffs, quillings, or ruches from the waist to the feet. Be careful that the fullness of puffs decreases toward the top.

These trimmings, however, mostly apply to ball dresses. In making transparent skirts, it is more convenient to leave one of the joins next the train open until after all the trimmings have been put on. If the trimmings be of net, tarlatan, grenadine, tulle, or gauze, flounces or puffs should be run on from the inside of the skirt. As the drawing threads and pins are plainly visible, and there is nothing in which the sewing cotton can be caught, the work becomes more rapid, and is less tumbled. Always use a long straw needle and avoid coarse cotton.

Banding the Skirt. Pins must be used to mark the center of the back and front breadths, and the two halves must be kept together. Thus prepared the skirt is folded into three parts. The first is for the front, the second for the sides, and the third for the back. Turn down the waist the 1/2 in. allowed in the cutting.

A band is now made of a strip of the material, and lined (see figure 88). Or the band may be made of strong ribbon. It should be as much longer than the waist, on the left side, as the placket hole's false hem is wide. The center is marked by a pin (not taking the overlap into account). The band has two strong eyes sewn to the exact edge, and one eye 1 1/2 in. distant from these. Two hooks are sewn on the under part of the right side of the

band, and one hook 1 1/2 in. distant from these. The band (excluding the overlap) is folded into three parts, corresponding to the three parts of the skirt.

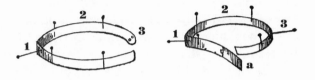

Figure 88. Waistband for back fastening and one for side fastening

For a gathered skirt, a running is made from the front to each side and from the back to each side, using two rows of thread. By drawing these threads the gathering is made to fit the waist (see figure 89). The size of the gathers depends on the quantity of the skirt to be gathered into a certain space. But the stitches are usually made 1 in. long on the wrong side, and very small on the right. When the gathering thread is drawn up, the 1 in. is folded in half, and makes gathers 1/2 in. deep. Sew these to the band at their threaded edge. Then sew them over at the opposite one, to keep all the corners regular, and make the gathers set in uniform folds.

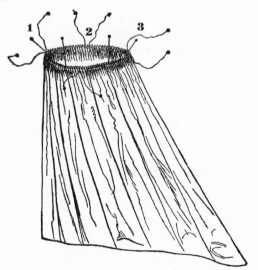

Figure 89. Gathered skirt drawn up

A pleated skirt, or each of its three divisions, can have as many pleats as desired. The waistband must be folded to correspond. Naturally each fold of the dress contains more material than a fold in the waistband. A fold, therefore, of the band is taken for the width of each pleat, and what remains is folded behind the pleat. The pleats are fixed one after another, first by pins and then by tacking. The skirt size must be verified by the waistband size. Then the skirt is sewn onto the band, with the three parts of the band corresponding to the three parts of the skirt. If the skirt has a back seam, this must carefully be hidden underneath a pleat.

A plain skirt is placed in the waistband without either gathers or pleats, and for this reason is gored to the figure. For this style the waistband is folded into as many parts as there are skirt gores. The straight end of each gore ought to be the same width as a fold in the waistband. The two side gores falling over the hips should be rather wider at the top than the back breadths. Without this precaution a plain dress is liable to ruck at the sides of the waist. The folds of the waistband on the hips will of course correspond to the width of the side gores.

Often dresses are plain in front and at the sides. In this case only the plain breadths are measured on the waistband. Small pleats may be put between the front and first gore, and again between the first and second gores, to hide the seams. The remaining fullness is gathered or pleated into the waist at the back of the skirt.

The present mode demands that the front and side breadths be put in the band as plainly over the figure as the contour will permit, only one or two slight pleats being allowable to make the skirt set easily at the waist. The whole fullness is at the back, where a double box pleat from 3 to 4 in. wide, called the bulgare pleat, is placed.

To keep all fullness quite at the back, pieces of wide elastic are sometimes sewed at intervals down each side breadth on the wrong side. On this elastic are placed buttons and strong loops or buttonholes, which, when fastened, keep the dress quite tight to the figure. Strings may be substituted for elastic, but the latter is the more secure

arrangement for holding the long folds in position. A piece of lining should always be sewed on where the elastic is fastened, as the strain upon the single material would soon tear it out.

Making Different Skirts and Overskirts. By referring to the current fashions the different lengths in vogue can be seen. It must be remembered that, however trimmed (and therefore apparently greatly differing from each other) all skirts are cut as explained above. By following these directions it will be easy to make every variety of dress, whether as short as a walking costume or as long as a riding habit. Fashion exacts various alterations such as puffs and fullness in different parts of the skirt. But these are always made separately as in the case of tabliers, and drawn up at the side or back. The breadths by being separated from the top to the bottom can be draped by being gathered or raised after any style. They can be fastened back on the outside by any trimming suitable to the dress, or on the inside by strings underneath. They can also be cut away or scalloped in any manner—in fact, trimmed according to any particular taste or fashion.

Tunics, tabliers, peplums, double skirts, polonaises, or whatever the top or overgarment is called, are all cut in a similar way to skirts. Double-width materials are folded at the center, and the fronts of tabliers and overskirts are placed along the fold.

Lining a Skirt. Skirt linings are of various materials, selected to suit the dress for which they are designed. As a rule, alpaca and silesia are the principal materials in use. For black velveteen silesia, striped or checked, is the best suited. For a pale-colored silk, the silesia should be plain white. For dark materials and quilted petticoats figured silesias are preferable. In this case make a facing of alpaca to cover the lining at the lower part of the skirt, about 6 in. or rather more deep. Owing to the spring, as well as the stiffness in alpaca, it is recommended for use in the same way round the extreme edge of dresses and trains, 10 in. deep. The dress is less likely to roll the wrong side up-

ward when the wearer turns round. Besides, a light-colored lining becomes so quickly soiled when sweeping the ground.

The lining of a heavy poplin or woolen dress should be restricted to a mere facing about 10 or 12 in. deep. When there are trimmings or flounces, extend the lining upward as high as the top of the trimmings, but so that all stitches will be concealed underneath them. The material employed for mourning called paramatta should have a lining of black mull muslin.

Instead of adopting the usual plan for lining a bodice, cut out the skirt first and tack it on the lining. If the skirt be gored, cut the lining to fit the gores exactly, as otherwise the skirt will set stiffly over the triangular pleats that will have to be made.

When the skirt breadths have been cut out, pin the raw sides of each flatly together at the bottom. Fold the skirt in half on a table, to expose half the front, and half the back breadth, the hem being toward you. Then lay the lining muslin with one selvage up the folded edge of the skirt front, the torn part of the muslin being at the hem. Slope off the right-hand corner of the muslin even with the dress. Measure the depth of the facing, placing pins at the upper part to mark it; and cut off by them. Next lay the piece so cut on the top of the remainder of the muslin, in exactly the same position. The hollowed-out upper part of the first will give very nearly the proper curve for the lower part of the second. The two pieces, when joined by the selvages in front, will extend nearly half round the skirt. The rest is taken piece by piece in the same way. The selvages are always joined together, although they lie very slantingly after the first, where the skirt front was straight.

When the middle of the back breadth is reached, allow about 1 in. for joinings. Cut off what is not wanted in a line with the folded skirt, so that the center join there will set upright, like the front. But owing to the increase of slope as the muslin nears the back, the join will neither lie exactly on the straight, nor on the cross of the muslin.

If alpaca be used, the joins must be opened and pressed flat before the lining is sewn into the skirt.

Mounting the Skirt on a Lining. An excellent plan is to cut a plain, close form out in lining, and mount the dress material upon it. This method is especially suitable for dresses consisting of trimmed skirts and basques. Cut your skirt lining after the pattern of the walking skirt or demitrain. Then add flounces of the dress material, a draped tablier, or folds across the front, as preferred. The back may be draped or kilt pleated, and either made in two parts, or divided by a strap, to form a slight pannier at the top, which falls over the smallest possible tournure.

Making Separate Pockets. Many ladies prefer the flat pocket that is separate, and can be worn under any dress, instead of one that is sewn into the skirt. Some ladies appreciate it because they can easily turn it to bring it just in the lap, and thus make it safer when traveling and shopping in cities. Strings are always sewn at each end. It is tied around the waist before putting on the skirt. Figure 90 shows a pocket before the strings are sewn on.

Adding a Balayeuse. The balayeuse flounce, coming below the edge of the dress, is set on all dresses for day as well as evening. It is designed to protect somewhat the bottom of the dress. Figure 91 shows a balayeuse that can be buttoned on a short walking skirt. The size of the band, and the fullness and length of the flounce, depend on the dress with which it is to be worn. The upper part of this balayeuse is made of muslin, and the frill of nainsook, with lace insertion and edging. Either Valenciennes or torchon is best, as they bear the washing.

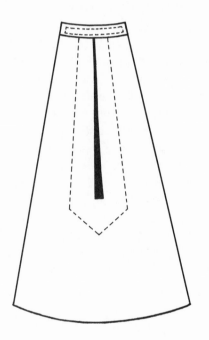

Figure 90. Separate pocket

Figure 91. Removable balayeuse

473

Making Overskirts and Polonaises

In most imported suits the overskirt is sewed in the same waistband with the lower skirt, and draped directly upon it. That plan is not popular here. It is preferred to leave the lower skirt separate so that it may be used with various overdresses. Figure 92 shows a tunic and panniers arranged on a band (the looping is accomplished by strings underneath).

Making a Tablier. Much of the style of the costume depends on the way the tablier sets at the waist. A good slope must be taken in front, and in sewing it on the band, care must be taken to follow the slope equally on both sides. Otherwise the tablier drags and looks crooked.

The tablier should be lined 2 in. deep all round with bias silk. The cashmere tablier must be trimmed with a narrow close silk pleating, unless fur, tape, fringe, or other trimming is preferred. The trimming is sewn on over the lining.

Draping an Overskirt or Polonaise on a Lay Figure. In the proper looping of the surplus length and fullness in overskirts, polonaises, and drapery of trained skirts, consists the grace and beauty of dresses. Yet it is not possible to give more than a few general directions on this subject, for it all depends on the artistic perception of the dressmaker.

Before cutting the garment, ascertain the style of looping desired. If you wish to copy the looping from a pattern, place the pattern on the lower part of the skirt, and cut by the pattern.

If you wish to copy a style of looping from a picture or fashion plate, practice with material or paper until you get the desired effect. Get a lay figure (see figures 93 and 94) and about 2 yd. in length and 1 1/2 in width of some soft and pliable material. Merino, for instance, or even common cheese-cloth, which, however, must be washed to render it soft, that it may fall into perfectly graceful folds. A large sheet of tissue paper may instead be used. Adjust the upper part of this to the waist of the figure in so many pleats as would be necessary for the back part of an overskirt. Then take a reliable fashion book, and a paper of pins, and choosing a simply draped skirt as a model, proceed to loop the skirt into the same folds. You will not be apt to succeed at the first trial, but at last you will have looped your drapery like the model.

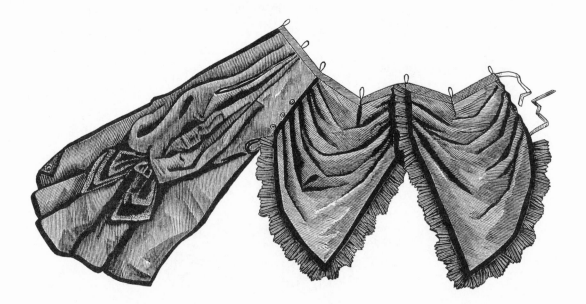

Figure 92. Overskirt mounted on separate band

Figure 93. Adjustable lay figure without padding

Figure 94. Lay figure with padding

The skirt or part to be draped should not be cut, but left the full width of the paper. When the draping is completed, cut the material or paper

when thus pleated, and folded and looped. Mark with pins where the loop or draping is formed; otherwise you may have difficulty in relooping. Remove the pattern from the figure. Open it and give the sharp points a rounded finish. Cut the material below the lining by this pattern, joining the lines at the top neatly and accurately.

All kinds and styles of drapery can be arranged by simply leaving the entire outlines of the material below the lining in the form of plain parallelograms, and folding it underneath, where not needed. This often enhances the appearance of the outside drapery, aside from leaving the silk or velvet whole for remaking or remodeling the dress at some future time.

Draping a Polonaise on the Cutting Table. Although the process of draping a polonaise, as described, at first may seem intricate and somewhat difficult, the very opposite is true.

In deciding on the style of drapery, much depends on arranging it so that it will enhance the given form. The styles of drapery may be classified as to position, as high drapery, low drapery, medium-high drapery, front drapery, back drapery, and side drapery. As to the kinds of drapery, they come *a la Française. Bonfante* drapery is known to all. *En biais* drapery is on the cross, or diagonal folds. *En châle* drapery has shawl-like folds. *En coquille* drapery is folded backward and forward, in zigzag shape, forming shell points. *En echelle* drapery has a ladderlike appearance, in uniform interval folds. *Pannier* drapery represents panniers at the sides. *Flots coques* drapery has quantities of lace or ribbon looped, and arranged to fall over each other. *En eventail* drapery has folds that show an apparent center, giving a fanlike appearance. *Cascade* drapery has an arrangement of lace or in the material representing a cascade. This catalog is by no means exhaustive, but represents the principal standards.

Suppose the polonaise has been basted and partially stitched, and is now ready for draping. Place it lengthwise on the cutting table, drawing it down neatly and smoothly, in a lengthwise manner.

475

The example design calls for medium-high drapery at the back and a series of shell puffs at each side, with the points two-third ways from the waist, each side. The shell puffs are to be in alternate positions, as to their height and depth; instead of each row or series being on the same horizontal line.

Notice how far down below the waist the polonaise is drawn to its closest degree, toward the back of the form, on the given design. This is usually on the hipline. Mark these points, equidistant from the waistline at each side of the polonaise, with chalk or pins. This should be done very accurately, and only by actual measurement. Sew on the elastic at each respective side. This is afterwards to be drawn to the desired degree of closeness when upon the lay figure.

Now locate the required points on the exact center fold of the back, either only below, or above and below said line, upon which the first points were located, and where the intervals occur, that secure and form the shell puffs. This distances are usually from 10 to 14 in.; but often only from 4 to 6 in.

On a direct perpendicular line, halfway between or equidistant from the center fold at the back and the lines on each side, and upon which the elastic is adjusted, locate points as above; also, of equal and uniform distances apart. This is done either on the same horizontal line, with the former locations, or on alternate heights, and on different and alternate horizontal lines, as the design may call for. Locate these points and those on the center fold, at the desired depth.

If it is desired to continue the shell puffs, locate the points on a slightly curving line. If the opposite, locate the points between the former.

Fasten loopings, by means of tape, at each respective point. Run through these loopings a runner, by means of another tape. This can be drawn to any degree of closeness desired for the shell puffs. If a double series of shell puffs is wanted, use a second runner of tape. Then cut the tape the required lengths. Secure each to its respective point, on the center line of the back.

Tapes should be adjusted at the side seams of the skirt part to hold it back firmly, and should be neatly and firmly joined together. These should be concealed under the draperies at the back when the work is completed.

Now place the polonaise on the lay figure. It should be arranged to the proper sizes at the bust, waist, and hips, and the length of the skirt. Draw the elastics to the proper degree of closeness. Study to bring everything into the position called for in the design. Secure everything as arranged for on the cutting table.

Making Outdoor Garments

Tailoring is marked by its perfect accuracy, its firmness, strength, and durability of workmanship. It is a style of work adapted, indeed requisite, for heavy materials. The home tailoress will find an incessant need of hot, heavy irons. But there is something satisfactory about the work, for it looks so beautifully neat when finished.

Making Outdoor Jackets and Mantles. The modern styles are almost invariably short in back and long in front. Some have sleeves. In others, the sleeve is simulated by a deep fold of the material, as in the dolman form.

The general principles for cutting out are the same as for a jacket bodice. However, a great deal must be allowed for turnings. One great error in cutting out fitting jackets for street wear is that of making them too tight at the waist. If this is done, the jacket never wears so well. It is, besides, almost impossible to make the basques set properly. With loose jackets, there is, of course, no temptation to commit this blunder. Here the principal difficulty is making the sleeves set well, particularly if the material is thick, as cloth, sealskin, Astrakhan, etc. A tailor always gives abundance of width on the chest and across the back, and we must imitate the fraternity. Much of the style depends on the set of the collar. On no account should the neck be cut away until the collar has been cut out, made, and tried on.

There are some differences in the mode of finishing off compared to a dress bodice. The fronts must be lined for a breadth of about 2 in. with silk,

476

before the buttonholes are worked. This lining not only gives strength to the buttonholes, but also affords a neat finish. The basque must be finished in the same manner. With cloth and other thick materials, braid is substituted for silk, as it is stronger and wears better.

The inside of the sleeves at the cuff is finished to correspond. The sleeves are not piped into the jacket as in a dress bodice. They are very firmly stitched in. If the material is cloth, the raw edges are afterwards parted and lightly tacked down on either side. The stitches are not taken through to the right side.

The collar is lined with silk, the lining being hemmed down on the inside after the collar has been stitched on.

The foregoing remarks have applied more particularly to the jacket form of mantle, but there is very little difference in making a dolman. The lining must be of silk, but no buttonholes are necessary. The trimming round the edges may consist of fringe, lace, or silk plissés. But it is not indispensable to have any of these, especially if the dolman be braided or embroidered.

In cutting out a fichu, the width of the material seldom admits of the whole being cut without a join. These joins should be managed so that they will come at that portion of the fichu that crosses over under a bow. Fichus are finished off similarly to dolmans, but it is quite necessary that they should have a fringe, or plissés of silk or cashmere. Otherwise they look not only unfinished, but ungraceful. These plissés need not be made of very good silk. It is difficult to make them at home, and is a tedious business even with a sewing machine. I should advise those who think to this trimming to put it out to be done.

Fitting a Dolman. To fit perfectly a dolman should hang lightly from the shoulders, delicately defining the outline of the figure. The most difficult part of fitting a dolman is the sleeve. A slight variation in putting it in will make a material change in the appearance of the garment.

Procure a reliable pattern. Then cut a muslin by this, baste it together, and fit it on. The sleeves should fall gracefully without a wrinkle. The hand should then be raised upward even with the waist. If the sleeve draws upon the forearm or forms a wrinkle, it is too long between the forearm and the shoulder. To remedy this, a pleat should be taken up in the sleeve from front to back, halfway between elbow and shoulder, and deep enough to allow the sleeve to hang perfectly easy on the arm. The pleat should be fastened with pins. The sleeve should then be ripped out, leaving the pins still in the pleat. A new sleeve pattern should be cut from the muslin sleeve. On no account must the top of the sleeve be changed.

The sleeves to dolmans in the mantle style should be cut bias down the middle.

When the dolman is made and before the sleeves are sewn in, the garment should be fitted on and the sleeves pinned to the armhole to get the fullness in its proper place.

Making a Pocket. To bind a pocket slit in all heavy materials, for a vest, jacket, Newmarket, Ulster, or coat: Cut the slit the desired length. Then make small slits, the width of a narrow seam, in each end, the opposite way (see figure 95). Bind the edges. Sew to the upper edge a piece of the material, 3 in. deep. Bringing the pieces through, to the wrong side, stitch it the width of a cord above the edge (see figure 96). On the right side of the lower edge, run a bias strip. Lay it over on the wrong side, and neatly stitch it down 3/16 in. from the edge. Stitch a pocket to said pieces. Then fasten down the end of the cut, over the top piece. This is most neatly performed with the buttonhole stitch.

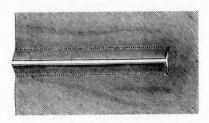

Figure 95. Pocket slit

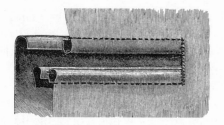

Figure 96. Binding pocket slit

If a corded finish is desired, first sew in a cord, adding the small strips as already described. In this case the stitches should not pass through on the outside. Sew the pocket piece on from the under side (see figure 97). The ends are finished with the buttonhole stitch.

Figure 97. Cording pocket slit

Adding a Quilted Lining. For a garment to be worn in cold weather, such as a mantle, dressing gown, or underpetticoat, it is usual to trim with quilting. This is of cotton or carded wool, which is sold in sheets of different sizes and two colors, white and violet.

When drawing the outline of the pattern on the material or lining, an allowance of 1 to 2 in. must be made all round for the wadding. This is in addition to the seam allowances.

Cut out the lining and outer material. Baste up the lining and outside separately. Try the lining on the wearer. If it is all right, stitch the outside up. Press or baste open every seam. Clip every seam at each point where it either springs out or rounds. Lay the lining on a table. The wadding must be placed on the wrong side of it. Tack the wadding to the lining in rows spaced according to the garment

shape; for example, closer together for a bodice than a petticoat. The stitches will be very small, almost invisible, on the right side of the lining, while they are very long on the wadding. It is well to take the stitches from left to right, so that the stitch being crossed is thus rendered stronger.

With a little more trouble the lining can be quilted on the wadding. This is done by first evenly tacking down where the lines of stitches are to be. They should be about 1 in. or more apart. Then the stitching is done by hand or machine. The first lines can have others made transversely across, and this makes the quilting somewhat in a lozenge shape.

The lining for an opera cloak is always stitched in lines or to any pattern, such as lozenges, squares, zigzags, etc. It is necessary to be very careful to draw the design to be stitched with a thread or better still, chalk. Running the lines using very small stitches answers as well as the backstitch for the lining of an opera cloak, or any other article in which wadding must be quilted into the lining.

When the lining is wadded (whether quilted or not), baste it to the outer material. Do so piece by piece, until the entire lining is basted smoothly on the outside. Be sure to first make the lining edges and the seam edges come even. Baste the lining with a short stitch, only a few inches from the seams. When it is all firmly fixed the wadding is slightly torn away at the edges to thin it at the seams. Then turn the garment right side up and baste through each seam into one side of the lining. Always leave one edge of the lining loose so that it may be turned in and felled over the other.

Leave the shoulder seams open until all the others are completed. Then stitch them and open them the same as the other seams. The sleeve must be entirely finished before it is put in. Do not sew the lining in with the sleeve. Baste or press open the armhole seam before sewing the lining.

If a cloak is silk, velvet, or any soft material that will flatten down or crease at the bottom and front edges, baste in a piece of wadding before the edge is turned up and the lining is felled to the outer material. This will cause a round, plump edge.

Making Undergarments

Making Undergarments

All linens and calicoes should be washed prior to cutting out. All linens, including lawn, cambric, and Holland, should be cut by the thread, one or two strands being drawn to guide the scissors. All calicoes, muslins, and flannels may be torn, but the material should be rolled over on each side at each tear that is given. All portions of underclothing liable to be stretched in wearing, such as skirts, sleeves, wristbands, shoulder straps, collars, and waistbands, should be cut with the selvage or straight way of the material. Frills and pieces gathered or fulled between bands and flounces should be cut across the material, from selvage to selvage.

For ordinary underlinen for adults, the average quantities required follow. For a chemise, from 2 1/2 to 3 1/4 yd. longcloth, and from 2 1/2 to 3 1/2 yd. embroidery edging. For a combination garment, about 3 yd. longcloth, 2 3/4 yd. embroidery for the neck and arms, and 1 yd. 4 or 6 in. ditto for the legs. For drawers, 2 1/2 yd. longcloth and 2 1/2 yd. frillings. For flannel knickerbockers, 2 3/4 yd. For a square-cut petticoat bodice, cut the same behind as in front, 1 1/4 yd. longcloth and 2 1/4 yd. trimming for the neck and armholes. For a high petticoat bodice cut down V shape in front, 1 1/4 yd. longcloth, and 1 3/4 yd. trimming. For a white petticoat of longcloth, of walking length with four gores, about 4 1/2 yd. For a nightdress, 4 yd. longcloth, the trimming depending on the pattern and the fancy of the wearer.

Cutting Out and Making a Chemise. Place the roll of material from which you intend to cut out on a chair at the end of a long dining-room table. Pull out as much material as will lie all along the length of the table. Stand at the side of the table, so that the piece of material lies selvage-ways across you.

In cutting out all underlinen, great care must be taken to note beforehand any alterations that may be required to the length or width of the garment. The pattern must be laid perfectly straight on the material, and all folds and creases smoothed out. Turnings must be allowed for everywhere,

except where the selvages are seamed together, as in joining on gores, etc. Tucks in drawers must be allowed for.

Before cutting out a chemise, it must be ascertained what width it is to be at the hem, as the size of the gores and the method of cutting depend

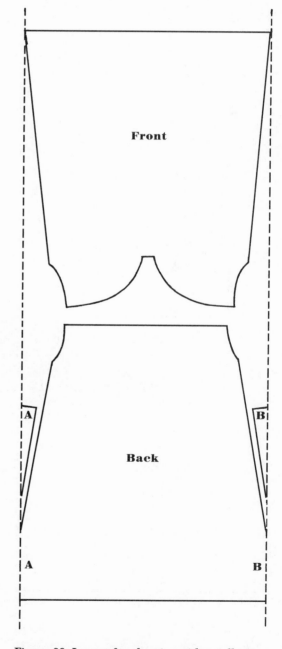

Figure 98. Layout for chemise with small gores

479

entirely on this. Figure 98 shows the way to cut a chemise with small gores only from an ordinary 36 in. material. This gives a width of 2 yd., which is generally considered sufficient.

Supposing, however, that the material is narrow, or a greater width is required, the chemise and gores must be cut as in figure 99.

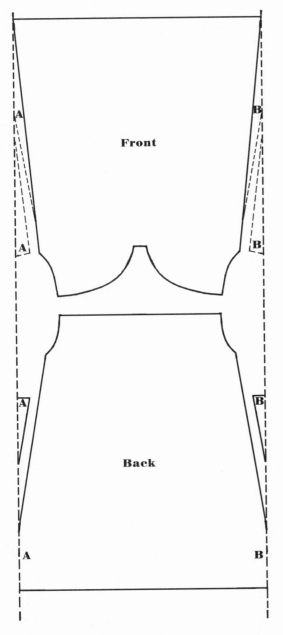

Figure 99. Layout for chemise with large gores

The gores can always be cut from the pieces of material at the top of the chemise. They must be neatly seamed on, leaving of course the wider part at the hem. When the gores are joined at the sides, the seams should be run and felled. A hem from 1/2 to 1 in. wide is made at the bottom.

The yokes and sleeves are placed on the material as shown in figure 100. The sleeves must never be cut across the material—that is from selvage to selvage—but always lengthways, as they wear much better. They are joined and put into the armholes of the chemise, with the pointed part toward the lowest part of the armhole.

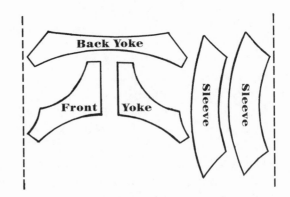

Figure 100. Layout for smaller pieces

The right side of the front should button over the left. The back and front of the chemise must be gathered. The back and front yokes are joined at the shoulders. They are then fitted onto, and stitched to, the chemise top and sleeves.

Some chemises and combination garments have no yoke or sleeves. Narrow bias facings for shaped edges are found to sit more neatly than those not cut bias but shaped precisely like the seam. Though nearly tight fitting, princess chemises have a tape run in a casing to draw them closely around the neck.

Chemise sleeves may be trimmed with lace or embroidery. The yokes may be plain, tucked all over, or made of alternate strips of tucks and embroidered insertions. The top edge of the yokes may be trimmed with lace or embroidery. The most

durable trimming for underclothing is Madeira work. But this is costly, and not within the reach of all. The Excelsior and the Beau-Ideal embroideries are a most excellent and durable substitute. Real Valenciennes lace is sold by some houses at little more than cost price. The make is strong, and very suitable for trimmings.

Cutting Out and Making a Nightdress. The mode of cutting out a nightdress is similar to that for cutting out a chemise. The required length must be calculated, and the pattern pinned onto the material. The simpler pattern shown in figures 101 and 102 will be described first. The front piece for a person of medium height should be 1 1/2 yd. long from the shoulder to the hem, and the back piece 6 in. less. (Figure 101 shows only part of the length.)

Before beginning to make up the nightdress, the gores must be cut out, and with them the sleeves and yoke pieces (see figure 102). The gores are joined to the lower part of the nightdress on either

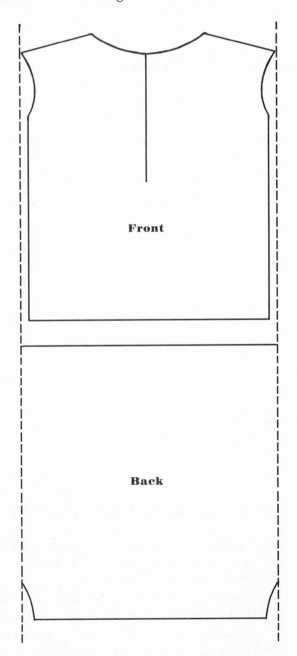

Figure 101. Layout for simple nightdress

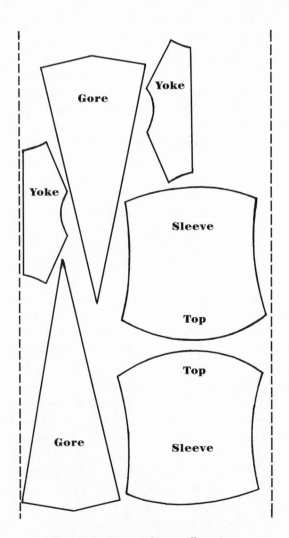

Figure 102. Layout for smaller pieces

481

side to give it additional fullness round the skirt. The side seams should then be run and felled up to the armholes. A tolerably wide hem, usually about 1 1/2 in., completes the lower edge of the night-dress.

At the top the back is gathered between the two small marks on the illustration. In the front the line down the center from the neck represents the opening, and is from 16 to 18 in. long. The front on either side of this opening is tucked to within 4 in. of the armhole, the tucks being continued a little lower than the opening, until the width is sufficiently reduced to make the shoulder fit exactly to the yoke. The right side of the opening should fold over the left. It will require an extra piece put on, and the hem on the left must be lined. This hem, and the piece folding over it, which is double, are usually about 1 in. wide.

The sleeves should next be joined, and the narrower and straighter end gathered into a wristband. The upper part is put plain into the armholes, any extra fullness being gathered at the shoulder. The yokes must be tacked together a little way from the edge. They are first hemmed on the wrong side to the back, sleeves, and front shoulders, then stitched to the right side. A straight band round the neck, and buttons and buttonholes down the front, complete the nightdress.

The nightdress shown in figures 103 and 104 differs little from the previous one. The back breadth is precisely the same. The front breadth is cut to fit into a pointed yoke, and is only 3 in. longer than the back.

In figure 104, the piece of longcloth left between the second yoke and the selvage will come in for cutting out bands, linings to hems, etc., all of which must be cut lengthways.

The mode of putting in the gores and sleeves is exactly similar to that already described. The back and front are gathered at the top. The two yoke pieces are tacked together; hemmed to the back, front, and sleeves on the wrong side; and stitched on the right side. The gatherings in front should not be continued beyond the marks on the illustration, but between them on both sides, leaving plain

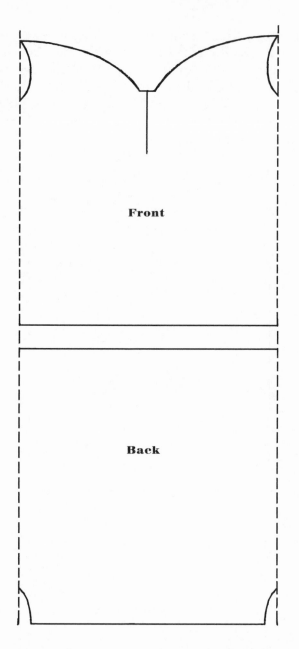

Figure 103. Layout for nightdress with pointed yoke

spaces near the front and armholes. A narrow band is put round the neck, and the collar joined to it.

Sleeves wear better if the armholes are lined. This is done by cutting pieces of material about 2 in. wide, but the exact shape and size of the armholes, and hemming them on the wrong side. The sleeve is then slipped between the nightdress and lining, and joined to both by fine hemming.

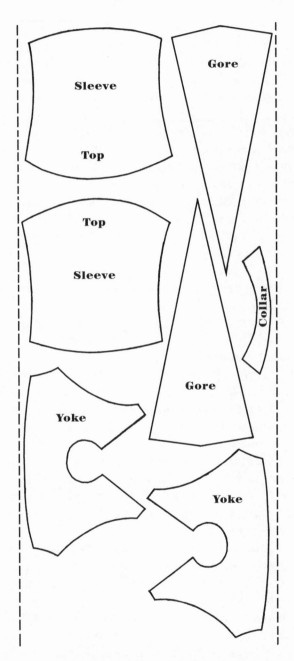

Figure 104. Layout for smaller pieces

Featherstitching is a very pretty way to finish off bands and yokes. Nightdresses are frequently trimmed with embroidery, which is put on with a cording by most makers. This plan, although beautifully neat, is not altogether to be adopted. When the embroidery is torn or worn, the cording must be removed to replace it. A better plan is to cord

the nightdress at the collar, front, and cuffs; whip the edge of the embroidery; and draw it up to the fullness required to tuck in place. Hem down the whipped edge just below the cord. By this means the work can be removed and replaced with little trouble. The same remarks apply to putting on lace, which should be sewn on the edge of the nightdress, and not put on with the cording. Before using any cord, it should be scalded in boiling water to prevent shrinking when washed.

Making a Chemisette or Habit Shirt. If the front is to be ornamented with pleats, allowance must be made on either side of the chemisette for them. To join the fronts to the back it is requisite to make a run and felled seam, or a tiny rolled hem, according to the texture of the material. Any sort of collar can be fastened by a seam (for a sloped collar) or a band (for a high, turned-down collar). The edge of the chemisette is hemmed all round. Generally narrow strings are fastened to the back to tie it firmly round the waist.

A bib is simply the body of a habit shirt, of which the front is cut in one piece and the back in two to fasten down the center. Sometimes the bib fastens on one shoulder, the back being cut in one piece like the front. The bib is shorter than the habit shirt, as it is seldom intended to reach the waist.

Making Drawers. Drawers are made of linen, muslin, and Canton flannel. The latter is indispensable for cold weather, unless knitted or flannel drawers are worn under the muslin ones. These garments vary in style. Closed drawers opening on the side are preferred by some. Others join the two fronts, and leave them open in back. The French pattern, which is entirely open—each leg being made separately and faced all around—is particularly comfortable. But even this has its back and front. Drawers should reach a little below the knee. When they are too long, the effect is very slovenly.

Each half of the drawers is joined by a run and felled seam. The bottoms are finished according to individual taste. If tucks are wanted (and narrow tucks above a hem and ruffle are exceedingly neat), room must be allowed for them in cutting out. Puffings and Hamburg edgings are also

483

used, while some prefer a simple hem with button-hole scallops.

The two halves are joined in the front by a strong seam from the waist, *e* to *h,* where the slope begins (see figure 105). The two back halves re-main separate from *e* to *f.* These, with the remaining open portion, have a strong facing of the material, 2 in. wide at the widest part, which is about the middle of the whole, and tapering off to half that width at the top of the back. Some persons use nothing stronger for facing than a moderately wide tape. Others, again, only use this for the middle, merely hemming the backs, the strong facing being "too much trouble." But it is a trouble that pays, as this portion of the garment is sure to wear out first.

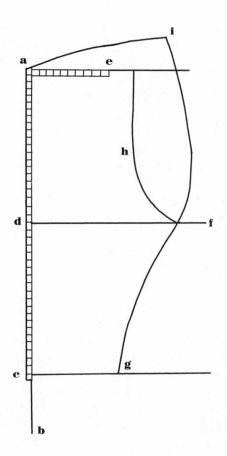

Figure 105. Diagram of drawers

In preparing the band for the waist, it is quite customary to tear off a straight piece of muslin, about 1 in. wide when doubled, and to fasten this with one large button and buttonhole. A better way is to slope up the band to 2 in. at the middle of the back, this wider portion being about one-third of the band. The other two-thirds of the band are 1 in. wide. The slope is made at the bottom, where the band is joined to the garment; the upper, or folded, edge is of course straight. In putting on the band, there are scarcely any gathers until the slope be-gins, and most of the fullness is put in the back. Two medium-sized (not small) buttons and button-holes bear the strain better than one large one on a narrow band. They should be sewed on three thick-nesses of material, one being placed on the double binding.

If a drawstring is preferred to buttons, the band is made with a running from *a,* where the string is placed on the inside.

Drawers can be fastened into a band below the knee, knickerbocker style. The band is made to fit the leg comfortably. It has a button and but-tonhole on the inner side of the leg, a small slit being made in the seam to enable this to fit properly.

Making Petticoats. White skirts are made very much like the underskirt of a dress. They are about as wide, but somewhat shorter. The breadths are very much gored, and run up like the breadths of a dress.

Sometimes the back breadth only reaches halfway from the binding, and is finished with a deep ruffle, making it the full length. The ruffle is finished where it is joined by a narrow bias band stitched on either side. The bottom of the skirt has a deep hem, over which there is often a scant ruffle of the same depth, headed by some narrow tucks in the skirt—sometimes a second ruffle and a sec-ond heading of tucks.

The opening is invariably in the back. It is finished by a broad hem on the upper side and a narrow one underneath. A straight binding fastened by strings is in most common use. But this implies tying the skirt around the waist—whereas it is desirable to have as few layers there as possible.

The yoke, which rests on the hips, is a far better invention. With the aid of a princess dress pattern, it is very easy to cut. The yoke is joined in front at the straight ends, and the back should be bias. It should be stitched all around, and finished with two buttons and buttonholes of about the same size as those used for drawers. The breadths of the skirt are cut shorter than when a binding is used.

The amount of material required varies with the style of the skirt and the height of the wearer. For the kind of skirt described, with cut breadth at the back, yoke, and one ruffle at the bottom, with deep hem and small tucks above, from 4 1/4 to 4 1/2 yd. of cambric muslin would be the medium limit.

A flannel skirt is made shorter and scantier, and has a muslin yoke. For this 3 yd., or even less, will suffice. The seams, after being run evenly together, are pressed open on the wrong side, and fastened down with herringbone or catch stitch. The bottom of the skirt is often finished with elaborate embroidery in silk. But a neat hem, headed with a row of chain stitching either in silk or linen floss, is sufficient for ordinary purposes.

Making a Corset

Corsets may be made of white or gray coutil; jean; black cashmere; or white, black, or colored silk. Corsets of cashmere or silk are lined with linen or muslin. Coutil corsets are made without a lining. On white and colored corsets the seams are worked with thread or white silk. On black and gray corsets the seams are usually worked with colored silk.

In cutting the parts of the corset, the lines indicating the lengthwise thread given on the *Harper's Bazar* pattern should be observed. When these lines are not given, lay the straight edge of the material on the straight edge of the pattern. On each part that is to be joined to another part, allow 3/4 in. on the edges, as the parts should overlap 1/2 in. at the seams. No extra material is allowed on the upper and under edges.

On the back edge of the backs 1 1/2 to 1 3/4 in. is sometimes allowed. This is then turned down on the wrong side and stitched through on the right side along the lines given on the pattern. The eyelet

holes should be punched. The joining seams are worked with two rows of stitching. To do this turn down the edge of one part on the wrong side, and the edge of the other part on the right side narrowly. Lay one part on the other, so the edges overlap 1/2 in., and join them on the right side. (See figures 106 and 107.)

Figure 106. Joining seam with whalebone–right side

Figure 107. Joining seam with whalebone–wrong side

The gussets with blunt points are set under the corset, either with two rows of stitching on the right side or one row of stitching and a felled seam on the wrong side. The breast gussets are fastened besides at the points and the hip gussets at the top with buttonhole stitches as shown by figures 108, 109, and 110. These stitches are worked on the right

side, in doing which the edge should not be turned down. On the wrong side sew the gussets to the corset with a close cross seam, without turning down the edge (see figure 109).

Figure 108. Setting in breast gusset–right side

Figure 109. Setting in breast gusset–wrong side

Figure 110. Setting in hip gusset–right side

For whalebone sheaths, set on a strip of material of the requisite width along the narrow lines on the pattern, stitching it on the right side along the lines indicated for the whalebones. (See figures

111 and 112.) Or else set linen tapes on the wrong side of the corset, which are then stitched on the right side. The whalebones should end about 1/2 in. from the upper and lower edges, but the tape or strip of muslin is generally extended to the edge.

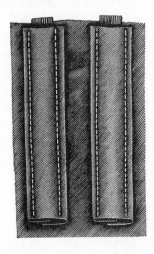

Figure 111. Stitching on whalebone sheaths

The ends of the whalebones are fastened by several long stitches, in doing which insert the needle in a broad hole bored through the whalebone. (See figures 106 and 112.) Or they are fastened by a crosswise row of stitching worked close underneath the whalebone.

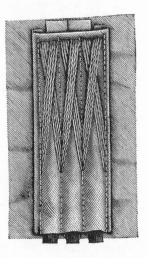

Figure 112. Fastening whalebones

To prevent the whalebones from showing at the top of the corset in back, several cords are frequently stitched in there as shown by figure 113. For busk sheaths stitch a linen tape on the wrong side of each front. This is indicated on the pattern by a straight line. The top and bottom of the corset are bound with linen, woolen, or silk braid.

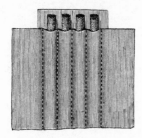

Figure 113. Stitching in cords

Trimming Garments

Certain materials should never be used as trimmings on others. Velveteen cannot be ornamented with velvet bows, but must have faille, or silk, etc. Grenadine cannot be used to trim washing materials. Nor is white embroidery appropriate for barege. Poplin looks best when velvet trimmed, but gros de Naples is not amiss with it. Turquoise and faille both add luster to cashmere, merinos, and all plain woolen goods. Clear materials, grenadines, and bareges look best self-trimmed, but foulard silk may be used with good effect. Passementerie, or gimp, is suitable on all opaque materials. Fringes are used to edge garments only, and should be placed under, not upon, the materials they ornament. Velvet bands are used to outline the borders of garments.

Binding Edges. *Binding* is used both as a trimming and as a secure finish, at the edges of dresses, etc. Figure 114 shows braid hemmed on both sides. However, binding is often run on one side and hemmed on the other. When binding scallops, make sufficient allowance, when running the braid, for the subsequent turning over. On thin materials the braid is simply folded in half and run on, taking

the stitches through on the other side. This mode is used in binding tarlatan flounces with satin ribbon, etc.

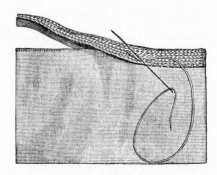

Figure 114. Binding

Figure 115 shows a *bias flounce,* finished at the edge by a narrow hem of bias silk. Both materials are cut strictly bias. The silk is placed right side downward upon the right side of the flounce. It is run on closely but lightly 1/8 in. from the edge, turned over, and felled on the wrong side over the turned-in portion. No stitch is of course seen on the right side.

Figure 115. Bias binding on flounce

Another mode of producing a similar effect is managed as follows. Cut the bias flounce a little longer than is actually required. Turn down on the right side of the material 1/8 in. more than is required for the rolled bind. Run closely at 1/8 in. from the edge, pulling the cotton rather tightly, and finishing off very securely.

Making Bias Folds. The *French fold* is usually made of the dress material, edged with satin (see figure 116). Cut a 3 1/4 in. wide strip of the material on the bias. Cut a strip of satin 1 in. wide on the bias. Fold the satin on the center line, and stitch it to the edge of the fold. Reverse the seam, and finish it by hemming it on the other edge, on the wrong side.

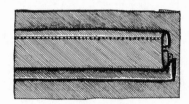

Figure 116. French fold

Figure 117 shows a *bias of two materials,* which forms a useful border for covering the marks shown on the removal of crape.

Figure 117. Bias of two materials

The *quadruple bias* is also called the "fourfold bias." That it folds four times should be remembered in cutting out the material; which, of course, is on the exact bias. Baste each fold down and finish on the wrong side of the material. Then removing the basting threads, continue this process until all the folds are stitched on (see figure 118). Fasten the top fold with slip stitches.

Crape is a difficult material for bias folds. It will stretch, no matter how careful you are. Crape bands should always be lined when not formed of double material. The band should be rather longer than the lining, which is otherwise apt to fall slightly below it. The lining is first placed on the right side of the band, and both are run closely together. Then the lining is turned over and tacked down to keep it in its place until the band is sewn on the dress.

Figure 118. Quadruple bias

Making Pipings. *Bias piping* is a useful and standard trimming. Although it is very narrow when completed, it should generally be cut 1 in. wide. Deep seams are required on the inside, which will take up the surplus width. It must be on the exact bias of the material. Turn the material, and place it with the edges turned to the inside, having the upper the mere width of a cord above the lower. Then finish it by close, firm invisible stitches (see figure 119).

Figure 119. Making piping

Double piping is formed by showing two different colors (see figure 120). Black silks are sometimes thus decorated, by heading the ruffle with a slight showing of some different shade. Cut the bias pieces as usual. Attach them by the ordinary seam. Open them and turn them over.

Figure 120. Double piping

For *double corded piping,* cut the two materials on the bias (see figures 121 and 122). Attach them by the ordinary seam. Instead of turning and hemming them on the wrong side (as for double piping), stitch near the bottom edge with silk of the same color. Into the upper, insert a medium-sized cord.

Figure 121. Double corded piping–right side

Figure 122. Double corded piping–wrong side

Making Cordings. Cording is extensively used in dressmaking, and for this work great nicety is required. Bodices are often edged with a double cording of the same, or contrasting material. Flounces are sometimes corded with another shade of color. Ball dresses of white tarlatan look admirable finished with satin cordings.

Cording can be made single, double, triple, or quadruple, though this is seldom done. The same rules are used for all. Cut the material in exact crossway or bias lengths. For single cording it should be narrower than for double. Join all the bias bands into one long strip by stitching or running the short diagonal seams. Press them open with a hot iron.

For *single cording,* place the cord in the center of the bias piece (see figure 123). Fold the material over it and baste. Run it in its proper place. Turn the edges under, and hem it down (see figure 124).

For *double cording,* lay a cord under each edge of a crossway strip 1 1/2 in. wide. Fold it to enclose the raw edges in the middle of the casing, allowing one cord to lie below the other (see figure 125). Run them together close to the lower. Place this face downward on the edge to be piped. Fix it to that part with an occasional backstitch, using the

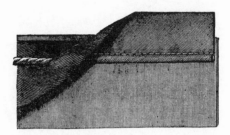

Figure 123. Sewing on cord

last row of running as a guide to sew by. The folded edge of the piping is then ready to be hemmed to the lining without making a turning.

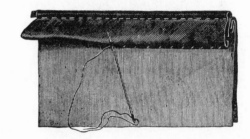

Figure 124. Hemming down cord

The above is a quick method, and answers for straight lines. But it will not do for curves, as the outer cord has to describe a wider circle than the inner one, and would be strained. For proper double or triple cording, tack each into its own casing (see figure 126). Run on separately by first putting on the one nearest to the dress. Then run the second cord over the first, projecting beyond it, and the third beyond the second in the same way. Finally lay a crossway piece over the last cording. Turn it over and fell it up on the inside, to hide the numerous raw edges.

Making Rouleaux. A *rouleau* is a large piping or rolled trimming, sometimes used as a decorative covering for the heading round a flounce, or any such kind of hem. Take a strip of material cut on the bias and 2 in. wide or more. Lay a strip, or even a roll, of lamb's wool or wadding along it. Fold the material over it and run it down at the back.

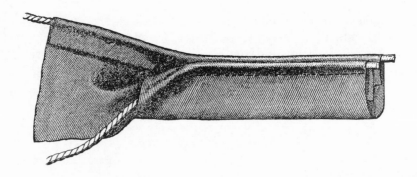

Figure 125. Double cording with one bias strip

Figure 126. Double cording with two bias strips

To conceal the stitches, it is better still to adopt the following method. Tack a piece of cord, and a length of wadding or lamb's wool, to the end of the bias strip. Fold the strip together, leaving the lamb's wool outside, and the cord inside. When the running is done, pull the cord. As it draws the lamb's wool or wadding inward, it will turn the covering material right side out at the same time, ready to lay on the dress.

Braiding in Patterns. Braiding patterns in Turkish style, arabesque, key bordering, and other designs, are more effective than flowers or leaves, which are apt to look stiff. Grape leaves and stems in braid, however, are very handsome for flannel work. If broad braid is to be used, the pattern must have longer curves than for narrow braid.

Both dresses and wraps should be fitted and basted before tracing the braiding pattern, so that it may not be uneven in crossing the seams. Trimming made by braiding the pattern upon a strip of the material is far easier than braiding the actual garment, and is very much worn. It can be put on as a heading for ruffles and flounces, or made into ruffling and flouncing. In the latter case it must always be finished with a buttonhole stitch scallop,

in thread to match the braid. The braiding pattern should be carefully traced upon tissue paper, basted down upon the material, carefully followed in thread in short, even stitches, and the paper torn away.

It is very important to select braid that is close and firm, as it will not stretch so much in working. The braid must be fastened upon the wrong side at the beginning of the work, carried through by being threaded in a coarse worsted needle. The stitches should then be taken very close, across the braid. If braid is sewed down with a sewing machine or carefully stitched by hand, a line in the exact center, of a contrasting color, is very effective.

The braid should be kept carefully on the lines forming the pattern, curving with very slight fullness. Points should be made by sharply folding the braid over, if alike on both sides, or turning it sharply if not alike. One stitch must always be taken across to secure the point. The difficulty is to keep the braid from spreading at turns or curves. Broad braid must be run on both edges, and have a close running under the fold to keep each point in place.

For *braiding in cord,* choose the softest and silkiest. The stiff, hard cord will never curve into graceful patterns, and is very difficult to sew on. Braiding in cord is best done with a rather strong straw needle. Lay the cord on the pattern, securing the end as for a flat braid. Holding it firmly, sew it down with stitches taken underneath, so as to be entirely invisible. Never cross the cord with stitches.

Raised braiding is produced by sewing the braid down on one edge only, if it is narrow. If wide, the braid is sewn upon both edges, which are pushed a little closer together than the actual width of the braid, so that it will stand up in relief.

All braiding requires to be pressed with a moderately cool iron when finished. Generally it may be done upon several folds of flannel, to ensure a very soft surface. Raised braiding must have the wrong side passed over an iron held upright.

Pleating Trimmings. *Kilt pleating* or *side pleating* is shown in figure 127. It may be either jointly bound and hemmed, or lined entire. It is most standard to line it entire and finish it with the invisible stitch.

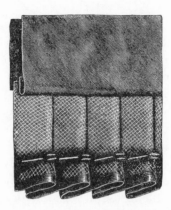

Figure 128. Pleated trimming—wrong side

Pleated belts are often used for loose garments. Cut the material twice the desired width of the belt, on the bias. Using a narrow seam, stitch the material to the wrong side of the lower part of said belt. Then turn it back and stitch the pleats to the belt, near the edge on the lower side. Fold the top edge over and hem on the wrong side. This is also one way to make a flounce heading.

Make *single box pleats* like two kilt pleats (see figure 129). Turn one to the right, the other to the left. Let the heels of each half of the pleat touch at the back, but not overlap. Single box pleats are rarely more than 1 in. wide, and are never separated by more than their own width. They take twice the length to be trimmed. For example, for a skirt 4 yd. around take a strip of 8 yd.

Figure 127. Pleated trimming—right side

Design the width of the pleats, which should be uniform. Lay the first pleat and baste it into position. Repeat for each succeeding pleat. Baste all the pleats across the lower edge. Press them on the wrong side. Join them with strong cotton. Remove the basting. This completes the work ready for adjusting and finishing (see figure 128).

Knife pleating takes its name from its appearance of being laid over a knife. The principle is the same as for all pleating. The pleatings, however, are much smaller, and are generally laid in regular successive widths, one way. This is called "plain knife pleating." It is sometimes varied by arranging the pleats in clusters at equidistant spaces, called "cluster knife pleating."

Figure 129. Pleated strip with middle box pleat

Double box pleats resemble two single ones of different widths, the smaller set upon the wider, which thus shows beyond the sides of the smaller. Place the edges of the upper pleat so as to meet at the back, as for single box pleats. But do not allow the lower one to meet in the center by as much as it projects beyond the face of the upper one at the sides.

Double box pleats are necessarily somewhat heavy. Although they make a handsome trimming, it is not suitable for all materials. Nor does it look well for flounces less than 7 in. deep. For a skirt of 4 yd., take a strip of 16 yd. for pleating. According to the thickness of the material, and width of the folds, place the lower ones farther apart at the back to economize the quantity. Nothing under 1 in. for the upper portion is heavy enough for this style.

Making Flutings. *Flutings* are piping or frill ornaments, shaped as a flute, the latter being gathered at both ends with great evenness and regularity. (See figure 130.) A collection of flutings resembles the pipes of an organ.

Figure 130. Fluting

Making Ruches. A *ruche* is a pleated or goffered strip of ribbon, net, lace, or other material, applied to a bodice, skirt, or headdress. The fluted ruche, or *ruche a la vieille,* is used as a dress trimming, and resembles a single box-pleated flounce (see figure 131). Make a number of small box pleats. Leave the distance between each pleat and a precisely equal amount of the pleating at the top and bottom of the ruche loose beyond the respective stitchings. This forms a sort of frilling above and below the pleats. For tarlatan, muslin, and thin materials the best size for each pleat is 1/2 in.; for silk, from 1/2 to 1 in. In tarlatan and grenadine

turn the edge down just past where the stitches confining the pleats will be made. Or snip out the raw edges in small points, tack several strips together, and cut through all at once. Silk needs a book muslin lining exactly as wide as the ruche when made, including the headings. The silk alone folds over the edges of the muslin to the depth of the headings.

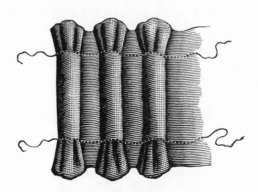

Figure 131. Fluted ruche

A *twisted ruche* is sometimes made on the straight, but looks best on the bias. Turn down the edges. Fold one of them in pleats about 3/4 in. wide, and let all respectively touch each other. Then make up the other edge in the same way, only turning the pleats in the opposite direction. This will give them a twist in the middle. Plissé flounces may be stitched at about 1 1/2 or 2 in. from the top, and the edge pleated to the opposite side. This gives a kind of heading to the flounces, and a spiral effect resembling a separate twisted ruche.

A *feather ruche* is produced by fringing out silk. Thus must be unraveled the width way, or across the material, but not along the selvage line, as the fringe would thus be too poor. Snip the depth the fringe is to be apart at every 2 in. If further than that, the threads are not drawn nearly so fast, and when the feathering is wide, the silk is liable to knot. Ruches on the straight need to be fuller than crossway ones; quite triple the finished length must be allowed.

Forming Quillings. Quillings are small round pleats made in lace, tulle, or ribbon. They are lightly sewn down with an occasional backstitch, the edge

of the trimming remaining in open flutelike folds. They are generally made for frills at the neck and wrists of bodices, and the fronts of caps and bonnets. Quillings are distinguished from kiltings by their roundness at the open or outer edge, kiltings being ironed down in flat folds. The name was probably given to this description of pleating because of its round form, just large enough to admit a goose or turkey quill.

Plain quilling is only used in the lightest materials, such as net, tulle, blonde, etc., and principally for tuckers. It is made up either single or double, according to the thickness required. Make single small box pleats at one edge, each rather overlapping the next at the back, and wrapping over the whole width of the pleat if the quilling be very thick. Hold the right side toward you and the quilling downward, the pleating being done at the upper edge. Use a long straw needle, and work it in and out as every pleat is formed, but do not draw the needle and cotton out of the quilling. As the needle fills, pass the pleats over the eye, onto the cotton, until the cotton itself is occupied by the pleats.

Shell quilling is one of the most effective trimmings when made of the same material as the dress. It is especially useful where a second color is introduced, as the material to be quilled is then lined with it instead of merely hemmed at the edges. Shells are never pretty if made too large; 2 in. is the best width, but they may be as narrow as desired. Shell quilling is also available for crape or gauze, but the strips must then be cut double the required width. They must be folded over on each side, so the edges may overlap down the middle, where it is tacked, while the doubled material is being pleated.

Stitch three little pleats in the middle of the strip, all one on top of the other, and the edge of each barely showing beyond the one above it. Start the next group of three, so the edge of its first pleat is as far from the edge of the last pleat of the last group, as half the width of the strip. When the length is pleated up, catch the two corners of the top pleat of each group together backward, and sew them to the middle. Done thus, every shell touches.

The shells may be spaced, which takes less material. It marks the kind of trimming better than when close, if a contrasting lining is used. The spacing, however, between the edges of the top pleat of the last group and the bottom pleat of the new group must never exceed the width of the strip.

Making a Trimming *en Coquille*. This is the French term to denote "shell shaped." The ribbon or lace is laid like a succession of scallop shells, one above or over the other, in groups of threes. It is previously lined and pleated, then drawn closely together at the top of each scallop, leaving the lower portion of the *coquille* to spread out in a half circle. When employed as a trimming for crape or gauze, the strips of material should be cut double the width required, and folded over on each side, so that the edges may overlap where it is tacked down the middle, while the double material is being pleated. The space between the edge of the top pleat of one group and the lower one of the next group must never exceed the width of the strip.

Making a Trimming *en Echelle*. This is a French term to signify "in ladder form." Applied to trimmings consisting of a succession of narrow pleatings laid on horizontally between two upright side folds or bands, forming a kind of insertion of ladderlike appearance.

Making a Trimming *en Eventail*. This is a French term to signify "in the form of a fan." Flounces at the end of a skirt are sometimes thus made. Openings are cut out at regular distances. A piece of material of a different color or type is pleated, and inserted into each opening so that it is closely confined together at the top and allowed to flare at the bottom. This gives much freedom, as well as a more ornamental character to the flounce.

Kilt Pleating a Flounce. The *kilt pleatings* now so fashionable require a great quantity of material. The allowance is three times the width of the portion to be trimmed. Silk for kilting must be cut across, but other materials are usually cut in the length. Kilt pleating sits closer when cut the selvage way, and is fuller and more fluffy when cut straight across.

To kilt silk, after having cut and joined the breadths, hem them with fine sewing silk. Do not put the stitches too close, and draw the silk as little as possible. Supposing the flounce be required to form its own heading, turn it down at the top and tack it along on the wrong side. With the exception of materials damaged by ironing, after the hem is made it is better to press it, as also the fold at the top, if it is not hemmed at each edge.

Decide upon the size of the pleats. Fold two or three, pin them and crease them firmly. Then take out the pins and measure the width between the folds. You must now fold and crease your length of silk, or should it be a very long one, a few breadths at a time. Take the width between the creases from the folds you have already arranged, so that when you begin to kilt you have every fold evenly and plainly marked. You will scarcely need to measure for creasing the folds, if the flounce be a narrow one, but be careful to get them even and straight.

Begin kilting with the top of the flounce to your right hand, turning the pleats away from you and pinning them both at the top and bottom with silk pins. This done—say 1/2 yd. at a time—tack it in the center on the right side, putting a stitch in each pleat, and again about 1/2 in. from each edge with a fine needle and thin white cotton. This done the flounce is ready for stitching. If you do not want to stitch it upon the dress, tack a tape underneath and stitch it down upon that. For a flounce it is better to put this tape about one-third of the depth from the lower edge, and stitch it before putting it upon the skirt.

Making Ruffled Flounces. The *plain gathered ruffle* or *flounce* is the most simple, common, and useful of skirt trimmings. It is, of course, cut on the exact bias. There are three distinct methods of finishing it. The first is to bind the edge by a strip 3/4 in. wide, stitching it to the right side, and taking up as small a seam as possible. Then turn it over and hem it down on the wrong side, putting the stitches in the first seam so that they are invisible on the wrong side. The second method is to turn the ruffle up on the wrong side and hem it

1/4 in. wide. The third method is to cut a lining of undressed crinoline, or some similar material. Sew both together on the bottom edge, then turn it so the seam is hidden between the two materials.

The *French ruffle* or *flounce* is formed as follows. Cut it, on the exact bias, 2 in. wider than it is to be when finished. Deep, broad points of the desired depths and widths are cut in the bottom. The points are sewed all around to a lining; which should be of silk, since it shows slightly. Fold it across the top in regular, small side pleats. Arrange it so that each pleat is taken exactly at the upper end of each respective point.

The *English ruffle* or *flounce* is a cousin to the French ruffle. Cut it like the French ruffle and give the points the desired shape. Instead of the points being lined, they are bound with a very narrow bias piece of material. Arrange the flounce at the top in a series of box pleats. Said pleats should be the same width as the spaces between them. The center of each pleat will thus become the center of each point.

The *corded ruffle* or *flounce* is cut 2 in. wider than you wish the flounce, and on the exact bias. The extra amount is taken up in the cording and the heading. The heading should be turned in double to the cord. It can be cut in points, or otherwise. It can then be finished by attaching it to a crinoline or silk lining. Before turning, the upper part of the point should be cut, so that you may easily turn it and draw it out. The cord should be inserted and the gathering done at the same time.

Finishing a Flounce with a French Hem. The *French hem* is employed in lieu of a silk binding. It is especially suitable for such materials as mohair and alpaca. It is made thus: Hold the right side of the flounce toward you. Turn the top edge down also toward you, so that its inside shows. The piece so turned down must measure 3/4 in. for silk, and 1 in. for materials that fray. Then make a close running, using an inappreciable quantity of the turned-down doubled edge that is over the left hand. When the whole has been run, turn the flounce wrong side toward you. Fell down the false hem on the line of running. The raw edge of the

hem must be turned in nearly halfway, so that it may make the hem of double material and not lose the appearance of a hollow roll.

To make a *double French hem:* Cut the flounce as wide as it is to be when finished, with the addition of 1 in. for turnings. Then cut off this hem and its 1 in. Line it with leno. Run the piping or silk fold upside down on the right side of the hem, so that all four raw edges may be laid together. Then run the other edge of the hem to the edge of the flounce, placing the right side of the former to the wrong side of the latter. The joining will be enclosed inside the hem when it is turned over on the face of the flounce, pinned in place, and sewn to it by running along the ridge made by the cording. This is done on the inside of the flounce, by feeling the ridge.

The hem must not be pulled up to its whole extent, as the actual edge of it must be of double material, and betray no signs of the join, which is 1/2 in. up on the inside. It is this 1/2 in., and 1/4 in. for joining the silk to it, and 1/4 in. for joining the hem to the flounce, which uses the 1 in. extra that was allotted. The hem now really projecting 1/2 in. beyond the depth the flounce was given, will be accounted for by 1/4 in. having been used at the join below, and the other 1/4 in. for turning at the top.

Gauging or Shirring Trimmings. *Gauging* is used to trim the bodice or sleeves of a dress or the head of a flounce. A series of close parallel runnings are made, and all drawn up to gather the material between them (see figure 132). Gauging may be made in groups at even distances. It is pulled nearly tight from row to row of the runnings, but not so much as to make the line of gathering threads take on an uncertain course. The beauty of this trimming depends on lines of extreme accuracy.

Forming Puffings. *Puffings* are bands of any material, cut straight or on the bias, and gathered on both sides. They are used as flounce headings, round sleeves, or down them. The method of making them depends on the current fashion.

Both tarlatan net and tulle require as much again as the space they are to cover. That is, a 4 yd. skirt needs a strip of 8 yd. for the puff. Grenadine

Figure 132. Gauging

and silk gauze, being slightly more substantial, do not need quite as much. For thick opaque materials, half again as much as the foundation is sufficient.

When skirts are much gored, it is impossible to make a group of puffs. But you may divide every two with a ruche, or other device. This admits of cutting the puffs asunder (rather than using one width of material) to lessen the length for the upper ones (which otherwise would be much fuller than the ones near the hem).

Run crossway puffs straight along a creased mark. Tack the thread, when drawn up, lightly down to the foundation. Fold the skirt into four, and put a pin at each quarter. Fold the strip into four, and do the same. Run a thread from pin to pin, fixing one on the puff to one on the skirt at each division. Spread the skirt over the corner of a table, far enough to distend a quarter at a time. Pull up the drawing thread and twist it round the pin. Equalize the fullness, and secure it with pins every few inches. Every quarter being so arranged, turn the skirt inside out. Run along on the inside to sew the puff to the dress, which is seen through. This saves much fingering, as the left hand underneath need scarcely touch the dress. A long straw needle is best for all trimmings made of clear tissues.

Puffs that hang over the bottom are called *falling bouillonées*. Crease them down on the wrong side. Make a running a little way in, to take up the material double. Sew each succeeding row, made on one piece, to the skirt by running the inside of the puff to the right side of the dress, the creased edge lying upward. The topmost puff may have the edge turned down. Make a running to gather it up into a little frill heading.

Puffs on the straight, not meant to hang downward, may not show the gathering thread. Crease them on the inside and whip them scantily over.

Stout woolens and silks may be gathered up better, and are more durable, if a small cotton cord is run in the crease.

Making Bows. *Bows,* whether for trimming sleeves or for dresses, are better cut on the cross. The ordinary or butterfly-shaped bow is in five pieces, two for the loops, one for the center, and two for the ends. These are preferably lined with the same material, the reverse sides being frequently visible. The material for the different parts should be cut rather larger than the lining, and tacked down over it, to form neat edges to the different sides.

Every Lady Her Own Milliner

Bonnets may be divided into two classes. One is the bonnet manufactured of straw, only requiring a little ribbon and feathers or flowers to make it perfect. The other is the millinery bonnet, made on a net or buckram foundation and covered and trimmed with fancy materials.

Making a Bonnet Foundation. For the millinery bonnet, you must first have your shape or foundation. This you may purchase at one of the little shops where such things are exposed for sale in the window. Or you may make one by adhering to the following rules.

Purchase a buckram foundation shape of the present fashion. Then obtain the following materials of a draper. One-quarter yard of illusion tulle, black or white according to the color of the material of which the bonnet is to be made. If a light shade, the shape should be white; if the opposite, black is more suitable. This is enough tulle for two shape fronts, as it is a double-width material, and half a width is sufficient for a shape. A ring of edge wire, one of support wire, and a pair of wire nippers are all now that is necessary. The rings of wire will make more than one shape.

Divide the tulle double; one of the pieces will be 4 1/2 in. deep. Run in a short thread to mark the center. Then run a thread lengthways of the tulle, at a sufficient distance from the doubled edge to admit an edge wire. Run another 3/4 in. from the first, then another at a sufficient distance to hold the second wire, which will be of support wire, not edge. Repeat this once more. Then turn up the raw edges of the tulle and run in another thread to admit the last wire. All the ends of thread must be left unfastened until the wires have been inserted and the tulle drawn up on the buckram shape.

Now the tulle is ready to receive the wires. Measure off enough edge wire to go round the edge of the buckram shape and round the back. Run this into the first runner of the tulle. Run in a support wire in each of the other spaces allotted to them, cutting them off just a little longer than the buckram, to admit of turning up or wrapping over. Put the center of the tulle to the center of the buckram shape. Roughly oversew the edge wire to the buckram shape wire, keeping the former to the exact form of the buckram wire. Draw up the remaining threads. Secure them firmly with the wires at the ears of the shape, or at its back, the place for which will be plainly indicated on the buckram shape. All the wires must be turned up over the edge wire and firmly sewn. Next short support wires must be cut a little longer than the depth of the front. One is run in across the middle of the tulle front, and two on either side of this one, at equal distances of 3 in., until the front is equally supported all round. The ends of these wires must be turned up over the edge wire and last support wire, and tied to the transverse support wires to keep them firm. Their use is obvious—to support the front to its proper form and width. After this is done, remove it from the buckram shape by unpicking the sewing at the edge, which has been keeping the front in place. Now it is ready for the crown.

If blocked crowns such as envelop the head are in use, one must be purchased at a shape shop, and being placed center to center with the tulle front, firmly sewn to it and to the back wire. If a soft crown be needed for a fancy make of bonnet, a little net or tulle pleated on to fit the crown of the head is all that is necessary.

These directions for shape making have been given in case some readers should require to make any shape they cannot buy. But it is better for the amateur milliner to buy the shape and save an unnecessary labor. It is less expensive, as it is impossible to buy materials for one shape only. When choosing a shape, see that the tulle is perfect and the wires firm and in place. Try it on, for the bonnet will suit you as well again if it rests easily on your head, and is chosen with regard to your face and figure.

Making an Old-Fashioned Bonnet. Millinery bonnets are of two styles. A few years ago the fashion was a bonnet enveloping the head with a blocked crown and curtain behind. It was plainly covered with velvet, crape, French crepe, or drawn silk, consisting of many runners and trimmed high in front. It had also a substantial cap border next the face and inside the edge front. The bonnet of the present day only rests upon the head. It usually has a soft fancy crown puffed or pleated, and is trimmed partly on the crown on one side and toward the back. Although the large bonnet with blocked crown has become the style of the past, that style will be treated first, for the capote so fashionable at present is merely a modification.

The front of the shape is either purchased or made, then, and the back part is composed of a firm or blocked crown. Now proceed to make the bonnet. If for summer wear it will be composed of silk, French crepe, tulle, or one of the numerous fancy materials always being introduced for millinery. If for winter, velvet, terry velvet, or English crape (if for mourning) would be more suitable.

When selecting velvet, be careful that it be soft and pliable, as it will give to the shape much more readily—in fact, set better. If silk, it should be substantial, but yield easily to the touch when taken by the cross corners. Tulle, black or white, should be fine and soft. If stiff it is on account of the dress in it, which it loses in the first heavy rain, and is spoiled. White or colored French crepes are much firmer, but should also yield easily when pulled gently on the cross. Black English crape is good when the rib is well defined yet close, and of a good jet black. The same rule applies to black French crepe. Bonnet silks and velvets from 18 to 21 in. wide can be had. Tulles and English crapes always double the width of velvets and silks.

To plainly cover a blocked crown bonnet, 3/4 yd. of velvet is sufficient on the straight. Cut off a small square piece from one corner just large enough to cover the round of the crown. All velvet shades dark or light when held down, and is placed on the bonnet to shade the dark way when seen from behind the wearer. The little square of velvet is stretched over the tip and pinned at each corner, one corner being on the top in the center, the others of course taking their places of themselves. Pull one of the corners with the left hand and commence sewing with the right, the bonnet shape resting on the knee. Each corner must be well pulled to make the square set nicely over the round. In sewing do not encroach more than 1/2 in. onto the crown.

When this is done take the pattern of the crown from the tip to where it joins the front. This is done in tissue paper and then cut out in the velvet, a little being allowed for turnings. Now fit this over the crown of the bonnet and sew in place, neatly turning it in round the portion that has already been covered.

Now take a pattern of the front in tissue paper, allowing more for turnings, for the front is usually turned in over the edge wire and hemmed down inside. Before covering the front it is well to bind the edge wire with a little crossway muslin doubled to take off the sharp marks of the wires. Indeed, many consider the shape had better be covered all over, and certainly this is advisable when it is at all rough. Old soft calico is very good for this purpose cut to the same tissue pattern as the velvet. When the front has been covered with

the velvet, it must be turned in where it joins the crown piece and hemmed down on the inside of the edge.

The remaining velvet will be required for trimming the bonnet and making the curtain. The latter is generally composed of a piece of crossway velvet, from 2 to 4 in. deep, and lined with stiff net and pleated with two or three pleats. The velvet at the edge of the curtain is first hemmed over the stiff net for neatness. When hemmed and pleated, place center to center and velvet to velvet at the back of the bonnet crown. Sew round to the ears on either side.

The bonnet needs a head lining. This may be either of Persian silk (1/4 yd. will line two bonnets) or a little old soft calico. The lining is just run to the net of the shape inside, but not taken through the velvet, as no stitches must be seen on the right side of the bonnet. A little strip of velvet, about 1 in. wide and on the cross, will bind in the rough edges of crown, curtain, and head lining. This is as necessary as it is easy, the raw edges being visible on the wrong side and at the back of the bonnet.

Now the bonnet is ready for its trimming. This may consist of pleatings of crossway velvet, silk, or tulle; or bows of ribbon with a feather or feathers; or flowers and lace. The place for trimming is indicated by the fashion. It is usually on the fore part and high up in this style of bonnet, whose great beauty is in the set of the velvet on the crown, which trimming on that part would hide.

There remain only the cap border and strings to complete the bonnet. The former being somewhat difficult work and a very trifling expense to buy ready-made, had better be procured of the draper, and it will be in character with the shape of the day. Cap borders are made of tulle, or quilling, and blonde. One-quarter yard of Mechlin is sufficient for one border, or 6 yd. of quilling, and blonde. This is pleated, directions for which appear below.

This style of bonnet may be made of English crape or French crepe, silk, tulle, or any fancy material, with this difference. French crepe requires at least two layers, the material being thin. English crape may do once covered, but must have a

covering of black mull muslin strained all over the shape first to prevent the shape from showing through the crape. English crape is only made in black, and is consequently only used for mourning bonnets. A yard of French crepe is enough for a bonnet and 1/2 yd. of English crape, the latter being a wider and better material.

Making a Mourning Bonnet. Mourning bonnets are trimmed with a series of folds of English crape laid one just within the other like a series of tiny steps. They are composed of strips of crape cut on the cross about 1 in. wide. They may be placed across the bonnet as a ribbon would be, or round the crown, or several tacked together make a rich-looking bow. A little silk cut in the same way may be folded in with the crape if not intended for the deepest mourning. In these cases no silk is introduced, as a rule, especially in the widow's bonnet. This is made as plain as it can be. It has a long crape veil attached to it either at the edge or halfway on the bonnet. The veil has a 6- or 8-in. hem, which is slip stitched with crape cotton. A crape flower is used in trimming any mourning bonnet except the widow's, as are feathers and jet. These with a little ribbon are all that is necessary to compose a crape bonnet.

French crepe can be had in black or any color. Being a rather thin material, it is, like tulle, often drawn in the same way that a shape is made, and may be used with or without wire. The material is double in this case, and of crepe 4 to 6 in. longer than the part of the bonnet to be covered. If tulle 9 in. is not too much for fullness, and some even prefer more.

Making a Drawn Bonnet on a Foundation. There is another style consisting of the stand-up runner or drawn tucks. You must allow the fullness mentioned. Run the threads or silks in one at a time, leaving the material at full length till all the threads are in. Each thread should remain unfastened, and a little longer than the material till all are run in. Then they must be drawn up to fit the crown or front of the bonnet, the bonnet being covered in two parts. Any lady will, with these hints, be

enabled to form a very pretty summer bonnet in any light material, including silk, turquoise, etc., the material of which her dress is composed.

Making a Modern Bonnet. The only difference between the old-fashioned bonnet and that of the present is the shape. This can be either purchased at a shape shop or made. If made a buckram foundation shape must be obtained of the present fashion, and the tulle shape made to it according to the instructions already given. The bonnet of the present is small and rests upon the head. The shapes are the "gypsy," the "coronet," the "rink," and the "capote," the latter more flat than the "coronet." All are more or less close to the head and placed rather far back.

The make of these bonnets differs from those just described in the following respects. The crowns are not often hard blocked, and consequently not plain covered. The material of which they are composed, which may be any one of those mentioned as used in millinery, is loosely drawn over in one or more puffs from front to back over the crown.

The edge is covered with a piece of crossway silk, velvet, or other material. This should be cut a little deeper than the front of the shape for turning in on the inside. It should also be cut 6 or 8 in. longer than the part to be covered, because it is put on full. Because it is on the cross, one width is not quite sufficient, and a similar piece must be cut and joined to it. Each edge must be gathered. Then it should be placed center to center on the bonnet and run on one way, say the inside edge of the bonnet, then turned over and tacked down to where the crown joins the front.

This style of bonnet has no curtain at its back, unless for very elderly ladies sometimes. Its place is filled by a bow of the material, and ribbon, with flower or feather, the place for which is plainly indicated on the shape. There is a little strip of gathered tulle double run inside the edge by way of cap border. If strings are attached they are sewn on quite at the back, and are brought loosely round under the chin. These nowadays consist of net, tulle, or crepe edged with narrow lace. The real fastening

of the bonnet is either an ornamental pin run through the hair, or an elastic sewn on just above the ears and fastened behind under the hair.

This style of bonnet may be made of any material according to the season. The material may be quilted or drawn, or arranged in any way you choose; but you will of course be guided by the fashion.

Making a Paris Chip Bonnet. These stand on the borderland of the millinery bonnet and the straw. Owing to their delicacy, they are almost exclusively confined to the use of brides and wedding parties. The material, being perfectly white, requires the most careful handling. It consists of a circular piece of chip, sold as a flat.

The pattern of the different bonnet parts must be carefully taken in tissue paper, then cut out in the chip. A tip for the little round end of the crown is sent with every flat, and only requires sewing on. The crown proper, or band, must be cut out to the pattern, as also the front. These two pieces must be bound all round with the narrowest braid, consisting of a piece of crossway white silk. It is lightly run on on one side, then slip stitched to the other. After this it is ready to be placed on the bonnet, the shape having first been covered with white mull muslin. A curtain or not, according to the fashion, is made in the same way and sewn on as directed. A white feather generally completes the beauty of this bonnet or hat.

Trimming Straw Bonnets, Straw Hats, and Felt Hats. Some straw bonnets are worn on the fore part and some toward the back of the head. Be careful to purchase one that fits the part of the head for which it is intended.

The edge of this bonnet is sometimes bound 1/2 in. deep with bonnet silk. This is cut on the cross and sewn on upon the outer and right side of the bonnet about 1/4 in. in. It is then turned in into the inside of the bonnet and hemmed down to a lining already tacked in, which should consist of a little muslin. The head or crown lining may also be of muslin or any little odd bit of silk.

The present bonnet is often trimmed with a wreath of small flowers and leaves. This needs only placing round the bonnet and securing with pins or a needle and thread. Sometimes a ruching forms the trimming. A piece of silk or a ribbon may be put round, and over that a long feather reaching quite round from back to back of the bonnet. This may be finished off with a ribbon bow; a small ornament of pearl, jet, steel, or silver; sometimes an ornamental pin fastening the bonnet to the hair, thus answering a double purpose.

The cap border is composed of a narrow strip of double tulle. One-quarter yard of tulle, cut in two, is sufficient. The two widths are needed for pleating double the length of the space to be trimmed or covered.

Straw hats are trimmed in the same way as bonnets–in fact, the bonnet of the present day is more hat than bonnet. When the inner edge of a hat is lined, the material is cut on the cross of sufficient depth. If one width is insufficient to go round the hat, another or part of one must be cut and joined to it. This must be sewn on the right side of the hat, then turned over and tacked round in place to where the head lining will be again sewn to meet it, thus making all neat. Generally, a ribbon, wreath, or feather completes the hat, whether it be felt or straw.

A hat may be made of any material by getting a shape and cutting patterns of the different parts as for a bonnet, and then covering with the material desired. Thus cloth may be used up or velvet that has done duty before in larger form.

Making a Cap. There are numerous head coverings bearing the designation of cap. Take an old cap your friend or relative has been wearing, and take the pattern of its foundation, which is composed of black stiff net and a support wire hemmed in to keep it firm. This will instruct you in making the foundation, and you will be sure it will fit and suit your friend.

Caps are worn only by elderly ladies, and each lady has her own particular style of cap. You have only to put the bows, laces, and flowers on in the same way, with any little addition or improvement

that may suggest itself. The best way to prove whether an addition be an improvement is to try the cap on with the bow, ruche, or flower just pinned in; after which, if it suits the wearer, it may be sewn in place.

Crowns of caps are sometimes drawn (see above for drawn bonnets) and sometimes composed of a lace or tulle fichu. The former is bought ready to put on the cap. For the fichu style, take a square of tulle, black or white, say 18 in. Fold it in a fold 1 in. wide across the piece, and then form another fold or tuck at a clear distance of 1 in. Repeat until the tulle is all folded. Then fold it across the other folds at the same distance and in folds of the same depth. Thus there is a square fichu of about 9 in. This is made neat round the edges by a trimming, upon which can be placed a narrow ribbon or velvet according to the make of the cap; the borders of caps are usually quilted or pleated.

The style may be altered by having recourse to a fashion book that tells of the newest materials and colors. Any cap can be made of any style whatever except the widow's cap. This cannot be made by a private individual, as machinery is put in force for its completion.

Cap springs are worn by some ladies who could not well do without them. Springs are all alike, with the exception of degrees in length. There are not two heads quite alike, yet these steel springs fall one into the other so exactly that two dozen will lie in the smallest compass. One of them sewn into the cap in its normal condition is nothing but a trouble to the wearer. The remedy is to study the lady's head and pull out and round the spring to suit it, giving it a slight curve inward at the ears. The cap then sets becomingly without strings. A cap with a spring will do very well without wire. The spring should have a narrow ribbon twisted round it to soften it.

Elderly ladies wear a bonnet cap instead of a cap border sewn into the bonnet. This is made of illusion tulle, with three or four tucks in for the crown. The measurements must be taken from back to front over the top of the head and round the poll, from the sides of the neck over the top of the head

on the crown, and round the face from ear to ear. The tulle is cut to these measurements, allowing for turnings and the usual fullness for the raised tucks on the crown–about half as much again as the length required. This piece of tulle is all in one, and forms the cap. The edges are bound right round, and two or more rows of quilling and blonde are then run on round the face. This cap has no wires, but sometimes a narrow ribbon is seen in running the tucks to give firmness.

Making a Headdress. A headdress may be composed of velvet or velvet and lace, with feathers or flowers, or lace and ribbons only. Again recourse must be had to one being worn by the person for whom the new one is required. Fichus generally form the chief part of an ordinary headdress. Sometimes a bow or two of ribbon is attached, inclining down and backward with lace ends, or toward the face, according to taste or necessity; for headdresses are ordinarily worn to protect that part of the head that is not covered by its natural adornment, hair.

Another type of headdress is the court headdress worn by ladies at court. This consists of a coronet fitting the head, upon which is the diamond, ruby, pearl, or other ornament, and which is always finished by the white ostrich or Prince of Wales's plume on the left side. This is a headdress not likely to be needed by the amateur at home, and a lady would scarcely trust her maid with such particular work. Were she to do so the maid must take the pattern in paper of a coronet. The coronet must be neat inside and out and without a crease.

Making a Veil. A veil is composed of French crepe, or black English crape if for mourning. It is hemmed more or less deeply according to the depth of mourning. Other veils are of net, plain or spotted, hemmed simply or lace edged, and sometimes beaded. They are either straight or rounded. One-half yard of spotted or plain net is sufficient for a straight veil, or 3/4 yd. for a round one. For a round one there must be an old veil as a pattern, or a paper pattern. Brussels net and illusion tulle veils are often worn instead of lace (which is more

expensive) by brides and at the rite of confirmation, in place of a little tulle cap. These are from 1 yd. square, with a 2 or 3 in. hem.

Forming Trimmings. To make a *rosette of broad ribbon* cut a small round in stiff net about the size of a two-shilling piece. Let the net be white for a light color of ribbon, and black if the reverse. Cut 12 strips of ribbon 3 in. long. Double one, and pinch the raw edges into two pleats or folds. Sew over once or twice to secure them, and so on until the 12 are sewn. Then place them round the edge of the circle of net, and sew them firmly to it in a standing position. Having put one row round, put another a little farther in, and let the bows come rather between the first row. Repeat until the net is covered. There will be just room enough in the center to put one loop more. This should be sewn on on one end, then turned over and slip stitched to the net in the opposite direction. This makes the whole neat. Any number of bows must be cut until the net is covered. The size of the rosette–in fact, of all rosettes–is determined by the size of the circle of net.

Rosettes of narrow ribbon only differ from the former in that they are made of narrow ribbon. Each rosette takes about 3 yd. of 1/2 in. ribbon. Do not cut the ribbon in this case, but use from the length. Now make a loop about 2 in. long, and place on the circle of net. Pass a stitch through it, and make another loop next it, keeping the satin side of the ribbon from you, and bending it backward. After forming the loop pass the stitch through, and so on till you have been round the circle. Repeat in an inner circle until finished, and filled in in the center. Thus you will have a round full shining rosette, the right side of the ribbon only being visible.

Bows are made like rosettes, a small piece of net being the foundation. But the ribbon, when pinched or pleated, is sewn onto the net flat. It consists of but two or four loops, two one way and two another, with two ends the length of which depends on the use of the bow.

Ruching is pleating ribbon, velvet, tulle, lace, or silk. There is single box pleating, double ditto, triple ditto, and half pleating. When the pleats are

in the center of the ribbon, it is called ruching. When at the edge of the ribbon they are simply called pleating. Single, double, or triple box pleating, folded and sewn at the edge, is called quilling.

For *single box pleating* allow just as much again as the part to be covered. For double box pleating double the quantity, and for triple box pleating triple it. Half pleating takes just half the quantity of single box pleating.

For a single box pleat a little more than 1/4 in. wide, take the end of the ribbon to be ruched between the thumb and forefinger of both hands, right side up. Make a fold in the center from your left toward your right hand about 1/4 in. deep. Put your needle through it threaded with silk the same color, taking care to make the tiniest stitch. Then fold your ribbon over toward your left hand and a little under the first fold at the back. This makes one pleat. Allow a space the width of the pleat just made, and repeat the process until the ruching is long enough.

Double box pleating is made by putting two folds each way one on the other, then the usual space, then another pleat, and so on. The same rule stands good for triple pleating. Half pleating is, as may be guessed from the name, only half a pleat, each pleat following or turning the same way as the last, and usually folded from left to right of the worker. This is much more scanty than the box pleating.

Bouillons are puffings of greater or less degree, and are arranged on the bonnet, cap, or dress. Gather one side or edge of the net or tulle, allowing for fullness. Then place the forefinger of the left hand under the tulle and throw up the tulle gently into a puff. About 1 in. at a time can be done in this way, and then secured by needle and thread. Several of these puffings in rows round a bonnet, especially if of tulle, may be very pretty, and the bonnet light.

Suppose the bonnet measures 22 in. round the edge. Two widths of tulle will be necessary to *bouillonner* the front. Each puff stands about 1 in. high, so there are 2 in. of material in the depth of each puff. If, therefore, four puffings are required, cut the material 9 in. deep. This allows for turning in, making the last puff neat. Net, tulle, and French crepe require much more fullness than velvet or silk, because of their thinness of texture. Net and tulle are used on the straight. Velvet and silk are cut on the cross.

Good millinery consists in neatness of stitch and arrangement, without the appearance of having been handled or pressed. It should be light looking, and as much as possible as if fingers had not touched it. Feathers and flowers should be placed in as natural a position as possible. They should not adhere too closely to the bonnet, yet be firmly secured at their base. The better the materials, the better the bonnet will look.

The Milliner's Art

Many home milliners depend upon their trimmings to give their work the right look. When these are plentifully used, the desired result may be obtained. But it is better to make the foundation right, and in a plain bonnet this is absolutely essential.

Making a Bonnet. The generally accepted idea in making a bonnet is, that a frame is to be bought and covered just as it is. However, a bonnet frame in the hands of the expert is bent in here, and pulled out there, and narrowed or deepened, until it has an entirely different expression. These alterations require taste and judgment, and would be decidedly rash for beginners without the advice and direction of someone who understands the matter.

It will be assumed, therefore, that the frame is ready to be covered—a process that begins with the crown. If the material is velvet, from 3/8 to 1/2 yd., cut on the bias, will be sufficient. An entirely round piece, rather more than 1 in. larger than the crown, is cut out. It is smoothly basted on the frame, the velvet being carefully pulled away from the bias when there is a disposition to fullness, as little pleats at this point are not desirable. A closer basting, very near the edge, is then made with the silk used in sewing the other parts of the bonnet, and the first threads are taken out.

Before putting on the fronts, the edge of the frame, over the wire, is carefully bound with soft paper or old silk, to prevent the wire from rubbing on the velvet and making the edge shabby. In

making a velvet bonnet, it is not necessary to place anything between the outside material and the frame except on the edge.

Two fronts are cut, one for the outside and one for the inside. In some cases a velvet binding is closely basted over the first binding, and both fronts slip stitched to this velvet binding. In others the outside and inside are slip stitched together without any intermediate binding. Slip stitching is done on the right side. The inside front is not quite so deep as the outside one, the silk crown lining meeting it; and the two are tacked together. The crown lining is then gathered and drawn to the proper size.

The outside front must be put on with great care, as this is the part of the bonnet that shows the most. A small pin here and there is better for holding it than basting threads. A smoother effect is produced by having a second piece between the front and the crown. When this is the case, the front reaches only to the point that marks the end of the slope upward and the beginning of the slope downward for the side and back. This second piece has the edge turned under, both where it meets the front and where it goes around the crown. It is usually secured by a few stitches at either end, as the trimming conceals it almost entirely.

Sometimes the bonnet is so shaped that there is no opportunity for this second piece. A bias strip of velvet, 4 or 5 in. wide, is gathered on one side (the outside edge). It is joined to the lining by turning it inside out and sewing it a little within the bonnet. It is then turned back over the front of the frame and pleated at the opposite edge, and fastened down at the joining of the crown. This piece is, therefore, the binding and outside front covering in one.

A shirred satin lining is suitable for a bonnet of this kind; or the lining may be plain, or of velvet. The crown should be high, and laid in pleats at the sides, or treated like a cap crown and pleated all across. Another way is to have the strings, which should be very wide, cross the crown (which is then plain) with two or three pleats in the middle and at each side. A bunch of feathers or flowers on the top (or at the side) will complete the bonnet.

In finishing a bonnet, the back is turned under and slip stitched to the back of the crown lining. A milliner never sews on feathers or flowers, but pins them; and everything depends on putting them just in the right place.

A bonnet of thin material, such as tulle, crape, lace, etc., has an undercovering of the same material inferior in quality. A white frame is used when the covering is light, and a black one for black material.

A gift for trimming hats and bonnets is sometimes possessed by those who do not yet venture on their manufacture. When the article is of straw, this makes a great difference in the expense.

To be able to trim your own hats is a great convenience in traveling, if you like a variety. Some ladies always prepare for a journey by stripping their hats and bonnets of every particle of trimming, and telescoping the naked frames together to fill some spare corner. Feathers, flowers, and ribbons are carefully placed in a box by themselves. Half-a-dozen bonnets are carried without taking up more space than one would under ordinary circumstances. These ladies' headgear is never tumbled at the end of a trip, but emerges as fresh as if just from the milliner's hands.

Making a Cap. An old lady's cap is a useful thing to be able to make. Professional cap makers say that caps should be made on a block. But this is not necessary when a foundation of stiff bobbinet is used. A slight point and depression in front is generally becoming; but some prefer a perfectly straight edge. The frame, or foundation, is cut in two pieces. For an old lady, rather than an elderly one, the crown is round, and cut large enough to pleat down on the front. It is in forming this crown that the block is used; but the wearer's head may be substituted, or the size taken from the crown of an old cap. The front piece should be about 1/2 yd. long and 2 1/2 in. deep at the sides, while the point is 1 in. or more wide.

The outside covering is cut by the foundation, the latter taking the place of a lining. This foundation is neatly put together before the lace is arranged on it. Wash blonde is a very nice material for a cap of this description, which should have a thick ruching of the same around the edge and at the join of the front and crown. The latter is sometimes further embellished by two rows of ruching placed lengthwise. This ruching is less troublesome to make if a wide footing is used in place of the blonde, as in using the latter it is necessary to roll the edge. A whipped roll, done with black worsted, is sometimes used. The ruching is made in double box pleats—for which three times the length is needed—and attached to the cap by running it on the wrong side with moderately fine cotton.

A bow and ends of the cap material ornament the back. The finishing touch is a pair of wide strings (also of blonde) 1 yd. long, with a hem nearly 3/4 in. deep at the sides and ends. This hem is done with very fine cotton, and the stitches should not show.

This is, of course, a very simple cap. But it is a very suitable one, and not so plain as a straight band of tarlatan with broad strings, in which some very sweet aged faces have been framed. The materials can be varied with this shape, and white and black used in combination. More elaborate caps are made with differently shaped crowns, some long and narrow, and others very full—double white silk tulle, with lace, ribbon, and even flowers, being used for materials.

Caps for nurses, waitresses, etc., are made of cambric or jaconet muslin, sometimes with a large crown closely gathered at the bottom and finished with a bow and ends. The short front is pointed and trimmed with a fluted ruffle. Another shape is that of a half-handkerchief tied behind with a long-ended bow, and no crown. It will save trouble to buy a cap ready-made and use it for a guide.

Home Millinery

Making your bonnets is almost as great a convenience as making your dresses, and quite as great a saving. The lady who makes her own bonnets is constantly appearing in new ones. It is the fancy work of plain sewing, if such a contradiction is admissible, and is therefore a far more interesting employment than dressmaking.

Making a Bonnet Front. When a bonnet is formed of two parts—the front and the crown—the method of making it is as follows. Cut a paper pattern. Lay it on the willow or buckram, cutting it by the outline supplied. Sew wired chip round the outer edge of the front, the wire being anchored between it and the front. Bind all with a strip of soft silk or muslin, cut on the bias, to cover all unevennesses. Proceed to wire the inside of the front next to the head—the chip inside, the wire outside, and the willow foundation between them. The willow will project beyond the chip and wire. It must be snipped at regular intervals to make it expand at the edge, and turned up to fit better to the head or crown, which will afterward be attached to it. Lay a piece of thin muslin smoothly over the willow front. On this place the silk or satin material of the bonnet, so as to lie the straight way of the web. Pin it on carefully, that it may not be drawn on the bias. Then tack down the silk on the inside to the chip. In the same way line the front, finishing the edge by slip stitching, or else with a plain binding or a cord edge.

Making a Bonnet Crown. The crown of the bonnet must be made next, either plain or full. Cut it out of the willow or buckram from a paper pattern. Join the extreme ends, so as to fit the front made for it. The upper edge (if a plain crown) must be stiffened with a wire chip. Crowns with plain round tops may be procured ready-made. Cover the top with a flat piece of wadding or muslin. Lay the silk covering over it, and tack it down to the sides. Then cover the sides. Take care to place the join so that it will be concealed under some trimming. Otherwise finish it with a cord. Let the joining at the top, as well as of the side, be finished precisely as the edge of the front.

The next business is to sew the crown and front together. This constitutes one of the chief arts of the trade, all depending on the degree of slant given—either forward or backward—to the crown.

Full or fancy crowns must be made on a dummy head. They are first cut out of buckram to a pattern, then pleated on the dummy.

Making a Drawn Bonnet with Bones. The old-fashioned drawn bonnets are no longer seen, although the backs of fancy ones are sometimes gauged. The front when drawn was made of a length of material cut the straight way, the selvage going round the outer rim of the front. Then a wide hem was made. In this from three to five runnings were made, to form casings for the wires, canes, or whalebones to be introduced into them. A stiff wire was run into the outermost, the better to maintain the shape. Then the wires, canes, or whalebones were secured at one end, the gatherings evenly drawn, and the other ends of the stiffeners were sewn down. The crown was drawn in the same way, and the circular form obtained by fixing it to a wired chip.

Making Crape and Lightweight Bonnets. To make any description of light, transparent summer bonnet, such as crape, gauze, muslin, or net, employ a foundation of Paris net. This material is thin and brittle, and needs careful handling. Sew a narrow, white, wired chip round the edge of the front. Lay on the transparent covering (cut on the straight). Tack it in position. Bind the edge with satin, as likewise the chips and joinings of the crown. These may be equally well concealed by folds of satin instead of bindings.

Bonnets worn in mourning must be made of crape, or of silk trimmed with it. If of crape only, cover the willow foundation with thin black silk to conceal it, as black willow is brittle. Make a broad hem on the crape bow and strings; the double hem being about 1 in. wide.

Lace caps must be made on a foundation of stiff, coarse muslin or wired chip.

A. Apportioning Scales

24 cm 9 7/16 in.	25 cm 9 13/16 in.	26 cm 10 1/4 in.	27 cm 10 5/8 in.
1	1	1	1
2	2	2	2
3	3	3	3
4	4	4	4
5	5	5	5
6	6	6	6
7	7	7	7
8	8	8	8
9	9	9	9
0	0	0	0
1	1	1	1
2	2	2	2
3	3	3	3
4	4	4	4
5	5	5	5
6	6	6	6
7	7	7	7
8	8	8	8
9	9	9	9
0	0	0	0
1	1	1	1
2	2	2	2
3	3	3	3
4	4	4	4
5	5	5	5
6	6	6	6
7	7	7	7
8	8	8	8
9	9	9	9
0	0	0	0

28 cm 11 in.	29 cm 11 7/16 in.	30 cm 11 13/16 in.	31 cm 12 3/16 in.
1	1	1	1
2	2	2	2
3	3	3	3
4	4	4	4
5	5	5	5
6	6	6	6
7	7	7	7
8	8	8	8
9	9	9	9
0	0	0	0
1	1	1	1
2	2	2	2
3	3	3	3
4	4	4	4
5	5	5	5
6	6	6	6
7	7	7	7
8	8	8	8
9	9	9	9
0	0	0	0

507

32 cm 12 5/8 in.	33 cm 13 in.	34 cm 13 3/8 in.	35 cm 13 3/4 in.
1	1	1	1
2	2	2	2
3	3	3	3
4	4	4	4
5	5	5	5
6	6	6	6
7	7	7	7
8	8	8	8
9	9	9	9
0	0	0	0
1	1	1	1
2	2	2	2
3	3	3	3
4	4	4	4
5	5	5	5
6	6	6	6
7	7	7	7
8	8	8	8
9	9	9	9
0	0	0	0

508

 # Apportioning Scales

36 cm 14 3/16 in.	37 cm 14 9/16 in.	38 cm 14 15/16 in.	39 cm 15 3/8 in.
1	1	1	1
2	2	2	2
3	3	3	3
4	4	4	4
5	5	5	5
6	6	6	6
7	7	7	7
8	8	8	8
9	9	9	9
0	0	0	0
1	1	1	1
2	2	2	2
3	3	3	3
4	4	4	4
5	5	5	5
6	6	6	6
7	7	7	7
8	8	8	8
9	9	9	9
0	0	0	0

40 cm 15 3/4 in.	41 cm 16 1/8 in.	42 cm 16 9/16 in.	43 cm 16 15/16 in.
1	1	1	1
2	2	2	2
3	3	3	3
4	4	4	4
5	5	5	5
6	6	6	6
7	7	7	7
8	8	8	8
9	9	9	9
0	0	0	0
1	1	1	1
2	2	2	2
3	3	3	3
4	4	4	4
5	5	5	5
6	6	6	6
7	7	7	7
8	8	8	8
9	9	9	9
0	0	0	0

 # Apportioning Scales

44 cm 17 5/16 in.	45 cm 17 11/16 in.	46 cm 18 1/8 in.	47 cm 18 1/2 in.
1	1	1	1
2	2	2	2
3	3	3	3
4	4	4	4
5	5	5	5
6	6	6	6
7	7	7	7
8	8	8	8
9	9	9	9
0	0	0	0

48 cm 18 7/8 in.	49 cm 19 5/16 in.	50 cm 19 11/16 in.	51 cm 20 1/16 in.
1	1	1	1
2	2	2	2
3	3	3	3
4	4	4	4
5	5	5	5
6	6	6	6
7	7	7	7
8	8	8	8
9	9	9	9
0	0	0	0

Apportioning Scales

52 cm 20 1/2 in.	53 cm 20 7/8 in.	54 cm 21 1/4 in.	55 cm 21 5/8 in.
1	1	1	1
2	2	2	2
3	3	3	3
4	4	4	4
5	5	5	5
6	6	6	6
7	7	7	7
8	8	8	8
9	9	9	9
0	0	0	0

56 cm 22 1/16 in.	57 cm 22 7/16 in.	58 cm 22 13/16 in.	59 cm 23 1/4 in.
1	1	1	1
2	2	2	2
3	3	3	3
4	4	4	4
5	5	5	5
6	6	6	6
7	7	7	7
8	8	8	8
9	9	9	9
0	0	0	0

60 cm 23 5/8 in.	61 cm 24 in.	62 cm 24 7/16 in.	63 cm 24 13/16 in.
1	1	1	1
2	2	2	2
3	3	3	3
4	4	4	4
5	5	5	5
6	6	6	6
7	7	7	7
8	8	8	8
9	9	9	9
0	0	0	0

515

64 cm 25 3/16 in.	65 cm 25 9/16 in.	66 cm 26 in.
1	1	1
2	2	2
3	3	3
4	4	4
5	5	5
6	6	6
7	7	7
8	8	8
9	9	9
0	0	0

B. Metric Conversion Table

English Measurement	Metric Equivalent	Metric Measurement	English Equivalent
1/8 in.	3.2 mm	1 mm	1/32 in.
1/4 in.	6.4 mm	2 mm	1/16 in.
3/8 in.	9.5 mm	3 mm	1/8 in.
1/2 in.	1.3 cm	4 mm	5/32 in.
5/8 in.	1.6 cm	5 mm	7/32 in.
3/4 in.	1.9 cm	6 mm	1/4 in.
7/8 in.	2.2 cm	7 mm	9/32 in.
1 in.	2.5 cm	8 mm	5/16 in.
1 1/4 in.	3.2 cm	9 mm	11/32 in.
1 1/2 in.	3.8 cm	10 mm (1 cm)	13/32 in.
1 3/4 in.	4.4 cm	2 cm	3/4 in.
2 in.	5.1 cm	3 cm	1 3/16 in.
2 1/4 in.	5.7 cm	4 cm	1 9/16 in.
2 1/2 in.	6.4 cm	5 cm	2 in.
2 3/4 in.	7.0 cm	6 cm	2 3/8 in.
3 in.	7.6 cm	7 cm	2 3/4 in.
3 1/4 in.	8.3 cm	8 cm	3 1/8 in.
3 1/2 in.	8.9 cm	9 cm	3 1/2 in.
3 3/4 in.	9.5 cm	10 cm	3 15/16 in.
4 in.	10.2 cm	15 cm	5 7/8 in.
4 1/2 in.	11.4 cm	20 cm	7 7/8 in.
5 in.	12.7 cm	25 cm	9 13/16 in.
5 1/2 in.	14.0 cm	30 cm	11 13/16 in.

English Measurement	Metric Equivalent	Metric Measurement	English Equivalent
6 in.	15.2 cm	35 cm	13 3/4 in.
6 1/2 in.	16.5 cm	40 cm	15 3/4 in.
7 in.	17.8 cm	45 cm	17 11/16 in.
7 1/2 in.	19.1 cm	50 cm	19 11/16 in.
8 in.	20.3 cm	55 cm	21 5/8 in.
8 1/2 in.	21.6 cm	60 cm	23 5/8 in.
9 in. (1/4 yd.)	22.9 cm	65 cm	25 9/16 in.
9 1/2 in.	24.1 cm	70 cm	27 9/16 in.
10 in.	25.4 cm	75 cm	29 1/2 in.
10 1/2 in.	26.7 cm	80 cm	31 1/2 in.
11 in.	27.9 cm	85 cm	33 7/16 in.
11 1/2 in.	29.2 cm	90 cm	35 7/16 in.
12 in. (1 ft.)	30.5 cm	95 cm	37 3/8 in.
1/2 yd. (18 in.)	45.7 cm	100 cm (1 m)	39 3/8 in.
3/4 yd. (27 in.)	68.6 cm	1.25 m	1 yd. 13 3/16 in.
1 yd. (36 in.)	91.4 cm	1.50 m	1 yd. 23 1/16 in.
1 1/4 yd.	1.14 m	1.75 m	1 yd. 32 7/8 in.
1 1/2 yd.	1.37 m	2.00 m	2 yd. 6 3/4 in.
1 3/4 yd.	1.60 m	2.50 m	2 yd. 26 7/16 in.
2 yd.	1.83 m	3.00 m	3 yd. 10 1/8 in.
2 1/2 yd.	2.29 m	3.50 m	3 yd. 29 13/16 in.
3 yd.	2.74 m	4.00 m	4 yd. 13 1/2 in.
3 1/2 yd.	3.20 m	4.50 m	4 yd. 33 3/16 in.
4 yd.	3.66 m	5.00 m	5 yd. 16 7/8 in.
4 1/2 yd.	4.11 m	5.50 m	6 yd. 9/16 in.
5 yd.	4.57 m	6.00 m	6 yd. 20 1/4 in.
5 1/2 yd.	5.03 m	6.50 m	7 yd. 3 7/8 in.
6 yd.	5.49 m	7.00 m	7 yd. 23 9/16 in.
6 1/2 yd.	5.94 m	7.50 m	8 yd. 7 1/4 in.
7 yd.	6.40 m	8.00 m	8 yd. 26 15/16 in.
7 1/2 yd.	6.86 m	8.50 m	9 yd. 10 5/8 in.
8 yd.	7.32 m	9.00 m	9 yd. 30 5/16 in.

 # C. Glossary

Definitions of fashion and textile terms change over time. The information used to write these was drawn from late 19th-century sources wherever possible.

Agrafe: A clasp, or a gimp fastening.

Alençon lace: A needlepoint lace with solid designs outlined with cord.

Alpaca: The wooly hair of an animal of the camel tribe. Usually mixed with silk or cotton to produce a thin, shiny dress fabric.

Alsatian bow: A term used in millinery to describe a large, flat bow, the loops and ends of even length on each side.

Arabesque: Fanciful ornamentation, copied from Arabian decorations, consisting of figures, lines, animals, and sometimes human beings combined in relief.

Astrakhan fur: The pelts from young lambs reared in Astrakhan, dyed black. Imitations are also made for trimmings.

Aumônière: A small bag carried in the Middle Ages and Renaissance. It hung from the belt or girdle.

Balayeuse: The frilling of material or lace that lines the extreme edge of a dress skirt to keep the train clean. It is allowed to project beyond the edge of the dress, to form a decorative trimming.

Balbriggan: Knit hosiery or underwear of unbleached cotton fiber.

Balmoral skirt: A cheap, but strong and heavy, cotton underskirt.

Barbe: A lace streamer or long lace tie.

Barege: A kind of gauze, composed of silk and wool, or of wool only. Cheap sorts are made with a cotton warp.

Bashlyk: A hood with long ends that are wrapped around the neck like a scarf.

Basket weave: A style of weaving that produces a pattern resembling the plaited work of a basket.

Basque: A short-skirted dress bodice or jacket. Or, the part of the bodice below the waist. It may be cut in one piece with the bodice. Or it may be added to it, either all in one piece or divided.

Batiste: A fine linen muslin made in various colors. It is used for dresses, dress linings, and trimmings.

Beaver cloth: A stout make of woolen cloth, twilled and compact, with only one face shorn.

Beige: Beige is made of undyed wool. It is an extremely soft textile, graceful in draping.

Belt: A belt may be made of leather, ribbon, silk, satin, or velvet. It may be made of the dress material, in which case it must be stiffened with buckram or stiff linen. It is fastened by a band, rosette, or buckle. The word "belt" is often used for the waistband.

Bertha: A collar resembling a cape, often made of lace.

Blonde lace: A general term for white and black pillow laces made with a network ground. The patterns are generally heavy—thick flowers joined together with a wide meshed ground.

Blouse: A loose-fitting dress bodice.

Bobbinet: A machine-made cotton netting.

Bolton sheeting: Otherwise workhouse sheeting.

Bourette: An effect in weaving that throws fancy yarns into knots or knobs that form designs or appear at regular intervals.

Bretelles: Ornamental shoulder straps.

Breton lace: An embroidered net. It can be worked in colored silks or floss, and the foundation made of colored net. Or it may be fabricated of Brussels net and cream-colored lace thread.

Broadcloth: The stoutest and best description of woolen cloth. It has a slightly napped face and a twilled back.

Brocade: A fabric woven of any material with a pattern of raised figures.

Broché: A velvet or silk textile with a satin figure thrown up on the face.

Brussels net: The best type of net that is made.

Buff: A light brownish yellow.

Bulgare pleat: A double box pleat, employed at the back of a dress skirt at the waistband, to produce an extra fullness.

Bunting: A thin, open-made kind of worsted stuff.

Busk: A broad flat steel employed to stiffen the front of a corset.

Bustle: An arrangement of puffed-out crinoline, or wire, worn to distend the back of the skirt from the waist.

Buttonhole twist: A strong, tightly twisted thread employed to bind and strengthen buttonholes in cloth stuffs.

Cabriolet: Shaped like a carriage top.

Cachemire: A name given to woven designs resembling Persian patterns.

Calico: A cotton fabric, which varies from coarse cloth to the finest muslin, and from the richest printed chintz to plain white.

Cambric: A beautiful and delicate linen textile. There is also a cheap cotton fabric manufactured for dress linings.

Camel's hair cloth: This material is thick, warm, light, and has a fine gloss. It is unshaved, and the long hairs are of a paler color than the close substance of the cloth. Camel's hair is often mixed with wool or cotton.

Camisole: A loose jacket; applied to dressing and morning jackets.

Canary yellow: A brilliant, slightly reddish yellow.

Canton flannel: A cotton cloth napped heavily on one side, used chiefly for undergarments.

Capote: A hooded cloak worn by soldiers and sailors; a long, loose mantle. Also a head covering.

Cap springs: These appliances are made of steel, in either round or flat form.

Carrick cape: A cape with one or several shoulder capes.

Casaque: A long, mantlelike garment.

Cashmere: A soft twilled cloth, made of the wool of the Thibet goat, mixed with sheep's wool. Other varieties are made entirely of sheep's wool, or of Angora rabbit fur.

Cashmere shawl: An expensive shawl made from the soft, fine hair of the cashmere goat of India, woven in figures or embroidered.

Chamois leather: The skin of the Alpine goat of that name. Used for riding breeches, undervests, and other garments, which are perforated to make them more wholesome wear.

Changeable: A textile may be made to change in color according to the different positions in which it is viewed. This is effected by using a weft of a different color than the warp.

Chatelaine: A chain fastened to the belt that supports such objects as a fan, vinaigrette, ball tablets, etc.

Cheesecloth: Thin, limp, loose-woven muslin, bleached or brown.

Chemise: A loose undershirt of linen, longcloth, calico, or silk.

Chemisette: A plain or ornamental underbodice, with fronts and backs unconnected at the sides.

Chenille: A type of cord used for embroidery and decorative purposes. The name means "caterpillar" in French, and denotes the hairy appearance of the material. Chenille is made of silk, of silk and wool, and of wool only.

Cheviot cloth: A rough description of cloth, twilled, and coarser than homespun.

Chignon: A hairpiece arranged in braids or coils and worn at the back of the head.

China crape: Thicker in texture than ordinary crape, remarkably fine, but weighty in substance. It is made in white and various colors.

Chiné: A term applied to fabrics in which the warp is dyed different colors at short distances, so that a mottled effect is produced; or in which a double thread, formed of two smaller threads of different colors twisted together, is used to produced a mottled or speckled appearance.

Chintz: A printed calico, in which several different colors are applied to small designs, and printed on a white or yellow ground, highly glazed.

Chip: Wood split into thin filaments, for bonnets.

Circular: A cape with a wide flare, cut from a circle or near-circle of cloth.

Clair de lune: A color that varies from pale greenish blue to lavender-gray.

Claret color: Deep red; wine color.

Cloak: Properly a loose outer garment without sleeves. At present, however, the term is used for any ladies' sleeved wrap, long or short.

Clocks: Ornamental embroidered finishes to the leg and instep of stockings and socks. They are worked with filoselle or washing silk of a color that either matches or contrasts with the stocking.

Cloth: A woolen cloth of several descriptions. Also a generic term applied equally to linen and cotton.

Coat sleeve: A two-piece sleeve that comprises an underam and an upper piece. Used for dresses and other garments as well as coats.

Cocarde: Rosette or knot of ribbon, often pleated, with ends extending; a cockade. Used to trim hats.

Coiffure: A headdress; manner of dressing the hair.

Combination: An item of underwear that combines two or more garments in one.

Cordelière: A knotted cord.

Cordon: A decorative lace, cord, or braid.

Corsage: Bodice.

Costume: Complete dress.

Coutil: A type of jean used for corsets. It has a small woven pattern, like chevrons or zigzags.

Crape or crepe: A delicate transparent crimped gauze, made of silk, silk and cotton, or cotton only. It may be had crisped and smooth, with or without a twill, and in white, black, and colors.

Crepe de chine: An extremely thin and highly lustrous crepe dress silk.

Crepe lisse: A thin description of crepe, like gauze. It may be had in white, cream, and other colors.

Crevecouer: A lock worn at the nape of the neck.

Crinoline: A stiff material woven of horsehair and linen, or of cotton. Also a hoopskirt.

Crinoline steels: Flat narrow bands of steel covered with a web woven upon them.

Cuirass basque: A close-fitting, long-waisted bodice.

Damassé: Woven with a rich pattern, as of flowers or large running figures.

Darned net: A lace with designs worked on a net ground with a needle handled as if in darning. It can be worked with fine lace thread, with colored purse silks, or with floss and filoselles, upon white, colored, or black net.

Dead gold: Unburnished, lusterless gold.

Dimity: A stout cotton fabric with a raised pattern. It may be striped or cross-barred, plain or twilled.

Directoire styles: Imitations of the styles of the French Directory, from 1795 to 1799.

Dolman: A style of ladies' wrap, in various lengths, and characterized by a hanging piece over the arm instead of a sleeve.

Drab: A dull brownish gray.

Drap d'été: A fine worsted goods for summer wear.

Drape: The decorative arrangement of folds.

Drilling: A stout twilled material of either cotton or linen, used for bodice linings, underwear, pockets, etc. Found in all colors.

Duster: A light outer garment worn to protect the clothing from dust.

Ecru: Having the color of unbleached silk or linen, hence by extension any similar shade. Much lace is sold of this color, a hue that may be more fully described as café au lait.

Elastic webbing: Garters, belts, and ribbons used for articles of women's dress, boot elastics, etc. It is made in bands from 1 to 12 in. wide. The warp of this textile is made of square threads of India rubber. The weft covering it is made of silk, cotton, mohair, or worsted thread.

Embossed velvet: Velvet with designs raised in relief, by shearing the pile to different levels or pressing parts flat.

Façon: Fashion or cut.

Faille: A soft, ribbed dress silk distinguished by a prominent grain or cord extending from selvage to selvage.

Fichu: Any small covering for the shoulders.

Filoselle: A loose, slackly twisted silk thread used in art needlework.

Flannel: A woolen stuff, loosely woven. To be had in various makes–heavy and plain, twilled and light, white and colored. The pile may be raised on one or both sides.

Floss silk: A soft, fluffy, untwisted embroidery silk.

Fly: A strip of material sewn under the edge of a dress, or coat, at the bottom side of the opening, extending sufficiently far beyond it to underline the buttonholes at their extreme ends. The fly thus conceals the clothing under the coat or bodice.

Folds: The draping produced by pleating or gathering a skirt waist. Also flat pleats on any part of a skirt, bodice, or sleeve, secured at each end to the dress to keep them in place. Also the doubling of any cloth so that one part lies over the other.

Foulard: A soft, thin washable dress silk, woven without twill. It is generally printed in colors on black or white grounds.

Foundation muslin: A very coarse description of muslin, of very open make, and stiffened with gum. It is employed for stiffening dresses, and may be had in black and white.

Foundation net: A coarse quality of net, made in large meshes, gummed and used for stiff foundations in millinery and dressmaking. It is to be had in black and white.

Fox: To cover the upper of a shoe with ornamental leather.

French cambric: A very superior quality of cambric, fine in quality and very silky in appearance.

French gray: A light greenish gray.

French lace: All laces of French manufacture.

French merino: A merino with an exceedingly fine twill. It is to be had in all colors.

Frieze: A thick, heavy woolen cloth with a nap on one side.

Frizette: Fringe or bangs, often curled, worn on the forehead.

Froufrou: Dress trimmings, such as ruffles or lace.

Gaiter: A leather or cloth shoe covering the ankle. Also a protective covering for the ankle and leg fastening at the side and held down by a strap under the instep. This is usually made of heavy cloth, felt, or canvas.

Galloon: One type is a narrow ribbon of wool, silk, or cotton combined with silk or worsted, used to trim and bind articles of dress, hats, shoes, and furniture. Another type is a strong, thick, gold or silver lace with an even selvage at each side.

Garniture: Trimmings.

Gauze: A delicate, transparent textile, of a gossamer appearance, woven of silk, silk and cotton, or silk and linen. The several kinds are plain made, brocaded, or spotted, the designs being composed of silk, or else striped with satin and velvet.

Gendarme blue: A greenish blue.

Gilet: French term for "waistcoat." Gilets are sometimes made separately from the bodice, but are as often merely simulated, the central portion of the bodice front being bordered to look like a separate article.

Gimp: An openwork trimming. It is made of silk, worsted, or cotton twist, having a cord or a wire running through it. The strands are plaited or twisted to form a pattern.

Gingham: A checked or striped cloth made of cotton or linen, the threads dyed in the yarn.

Gore: A piece of any material, cut somewhat wedge shaped, wider at one end than the other. It is let into a skirt, or any part of a garment, to increase the width more at one end.

Gray goods: Undyed, unbleached fabric.

Grenadine: An open silk, or silk and wool textile. It is made both plain and figured.

Gros de Naples: A thick silk somewhat similar to lustring, but less stout. It is made both plain and figured, in various qualities, and colored.

Grosgrain: A firm, close-woven, finely corded or grained dress silk, finished with but a slight luster.

Guimpe: A chemisette to be worn with a low-cut dress, with or without sleeves.

Guipure lace: This name is applied to all laces having large patterns and coarse, open grounds not filled with delicate work.

Hamburg: A kind of cotton embroidery worked on cambric, used as an edging or trimming.

Holland: An unbleached linen.

Homespun cloth: A coarse and rather loosely woven woolen material, often woven by machine.

Illusion: A thin and very transparent silk tulle.

Insertion: Strips of lace, or embroidered muslin or cambric, with straight edges.

Invisible green: A dark bluish green.

Jabot: Frilling of lace worn on the front of a bodice.

Jaconet: A thin, yet close cotton textile, thicker than muslin and slighter than cambric.

Jean: A twilled cotton cloth.

Kilt pleating: Flat single pleats placed closely side by side, so that the double edge of the pleat on the upper side lies half over the preceding pleat on the inside.

Lady's cloth: A class of fine, wide flannels slightly napped, used for ladies' light wraps and dresses.

Lappet: A free-hanging or overlapping part of a headdress or garment.

Lasting: A strong and durable worsted fabric. It is used for covering buttons, for the uppers of women's shoes, and for gaiters. It is woven either with a double twill or a satin twill. It is usually black, but may be obtained in other colors.

Lawn: A delicate linen. Some cloths called lawns are really muslins made of cotton.

Leno: A very thin linen cloth that imitates muslin. It is much stiffened.

Lingerie: Used collectively to describe all the linen, cotton, silk, and lace articles of women's underwear, such as the corset, undervest, drawers, chemise, petticoats, nightdress, hose, garters, collar, cuffs, cravat, etc.

Lisle thread: An extremely fine and hard-twisted linen thread. Used especially for knitting gloves and stockings.

Llama lace: A woolen machine lace.

Longcloth: A kind of calico of a fine texture. The surface is smooth, all the short filaments being removed. It is used for undergarments.

Lorgnette: Folding eyeglasses or opera glasses on long ornamental handle.

Louis XV heel: A heel with a curved outline, flared at the base, and placed slightly forward under the foot.

Louisine: A very thin plain silk material. It is to be had in all colors, and also woven in small checks and stripes.

Lustring: A very fine corded glossy silk fabric.

MacFarlane: An outer coat with separate capes and side slits allowing the hands to reach inner pockets.

Madeira embroidery: A fine hand embroidery with round eyelets and simple floral and foliage designs.

Madras handkerchief: A large handkerchief of silk and cotton, usually in bright colors.

Maize: A soft yellow.

Malines lace: A fine silk net.

Manila: A light yellowish brown. Also a fibrous material obtained from the leaves and stalks of a hemp plant that grows in the Philippines, and used for making hats.

Mandarin yellow: Orange or reddish yellow.

Mantelet: A small cloak or mantle.

Mantilla: A head covering of lace, falling on the shoulders and sometimes used as a veil. Also a light cloak or cape.

Mantle: An outer garment somewhat resembling a short cloak. It differs in being slightly fitted to the figure, and in having either a loose frilling over the elbows, where the arms protrude from under it, or sometimes a very short sleeve commencing from the elbow.

Marabou: A thin silk, very fine in quality, of which fancy scarves are made, having a white center and colored borders.

Marabou feathers: These are procured from a species of stork. They may be had white, gray, or dyed. They are employed as plumes for headdresses and bonnets, and as trimmings for dresses, fans, and muffs.

Marguerite: Daisy.

Marseilles: A stiff corded cotton fabric. The raised cord extends from side to side of the web.

Mastic: A light olive brown.

Matelassé: A silk or woolen textile with a raised figured or flowered design, having a quilted appearance. Those of silk are made in white and in colors, and are much used for opera cloaks.

Matinee: Dressing gown.

Mechlin lace: A fine, transparent lace, with the patterns outlined by a very narrow flat cord.

Merino: A thin woolen twilled cloth.

Mignardise: A fancy braid incorporated into crocheted lace.

Mohair: Fabrics composed of the hair of the Angora goat, mixed with silk or cotton warps. These fabrics have a luster equal to that of silk, are remarkably regular in texture, and are soft and fine.

Moiré: A wavy undulating effect produced on the surface of textiles by wetting, crumpling, and great pressure.

Moiré antique: A superior silk, stouter than ordinary, with a "watered" effect. Some inferior kinds have cotton backs.

Morocco leather: This leather is made from goatskins tanned with sumac. It combines great firmness of texture with flexibility, and a grained surface produced by an embossing process. The term is also used to describe fine lightweight leather in imitation of the above, made of sheep-, lamb-, and kidskins as well as goat.

Mousquetaire: A style of ladies' kid glove, distinguished by its long loose top and a lengthwise slit at the wrist.

Mousseline: French for muslin.

Mull: A very thin and soft variety of muslin.

Muslin: A thin and more or less transparent cotton fabric.

Nainsook: A description of muslin made both plain and striped, the stripes running the way of the warp.

Negligee: An informal robe for home wear.

Net: An open textile fabric of cotton, linen, hemp, silk, or other material, tied and woven with a mesh of any size.

Newmarket: A tight-fitting ladies' cloak, the skirt reaching quite to the ground.

Nile green: A yellowish green.

Nun's veiling: A wide untwilled woolen dress fabric, very soft, fine, and thin. It is dyed black, white, and in colors.

Oatmeal cloth: Under this descriptive name there are textiles of cotton, linen, and wool, with a corrugated face. These cloths are thick, soft, and pliant and may be had in all colors. Some varieties are employed as a foundation for embroidery in crewels and silks.

Oiled silk: Silk made waterproof by saturation in oil. It is semitransparent. It is much used in dressmaking to prevent perspiration from passing through, as at the armpits of garments and bonnet linings.

On the cross: On the bias.

Organdy: A fine variety of white goods, woven plain, cross-barred, striped, and printed with figures.

Oriental lace: Machine embroidery on machine net with coarse, soft thread.

Ottoman silk: A fine, soft undressed silk dress fabric, woven in large cords, extending from selvage to selvage.

Paletot: A loose overcoat.

Pannier: A description of puffed overskirt. Also a bustle.

Paramatta: A kind of bombazine, the weft of which is of worsted, and the warp of cotton. It is employed as a dress material for mourning.

Parement: A cuff sewn upon the outside of a sleeve.

Parure: A set of collars and cuffs, or a set of jewelry or ornaments.

Passementerie: Heavy embroidery or lace edgings and trimmings, especially those made of gimp and braid, or covered with beads and silk.

Pearl button: A button made of mother-of-pearl.

Peignoir: Dressing gown; dressing jacket.

Pelerine: A small mantle, rounded like a cape.

Percale: A very closely and firmly woven cotton fabric. It is printed in fancy patterns on white and colored grounds.

Picots: Little loops and bobs that ornament needle made laces of all kinds, and are often introduced into embroidery.

Piqué: A washable cotton material, woven with a small pattern in relief, usually a lozenge, cord, or rib. It may be had in many qualities, thin and thick. There are colored and figured varieties.

Plastron: A trimming for a dress front, of a different material. It may extend to the waist or to the hem.

Platina: Platinum. Also a pale bluish gray.

Plissé: Pleating.

Plush: A shaggy, hairy kind of silk or cotton cloth. It is sometimes made of camel's or goat's hair. The pile is softer and longer than that of velvet, and resembles fur.

Point d'esprit lace: Net or tulle with dots.

Pointillé: Dotted with small spots or polka dots.

Polonaise: A shorter version of the princess dress, worn over a skirt.

Pompadour basque: Bodice with a low square neckline.

Pompadour patterns: Small floral designs in delicate tints of pink and blue.

Pompon: A fluffy ball of silk or wool, used to trim bonnets and hats.

Pongee: A thin, soft, washable silk fabric, woven from the natural, uncolored silk.

Poplin: A kind of rep made of silk and wool or worsted, having a fine cord on the surface. It is produced brocaded, watered, and plain.

Porte-monnaie: Purse.

Postilion: An extension of the back pieces of a basque or jacket, or extra tabs set on at the back.

Pouf: A puffing of any material, used to ornament a dress or other garment.

Princess: A long, close-fitting gown with no waist seam.

Psyche knot: A hairstyle with a chignon at the back of the neck.

Quadrillé: A design showing a succession of small squares.

Redingote: Polonaise or long coat, with long straight basques open in front.

Renaissance embroidery: Cutwork embroidery.

Rep: This textile may be of silk, silk and wool, or wool only. It has a thick cord. There are figured kinds. Silk rep is used for dresses.

Reseda: A grayish to dark grayish green.

Reticule: A bag, of any material, carried in the hand or on the arm, and answering the purpose of a pocket.

Retroussé: Turned up or tucked up.

Revers: A part of the dress reversed, or turned back, such as a lapel, cuff, or corner of a basque. May show a lining of a contrasting color or material.

Roman stripes: A cloth of any fiber with vivid horizontal stripes in different widths.

Rosette: A collection of bows of narrow ribbon, arranged to form a circle, and attached to a circular foundation of stiff, coarse muslin or buckram.

Ruching: A pleating or shirring of net, lace, ribbon, or other light material into bands that are worn in the necks and wrists of garments and the facings of bonnets.

Running string: Drawstring.

Russian braid: Made respectively in two materials—mohair and silk. The former consists of two cords woven together. The silk is a braid of similar make, designed for embroidery work.

Russian embroidery: Embroidery in simple and formal patterns, especially on washable materials.

Russian lace: All laces of Russian manufacture. Much of the native designing contains colored tapes and threads.

Sacque or sack: A loose jacket or coat with sleeves.

Sarcenet: A thin silk that can be obtained either plain or twilled, and in several colors. It is used for linings, being fine and very soft.

Sarcenet ribbon: This is much like piece sarcenet of superior quality.

Sateen: A twilled cotton textile of satin make, glossy, thick, and strong. It is employed for corsets, dresses, and boots. It can be procured in black and white, various colors, and figured in many color combinations.

Satin: A silk twill, very glossy on the face, and dull at the back. Some satins are figured and brocaded.

Satin de Lyons: This satin has a grosgrain back in lieu of a twill.

Satin duchesse: A thick, plain satin, exceedingly durable. It is to be had in all colors.

Satin merveilleux: A twilled satin textile, of an exceedingly soft and pliable character, and having but little gloss.

Scarf: A band or strip of fabric.

Sealskin cloth: A variety of cloaking made of the finest kind of mohair, and dyed exactly the shade of the real fur.

Serge: A loosely woven, very durable twilled material. It may be had in either silk or wool. Wool serge may be rough on one or both sides of the cloth, or smooth on both sides. Serge is dyed in every color, besides being sold in white and black.

Serpentine braid: So called from its resemblance to the winding or sinuous motion of a serpent.

Sewing cotton: Cotton thread, which may be had on reels or balls, in every variety of color, glazed or unglazed.

Sewing silk: Of silk thread there are three classes—that for plain sewing, that for knitting, and that for embroidery.

Shells: Trimming arranged to form scallops.

Shirting: A cotton cloth used for shirts, dresses, and women's collars and cuffs. Shirtings may be had in stripes and fancy designs in various colors.

Sicilienne: A description of fine poplin, made of silk and wool, and especially used for mantles.

Silesia: A thin undyed linen, used for linings.

Silk sealskin: A heavy cloth with a pile of tussah silk, made in imitation of sealskin fur. It is dyed brown or golden color. It is designed for mantles, jackets, hats, and trimmings.

Skirt: The part of the garment below the waist. Also a petticoat. Also the edge of any part of the dress, border, margin, extreme part.

Skirt braids: These are made of alpaca and mohair. They are cut into lengths of sufficient quantity for a dress, and tied up for sale in knots.

Slate: Gray, usually a slightly bluish gray.

Snowflake cloth: A woolen cloth with small knots on the face that have the appearance, when white or light-colored, of a sprinkling of snow.

Soutache braid: A very narrow silk braid, available in several widths, and having an openwork center. It is produced in many colors, and employed for embroidery and the braiding of dresses, mantles, etc. It is also known as Russian braid.

Spanish embroidery: Executed for washing purposes on mull muslin with darning cotton, and for dress trimmings on black or colored net with filoselles. It consists of filling in the pattern with lines of herringbone stitches.

Spanish flounce: A deep gathered flounce joined to the edge of a short skirt.

Spanish lace: The most celebrated Spanish laces are the gold and silver laces known as point d'Espagne, the blonde laces, and the Spanish or rose points.

Spoon busk: Or spoonbill; a busk that widens below the waist.

Squirrel lock fur: The portion of the gray squirrel's fur that grows on the belly. It is yellowish white. Being cut out with a bordering of the gray fur of the back, it has a pretty variegated appearance when made up.

Stays: Corsets. Also boning in a bodice.

Surah: A fine soft twilled silk, employed for dresses. It is to be had in silver-gray and white, and various delicate colors.

Surplice effect: A bodice that overlaps diagonally in front.

Surtout: A coat with long skirts.

Swansdown: The soft, white, fluffy feathers of the breast of the white swan. Used for boas, ruffs, muffs, and trimmings for opera cloaks.

Swiss embroidery: A variety of needlework in white cotton on fine white linen or muslin.

Swiss muslin: A thin, transparent fabric, woven rather open, with simple patterns of dots, stripes, or sprigs.

Tablier: Part of a dress resembling an apron.

Tabs: A square-cut, loosely hanging border trimming of a bodice or skirt. It consists of regular cuts 1, 2, or 3 in. deep. The three raw edges of each square of material are bound, usually with the same material cut bias. Tabs are sometimes made on flounces.

Tacking: Basting.

Taffeta: A thin, glossy silk, of a wavy luster. It is to be had in all colors, some plain, others striped, checked, or flowered.

Tailor's twist: A coarse silk sewing thread.

Tape: A narrow, stout strip of woven cotton or linen, used for innumerable purposes.

Tarlatan: A thin gauzelike muslin, much stiffened. It may be had in various colors, and is much used for evening dresses.

Terracotta: Reddish orange.

Terry velvet: A textile made entirely of silk, and having fine cords or ribs on the best side. Inferior kinds have a cotton back. It has no nap or pile. When used as a trimming it is cut on the bias.

Thread lace: Made of linen as distinguished from cotton and silk.

Tilleul: A pale greenish yellow.

Toilette: A dress or costume.

Torchon lace: A simple thread lace with geometric patterns. Much of it is made by machinery.

Torsade: A twisted length of hair.

Tortoiseshell: The horny scales or plates on the outer shell of certain sea turtles. These are naturally of a beautiful mottled or clouded color. Tortoiseshell is largely imitated in horn and in artificial compounds.

Tournure: A bustle. Also the general appearance of a dress, costume, or person.

Tulle: A fine silk net, used for bonnets, veils, and dress trimmings. It may be had in black and white, and every color. It is made with spots of different sizes, and varying in closeness to each other; also plain.

Tunic: An overskirt that is shorter than the skirt.

Turquoise silk: This silk is slight in substance and has a very small rib. Used for bonnet linings.

Tussah: A "raw" silk, plain made, without any cord or woven pattern, although some are stamped or printed. It is very suitable for summer costumes, and will bear both cleaning and washing.

Tweed: A twilled woolen cloth. It is soft, flexible, and durable.

Twill: A weave of any fiber, where the weft threads pass over two and under one, or over three or more warp threads. Many different patterns or surfaces can be produced by changing the order of passing the weft.

Ulster: A loose overcoat, the breadths of which are cut straight, and confined by a belt of the same material. Ulsters are well furnished with pockets, and sometimes have either a hood or a cape of the same stuff.

Underskirt: An inner skirt beneath the dress skirt. Also a petticoat. Also the main skirt over which an overskirt or other drapery may be arranged.

Valenciennes lace: A narrow, cotton or linen lace.

Vandyked: A series of pointed forms cut out as a decorative border or trimming.

Velvet: A closely woven silk that has a very thick, short pile or nap on the right side. Inferior sorts are made with a cotton back.

Velveteen: Cotton velvet.

Venetian embroidery: Embroidery on linen in which the spaces between the figures are cut away and then joined by threads, giving a lacelike appearance.

Vest: A waistcoat, a part in the front of a bodice that simulates a waistcoat, or a knit undershirt.

Vigogne: A delicate wool textile, twilled, and produced in neutral colors—grays, lavenders, and steel—as well as black. It is very suitable as a summer dress material.

Vinaigrette: A small ornamental bottle to hold smelling salts.

Wadding: Carded cotton wool. It is available bleached, unbleached, slate colored, and black, cut into sheets of various sizes. It is placed between the outer material and the lining of any garment.

Waist: A garment covering the waist or trunk; the bodice of a dress, whether separate from the skirt or joined to it; a corsage; a basque; a blouse. Also the waistline.

Wash blonde: A species of narrow bobbinet or Brussels net, suitable for quillings.

Wash leather: An imitation of chamois leather, made of split sheepskin, from which gloves and linings for waistcoats, bodices, and petticoats are produced.

Waterproofed fabrics: An extensive variety of textiles rendered impervious to moisture, without being injured in texture or color. They may be had in thick and thin woolen cloths, in silk and alpaca.

Watteau pleat: An arrangement of the back of a woman's dress in which broad pleats or folds hang from the neck to the bottom of the skirt without interruption.

Wigan: A very coarse and heavy sized cotton cloth, used to line the bottom of ladies' dresses, to make them keep the shape desired.

Workhouse sheeting: A coarse, twilled, and unbleached cotton cloth, much used for embroidery.

Wrapper: A loose, one-piece house dress.

Zephyr ginghams or prints: These are delicate textiles, resembling cotton batiste, and produced in pink and blue.

Zephyr yarn: Manufactured for knitting and embroidery. It is to be had in two sizes, the single and the double. It is very evenly twisted, smooth and soft.

D. References

The bibliography lists (mostly antique) books, periodicals, and booklets from which I drew text, fashion illustrations, and patterns. The "further reading" section lists (mostly modern) books that contain additional historical information, period fashion illustrations and photos, and photos of surviving period garments.

Bibliography

Caulfeild, Sophia Frances Anne and Blanche C. Saward. *The Dictionary of Needlework: An Encyclopaedia of Artistic, Plain and Fancy Needlework.* 1882. Reprint, Arno Press: 1972.

Charles J. Peterson. *Peterson's Ladies National Magazine,* Vol. 72. Philadelphia: Charles J. Peterson, 1877.

Charles J. Peterson. *Peterson's Ladies National Magazine,* Vols. 75–76. Philadelphia: Charles J. Peterson, 1879.

Christner, Prof. D. C. *The International Encyclopedia of Scientific Tailor Principles . . . .* Philadelphia: Samuel M. Larzelere, 1885.

Church, Ella Rodman. *The Home Needle.* New York: D. Appleton & Co., 1882.

Demorest, Mme. *What to Wear and How to Make It.* New York: W. Jennings Demorest, Autumn/ Winter 1878–1879.

Doughty & Co. *Doughty's New Standard Work on Garment Cutting and Dress-Making.* Cincinnati: Doughty & Co., 1887.

Duffey, Mrs. E. B. *The Ladies' and Gentlemen's Etiquette: A Complete Manual of the Manners and Dress of American Society.* Philadelphia: Henry T. Coates & Co., 1877.

Frost, S. Annie. *The Ladies' Guide to Needle Work: Being a Complete Guide to All Types of Ladies' Fancy Work.* 1877. Reprint, Washington: R. L. Shep, 1986.

Grimble, Frances. *After a Fashion: How to Reproduce, Restore, and Wear Vintage Styles,* 2nd ed. San Francisco: Lavolta Press, 1998.

Harper & Bros. *Harper's Bazar,* Vol. 10. New York: Harper & Bros., 1877.

Harper & Bros. *Harper's Bazar,* Vol. 11. New York: Harper & Bros., 1878.

Harper & Bros. *Harper's Bazar,* Vol. 12. New York: Harper & Bros., 1879.

Harper & Bros. *Harper's Bazar,* Vol. 13. New York: Harper & Bros., 1880.

Harper & Bros. *Harper's Bazar,* Vol. 14. New York: Harper & Bros., 1881.

Harper & Bros. *Harper's Bazar,* Vol. 15. New York: Harper & Bros., 1882.

Hecklinger, Charles. *Women's Costume 1877–1885.* Fort Bragg, CA: R. L. Shep, 2002.

International News Co. *The Young Ladies' Journal,* Vol. 16. London and New York: International News Co., 1879.

J. Henry Symonds. *Guide to Needlework, Containing Explicit Instructions for Every Kind of Stitch in Plain and Fancy Needlework . . . .* Boston: J. Henry Symonds, 1876.

J. S. Robertson & Bros. *Guide to Dressmaking and Fancy Work . . . ,* n.d. Reprint, Burlington: Eileen Collard, 1977.

Klemm, Heinrich. *Vollständige Schule der Damen-schneiderei...*, 11th ed. Dresden: H. Klemm's Verlag, 1883.

McCall, James. *Instruction Book for the French and English Systems of Cutting, Fitting, and Basting.* New York: James McCall, 1881.

Myra. *Dressmaking Lessons.* London: Myra & Son, n.d.

Oakey, Miss. *Beauty in Dress.* New York: Harper & Bros., 1881.

Smith, Madame A. Burdette. *Practical Lectures on Dressmaking.* New York: A. Burdette Smith, 1879.

Ward, Lock, & Co. *Handbook of Plain and Fancy Needlework ....* New York: Ward, Lock, and Co., n.d.

Ward, Lock, & Co. *Ward and Lock's Home Book: A Domestic Encyclopaedia.* London: Ward, Lock, and Co., n.d.

Ward, Lock, & Tyler. *The Englishwoman's Domestic Magazine*, Vol. 22. London: 1877.

W. Jennings Demorest. *Demorest's Monthly Magazine and Mirror of Fashions,* Vol. 13. New York: W. Jennings Demorest, 1877.

W. Jennings Demorest. *Demorest's Monthly Magazine and Mirror of Fashions,* Vol. 14. New York: W. Jennings Demorest, 1878.

W. Jennings Demorest. *Demorest's Monthly Magazine and Mirror of Fashions,* Vol. 15. New York: W. Jennings Demorest, 1879.

W. Jennings Demorest. *Demorest's Monthly Magazine and Mirror of Fashions,* Vol. 17. New York: W. Jennings Demorest, 1881.

Further Reading

Blum, Stella, ed. *Victorian Fashions and Costumes from Harper's Bazar: 1867–1898.* New York: Dover Publications, 1974.

Buck, Anne. *Victorian Costume and Costume Accessories.* Carlton: Ruth Bean, 1984.

Byrde, Penelope. *Nineteenth-Century Fashion.* London: B. T. Batsford, 1992.

Coleman, Elizabeth Ann. *The Opulent Era: Fashions of Worth, Doucet, and Pingat.* New York: Thames and Hudson, 1989.

Ginsburg, Madeleine, ed. *Victorian Dress in Photographs.* New York: Holmes & Meier, 1983.

Hornbostel, Wilhelm et al. *Voilà: Glanzstucke Historischer Moden 1750–1960.* Munchen: Prestel-Verlag, 1991.

Kidwell, Claudia. *Cutting a Fashionable Fit: Dressmaker's Drafting Systems in the United States.* Washington, DC: Smithsonian Institution Press, 1979.

Lord & Taylor. *Clothing and Furnishings.* 1881. Reprint, Princeton: Pyne Press, 1971.

Olian, JoAnne, ed. *Full-Color Victorian Fashions 1870–1893.* Mineola: Dover Publications, 1999.

Olian, JoAnne, ed. *Victorian and Edwardian Fashions from "La Mode Illustrée."* Mineola: Dover Publications, 1998.

Rothstein, Natalie, ed. *Four Hundred Years of Fashion.* London: Victoria and Albert Museum, 1984.

Severa, Joan L. *Dressed for the Photographer: Ordinary Americans and Fashion, 1840–1900.* Kent: Kent State University Press, 1995.

Tarrant, Naomi A. E. *Great Grandmother's Clothes: Women's Fashion in the 1880s.* Edinburgh: National Museums of Scotland, 1986.

Thieme, Otto Charles, ed. *With Grace and Favour: Victorian and Edwardian Fashion in America.* Cincinnati: Cincinnati Art Museum, 1993.

I. Patterns by Enlargement Method And Needlework Technique

This index is for both volumes of *Fashions of the Gilded Age*. For each entry, the volume number is given, followed by a colon, then by the page number(s); then, if appropriate, by a semicolon, another volume number, then page number(s). References to the introduction and chapter 1 are given as 1 & 2, since this material is repeated with the same page numbers in both volumes.

Numbers in parentheses distinguish different patterns with the same name.

Index I

 **Patterns by Method**

II. Text Other Than Patterns

This index is for both volumes of *Fashions of the Gilded Age.* For each entry, the volume number is given, followed by a colon, then by the page number(s); then, if appropriate, by a semicolon, another volume number, then page number(s). References to the introduction and chapter 1 are given as 1 & 2, since this material is repeated with the same page numbers in both volumes.

Text Other Than Patterns

chatelaine fan holders, 2: 335–336

chemises, 1 & 2: 1; 1: 98–102; 2: 377–381, 479–481

chemisettes, 2: 483

chignons, 2: 250, 253

cloaks, 2: 149–150. *See also* wrappings

coat basque, 1: 159

coats, 1: 160; 2: 149, 476–478

coiffures, 2: 259–260, 262. *See also* hairstyles

collars

    for dresses, 1 & 2: 4; 1: 246, 345–347; 2: 91, 286–298, 462

    for mantles, 2: 477

    for sports outfits, 2: 112–114

colors, 1 & 2: 3–4

    for accessories, 2: 245–246

    for corsets, 1: 50

    for day, 1: 158, 160, 345–347

    for evening, 1: 246; 2: 50–51

    for outerwear, 2: 149–150

    for sports outfits, 2: 112–114

    for wedding party, 2: 90

combination costumes, 1: 310

combination garments, 1 & 2: 1; 1: 71

combs, 2: 257–258

Complete Guide to Ladies' Garment Cutting, 1 & 2: 5–6

corded ruffle, 2: 494

cordings, 2: 461, 464, 466–467, 483, 489

cord seam, 2: 430–431

corsage bouquets, 2: 262–263

corset covers, 1 & 2: 1; 1: 310; 2: 382

corsets and alternatives, 1 & 2: 1; 1: 50, 71; 2: 485–487

covered button, 2: 440

cravats, 2: 299–308

crocheted trimmings, 2: 374–376, 379, 386–389

croquet costumes, 2: 112–113

cross–stitch. *See* herringbone stitch

cuffs, 2: 286–287, 291, 293, 296, 463

curtain overskirt, 1: 277

D

Derby coats, 2: 149

dinner dresses, 2: 50

dolmans, 1 & 2: 3; 2: 477

double box pleats, 2: 492

double corded piping, 2: 488

double cording, 2: 489–490

double French hem, 2: 494

double piping, 2: 488

double seam, 2: 430

double-stitch buttonhole, 2: 437–438

draping, 2:418–419, 474–476

drawers, 2: 374–376, 483–484

drawn bonnets, 2: 498–499, 505

dresses, cutting out, 2: 454–460

dressing sacques, 2: 384

E

earrings, 2: 320, 322–325, 328

elastics, for skirts, 2: 471–472

embroidery

    for dresses, 2: 370, 372, 403–405

    for lingerie, 2: 377, 380–381, 384–385, 388, 391–392

    for wrappings, 2: 409, 413

English ruffle, 2: 494

English stitch, 2: 427

Englishwoman's Domestic Magazine, 1 & 2: 6, 8

evening dresses, 1: 246; 2: 50–51, 464, 466, 470

eye button, 2: 441

eyelets, 2: 428, 466, 485

F

fabrics. *See* materials

false hem, 2: 435–436

fans, 2: 51, 245, 342–345

fashion, international influences, 1 & 2: 4; 2: 50, 90

fashion plates, copying styles, 2: 418–419

feather ruche, 2: 492

feather trimmings, 2: 372

felled seam, 2: 429

fichu–collars, 2: 287, 291, 293, 296–297

fichus, 2: 244, 310–314, 477

flat button, 2: 440

flat seam, 2: 428–429

flounces, 1: 143; 2: 370, 487, 493–495

flower trimmings, 2: 373

Other Books by Lavolta Press

Fashions of the Gilded Age, Volume 1: Undergarments, Bodices, Skirts, Overskirts, Polonaises, and Day Dresses 1877–1882, by Frances Grimble

Women's patterns and instructions from *Vollständige Schule der Damenschneiderei, Harper's Bazar,* and other sources. Includes rulers for a German drafting system.

469 pages, 200 illustrations, $49

After a Fashion: How to Reproduce, Restore, and Wear Vintage Styles, by Frances Grimble

Covers medieval through Art Deco styles for women and men. Guides readers through each stage of a reproduction project and advises them on all aspects of collecting vintage clothes.

356 pages, 147 illustrations, $38

Reconstruction Era Fashions: 350 Sewing, Needlework, and Millinery Patterns 1867–1868, by Frances Grimble

Women's patterns and instructions from the first 14 months of *Harper's Bazar.* Includes articles on needlework techniques and fashion trends.

529 pages, 609 illustrations, $45

The Voice of Fashion: 79 Turn-of-the-Century Patterns with Instructions and Fashion Plates, by Frances Grimble

Women's patterns for 1900 through 1906, selected from *The Voice of Fashion.* Includes rulers for the Diamond Cutting System.

463 pages, 93 illustrations, $42

The Edwardian Modiste: 85 Authentic Patterns with Instructions, Fashion Plates, and Period Sewing Techniques, by Frances Grimble

Women's patterns for 1905 through 1909, selected from *The American Garment Cutter Instruction and Diagram Book* and *The American Modiste.* Includes chapters of a 1907 dressmaking manual and rulers for the American System of Cutting.

430 pages, 112 illustrations, $42

Further information is available on our web site, http://www.lavoltapress.com.

Our books can be purchased in bookstores or ordered from Lavolta Press at 20 Meadowbrook Drive, San Francisco, CA 94132. If mail ordered, shipping is $4 for the first book and $2 for each additional book (for book post within the US). California purchasers must add sales tax. Prices subject to change without notice.